RECONSTRUCTING
SOUTHERN RHETORIC

RACE
RHETORIC
& MEDIA

Race, Rhetoric, and Media Series
Davis W. Houck, General Editor

RECONSTRUCTING SOUTHERN RHETORIC

Edited by Christina L. Moss
and Brandon Inabinet

University Press of Mississippi / Jackson

The University Press of Mississippi is the scholarly publishing agency of
the Mississippi Institutions of Higher Learning: Alcorn State University,
Delta State University, Jackson State University, Mississippi State University,
Mississippi University for Women, Mississippi Valley State University,
University of Mississippi, and University of Southern Mississippi.

www.upress.state.ms.us

The University Press of Mississippi is a member
of the Association of University Presses.

First printing 2021
∞

Library of Congress Cataloging-in-Publication Data

Names: Moss, Christina L., editor. | Inabinet, Brandon, editor.
Title: Reconstructing southern rhetoric / edited by Christina L. Moss
and Brandon Inabinet.
Other titles: Race, rhetoric, and media series.
Description: Jackson : University Press of Mississippi, 2021. | Series: Race, rhetoric,
and media series | Includes bibliographical references and index.
Identifiers: LCCN 2021031178 (print) | LCCN 2021031179 (ebook) |
ISBN 9781496836144 (hardback) | ISBN 9781496836151 (trade paperback) |
ISBN 9781496836168 (epub) | ISBN 9781496836175 (epub) |
ISBN 9781496836182 (pdf) | ISBN 9781496836199 (pdf)
Subjects: LCSH: Rhetoric—Southern States—History. | Southern States—
Intellectual life—1865– | Southern States—Social life and customs.
Classification: LCC P301.3.U6 R43 2021 (print) | LCC P301.3.U6 (ebook) |
DDC 808.00975—dc23
LC record available at https://lccn.loc.gov/2021031178
LC ebook record available at https://lccn.loc.gov/2021031179

British Library Cataloging-in-Publication Data available

CONTENTS

I. Reconstructing the South, Banishing Nostalgia

II. Reconstructing the South in Relational Identity: Decentering the White Victim

III. Reconstructing the South in New Locales

ACKNOWLEDGMENTS

This volume has been forming in our minds since we first met in 2014 at the Southern States Communication Association Conference during a double panel of the Southern Colloquium on Rhetoric. The panel was put together by James Darsey and focused on the speeches of current-day southern politicians. It was our dear friend Mary Stuckey who introduced us with a declaration of "You two should know each other." As we've come to know, that is just one of many things about which Mary was right. To Mary and James, we owe our friendship and our continued dedication to understanding and reconstructing southern rhetoric.

We would also like to thank Kathleen Turner, whose own work is an excellent example of editing and who gave keen advice and savvy instruction along the way. Her friendship and council remain most dear.

A very special shout-out goes to Catherine Eakin, whose work as a graduate research assistant at the University of Memphis was most helpful in organizing and completing this project. At times she adeptly turned chaos into order, for which we are very grateful.

The contributors to this volume are a dream team of scholars at various stages in their careers and from a variety of viewpoints about the South. Their chapters made this volume a pure joy to put together. We thank them all for their insights, patience, and care. They made us better scholars, editors, and people.

The team at University Press of Mississippi believed in this project from the beginning, and for that we are most grateful. To Vijay Shah, we owe much gratitude for first discussing the project with us and for continuing interest when we weren't sure we could pull it off. We were sad to see him leave UPM for other interests. However, Emily Bandy hit the ground running, and we appreciate her for continuing the enthusiasm and seeing us through to the end.

Christi would like to thank the people at the University of Memphis Department of Communication and Film who have supported this and many other projects and to thank both Wendy Atkins-Sayre and Tony de Valesco for continually discussing the South and its complexities. Thank you to the

#WriteOrDie writing group and Andre Johnson and Amanda Edgar for their support and company over several cups of coffee, pub grub meals, and the occasional bourbon. I am indebted to other mentors. Ron Jackson shared how to edit, but more importantly, who to be as an editor. Special gratitude to Bill, Olivia, and Mitchell Hayes, who keep things real in all the best ways. And, of course, to Brandon I am indebted, for being such a smart and humane partner on this project.

Brandon thanks his wife, Rachel, for abiding his terrible schedule (editing happens from 2 to 3 am); his mentors at Furman and Northwestern for lessons in southern themes and reckoning (Angela Ray, Eric Cain, Cynthia King, Sharon Morgan, and Claire Whitlinger); and especially Roger Sneed, who regularly gave counsel to make "good trouble" while embracing roots and place. For original lessons on treating all people with good humor and fairness, thanks to his parents, Michael and Rosemary, grandparents (Lois, Willie, Ethel, and Rufus), Uncle Rufus and Aunt Phyllis, and teachers Ms. Milly, Ms. Anne, and Ms. Nancy. And to Christi, who helped aim all of this energy and upbringing toward the South's rhetorical tradition.

RECONSTRUCTING
SOUTHERN RHETORIC

RECONSTRUCTING SOUTHERN RHETORIC

CHRISTINA L. MOSS AND BRANDON INABINET

As a white female growing up in Kentucky, I never thought of myself as southern per se, but I was very aware of rural and urban divides. The granddaughter of tobacco farmers, a schoolteacher, and a factory worker, I was taught to "neutral-ize" my hick accent but had to be able to "switch over" at certain friend or family gatherings for fear of being considered uppity. My interest in the South came as I moved throughout Kentucky, Alabama, Georgia, Florida, North Carolina, Louisiana, and now Tennessee as an adult. With those moves, I observed my own navigations and those of others and realized the complexities that continue to keep hierarchies and exclusions in place. I've dedicated my work to revealing those power structures and whom they serve in everything from television shows to public address to civil rights histories.
—*Christina L. Moss*

Born in rural South Carolina, sent to a segregation academy named for John C. Calhoun, and baptized Southern Baptist, I know it should be hard to say I'm an "outsider." And yet my work with interracial dialogue and calls for reckoning and reconstruction are taken as a divorce from my white southern roots. One cousin went so far recently as to threaten to beat me up if I came to a family reunion, suggesting I thought myself better than "illiterate rednecks." Estranged insider it is, for now.
—*Brandon Inabinet*

Ibram Kendi's best-selling *How to Be an Antiracist* begins with his story of the Martin Luther King Jr. Oratorical Competition at Manassas, Virginia's Stonewall Jackson High School, named for the Confederate general. Kendi is ashamed to admit that, in the competition, he rephrased King's speech to attack Black youth for being the root of their own problems (2019, 3–7). To do so, he pulled language and rhetorical depictions from King's most famous speeches, yet he did so with the systemic bias of a society that honored all the iconography, ideas, and heroism of slaveholders. In such a layered world, Kendi had maintained a racist environment without even realizing it. Later in the book, motivated to amend his youthful mistake, he cuts through distinctions like "structural" and "institutional" racisms, bluntly calling such terms solipsisms; all racism is deeply embedded, he argues, or else it would not be an ideology. To change things, he advises active knowledge of how symbols, attitudes, and structures operate.

This volume examines these structures of southern rhetoric and regionalism. And it uses the region to claim that the violence of trauma and solidarity of reconstructive healing need to redefine critical regionalism. It puts into conversation what we know from experience—that southern rhetoric matters in ways far beyond geographical borders and a war fought more than 150 years ago. While studying the history of southern communication rhetoric, we've found case studies, defensive history, and a primarily white male viewpoint that limits the understanding, imagination, and relevance of southern rhetoric (Inabinet and Moss 2019). Both of us have, in a variety of ways, gained privilege from the hierarchies and power differentials of the southern past, even as others have suffered from those differentials. We both, at various points in our academic careers, have been asked why people still study the South. The question has come with an undercurrent that the presence of regional interest is parochial, working against national and global trends.

Therefore, we started this volume asking the question of what southern rhetoric and southern rhetorical critique would look like if constructed differently, i.e., (re)constructed? Following the work of Patricia Davis (2016), how could southern rhetoric be more inclusive of actual-existing southern history and tradition, with its rich tapestry of southern culture and people? How can we disrupt the limited view of southern rhetoric and its subject matter as Confederate and neo-Confederate whiteness? How can we connect regional dynamics with a global system of discourse and circulation? The chapters in this book help answer and situate that conversation. Disposing of white guilt (McPherson 2003, 11), we work to shift focus beyond white feeling and white affect studies and look instead to a broader view of southern rhetorics. Not only is this creating a "new diversity" of who counts as southern—a very old but important concept in this area of New South studies—and not only is it attentive to inclusivity and equity as important values for reconstructing the region, but this approach uses the South to redefine regions and regionalism as a new paradigm for the study of discourse. For this, we turn to the genealogy of critical regionalism.

CRITICAL REGIONALISM

In our prior work, we found that regional criticism tended to hinge on the validity and authenticity of the region and its connoisseurs. What is "truly" southern? Was it okay (ethically, aesthetically, or pedagogically sound) to study the South, or was that a more nostalgic focus than American discourse? Should academics know the South well, as "insiders," to unravel its myths? Or was it the duty of "outsiders," with their more objective foothold? Or, in complex cases like Waldo Braden or Richard Weaver, should it be the subset who had a leg in both? Although limited at the time to a debate among elite white men, these are important questions that most critics face. Yet they stunt the actual outcomes and reception of the studies. The theory of critical regionalism nicely pushes beyond the impasses that made regions parochial.

Critical regionalism recenters the study of power, specifically "whose interests are served by a given version of region" (Powell 2007, 7). To each of the questions above, the critic becomes part of this larger power constellation. Thus, in this volume, we have gone to the extra effort of asking every author to disclose their relationship to the South as they see it. The contributions all evidence the complexity of what it means to be an insider/outsider in the South and how that may inform the focus of these authors' scholarship. Regions are manifestly persuasive, without civic legitimation processes that nations enjoy. Who is part of the South? What are its symbols? When did it form? Where are its boundaries? Why is it important? There is no assembly, no government. Space and time are constructed through complicated relational identities, layering, and rhetorical shifts in power constellations. The enduring focus on the South (back to Dallas Dickey in the early days of public address study), as well as the recent focus on critical regionalism outside the South (by Rice and participating authors in the 2012 special issue of *Rhetoric Society Quarterly*), points our way.

In addition to the definitional work noted above, this collection of chapters is a significant step forward for our field's theorization of "critical regionalism." This term, from architectural theory, was coined by Alexander Tzonis and Liane Lefaivre in a 1981 article ("The Grid and the Pathway") and later traced intellectually in a 2003 book with the title *Critical Regionalism*. Specifically, those authors were worried that the force of globalization, with its competitiveness and mass consumption, obscured the potential for local design options. To put it in rhetorical terms, people begin to lack capacity for prudential judgment, or what Kant called practical reasoning. On the one hand, one should revalue the region as a positive force against neoliberal pressures—building the kindred ties, the dialects, and the localized practices that make the place something other than the homogeneous West or "developing" to be so. On the other hand, this effort should be situated within a field of regionalisms, so it does not slip into unreflective praise, historical solipsism, or essentialist claims of uniqueness. After all, in the South, we have enough new suburban neighborhoods with the name "Plantation" in them and enough corporate buildings that attempt to recall a mythic "simpler time." Simply elevating the region against the global, without the critique and the promise of *phronesis* (situational judgment), is a mistake.

Kenneth Frampton (1983) further elaborated the idea of critical regionalism through Paul Ricoeur's hermeneutics and Heidegger's phenomenology, popularizing the concept while removing some of the Enlightenment assumptions about the universal and particular. Frampton encouraged a focus on the tectonics revealed by lived experience. In architecture, this might mean one still sees the beam, creating the tactile sense that one could actually reach out and understand the joints of the structure, once hidden by modern commercial drop-down tiles; however, the beam might slant according to regionally specific practices like the Swiss chalet or the flat adobe home. The South should be exposed for its power structures and the mundane ways it is supported; and, with that knowledge, we can study and rebuild regional structures. The chapters in this volume center such power structures revealed by everyday experiences, from food to music to architecture.

Judith Butler and Gayatri Chakravorty Spivak's *Who Sings the Nation-State? Language, Politics, Belonging* (2007) signals the fuller cultural turn of the phrase when they turn to the postnational landscape. Still retaining the earlier meanings, Butler and Spivak cite the term to consider the solutions that regions offer when issues (including conflict management) cannot be solely state-determined. They assert that whereas Hannah Arendt saw this situation as a "problem" (with stateless persons and issues that fall outside of national legitimation unresolved), critical regionalism sees it as a solution: that the architects have offered a broader way to visualize emancipation outside of national systems and Western-legitimated borders.

Rather than thinking the future is fully transnational and solved by global governance, we need to instead focus on local resistive practices that work together and around the global architectonic system to make it more caring. Regions emerge to the primary scene when, for example, Western ideas of birthright citizenship break down over porous borders. Genealogies of influence move more adeptly through families and communities than according to nation-state civics. In Butler and Spivak's words, rather than the state being born *ex nihilo* as Hannah Arendt suggested, revolutions come from regions "because they've criticized and because they've bonded together for various reasons and produced solidarity on the basis of an analysis and a history"

(2007, 119). As the chapters in this volume show, trauma and resilience through transnational flows become the basis for regional articulations. Although we embrace a broadly pluralistic, multivocal South, Black women become a frequent paradigm for the South in this book. Because of their attention to family care, memorial activism and public memory work, everyday activism regarding race and equity, and bearing witness to the global flows of African ancestry and Black diaspora into southern places, the critical perspectives and the rhetorical performances of southern Black women are uniquely productive for the study of region as a site of solidarity and trauma resilience on a global stage.

One final text in this genealogy bears mentioning, if only because nearly every author in the volume returns to it. Douglas Reichert Powell (2007) has already used ideas of critical regionalism for his study of the South. Powell tours regions of the South, specifically Appalachia, as texts and as rhetorics, and he understands each as a metaphor. Regions are a little like mapped places, a little like heritage museums, a little like films, a little like images, and so forth. In each case, a quaint or marginalized community (like southern Appalachia) picks up a little revelation of a broader global cultural trend. Powell, in other words, finds a tactile tectonic, a recognizable architecture, in each place he critically visits in the South. Each reflects a much broader global issue.

The argument of this book is that critical regionalism is exactly what Powell says, but also more. Yes, the South is usefully understood as a local citation of a global phenomenon—fueled by power dynamics, relationally experienced, layered in time. But we cannot walk away with a *Hillbilly Elegy* mentality, in which the goal is just to say that the poor or marginalized of every sort are more like some global category: impoverished whites, resentful or racist, are still linked to broader globally impoverished peoples, for example, and are not just inept at gaining white American privileges. Rather, critical regionalism calls us to critically interrogate power, trace tectonics, and offer something on a global stage. We believe each author contributes significantly in this vein, pointing to regions as a new paradigm of rhetorical criticism outside the national civic horizon.

In the South, understandings of trauma lead to new solidarity, as Butler and Spivak (2007) pointed out; this leads to new place making, new public memory, and new pedagogy. The South offers no end to stories of traumatic, intergenerational racism, exhibited in those chapters that center the African American experience in the South. But critical regionalism inverts this into potentiality, given the architectural metaphor of inhabiting a shared space at its base. Belonging and identity can be tied more to placed trauma (which can be healed), rather than the place as timelessly or mythically wounded and impossible to cure. Critics need to understand the South as a place where new solidarity emerges, not just where trauma occurred; as a place where actual trauma by Indigenous and enslaved people and their descendants was repeatedly co-opted by white demagogues, who claimed to "lose their freedom" or have been "treated like slaves" by the North, by science, by justice, or by equality. Resistive feelings and solidarity are birthed in regional trauma and often co-opted; regional rhetoric and rhetorical studies have too often treated the co-optation at the center of the action, rather than its mutant spawn. Critical regionalism, under this new definition, lays bare the site of the trauma, the resistance, and the healing as symbolic action.

THE TURN SOUTH

Refocusing on the South may, despite our intentions, still lead to unwarranted glorification or essentializing of the region in ways that are problematic. And yet it deserves study. In the speech communication discipline, southern rhetoric and oratory are arguably the first recognized regional rhetoric, and the region of the US most in need of disruptive, healing criticism. In 1947, Dallas Dickey declared southern oratory an area in need of attention and scholarship: "The field of Southern oratory is almost completely unworked, and offers great opportunities for the student of rhetorical history and criticism. If we are to have in our day a body of research on significant and influential speakers, we should not delay in our activities" (459). The call for regionally recognized scholarship was direct and intentional (Moss, forthcoming).

From Dickey's call forward, scholars such as Waldo Braden, Kevin Kearney, Howard Dorgan, Calvin Logue, and Stuart Towns wrestled with definitions and parameters surrounding what made oratory or rhetoric southern and what it meant to be identified as southern (Inabinet and Moss 2019). These scholars struggled with three main obstacles: 1) the "othering" of the South from the rest of the country, 2) the resulting defensive positioning of scholars about the South, and 3) the challenge of varied southern cultures at a time when racial, gender, and class diversity was minimally noted by the communication discipline (Moss, forthcoming).

These structural systems resulted in the erasure of the multiple identities associated with the diverse rhetorical culture of the region. A primarily Black and white dichotomy has downplayed Latinx and other marginalized communities (Calafell 2004). Although a few chapters in this book push boundaries in terms of those other marginalized communities, the focus on trauma and reconstruction has centered our eyes largely on the Black experience. But even that work is needed, within a public address discipline whose notions of social significance, usually white and male, were the measure of what made rhetoric and public address relevant as a study and an art. This hegemony enabled white southerners generally, and scholars in particular, to use the privilege of regional and relational power while communicating their "imagined marginality" (Inabinet and Moss 2019). Critical regionalism allows for the potential for a non-nostalgic rendering of a regional past, rooted in architectural metaphors of place.

For example, rather than looking for an essential attachment to a unique land, we see "overlapping spheres" (Rice 2012, 204) between global and local, national and subnational. Creole spaces are confluences of constantly moving peoples and texts across and against any attempt at distinct powers and borders. Defined as "weak counterpublics" (Inabinet and Moss 2019), regions are not legitimated as formal public spheres with clear channels of political power. Instead, they negotiate relational identities (Moss 2011), anxiously circulating texts, bodies, and symbols with accents of a layered past. Often they do this against the presence of a more powerful and legitimated power structure.

These same obstacles appear in the historical development of southern rhetoric and public address. Rarely have we taken the opportunity to understand how southern rhetoric operates globally—for example, as African American culture influences the world, or as Confederate ideas of racial superiority and rebellion circulated outside national boundaries. Neither have we embraced the idea of an actively antiracist rhetorical pedagogy to remake regions. Too often we have focused on national civic practices and how the South did or did not keep pace.

But as we see around the globe, stoking regional relational identities is often the toehold to power. Knowing how to eat the local barbeque, mock the national power structure with a regional accent, or position the region in a global system certainly matters to social change more than the relatively rare instance of soaring eloquence on a national stage. Scholars of public address must work to demystify regions and regional practices across boundaries.

This is not easy, though, because regions are not monoliths. There is no singular southern region or southern rhetoric. The symbols of white southern rhetoric (sometimes referred to as the traditional South) remain obstacles to be negotiated today (Davis 2016). For example, Greek Revival columns on large front porches are differently remembered and acknowledged by southerners of various sorts. Plantation tourist sites often offer their porches for weddings. Some are managed by people of color who push back against the monolithic expectation and see a site of ancestral labor and cruel wounding. LGBTQIA+ communities question the heteronormative remembering of the space for weddings, refocusing our gaze on a historically queer South. Southern regionalism is a living and ongoing layering of "texts, experiences, and interpretations of specific locales that produces, in its ongoing processes, a place" (Powell 2007, 35). We especially ask the field to consider the ways in which those symbols circulate across publics and counterpublics, then manifest in communicative acts.

The reconstruction of southern rhetoric is a disruption of the complicity of past scholarship. This collection strives to use the voices of diverse critics and subjects to reconstruct the South as a region. *Reconstructing* the South, we realize, is a loaded term. We found from our call for chapters that some scholars mistakenly read the word "reconstruction" as being more like the term "redemption" used by many nineteenth-century white southerners to call for the reversion of the South to white supremacy after the period of Reconstruction and thus suggesting a redevelopment of (white) southern power and economics through the act of racial forgetting. In other words, they somehow read a project on reconstruction as a claim that "the (white) South shall rise again." We, as editors, were more interested in reconstruction as a concept related to new explorations of the historical era of Reconstruction by groundbreaking historians Eric Foner (1988) and David Blight (2001). In its best light, the Reconstruction era saw a mass overturning of society, in which formerly enslaved persons became political elites, Black children from the plantation fields were afforded educational opportunity (including higher education), and persons with power intentionally named the wounds of slavery and inequity. Even more importantly, we were inspired by how Reverend William Barber (2016) appropriated the term for his goal of igniting a Third Reconstruction, a multiracial grassroots movement to address the economic and social roots of racial inequality and poverty. Our use of the term thus signifies the historical as well as the contemporary struggle to complete the unfinished work of a new birth of freedom and equity for all.

In scholarship regarding the South and cultural consideration of what constitutes southern regionalism, we need a similar project. We believe transformation and historical reconstruction have much to teach us today, whether about the capacity of a marginalized group to find power, the rethinking of what it means to be "southern," or the radical potential that lies in activist pedagogy and critique. Scholars in communication are uniquely qualified to study, redefine, and actively address regionalism. The South, with its traumatic past and need for new solidarity and healing, offers the paradigmatic case.

OUTLINE OF STUDY

We argue that southern rhetoric, like all regional rhetoric, is fluid and migrates beyond geography; that southern rhetoric, like all regional rhetoric, is constructed in weak counterpublic formation against legitimated power; that southern rhetoric, like all regional rhetoric, creates a region that is not monolithic; and that southern rhetoric, like all regional rhetoric, is in need of rhetorical criticism that nourishes reconstruction based on trauma, solidarity, and healing in symbolic action—a new project of critical regionalism. We hope this same framework will be useful in the broader critical study of critical regionalism whether internal to the nation (North, Midwest, Southwest, West) or global (Global South, Southeast Asia, etc.). After all, the very basis for regional identification is shared trauma and harm that create a sense of solidarity and humanity, as well as the resources of place and time to heal.

To this end, this volume is divided into sections that structure a reconstruction. This path of communicative reconstruction functions not just at an abstract or theoretical level, but also as a conversation process, a social movement builder, and a classroom plan. The first step, and the focus of the first section, is to disrupt nostalgia: the myths of the past are often a hindrance to understanding power relationships. They are still there—informing practices from the mundane to the extraordinary. But one should move beyond them as the "essence" of the place and time, seeing instead fluid identities tied to place. The second section works to decenter the martyrs and carve out new archetypal identities. It seeks to name the harmful aggression among the so-called heroes, mark the new space for recentering, and consider alternative acts of identification that create meaning and purpose within the rhetorically constructed space. The final chapters work to find interventions. Boundary objects, icons, or remembrance sites articulate a new power differential. In that way, we begin a conversation rooted in a potential for symbolic action and active healing from cycles of aggression and victimization.

The first set of chapters attempts to banish nostalgia. We begin this process with two autoethnographic reflections. Patricia Davis takes us to the National Memorial for Peace and Justice built by the Equal Justice Initiative. In doing so, she prepares our minds for reckoning with an often hidden past and the emotional trauma of doing so. A non-nostalgic look at the South is especially painful for African Americans, and Davis helps us see that pain—alongside the potential for healing—in her experience of the site with students.

Next, Dave Tell describes his encounters with the memory makers and residents of Tallahatchie County, Mississippi. The Emmett Till Memorial Project has been in the national and international headlines for years, as the signs commemorating Till continuously absorb the bullets of white supremacists. Dave Tell takes us through his early encounters with the memorial committee in this economically devastated part of Mississippi, exploring the ways that biracial alliances are formed by seeking out ways to build tourism in the area. Tell highlights how the group warmly embraced scholarly assistance once they realized Tell was also willing to be part of the economic project, not just using study of the past as another means for elite scholars to marginalize Mississippi living.

Although both of these chapters claim as significant the new relationship to southern memories, neither of them participates in the rhetoric of the "New South." That is to say, unlike prior conversation and scholarship, neither scholar tries to claim that simply by including African American voices in the anthology, the South has somehow dramatically altered and advanced to a new era. One source of frequent nostalgia, especially given the fiftieth anniversary of the US civil rights movement over the past decade, has been the substitution of inclusion for power. A pat on the back to white southerners, both from within and by national and international news, has been the story of white and Black individuals working together to "create a New South."

But this characterization includes several assumptions. First is the assumption that "the South" is what they are building, when in fact they may just be part of a global community of learning about trauma (in Davis's chapter) or an individual or family trying to make a few dollars from local memory (in Tell's chapter). Second, the term "New South" attempts to see race relations as distinctly periodized after the Civil War, rather than continually invested in white supremacist culture and the slow recognition of that culture as a globally circulated phenomenon. Both by the announcement of a "National" memorial and by the feature of the Till project globally, we realize that no longer is the South more than a dramatic locale and setting for global power. In this way, we need not celebrate "Dixie" in times "not forgotten" (as the lyrics have it) of the Old South, nor to put a salve on the trauma through the "New South." Instead, we find in contemporary relationships the means for navigating the four hundred years of recorded southern history so far.

The next two chapters handle nostalgia more directly through critique. In Jonathan Smith's chapter, two famous Memphis recording studios that gave birth to modern music are compared as sites of nostalgia. Sun Studio, the self-proclaimed "Birthplace of Rock 'n' Roll," narrates four myths of the white US South as counterpublic, following fairly closely the Old South schema, to articulate in exhibits that whites achieved innovation with African American singers as happy sidekicks to their building American greatness. Meanwhile, at Stax Records, Black artists and white artists are shown working hand in hand through each exhibit, to create a New South of racial cooperation. Neither exhibit, says Smith, acknowledges the theft of Black musical traditions, even as Stax at least succeeds in foregrounding social progress.

Similarly, Julia Medhurst takes on the southern nostalgia that has been mediated and circulated globally through an analysis of HGTV's *Fixer Upper*.

Like the other case studies focused on economically enriching a specific locale in the South (in this case, Waco, Texas), the show has created significant gentrification in west Texas. However, the television program, like the Memphis recording studios, excludes any complex understanding of contemporary southern issues like gentrification. It instead features diverse home buyers perusing homes in less developed neighborhoods (predominantly African American and Latinx) and bringing them back to their "former" (white) glory. Yet, as Medhurst points out, this process is all hidden behind the veneer of a fun HGTV trope of home buying and repair, propped up by the aesthetic of farmhouse chic that only pretends to be interested in antique restoration.

In all four of the first section's chapters then, we see how local economic imperatives drive the manufacture of regionalism. Montgomery, rural Mississippi, Memphis, and Waco are all places where re-creation of a particular past can drive the local economy. In the first two, we see commemorative landscapes that debunk nostalgia with painful histories of terror. In the second two, we see nostalgia lurking in the day-to-day experience of consumption. The projects of lynching and terror campaigns clearly need emphasis as southern inflections of global trauma. The possibility of truth-telling in the other two situations depends on the economic model that currently militates against it. Scholars' future engagement with Memphis museums can work to reveal the white co-option of African American musicians and musical history (Hughes 2015). Similarly, media and rhetorical literacy could create consumers who demand even their banal entertainment, like *Fixer Upper*, not sidestep local race issues and history.

Critical regionalism asks that we find ideas within regional and relational identities worth circulating in our globally interconnected world. Or, perhaps better put, in a world that needs local connection and difference to satisfy the human condition, regions provide rhetorical possibilities. In all four of these cases, we can imagine a world that takes seriously the southern roots of racial truth-telling. And we hope to see a world that is ready to hear the real story of the origins of modern music and notions of home, but is unfortunately still rooted in the exploitation of Black and Brown bodies and culture for white economic gain.

In the second section, chapter authors take on relational identity of regions through two moves: the decentering of iconically demagogic southern males in the first two, and the recentering of diverse identities in the next three. Ryan Neville-Shepard, first, examines the history of the Dixiecrats and "Southern Strategy," especially in the example of Strom Thurmond. Neville-Shepard, a scholar focused on third-party politics, tells us of how once-excluded politicians, not all that popular even in the whites-only electoral South, appealed to the racial threat of the era following racial advancement in wartime. However, after contentious and difficult progress and planting the seeds of virulent political racism, real success only came later when Republicans put a nonracist veneer over policies that served the legacies of slavery (e.g., "welfare queen" tropes, the war on drugs and mass incarceration, and tax cuts as the alternative to social fraud).

Critiquing Democrats, Jeremy Grossman studies Mitch Landrieu's famous call for Confederate monument removal in New Orleans. Grossman finds, like Neville-Shepard, that white males can develop successful political strategies by containing the threat of Black voices. In Landrieu's case, his goal to tell a more complete history is a spatial *revision* of the city, whereas Take 'Em Down NOLA (TEDN, a group dedicated to removing all traces of white supremacy from the monument landscape of the city) offers the rhetoric of a temporal *reconstruction* of the city. Grossman focuses on how the idea of reconstruction requires a destruction—of radical tearing down of existing totems, something Grossman sees as possible if politicians were willing to focus more on the long narrative of racial repair, rather than the questions of how to provide balance in city spaces.

Decentering white male speech in American politics, even when it is in the service of helping equality, is important here. Both authors give us ample evidence that the agenda-setting and systemic power of whiteness are subtle and multigenerational efforts to resist a more radical politics that would be possible otherwise. When we went into this project, we were more obviously concerned with the imagined marginality of the demagogic orator foregrounded in our historical anthologies of the southern tradition of speech. But these two chapters helped us see that imagined marginality is more nefarious than one-time eloquence and that it takes the form of decades-long partisan formations of how core political issues will be settled.

The next three chapters offer strong counterexamples of paradigmatic southern traditions. Perhaps most directly related to the iconic representations described above, Cynthia King argues for Black women's voices as a new "decentered center" of southern voice. After all, King argues, regional identities are best when performed as multiple consciousness—aware of both the nation and the regionally specific locale, for example. She uses the example of Mary Church Terrell's address on the race issue in Washington, DC, to represent this voice and the convergence and divergence of aspects of Church Terrell's identity through a reading of the text. For example, Church Terrell converges her Black and female identities to identify hard-working, polite, educated African Americans in the nation's capital, whose success would be guaranteed if it weren't for the pernicious threats of Jim Crow in the region. And yet, her classist views of education and employment opportunity diverge from her race, so that she cannot fully articulate a subject position for the masses of African Americans injured by racism. These kinds of problematic movements of convergence and divergence, King argues, make for a better center for regionalism as marginality, rather than the imagined victimization of the white demagogues of Church Terrell's era (like Ben Tillman or Huey Long).

Cassidy Ellis and Michael Forst extend that idea of a decentered identity when they reflect on their personal experiences with Lynyrd Skynyrd's song "Sweet Home Alabama." This international signifier of the South contains lyrics that disturb the authors' sense of place, especially as dominant ideas about gender and sexuality determine what it means to be a southern man or woman. Queering the South, they argue, will require marking these negotiated regional identities. Similarly, Jason Edward Black calls us to consider Indigenous identity. Black's turn toward the legal records of Indian Removal in the early nineteenth century reminds us of the nearly total loss of early Native voices and speech texts, but the compelling legal argument (often by southerners like Justice John Marshall and Andrew Jackson) that determined what federal control over regional problems really meant. Black's chapter is an especially good reminder that "state's rights" as a rhetoric is so obviously an argument of (racist) convenience when federalism itself was weaponized against the original southern rights of land control held by Native peoples. In addition to southern control of tariffs and slavery, Black asks that we recenter Native people and Native land back into understanding the rhetoric of "state's rights" and, in turn, southern regionalism.

In short, all of these chapters help to argue that a radical reconstruction in rhetoric must overturn the racist takeover of southern identity, foregrounded in southern strategies. White male totems have been repeatedly used as outposts of an alien political force, one that has attempted to strangle regional plurality. Once this decentering has occurred in our theory and case studies, we begin to offer to the broader public a basis for regionalism that goes beyond white control. To put it another way, the Southern Christian Leadership Conference of Martin Luther King Jr. was just as much or more southern than the terrorist choke hold of the white supremacist League of the South; yet, the iconography of the latter circulates as southern while the former does not. Scholars can and should do more to decenter and recenter texts to radically resituate the complications of southern identity in multiple consciousnesses.

The last section calls for various actions, via the boundary objects and circulated icons that could make understanding, education, and civic engagement possible. Whitney Adams starts this off with her focus on the white fraternity Kappa Alpha (KA) as a site for "frozen loci," or frozen arguments that can be overturned by disruptive classroom pedagogy. An online forum, mostly by self-described KA brothers, demonstrates almost no understanding of the deeper symbolism or meaning of the Old South. Rather than use these "loci" as seats of resentment—places to launch anti-woman, anti-Black, anti-liberal invective—Adams asks students to turn to simple relational bonds to bridge the gap and invite self-understanding.

Ashli Stokes and Wendy Atkins-Sayre then take us to the kitchen to feature the skillet as conversation starter for dialogue. As with Memphis recording studios and HGTV in earlier chapters, Stokes and Atkins-Sayre call out major companies for a nostalgic white-centered mass marketing of southern cuisine (Cracker Barrel and Lodge being obvious culprits). Yet unlike a museum or performance, the skillet is radically situated in individual home experience and can recall very personal journeys through southern experience. In doing so, many of these broader challenges to speaking across differences become easier—and the sharing of a meal helps.

Carolyn Walcott brings global ethnography to the US South, similar to where the book started, but this time from the eyes of a young Guyanese woman. Rather than being satisfied with local progress, Walcott reminds us that even the most well-intentioned spaces—like the National Center for Civil and Human Rights in Atlanta—often foreground a particular public memory for civic purposes, at the expense of a broader regional identity of the Global South and the Black diaspora. Walcott tells about her own "flashbulb" memories from back home as she observes white segregationists and Black movement leaders and highlights the focus on global human trafficking in the final room of the museum. Still, Walcott argues, a more coherent attachment of the US South with the Global South and Black diaspora, rather than a completed national narrative of "giving" Black people their rights, will help the museum space become more coherent and focused on social memory and trauma as a global—especially a Global South—experience.

Lastly, Megan Fitzmaurice foregrounds an African burial ground in Richmond, Virginia, to remind us that the struggles of liberation are transnational, and if critical regionalism is to be successful as a project, it has to start foregrounding global resistance inflected through regional advocacy. For example, rather than being afraid or backing down to the traditional control elements of the city known as the "Capital of the Confederacy," Black activists proved themselves to be noncompromising and successful in challenging the memory landscape. As with the prior chapter, pan-African alliances with the Global South help. Multiple generations are invited to think and talk about how pavement can be put over one's ancestors and how educational institutions have been active in that erasure. A reconstruction will begin with reparative reinvestment in nonwhite communities.

INITIAL CONCLUSIONS

We realize this volume only starts to open the door to reconstructing southern rhetoric and its regional tropes. Even as rhetoric and communicative practice are infused throughout the book and regional study might have made the original Reconstruction era successful, the stakes even now must be a broad program of social, political, and cultural emancipation in real terms. Incredibly significant members of the US South have not merely come to the courthouse or Capitol to express imagined marginality (meaning all marginality circulated through texts), but have actually experienced empirical marginalization (the subset of imagined marginality legitimated not just in cultural circulation, but also in a lack of power). The hot air taken by imagined marginality has been especially pernicious for certain groups. Undocumented border crossings in the South contain stories of social vulnerability and extreme resilience (Córdova Plaza 2009). Latinx migrants are literally reconstructing the South, building rural and urban America despite incredibly low wages. Often such people exist in a "silent bargain," whose hard work with a local farmer or construction operator protects them from law enforcement, as long as their presence remains minimally felt in the community (Torres, Popke, and Hapke 2006; Stuesse 2016).

Indigenous removal and the Cherokee Trail of Tears (Smithers 2019) speak to a cultural genocide that rarely gets communicative space. Meanwhile, those who avoided removal to continue inhabiting the South (most notably, the Eastern Band of the Cherokee, but also the Lumbee, Coharie, and Haliwa-Saponi in North Carolina; Seminole and Miccosukee in Florida; Tunica, Houma, and Chitimacha of Louisiana; Poarch Creek of Alabama and the Mississippi Band of Choctaw Indians; see Snyder 2016, 327) are not archetypally southern; rather, they are co-opted by white conservative politicians, who pretend the plight of indigenous peoples is equal to whites who were "similar" victims of Sherman's March and Reconstruction (Taylor 2011, 10–11). People like the Lumbee Indians of Robeson County, North Carolina, created an archetypal southern identity and were subject to and then appropriated segregation to carve out their own sense of nationhood and to (re)create distinct identity (Lowery 2010). These must be elevated as well in the meaning of the South, beyond what this book accomplishes.

Where Friday night football and other norms of masculinity can be suffocating, the place of being a "tomboy" lesbian or a "sissy" gay man can result in staggering numbers of suicides in rural communities (Sears 1989; see also Howard 1997 and Whitlock 2013). Further intersections include Black masculinity (Richardson 2007) and Black Queerness in the South (Johnson 2015), as well as Native heritage in Appalachia (Tate 2009). In short, this kind of study is well under way, but we hope to have refocused it as southern rhetoric and as critical regionalism in the pages that follow. In each case, this book outlines a critical regionalism that centers trauma from historical harm and repair that might become the model for rhetorical study. We cannot simply leave behind moonlight and magnolias or include new voices; instead, we must call for a vulnerable and open conversation of consequence as to what the South can be beyond exclusionary practices of imagined marginality. Critical regionalism asks scholars to point out the locally significant practices occluded by global "anywhereness" under settler colonialism and capitalism.

The chapters that follow give us cause for optimism not only that these regional tropes are there for identity and study, but that the southern United States is poised to be a powerful resource for reckoning globally with historical harms and creating a beloved community. Until then, there is much more work to do, especially among those of us with the privileged position to write about these stakes.

REFERENCES

Barber, William. 2016. *Third Reconstruction: Moral Mondays, Fusion Politics, and the Rise of a New Justice Movement.* Boston: Beacon Press.

Blight, David W. 2001. *Race and Reunion: The Civil War in American Memory.* Cambridge, MA: Harvard University Press.

Butler, Judith, and Gayatri Chakravorty Spivak. 2007. *Who Sings the Nation-State? Language, Politics, Belonging.* London: Seagull Books.

Calafell, Bernadette Marie. 2004. "Disrupting the Dichotomy: 'Yo Soy Chicana/o?' in the New Latina/o South." *The Communication Review* 7, no. 2 (Summer): 175–204.

Córdova Plaza, Rosío. 2009. "New Scenarios of Migration: Social Vulnerability of Undocumented Vercruzanos in the Southern United States." In *Latino Immigrant and the Transformation of the U.S. South,* edited by Mar E. Odem and Elaine Cantrell Lacy. Athens: University of Georgia Press.

Davis, Patricia G. 2016. *Laying Claim: African American Cultural Memory and Southern Identity.* Tuscaloosa: University of Alabama Press.

Dickey, Dallas. 1947. "Southern Oratory: A Field for Research," *Quarterly Journal of Speech* 33: 459.

Foner, Eric. 1988. *Reconstruction: America's Unfinished Revolution, 1863–1877.* New York: HarperCollins Perennial Classics.

Frampton, Kenneth. 1983. "Towards a Critical Regionalism: Six Points for an Architecture of Resistance." In *The Anti-Aesthetic: Essays on Postmodern Culture,* edited by Hal Foster, 16–30. Port Townsend, WA: Bay Press.

Howard, John, ed. 1997. *Carrying On in the Lesbian and Gay South.* New York: New York University Press.

Hughes, Charles. 2015. *Country Soul: Making Music and Making Race in the American South.* Chapel Hill: University of North Carolina Press.

Inabinet, Brandon, and Christina Moss. 2019. "Complicit in Victimage: Imagined Marginality in Southern Communication Criticism." *Rhetoric Review* 38, no. 2 (April): 160–72. https://doi.org/10.1080/07350198.2019.1582228.

Johnson, Patrick E. 2015. "Southern (Dis)Comfort: Homosexuality in the Black South." *Creating and Consuming the U.S. South*, edited by William A. Fink, David Brown, Brian Ward, and Martyn Bone, 97–116. Gainesville: University Press of Florida.

Kendi, Ibram X. 2019. *How to Be an Antiracist*. New York: Penguin Random House.

Lowery, Malinda Maynor. 2010. *Lumbee Indians in the Jim Crow South: Race, Identity, and the Making of a Nation*. Self-published, with funding from UNC-Chapel Hill and the Andrew Mellon Foundation.

McPherson, Tara. 2003. *Reconstructing Dixie: Race, Gender, and Nostalgia in the Imagined South*. Durham, NC: Duke University Press.

Moss, Christina L. 2011. "A Nation Divided: Regional Identity, National Narratives, Zell Miller and the 2004 Presidential Election." *Southern Journal of Communication* 76, no. 1 (Spring): 76–96.

Moss, Christina L. Forthcoming. "A Rhetorical History of Southern Rhetoric." In *Returning to Rhetorical History*, edited by Jason Black and Kathleen Turner. Tuscaloosa: University of Alabama Press.

Powell, Douglass Reichert. 2007. *Critical Regionalism: Connecting Politics and Culture in the American Landscape*. Chapel Hill: University of North Carolina Press.

Rice, Jenny. 2012. "From Architectonic to Tectonics: Introducing Regional Rhetorics." *Rhetoric Society Quarterly* 42, no. 3 (June): 201–213. https://doi.org/10.1080/02773945.2012.682831.

Richardson, Riché. 2007. *Black Masculinity in the US South: From Uncle Tom to Gangsta*. Athens: University of Georgia Press.

Sears, James T. 1989. "The Impact of Gender and Race on Growing Up Lesbian and Gay in the South." *NWSA Journal* 1, no. 3 (Spring): 422–57.

Smithers, Gregory D. 2019. *Native Southerners: Indigenous History from Origins to Removal*. Norman: University of Oklahoma Press.

Snyder, Christine. 2016. "The South." In *The Oxford Handbook of American Indian History*, edited by Frederick E. Hoxie. New York: Oxford University Press.

Stuesse, Angela. 2016. *Scratching Out a Living: Latinos, Race, and Work in the Deep South*. Berkeley: University of California Press.

Tate, Linda. 2009. *Power in the Blood: A Family Narrative (Race, Ethnicity and Gender in Appalachia)*. Athens: University of Ohio Press.

Taylor, Melanie Benson. 2011. *Reconstructing the Native South: American Indian Literature and the Lost Cause*. Athens: University of Georgia Press.

Torres, Rebecca M., E. Jeffrey Popke, and Holly M. Hapke. 2006. "The South's Silent Bargain: Rural Restructuring, Latino Labor, and the Ambiguities of Migrant Experience." In *Latinos in the New South: Transformation of Place*, edited by Owen J. Furuseth. Boston: Routledge.

Tzonis, Alexander, and Liane Lefaivre. 1981. "The Grid and the Pathway: An Introduction to the Work of Dimitris and Suzana Antonakakis, with Prolegomena to a History of the Culture of Modern Greek Architecture." *Architecture in Greece* 15: 164–78.

Whitlock, Reta Ugena, ed. 2013. *Queer South Rising: Voices of a Contested Place*. Charlotte, NC: Information Age Publishing.

Part I

Reconstructing the South, Banishing Nostalgia

Chapter 1

OUR STORIES IN STEEL

An Autoethnographic Journey to the
National Memorial for Peace and Justice

PATRICIA G. DAVIS

Patricia Davis was born and raised in Virginia and, in spite of past residencies in Ohio and California and her current residence in Boston, considers the South to be her "forever home." Indeed, it is her African Americanness, *combined with her background, that provides the link that ties her indelibly to* southernness. *From this position, she is happy to engage in conversation about southern history and culture, and especially about the institutions that sustain both. Her book* Laying Claim: African American Cultural Memory and Southern Identity *was published by the University of Alabama Press in 2016.*

The demographic shifts that have characterized the South during the last few decades have long necessitated a corresponding evolution in rhetorical analyses of its culture and history. While the region remains culturally distinct in many significant ways, its ongoing transformation from a unitary bastion of reactionary sentiment to a diverse set of places and publics exemplifying varying degrees of consonance with modernity suggests a reevaluation of long-held assumptions about its sectional identity. This conceptualization of the "reconstructed" South calls for an intellectual reimagining of its myriad identities, including a broadening of the parameters of what we regard as "southern rhetoric."

This new approach to southern rhetoric involves two interrelated features. First, it resists the centering of whiteness as the default category constitutive of dominant notions of southernness and instead engages the underdeveloped perspectives of those historically marginalized from analyses of southern culture and history, particularly African Americans. Secondly, it must also offer nontraditional ways of analyzing southern discourse, including a move away from the more conventional modes and subjects of scholarly inquiry. Autoethnography presents an analytical approach that combines these two features. As a methodological intervention that "uses a researcher's personal experience to describe and critique cultural beliefs, practices, and experiences" (Adams, Jones, and Ellis 2015, 1), it offers a "richer understanding and account" of those experiences (Lauricella 2018, 65). More importantly for the purposes of a critical regionalism, autoethnography's provision that the researcher become the subject of her own research opens up a space for critical reflection on her experiences with a rhetorical text, thereby expanding the boundaries of authoritative voices on the meaning of that text. The positionality embedded in this approach is particularly meaningful when it comes to analyses centered on articulations of southern memory.

Regionalism has always been an important aspect of southern culture, as the people of the South have historically seen themselves as distinct from the citizens of the rest of the country. In this sense, southerners see the region's importance as extending well beyond geography to constitute a significant aspect of how they see themselves. It has thus been constructed as a homeplace, a site for identification. This sectionalism, reflected in the historical narratives they, and others, have constructed and articulated about the South, invokes a regional subjectivity when sociopolitically productive to do so, while retaining an unquestioned identification with the broader national identity when convenient. The basis for this dualism is, and has always been, race. The assumed white-centeredness of southern and American identities has enabled whites to claim both southern regionalism and national identity. These assumptions have traditionally formed the basis for the subjects, texts, and interlocutors of a southern rhetorical criticism developed in response to the perceived marginalization of white southern critics from the dominant culture. This counterpublic, comprised primarily of white male critics and audiences, has operated from its position of marginality devoid of the relevant historical context, particularly that associated with the systems of exploitation and racial domination indelible to southern memory and identity (Inabinet and Moss 2019).

Black southerners, in contrast, have been excluded from both regional and national identities, yet have, ironically, mobilized southern memory as a means of forging a sense of belonging to both the South and the nation. Though these efforts have occasionally been acknowledged, the "imagined marginalization" inherent in southern rhetorical criticism has largely disregarded African American experiences (Inabinet and Moss 2019). Furthermore, the conception of African American rhetoric does not directly address issues that might correspond to a regional identity.

A critical regionalism accounts for, and attempts to rectify, these erasures. Though Blackness has always been an important—if often unarticulated—element of hegemonic memories of the region's past, more conventional accounts of its production and expression have only rarely been occupied with questions foregrounding the perspectives of African Americans or the more critical standpoint such a focus entails. Autoethnography performs the work of enabling those who have often been regarded as, at best, historical objects within inquiries into southern discourse to situate themselves as historical subjects. It is through an autoethnographic lens that the racial *others* become the center of the narrative, enriching rhetorical analyses of the South in the process.

With these features in mind, I offer an autoethnographic reflection on my experiences with the National Memorial for Peace and Justice in Montgomery, Alabama. The memorial consists of two structures: a monument with the names of more than four thousand known victims of lynching in the US, and a museum that provides important historical context to the phenomenon of lynching, including its contemporary legacy.[1] As a critical and cultural rhetorical scholar who studies the ways in which monuments and museums construct, sustain, and contest hegemonic southern memories, I examine both structures through an analytical lens centered on the rhetorical work they perform in destabilizing canons with respect to southern discourse. I am also an African American woman who grew up in Virginia and who has lived and worked in the South for most of my life. My perspective on the memorial, as seen through the eyes of an African American reflecting on its meanings vis-à-vis the identities to which I lay claim, further enriches an intellectual perspective developed through many years of researching and writing about monuments and museums. As I have made clear in my other work, one perpetually informs the other (Davis 2016). In this case, the connections between the professional and the personal will be made more explicit as a means of constructing an analytic autoethnography, which enlists five key features: 1) membership in the group under study, 2) analytic reflexivity, 3) narrative visibility of the researcher's self, 4) dialogue with informants beyond the self, and 5) commitment to theoretical analysis (Anderson 2006).

This critical autoethnographic analysis represents a compendium of two visits to the monument and museum. In the first, I visited by myself and constructed my initial reflections based on my thoughts as a visitor viewing the monument and experiencing the museum for the first time. I engaged the second visit as part of a large group comprised primarily of students from the Religious Studies Department, the African American Studies Department, and the Multicultural Center at my university. I brought these two visits together in order to engage the extended dialogues with visitors integral to a critical autoethnography and to further enrich my self-reflection by noting the ways in which viewing the monument and museum exhibits as part of a group impacted my own experiences of them, as well as my thoughts about their meanings.

I develop this analysis through three sections. In the first, I discuss the evolution of the National Memorial for Peace and Justice and situate it within a more theoretical discussion of the rhetorical work of museums and monuments. In the subsequent section, I offer my autoethnographic reflection of my visits to both structures. In the final section, I conclude with a reflection on the possibilities that the memorial specifically and Black-centered memories in general offer to the production of a critical regionalism.

THE NATIONAL MEMORIAL FOR PEACE AND JUSTICE AS A RHETORICAL TEXT

There are two features of the National Memorial for Peace and Justice that render it one of the most unique memorials in the country. The first is that it highlights the history of lynching, serving as a material remembrance of the "4400 African American men, women, and children [who] were hanged, burned alive, shot, drowned, and beaten to death by white mobs between 1877 and 1950" (Equal Justice Initiative). This uniqueness lies not only in the fact that it is the only large-scale memorial to one of the most sordid chapters in American history—indeed, it is often colloquially referred to as "the lynching memorial"—but also in the fact that, in dredging up the ghosts from an era in which racist violence was considered the "normal way of doing things," it undercuts hegemonic regional narratives about whiteness, benevolence, and the rule of law.

The other distinctive characteristic of the memorial is that it consists of both a monument and a museum. While it is certainly not the only memorial institution in which a monument and a museum exist in conjunction, it is one of a small handful of such structures, with its distinctiveness lying in the dialogic relationship between the two and the combined narrative they craft linking the racial violence of the past to that of the present. In addition to the eight hundred pillars of Corten steel monument spread over four acres featuring the names of lynching victims by county, there is another edifice, the Legacy Museum, which emphasizes the history preceding and following the timeframe embodied on the monument, providing important context for the meanings visitors may expect to derive from it ("Confronting the Past" 2018).

These visitors may buy tickets to see one or both structures and can walk or take a short shuttle bus ride between them. While one may choose to begin the tourist experience with either structure, staff members encourage all to visit the museum before viewing the monument.

The National Memorial for Peace and Justice thus mobilizes the rhetorical features of both museums and monuments. History museums are educational in nature, serving as a pedagogical resource, through both displays for visitors and the workshops, special exhibitions, lectures, and other events they often host (Hooper-Greenhill 1999, 3). Indeed, through the use of material objects, space, interaction, technology, and other aspects of the museum experience, combined with the cultural authority assigned to museums, visitors often get a more meaningful education in history than is typically acquired through other means of historical production. However, this pedagogical function raises an important question, one that Fleming has posed: "How do museum professionals determine what lessons from history the museum visitor must learn?" (1994, 1020). The answer to this question lies in another important function of museums. Beyond their capacity to bring history to life through the display of artifacts from the past, museums advance particular historical narratives, creating memories that help define and respond to the values of the communities in which they are located and the constituencies they hope to attract. As such, they are civic institutions occupying a multitude of roles: spaces for cultural interchange and negotiation of values, operations for the creation of citizens, places of empowerment and recognition, and sites for the revitalization and economic development of communities, among other functions and expectations (Kratz and Karp 2006).

This civic identity of museums renders them inherently rhetorical institutions. They are decidedly partisan enterprises that attempt to persuade us that a particular era of history is important and relevant to the present while deploying a multitude of display strategies through which they make this connection. In engaging these strategies, they construct our memories of the past—both those of the history itself and of our experiences visiting the museum. Their rhetoricity lies in their capacity to build these memories, as the individual memories they shape become collective memories and, through their development within a community institution representative of its shared values, evolve to become *public* memories. As Weiser has suggested, history museums might be more appropriately termed "public memory" museums, in that they "bring present-day values to bear on their selection of past events" (2017, 151). These values may be seen in any of a variety of exhibition strategies the museum employs to construct the memories crucial to advancing its mission, including the selection of display artifacts, the public faces it deems representative of its historical focus, the use of technology to engage visitors interactively, the use of space inside the museum to encourage visitor dialogue, and the use of space and place outside of it (Davis 2016).

While the rhetoricity of museums is an important factor in building and maintaining a sense of shared identity based on assumed dominant values, it is particularly important for what Weiser (2017) refers to as "alternative museums," or those that present memories that destabilize, rather than maintain, dominant values. These institutions represent the memories of marginalized groups whose historical experiences often run counter to society's dominant values. As Weiser explains, the sense of identity constructed through these institutions is one that foregrounds opposition and builds a sense of civic duty that relies on the elaboration of new narratives intended to change the master narrative. As such, they perform the cultural work of attracting "nontraditional" visitors and complicating the civic identity of the places in which they are located. As is the case with museums, monuments are rhetorical structures "to the extent [that they] are intended by their creators and/or perceived by audiences to perpetuate values, admonish as to future conduct, and affirm or challenge existing power relations" (Gallagher 1995, 112). Like museums, they thus "speak," through their very existence, of the presumed place meanings of their surroundings. However, in comparison to museums, the rhetoricity of monuments operates in a different, and perhaps more powerful, manner.

The public nature of monuments is much more imposing; unlike museums, they are often the results of public input as to their form and content, unveiled in relatively high-profile public ceremonies and typically maintained with public funds. More importantly, while visitors must deliberately enter—and typically pay admission—to experience a museum, monuments advance unabashedly partisan memories upon anyone who encounters them in the often-prominent public spaces they occupy. Though they can be removed—and sometimes are—their presumed permanence ensures that the versions of history they represent are, quite literally, etched in stone.

The rhetorical work monuments perform serves to not only concretize particular historical narratives, but to venerate them. This lends an element of the sacred to the monument, such that any critique leveled at them may be discursively positioned as an act of desecration. In part, this is because of their role in commemorating death in some manner, often in terms of memorializing deceased figures or the scenes of trauma and suffering. However, there is a powerful ideological element to the cultural and political projects that discourses of reverence perform: they may situate monuments as material reminders that, of all of the interpretations that may exist about a particular historical event, person, or era, it is the specific event memorialized in stone that is being elevated above all the others and stands as inviolable. In conjunction with their very public nature, the notion that these structures are sacrosanct asserts even more powerful claims about the assumed values and collective identity of a community. In this role of linking the past to the present, they are often erected and maintained as means of preserving the social and political status quo, as "material devices for social control" (Molyneux 1995, 18; see also Stevens, Franck, and Fazakerley 2012).

Monuments located in urban areas, in particular, are significant products of the complex tapestry of social, cultural, political, and economic relationships characteristic of cities. Rosalyn Deutsche has situated cities as the products of social practices, a social form that "affirms the right of culturally excluded groups to have access to [it]—to make decisions about the spaces they use, to be attached to the places where they live, to refuse marginalization" (1996, 52–53). Urban monuments, then, often serve to "bring to the fore and critique what is often forgotten, omitted or silenced by the collectivity—especially in relation to its collective history—in the official narratives of the past. . . . [they] re-enact discourses of memory that were rejected, omitted or outright silenced by the [urban/local/national] collectivity and make virtue of what would otherwise be deemed difficult or inconvenient past" (Krzyzanowska 2016, 471). This role ensures that urban monuments may also serve a more dialogic function, providing for a mode of contesting rather than advancing the status quo. These structures are thus implicated in the formation of alternative place meanings and identities for the community.

The National Memorial for Peace and Justice combines the rhetoricity of alternative museums and counter monuments to recover narratives from an era of history often buried in other memory texts. In so doing, it builds a sense of cultural trauma in visitors.

Historian Spencer Crew (1996) has suggested that African Americans have unique concerns with preserving their history, as the erasure of memories highlighting the breadth and depth of Black achievements in America is crucial to their continuing marginalization. While the recognition of these contributions is paramount to questions of identity, citizenship, and belonging, it is also important to acknowledge them within a broader context concerned with cultural trauma. As a theoretical framework, cultural trauma extends beyond the collective trauma the members of a group may experience in the wake of an event to encompass its remembrance generations after those directly impacted have passed on. As Jeffrey Alexander and his coauthors explain, cultural trauma occurs when members of a group "feel they have been subjected to a horrendous event that leaves indelible marks upon their group consciousness, marking their memories forever and changing their future identity in fundamental and irrevocable ways" (2004, 1). Further, the construction of cultural trauma encompasses the broader collectivity—including entire societies—in the identification and assumption of social responsibility for the suffering. In the US, this includes the production of material structures that highlight memories designed to encourage visitors to forge connections between the racial terrorism of the past and its contemporary legacy in mass incarceration.

This is the goal of the National Memorial for Peace and Justice. A project of the nonprofit Equal Justice Initiative (EJI), it is an outgrowth of the organization's commitment to ending mass incarceration and excessive punishment, relieving poverty, challenging discrimination, and protecting basic human rights (Equal Justice Initiative). Bryan Stevenson, who founded the EJI and serves as its director, is a Montgomery-based human rights attorney who has spent his career defending African American men sentenced to harsh punishment in Alabama's prisons, up to and including the death penalty. Aware of the historical continuum between the decline of public lynchings and the institution of legal capital punishment, Stevenson conceived of the memorial as a visible reminder of the interconnectedness of the two. As he explained in an article about him in the *New Yorker*, "'One factor, to be honest, was that we started talking about a memorial to 9/11 victims within five years,' he said. 'It's not as if we haven't waited long enough to begin the process of a memorial to lynching. So, that's when it became clear to me that, in addition to the markers, we needed to be talking about a space, a bigger, deeper, richer space. The markers will give you a little snapshot, but we need to tell the whole story'" (Toobin 2016). In deciding that a monument was the most compelling way to provide visitors with a sense of scale of the violence, bloodshed, and terror induced by lynching, Stevenson drew inspiration from the Holocaust Memorial in Berlin and the Apartheid Museum in Johannesburg (Robertson 2018). Staffers at the EJI set to work in archives and county libraries, identifying lynching victims in twelve states. They eventually discovered approximately eight hundred more than had been previously known (Toobin 2016). Further, because cultural trauma impacts entire societies, not just its direct victims, Stevenson makes clear that the memorial's discursive focus on lynching is meant to construct a set of memories mobilized in the service of redemption. As he has explained, "'I'm not interested in talking about America's history because I want to punish America. . . . I want to liberate America'"; "'If I believe that each of us is more than the worst thing he's ever done,' he said, 'I have to believe that for everybody'" (Robertson 2018).

The memorial is also part of a project to spur revitalization of Montgomery's downtown district and its historic Black neighborhood of West Montgomery, which house the museum and monument, respectively. According to a local city planner, the once-thriving West Montgomery neighborhood's decline was precipitated—intentionally—with the construction of a freeway in the early 1970s. Thus, even in its role as an engine of tourism and economic investment, the memorial seeks to recover traumatic memories that extend beyond its display of lynching and engages another of its many legacies—in this case, those associated with economic disinvestment[2] (Blumgart 2018). Because the public representation of African American-centered historical narratives is a relatively new phenomenon, the institutions responsible for their recovery may be situated as vehicles that bring in new audiences eager to see their own memories reflected in our urban landscapes.

It is in the spirit of the knowledge that African American history museums and memorials—and Black memory practices in general—serve a multitude of functions that I began my autoethnographic journey to the memorial. As the museum and monument themselves represent a centering of Black historical experiences, African American self-reflections on visiting them represent a similar emphasis. However, an important qualification is in order. The construction of memory is an inherently social process not only in terms of the ways the past is brought to life in the present, but also in the ways in which we recollect our engagement with historical texts. Furthermore, one of the shortcomings of more traditional approaches to southern rhetoric is the problem of voice; when African American perspectives are acknowledged at all, Black voices are often presumed to be monolithic. While I evaluate my own insights into my visits to the museum and monument partially in terms of my interactions with others, I cannot—and do not—claim to speak for their experiences. My reflection is mine, and mine alone.

AN AUTOETHNOGRAPHIC JOURNEY TO THE NATIONAL MEMORIAL FOR PEACE AND JUSTICE

When I arrive outside of my office building in downtown Atlanta to await the arrival of the bus that will transport us on the two-hour trip to Montgomery, I take a quick visual inventory of exactly who is going. My previous research on Black vernacular historians—Civil War reenactors, museum staff and visitors, and others—had indicated two primary objectives they sought in their work: to pass along little-known Black history narratives to young African Americans, and to ensure that these narratives were situated as part of American history, rather than relegated to the much narrower confines of "Black" history.[3]

With this in mind, whenever I participate in any activity related to public history, I am pleased to see diversity in the visitors who, I hope, are learning from the experience. With this group of forty-six fellow travelers, I am not disappointed. Our group is multiracial and representative of various ages; most are young undergraduates, but there are a handful of folks who are middle-aged and older. Some of the students are coming as part of a "Theories and Concepts in Africana

Studies" course, while others are participating through their engagement with the Multicultural Center. Many of the members of our group are students in a religious studies course entitled "Religion in the American South."

I was particularly intrigued by the connection between the history of lynching and religion. Bailey and Snedker's examination of institutional religion and lynching found that religion, as a significant social institution in the South, "influenced the shape of local racial conflict and thus played a mitigating or exacerbating role in the incidence of lynching" (2011, 848). The embeddedness of religion in white southerners' collective consciousness, and especially its role in the formation of a moral community committed to white supremacy, they argued, was central to the activation of solidarity-enhancing rituals such as lynching. The activities that turned lynching into a public spectacle—the large crowds, the angling for photos with the corpse, the disfiguring of the body for souvenirs, the postcards—were all processes designed to sustain racial solidarity among white people and teach a "moral" lesson to Black people.

While this framework constitutes one way to examine the role of religion in racial violence, there is another perspective, one that shifts the analytical focus onto African Americans and is rooted in the remembrance, rather than the act, of violence. The element of the sacred assigned to monuments constructs the memorial as symbolic of African American suffering and death, while positioning the victims as martyrs to the cause of equality and freedom. As I would later realize upon my entry to the monument, visitors' initial experience with it is discursively geared toward viewing it in these terms, as they are encouraged to remain quiet, to resist taking "selfies" with the sculptures at the start of the exhibit, and to generally regard the area as a sacred space. Additionally, as I would also find out, the jars of soil taken from the actual sites of lynching and displayed in the museum serve a similar purpose.

During the two-hour ride to Montgomery, we watch the film Black Panther *on the televisions on the bus as a means of psychologically preparing ourselves for the emotional toll that the museum and monument might exact on us. How fitting that we might be expected to find—in Wakanda!—the psychological strength to endure the visual and material displays of racial violence and death that await us in Montgomery. We first head to the Peace and Justice Monument. Because of a glitch with our lunch reservation, we have to reschedule our appointed time to visit the Legacy Museum for later in the afternoon, and instead tour the monument first. Upon disembarking from the bus, we stand in line to gain entry to the monument. In addition to the unusual fact that one has to pay admission to view it, it is the only such edifice I have ever visited that requires all who enter its space to go through a security screening, including having our bags checked and walking through a metal detector. This, to me, is highly significant, as it demonstrates just how controversial the remembrance of lynching is, the intensity* of the opposition to the disruption of the status quo such a monument represents, and most importantly, the necessity of its existence.

Once we have gone through the security screening, we enter the grounds; there is a beautiful walkway leading up to the monument, with sculptures and a wall featuring descriptions of the historical context of lynching etched in stone. Before we begin our journey up to the steel columns containing the names of the victims, museum staff instruct us on the proper decorum when viewing the monument. Though we are allowed to take photos of the sculptures, wall, and columns, we are not permitted to take "selfies" with the "family in chains" sculpture at the beginning of the walkway. "We have to respect the monument as a sacred place," the staff member cautioned us. "No laughing, no running." The sculpture, which depicts a life-sized African family in chains, presumably about to embark on the transatlantic slave trade, immediately strikes me as an important part of the story of racial terrorism in America that is often left out of narratives focused on lynching. Its location at the beginning of the walkway to the monument establishes it materially as an antecedent. "That's kind of deep," one of the members of my group exclaims as she reaches out and rubs the mother and child sculptures. Though I occasionally see people breaking the proscription and posing for selfies with it, most everyone appears to respect the position of sanctity assigned to the sculpture.

The walkway up to the columns provides a brief history lesson on lynching, offering an explanation as to what it was and the cultural trauma it inflicted on Black people and the psychological damage it imposed on the white people who participated in it. In linking the past to the present, this history reminds us that the "enduring national and institutional wounds" have not healed and that the communities in which lynchings took place remain the sites of Black economic, social, and political marginalization. I am happy to see that this connection is "driven home" in such a way, as it not only provides important context for viewing the columns as more than just "names written in steel" would be (which, when viewed without context, might serve merely as an abstraction for some). In terms of the particular group of which I am a part, it also enables young folks—of all races and ethnicities—to see how they might be impacted in some way by this history. Later, on the bus trip back home, I would be able to see the effectiveness of this.

Visitors follow the walkway up a low hill to the steel columns themselves. The columns, or "mini" monuments, are hanging from the ceiling, in much the same way that the bodies of lynching victims hung from trees. Each represents a county where one or more lynchings took place and lists the name(s) of the victim(s), if known. This enables us to imagine the victims in more human terms—through learning of their actual names—and to better envision the scope of lynching in terms of when and where it occurred. One of the things I find most striking

Outside view of memorial. Photo by Christina L. Moss.

Outside view of monuments, each representing a county where one or more lynchings took place. Notice text designating names, where known, of those lynched. Photo by Christina L. Moss.

about this is the number of names that appear to be those of women. While I was aware that there were women who were lynched, I was not aware that there were so many. This, of course, undermines the master narrative of lynchings, which suggests that they typically occurred as retribution for Black men's alleged sexual assaults against white women.

Many of the visitors in our group, including myself, are curious about the record of lynching in the places where we have lived. Two white students, a male and a female, are staring intently at the column listing the lynchings in Tulsa, Oklahoma. In terms of the number of lynchings that took place there—about three dozen—this is one of the more intriguing columns. As I walk past them, I hear the female student exclaim to the male, "Wow, we don't really think of Oklahoma in this way," to which he responds that not all lynchings occurred in what we think of as the South. I double back to ask them if they are originally from Oklahoma. The man says he is from Memphis. "It was really bad there," he says of his hometown. "But [Oklahoma] was twice as bad." As I continue to walk through the columns, I see one student using a piece of paper and a marker to trace one of the names located on the column for Shelby County, Tennessee.

I look for the county of my hometown in Virginia and the county in Atlanta in which I currently reside. Unsurprisingly, I find that both are represented on the columns. There are rows of similar columns displayed outside of the monument; county officials are allowed to negotiate with the EJI to take them and officially display them in their own communities.

There are two aspects of the monument that I find particularly striking. The first involves its use of space. There is a large grassy area in the middle of the structure that houses the columns. As I look at the columns, I hear a staff member explaining the significance of the area to a group of about twenty visiting high school students. "This grassy space symbolizes those who watched and did nothing," she explains to them. "This provides a small sense of justice in its design." I later catch up with her and ask her to elaborate on the space, which is called Memorial Park. "It is dedicated specifically to victims of the public spectacle of lynching," she tells me. "It's a reversal—having them in the center surrounded by the victims [promotes a] sense of social justice. It is our most powerful space, for me, really interactive. People are really learning; it's causing them to dig deeper."

The Memorial Park represents an especially innovative use of space and is consistent with the rhetorical strategies African American history museums often deploy in their objectives to destabilize dominant historical narratives and recover silenced memories. However, this particular use of space is quite a bit different from the spatial discourses a slavery museum might mobilize to demonstrate the ways in which an entire community was implicated in the associated violence. Because many lynchings were public spectacles, the use of space to symbolically turn the tables on those who witnessed the events is a powerful rhetorical strategy in that it refocuses the visitor's attention away from the victims onto the perpetrators—those whose smiling visages in the face of unspeakable cruelty typically escape critical scrutiny in historical accounts of lynching (Hale 2002). It also enables visitors to momentarily occupy the physical and spatial position of witnesses gazing upward, bringing

View of hanging monument display from the ground looking up. Photo by Christina L. Moss.

View of monument from grassy "witnessing" area. Photo by Christina L. Moss.

racial identity to the forefront as white and Black people experience this role differently.

The second especially striking aspect of the monument involves the placards providing details on the reasons specific victims were lynched. David Hunter was lynched in Laurens, South Carolina, in 1898 for leaving the farm where he worked without permission. William Donegan was killed in 1908 in Springfield, Missouri, for having a white wife. David Walker, his wife, and four children were lynched after he was accused of using inappropriate language with a white woman. One woman was lynched in Rome, Tennessee, in 1908 by a mob looking for her brother. The reasons for the violence ranged from the merely ridiculous to the astoundingly ridiculous: for complaining about being refused service in a store . . . for walking directly behind his white boss's wife . . . for refusing to abandon their land to white people . . . for annoying a white woman . . . for suing a white man who killed his cow . . . for asking a white woman for a drink of water . . . for organizing local sharecroppers . . . for testifying against a white man accused of raping a Black woman . . . for walking past a window while a white woman was inside the building . . . for registering Black voters . . . for voting. The list of transgressions against the racial order for which African Americans were subjected to brutal violence and death goes on and on. I find myself picturing what the person looked like and wondering what each one thought and felt just before the moment of death, knowing that he or she was about to leave this world because he or she had the audacity to respond to insults or injustices in remarkably human ways or to engage in the same mundane activities we now perform without thinking. Because of the monument, they are presented as individuals rather than subsumed into the broad category of "lynching victim"; through it, they evolve from historical objects to historical subjects. Now, here—immortalized in stone on a wall—they are still victims, but through a brief glimpse of their names and stories on the memorial, they have all recovered in death the humanity they were denied in life. Through this recovery, they are afforded agency as the responsibility (and accompanying disgust) is finally placed where it belongs: on the killers.

This, along with the fact that women were also lynched in significant numbers, refutes the historical myths that have underlined dominant memories of lynching. Though the history of lynching had not been hidden from me as a young person, I had been taught that the violence was exacted as retribution, a form of extrajudicial "justice" for an actual crime a Black person had been accused of committing. Though I'd long known that this was not the case, I was still astonished by the "offenses" that would bring terror upon the entire community. Further, when one calls forth the images of the carnivalesque nature of the rituals in which some of this violence was carried out—the sneering faces in photos from the era, the dissemination and collection of body parts as souvenirs, the proud boasting about attending "barbecues"—it is emblematic of the violence associated with whiteness, the savagery that whites have expended considerable cultural, political, and social resources projecting onto others. Such deadly "pettiness" is revealing, not in terms of what it tells us about Black people, but in what it tells us about whiteness.

These brief descriptions of individual instances of lynching destabilize contemporary discourses positioning whiteness as benevolent and innocent—crucial assumptions in the sustenance of racial hierarchies. To the extent that racism is acknowledged as a white problem, rather than a Black problem, it is often individualized, which creates separable white villains in the service of leaving dominant ideas about whiteness itself intact. Memories of lynching (as does much of southern history) tend to undermine this project, and not just in the sense that large numbers of people may be seen in photos of the events. This is also in the sense that the entire justice system—in its refusal to hold the participants accountable in any meaningful way, in spite of photographic and testimonial evidence—as well as the broader society—in its long-time refusal to pass antilynching legislation and its continuance of racial terrorism in the form of contemporary police violence—become structurally implicated in the sustenance of racial hierarchies. Marshaling the past in the service of interrogating the present is part of the social and political work Black memorial institutions perform and, to the extent that their presentation of marginalized memories subverts dominant discourses about racial identity, is part of the underlying missions of alternative museums in general. It is this subversion that undergirded the 2002 controversy over the "Without Sanctuary" exhibit of lynching photographs and postcards. The exhibit, which had been displayed in the North, had trouble finding an exhibition space in Atlanta until the Martin Luther King Jr. Historical Site stepped in and provided it. The lynching monument resumes the work of forcing critical reflections on whiteness, in line with Ida B. Wells-Barnett's entreaty to foreground violence as one of its defining characteristics (Hale 2002).

Upon exiting the monument, the visitor is able to see replicas of all the columns inside, laid flat for easier viewing. I pass a student from our group who looks at several of those from Georgia and expresses skepticism that they tell the whole story. "You know Cobb [County] must have more than one; they must not have cooperated," she says. "My home county, Barrow—one name. I can guarantee you that's not true. That's definitely not true. I came a long way just to see this." She continues, "There were lynchings in Walton County—the next country over, in the seventies. So, you know there were more in Barrow. None of these are surprising. Nothing's changed."

During the short shuttle ride to the museum, with the Eyes on the Prize *television series showing on the video screen, the driver offers a short narration of Montgomery's city streets, pointing out the fact that the building housing the museum, along with those surrounding it, were once warehouses for enslaved persons. We enter the museum and go through yet another metal detector, a final reminder of the ironies inherent in the fact that the memories therein are meant to revitalize the city's downtown area, but are still perceived as "threatening" to the status quo.*

Upon beginning the tour of the museum, which is completely self-guided, one is confronted with the systemic nature of the racial subjugation that culminated in lynching through the display of slavery as its antecedent. The tour begins with a description of slavery in Montgomery, which is an aspect of the city's history of which few people are aware—as it is associated in the popular imagination with civil rights history. The display describes Montgomery as "one of the largest slave-trading cities in the country" and informs visitors that the spot where they are standing was the site where enslaved people were warehoused. It includes a dramatized video, without dialogue, depicting the march of enslaved persons to the warehouse. Most interestingly, the display describes the importance of slavery to Montgomery's economy, noting that Montgomery is "a city shaped by slavery." It also notes how whites became wealthy through the institution and remain so to this day, while descendants of the enslaved remain in poverty.

In addition to linking lynching to slavery, the description of Montgomery's antebellum history is very important for another reason: it works to change the place meanings of the city. Montgomery is associated in the popular imagination with civil rights history, including that displayed in many of its other museums, including the Freedom Riders Museum and the Rosa Parks Museum. The display complicates the symbolic meanings assigned to Montgomery, replacing the "triumphal" narrative associated with the civil rights movement with a set of memories that are not quite as settled. This is with respect to both the city's Confederate memorial landscape and the memories of the unpunished racial terrorism the monument and museum represent. The two work in conjunction to assign to Montgomery an air of "unfinished business" that may be in conflict with the image it is attempting to craft for tourists, but that its Black residents perhaps know all too well. When a person walks the streets of the commercial district in the area surrounding the museum, with its tourist-centered shops and restaurants, she could be forgiven for developing the impression that the city has evolved a bit more dramatically than its current reality might suggest. The museum's brief invitation to visitors to reflect on the contemporary racial wealth gap of the city's residents (and, by implication, the disparities characteristic of the entire country) serves as a reminder that the racial subjugation of which lynching was a part finds its present-day expression in their economic impoverishment. In broader terms, the reassignment of Montgomery's place meaning and the reminder of slavery's economic legacy work concomitantly to disrupt the "post-racial" narrative of progress advanced through the city's touristic urban landscape.

After reading the detailed descriptions of this history, I move on to the next exhibit, which was one of the two that resonated most memorably with me. The exhibit is a series of glass-encased "slave pens," each one containing a hologram, with audio, that activates when the visitor approaches. These ghostly images depict Black women, men, and children speaking of the pain of familial separation, one of the most profound traumas of enslavement. I am especially intrigued by this exhibit, as this is where my dual identities as an academic and an African American come together. As I look at the images and listen to the anguished cries emanating from them, I am hyperaware of the power of combining first-person narratives with technology as a means of enabling visitors to engage museum displays interactively. As a Black woman who is also a mother, I can't help but think that, had I been born in an earlier time, I could have been one of these women.

The atmosphere inside the museum is quite somber, save for a group of young high school students who occasionally erupt in fits of loud laughter during conversations among themselves. One of the things I first notice is that there are very few objects. Instead, we see a chronological mapping of the "evolution" of slavery into the convict leasing system, racial segregation, and the Jim Crow era more generally. The spatial trajectory continues with the Great Migration, the War on Drugs, and mass incarceration. Most of these exhibits consist of images on the walls, rather than artifacts.

The Legacy Museum relies less on objects and more on its spatial arrangements in the production of visitor memories of lynching. In this particular case, however, space is not primarily deployed in the service of enabling museum staff to control the interpretation of the displayed history, but rather in the crafting of a chronological/visual narrative. This is important because space, perhaps as much as artifacts, is an indelible part of visitors' cognitive and affective processing of the displayed history, an aspect of the "internal understanding" they are expected to share and develop through their movement throughout the structure (Storch 2014). Space thus becomes an "interpretive agent, active in the making of meaning" (MacLeod 2005, 1). In the case of the Legacy Museum, interior space functions to enable visitors to conceptualize lynching not as a series of isolated events, but as part of a broader system of racial subjugation that continues to this day.

The museum makes productive use of technology, with an interactive electronic map of the United States that enables visitors to touch particular places to see where lynching occurred. One of the more interesting uses of this technology involves booths wherein visitors can pick up a "telephone" and "speak" to an imprisoned person, who tells his or her story in vivid detail. Despite my urge to move on to other displays, I am fascinated enough to play the role of a visitor to the "prison" and listen to all of them. There is also a display case with brief descriptions of Supreme Court cases pertaining to race and civil rights, as well as a wall with an exhibition of racial segregation signs from the Jim Crow era. As was the case with the monument and the plaques describing the reasons for lynching, I am simultaneously amused and angered by the absurdity and cruelty of white supremacy: "No negroes or apes allowed in this building" . . . "Negroes not wanted in the North or the South. Send them back to Africa where God Almighty put them to begin with. That is their home" . . . "Clark's Café: All-white help, a good place to eat" . . . "No n-----s, no Jews, no dogs."

The museum is not completely devoid of objects, as there is a set of artifacts that is quite innovative. I'd read about this particular exhibit and was looking forward to viewing it. To the right, as I enter the museum, I see the wall of jars containing soil from various lynching sites, collected from the descendants of the victims. This display is the result of the EJI's Community Remembrance Project. Though I find the display intriguing in its originality and find myself looking to see if there are jars from the various places I have inhabited during my life (there are), it is not the most compelling exhibit in the museum for me—either personally or professionally.

I am far more interested in two displays that comprise the exhibit on incarceration that, in addition to the holographic slave pen images, resonate with me most powerfully. The first involves a series of letters from incarcerated individuals in Alabama's prisons. Part of the display takes up the entire back wall of the museum and contains plaques with the letters, while excerpts from them are projected on the wall above. The anguished pleas from the prisoners are heartrending: "It's getting harder to survive in here with my humanity intact"; "I am 20 years of age and I've been incarcerated since I was 14 years old. I'm to the point where I just want to give up"; "I am the youngest person in the whole jail . . . I'm only 15 and fearing for my life. Please don't let them throw me away"; "It's odd that humans created these conditions and treat me like this." Though these entreaties are affecting, the emotion they inspire in me is anger, rather than sadness. I get the sense from others in our group that they are affected in much the same way. While this is a more personal rumination, the other element of the incarceration exhibit resonates with me on both personal and professional levels. One of the prisoners whose story is featured on the "prison telephone" display is actually there in the flesh, telling his story to visitors. A group of young women college students, including some from our group, listen raptly as he speaks.

This exhibit, whether taken as a whole or separated into its component parts, is particularly poignant, as those who are most intimately impacted by mass incarceration are virtually invisible, shut out of most mainstream modes of representation. Within the contemporary prison industrial complex, there are often two sets of victims—those who are the victims of crimes committed by the incarcerated, and the individuals and entire communities subjected to the violence perpetrated by and through the carceral state.[4] The museum's presentation of mass incarceration as an extension of lynching mobilizes the rhetorical powers of testimonial. As Lopez (2005) has suggested, there is a third player in these stories of violence: witnesses, both passive and active. Through the display of these letters and the first-person narratives of a flesh-and-blood former prisoner, the museum mobilizes the pathos implicated in prisoner narratives to encourage visitors to adopt the role of witnesses and, presumably, agents of social change. This is a particularly compelling display strategy for a museum with activist goals.

Once visitors have served as "witnesses" in these exhibits, the museum's layout leads them to a series of videos displaying documentary-style first-person narratives, one of which is centered on the stories of Alabama's prisoners and the brutality of its prisons. I watch them with some of the students from our group. "Jesus . . . it's a shame," exclaims one. "Oh, it's gonna make me cry," says another. As the video ends, one student mutters "tough stuff," as she gets up to leave. Another student offers an extended reflection on the impact of the display. "It made me think a lot. A lot of the points made me mad," she says. "The more I get mad, the more . . . I don't know what to do with my anger. I want to go into law. It's like you [have] invisible chains. My short-term goal is to be a civil rights attorney." My hope, which is that the combination of these scenes, the prison letters, and the dialogue with the former prisoner would move at least some of them to action with respect to prison reform, is aligned with the EJI's goals. The affect and effects I observed here offer some hope.

While walking through the museum's exit hall, I read the series of plaques posing questions for visitors to ponder upon their departure. One in particular catches my eye. It references the ongoing debates over the removal of Confederate monuments and notes that most states have done nothing to acknowledge the history of slavery or to recognize its legacy. What, it implores, should be done about this? Because I write about Black memory practices as counternarratives to Confederate monuments and other white supremacist artifacts, I am pleased about this call to action.

Once we are back on the bus and headed home to Atlanta, we reflect as a group on our experiences at both memorial structures; the students are asked to do so in light of their classes. One religious studies student comments on the role religion played in both enslavement and lynching. "One thing I have learned in class is the role religion played in slavery," she says. "The lynching museum [suggested that] some of these people had probably come from church and were lynching folks. Very distasteful, very selfish. Not what religion is supposed to be about." In response to this, one of the professor-organizers of the trip reminds the students of one of their readings, referring to James Cone's identification of lynching with crucifixtion, likening the victims and Black people more generally to Jesus. As I am not an especially religious person, I admit—to myself—that I had not considered this interpretation. Nevertheless, I find it sufficiently intriguing to explore it a bit further and later—back at home—find that this view, foregrounded in Cone's book, The Cross and the Lynching Tree, *is consistent with Black liberation theology. This represents a much different intervention of religion into narratives of lynching, and certainly into what we regard as canonical southern inquiry.*

Another student on the bus situates her experiences in light of what it reveals about whiteness: "The psychology of white people—what motivates the things we saw?" "Do you mean the psychology of white people or the psychology of whiteness," one of the professors interjects. "The psychology of racism," the student clarifies. The professor responds by briefly discussing the trauma the white onlookers— particularly the children—must have experienced in witnessing such a horrific event, their grinning, leering faces in lynching photographs notwithstanding. I can't help but imagine the lifelong psychological damage with which I would have to grapple had my parents participated in such barbarity, much less brought me and my siblings along, as if it were a normal family outing.

Others on the bus choose to focus more on the economic forces that propelled the system of racial subjugation. "Some of the displays suggested it was really a monetary incentive," a male student explains. "Capitalism and racism are linked. We need a revolution to change the system." At this point, the professor asks the students to forge connections between the displayed memories and their own lives, pointing out that much of the segregationist rhetoric featured in one of the museum displays is echoed in our contemporary political discourse. One student responds with an expression of gratitude for what the Freedom Riders accomplished, suggesting that she is able to ride MARTA (Atlanta's public transportation system) because of what they did. Another student, who self- identifies as Black but not African American, expresses her appreciation for being invited to attend the trip as part of her honors government class. "My mom and dad did not tell me about this. These things are still prevalent and still matter," she says. "It's good we're able to remember this." As I listen to these responses, I am not only very proud of our students, but also grateful for the vision of the EJI in conceiving and constructing both institutions.

These reflections illustrate the work that African American archival institutions perform. On a more general level, they prompt visitors to forge more direct connections between the past and the present and to examine the ways in which historical narratives are never just a set of objective facts, but rather social constructions designed to achieve contemporary agendas— whether those agendas are concerned with maintaining or challenging the status quo. The National Memorial for Peace and Justice enacts that agenda, with the specific goal of stimulating visitors to think critically about the meanings of racial terrorism, including those forms of it they may not have otherwise perceived as "terrorism" as we currently conceive of it. In so doing, it urges visitors to engage in social action and to view themselves as historical agents. New approaches to southern rhetoric must account for these goals.

CONCLUSION: TOWARDS A CRITICAL REGIONALISM
FOR THE TWENTY-FIRST CENTURY

Thompson and Sloan (2018) have noted that, while most academic treatments of southern identity have focused almost exclusively on the perspectives and experiences of white southerners, race is an indelible aspect of any comprehensive discussion of the "South" as a geographic region and an identity. Indeed, they assert, it is through labor, sacrifice, and blood that African Americans played an essential role in the development of the region. Thus, a critical regionalism must contest and account for this erasure. This includes the development of rhetorical analyses that decenter whiteness and destabilize its dominant assumptions, as well as the cultivation of nontraditional modes of scholarly inquiry. Though there are many forms this new approach may assume, two important elements stand out. The first involves the production of analyses grounded in critical memory that account for the multitude of historical experiences and interpretations of the past that have long characterized the region but have only recently begun receiving scholarly attention. The second involves the development of nontraditional modes of inquiry that seek out alternative ways of knowing, thereby empowering diverse voices to contribute to the so-called canon of southern rhetoric. Autoethnography presents such a method.

African American memorial structures represent not only the particular versions of the past they highlight, but also the changing demographics and shifting cultural norms of the South, as African American civic leaders understand the importance of recovering Black-centered memories that have been marginalized and overturning hegemonic white-centered narratives. Lynching memorials are especially important in this regard. In highlighting the triviality of the reasons for lynching and the casual—though spectacular—manner in which racial violence was perpetrated, they serve to undercut the righteousness that traditional regional rhetorics have implicitly or explicitly assigned to the idea of "southern justice." More importantly, in emphasizing Black resilience as a response to racial violence, they also serve as material interrogations of dominant assumptions of white moral superiority, rendering it as characteristic of Blackness rather than whiteness.

The National Memorial for Peace and Justice presents an excellent case study of an institution designed to raise these questions. In confronting, in vivid detail, the region's (and country's) history of racial violence, it forces us to rethink long-held assumptions about Blackness and whiteness, doing so through the visual and material reproduction of trauma. The cultural work the memorial performs—indeed its very existence—enables us to reimagine the South as a site of emancipatory politics rather than the reactionary politics

that history has baked into the idea of "southern rhetoric." Specifically, it uses
the cultural realm to continue the political work of the foot soldiers of the civil
rights movement, supplanting public address as the default assumption with
respect to popular notions of regional discourse. This is of great importance
to rhetorical studies more generally, as race remains one of the most potent
forces in American politics and culture. Though the South will always serve
as the primal scene for the production and sustenance of race as a relevant
social category, the positioning of mass incarceration and hyperpolicing as
the legacies of lynching ensures that the history and contemporary reality of
racial violence and the hierarchies that sustain it remain an indelible part of
the *American* story.

Finally, because this analysis foregrounds autoethnographic observations,
I will end with a personal reflection. Around the same time that I made my
second visit to the memorial, I read two op-ed columns in the *New York Times*,
both written by Black women who were mildly critical of Barack and Michelle
Obama. In the first, the writer criticized the former president's persistent
"finger-wagging" at young Black men for their perceived shortcomings vis-à-vis
toxic masculinity and assumed lack of assimilation into the wider culture, along
with his failure to adequately address institutional racism (Purnell 2019). In the
second, the writer expressed her desire that the former first lady would use her
global platform to encourage public expressions of African Americans' self-
empathy for their ongoing marginalization rather than continue to prioritize
white empathy and the appeasement of white sensibilities (Kaplan 2019).
Unfortunately, both columns spurred a flurry of angry self-righteousness from
the *Times*'s predominantly affluent, "liberal" white readers. Why, many of them
wondered, were the columnists so eager to criticize their own, so willing to
risk further divisiveness and continued right-wing governmental dominance,
in order to interrogate the motives of the (nonthreatening) Obamas? Amid all
of the fervent expressions of white fragility and angst, one comment adopted
a much different approach, and stood out in terms of its writer's ability to
historicize the columnists' perspectives:

> E. A. Kaplan's op-ed is the second column in two days taking the Obamas
> to task for not being sufficiently empathetic to blacks, and as a corollary
> being too willing to embrace a white worldview. In terms of electability
> the Obamas had little choice but to be American first and black second
> and in terms of electability the op-ed writers should have realized by
> now—if the comments to their columns typify the whole—that their
> black-first viewpoint is not going to win a sizable number of white votes.
> However, each writer notes an important point, especially when Kaplan
> raises the issue of empathy. In speaking this past week with two black

men, each separately used the word "trauma" to characterize his experience of being black in America. Watching videos of brutality against blacks during marches through Alabama and Chicago—which, in honor of black history month, run regularly on PBS—had one friend saying he felt as though he was experiencing PTSD. Trauma of any kind is not a subject of debate nor is it an experience easily articulated or easily empathized with because its pain reverberates far below the surface of polite conversation. When Rev Jeremiah [Wright] is still so easily disavowed by the Obamas, I too have to wonder about their sincerity or courage. Yes, his jeremiad was toxic to Obama's election hopes, but [Wright] was hewing to the model set by his Hebrew namesake, who scolded from the heart. Much racial healing still needed. (Gluscabi 2019)

While I was dismayed—though not surprised—by the negative tone of the comments generally, including the substantial number of "recommends" each one received, this one in particular made clear the importance memorials displaying traumatic history may play in connecting the past to the present. More specifically, it offers some hope for the role of such structures in encouraging white people to look beyond their own perspectives and empathize with the experiences and views of others. The acknowledgment of Black pain is indicative of the importance of a trauma-centered approach to American race relations. Such an approach would further strengthen the South's place meaning as the primal scene of traumatic racism and resituate the region as a paradigmatic site for memorials like the National Memorial for Peace and Justice. Ultimately, it underscores the need for the development of a critical regionalism that not only connects the South to larger narratives of trauma and race, but also uses them as starting points.

NOTES

1. I use the term "memorial" to refer to both the monument and the museum as a whole. When writing specifically about the monument, I use the term "monument"; when writing specifically about the museum, I use the term "museum."

2. Although I do not seek to equate the cultural trauma of the physical and psychological violence of lynching with that associated with economic violence, I am not overstating the case in making this connection. According to the American Psychological Association, exposure to trauma is directly related to socioeconomic status; this connection includes a direct link between and persistent psychological symptoms. For more, see Bradley-Davino and Ruglass (2008).

3. I have written my autoethnographic observations in italics in order to distinguish them from the theory and analysis with which they are interwoven.

4. As I was constructing this reflection, I read, in multiple news outlets, that the Justice Department had issued a report citing "severe, systemic" violations in Alabama's prisons, describing "a high level of violence that is too common, cruel, of an unusual nature and pervasive." For more, see Benner and Dewan (2019).

REFERENCES

Adams, Tony E., Stacy Holman Jones, and Carolyn Ellis. 2015. *Autoethnography*. Oxford, UK: Oxford University Press.

Alexander, Jeffrey C., Ron Eyerman, Bernard Giesen, Neil J. Smelser, and Piotr Sztompka. 2004. "Introduction." In *Cultural Trauma and Collective Identity*, edited by Jeffrey Alexander, 1–30. Berkeley: University of California Press.

Anderson, Leon. 2006. "Analytic Autoethnography." *Journal of Contemporary Ethnography* 35, no. 4: 373–95.

Bailey, Amy, and Karen A. Snedker. 2011. "Practicing What They Preach? Lynching and Religion in the American South, 1890–1929." *American Journal of Sociology* 117, no. 3: 844–87.

Benner, Katie, and Shaila Dewan. 2019. "Alabama's Gruesome Prisons: Report Finds Rape and Murder at All Hours." *New York Times*, April 3, 2019. https://www.nytimes .com/2019/04/03/us/alabama-prisons-doj-investigation.html.

Blair, Carole, and Neil Michel. 2000. "Reproducing Civil Rights Tactics: The Rhetorical Performances of the Civil Rights Memorial." *Rhetoric Society Quarterly* 30, no. 2: 31–55.

Blumgart, Jake. 2018. "Lynching Memorial Spurs Revitalization." *Planning News* 10: 10–11.

Bradley-Davino, Bekha, and Lesia Ruglass. 2008. "Trauma and Post-Traumatic Stress Disorder in Economically Disadvantaged Populations." American Psychological Association, Division 56: Trauma Psychology.

Cone, James H. 2013. *The Cross and the Lynching Tree*. Ossining, NY: Orbis Books.

"Confronting the Past: The New National Memorial for Peace and Justice." 2018. *Architectural Digest*, May 27, 2018. https://www.architecturaldigest.com/story/confronting-the-past -the-new-national-memorial-for-peace-and-justice.

Crew, Spencer R. 1996. "African Americans, History, and Museums: Preserving African American History in the Public Arena." In *Making Histories in Museums*, edited by Gaynor Kavanagh, 80–91. New York: Leicester University Press.

Davis, Patricia. 2016. *Laying Claim: African American Cultural Memory and Southern Identity*. Tuscaloosa: University of Alabama Press.

Deutsche, Rosalyn. 1996. *Evictions: Art and Spatial Politics*. Cambridge, MA: MIT Press.

Equal Justice Initiative. n.d. "The Legacy Museum" and "The National Memorial for Peace and Justice." Accessed September 1, 2019. https://museumandmemorial.eji.org/.

Fleming, John E. 1994. "African-American Museums, History, and the American Ideal." *The Journal of American History* 81, no. 3: 1020–1026.

Gallagher, Victoria. 1995. "Remembering Together: Rhetorical Integration and the Case of the Martin Luther King, Jr. Memorial." *Southern Communication Journal* 60, no. 2: 109–119.

Gluscabi, February 25, 2019, comment on Erin Aubry Kaplan, "Michelle Obama's Rules of Assimilation," *New York Times*, February 24, 2019, https://www.nytimes.com/2019/02/24 /opinion/michelle-obama-becoming.html.

Hale, Grace Elizabeth. 2002. "Without Sanctuary: Lynching Photography in America." *The Journal of American History* 89, no. 3: 989–94.

Hooper-Greenhill, Eileen. 1999. *The Educational Role of the Museum*. New York: Routledge.

Inabinet, Brandon, and Christina Moss. 2019. "Complicit in Victimage: Imagined Marginality in Southern Communication Criticism." *Rhetoric Review* 38, no. 2: 160–72.

Kaplan, Erin Aubrey. 2019. "Michelle Obama's Rules of Assimilation." *New York Times*, February 24, 2019. https://www.nytimes.com/2019/02/24/opinion/michelle-obama -becoming.html.

Kratz, Corinne A., and Ivan Karp. 2006. "Introduction." In *Museum Frictions/Global Transformations*, edited by Ivan Karp, Corinne A. Kratz, Lynn Szwaja, and Tomas Ibarra-Frausto, 1–31. Durham, NC: Duke University Press.

Krzyzanowska, Natalia. 2016. "The Discourse of Counter-Monuments: Semiotics of Material Commemoration in Urban Spaces." *Social Semiotics* 26, no. 5: 465–85.

Lauricella, Sharon. 2018. "Bam! Pow! Vanish? A Feminist Autoethnography of Gender Performance and Covert Influences on Twitter." *Women and Language* 41, no. 2: 62–78.

Lopez, Tiffany Ana. 2005. "Critical Witnessing in Latina(o) and African American Prison Narratives." In *Pros and Cons: Essays on Prison Literature in the United States*, edited by D. Quentin Miller, 62–80. Jefferson, NC: McFarland and Co.

MacLeod, Suzanne. 2005. "Introduction." In *Reshaping Museum Space: Architecture, Design, Exhibitions*, edited by Suzanne MacLeod, 1–7. New York: Routledge.

Molyneux, John. 1995. "A Modest Proposal for Portsmouth." In *Art and the* City, edited by M. Miles, 16–18. Portsmouth, UK: University of Portsmouth Press.

Purnell, Derecka. 2019. "Why Does Obama Scold Black Boys?" *New York Times*, February 23, 2019. https://www.nytimes.com/2019/02/23/opinion/my-brothers-keeper-obama.html.

Robertson, Campbell. 2018. "A Lynching Memorial Is Opening: The Country Has Never Seen Anything like It." *New York Times*, April 25, 2018. https://www.nytimes.com/2018/04/25 /us/lynching-memorial-alabama.html.

Schorch, Philipp. 2014. "Cultural Feelings and the Making of Meaning." *International Journal of Heritage Studies* 20, no. 1: 1–14.

Stevens, Quentin, Karen A. Franck, and Ruth Fazakerley. 2012. "Counter-Monuments: The Anti-Monumental and the Dialogic." *The Journal of Architecture* 17, no. 6: 951–72.

Thompson, Ashley B., and Melissa M. Sloan. 2018. "Race as Region, Region as Race: How Black and White Southerners Understand Their Racial Identities." *Southern Cultures* 18, no. 4: 72–95.

Toobin, Jeffrey. 2016. "The Legacy of Lynching, on Death Row." *New Yorker*, August 22, 2016. https://www.newyorker.com/magazine/2016/08/22/bryan-stevenson-and-the-legacy -of-lynching.

Weiser, M. Elizabeth. 2017. *Museum Rhetoric: Building Civic Identity in National Spaces*. University Park: Penn State University Press.

Chapter 2

MEMORY MAKING IS REGION MAKING

Emmett Till in Tallahatchie County

DAVE TELL

In 2015, I purchased a book about Mississippi history from Turnrow Books, an independent bookseller in the heart of the Mississippi Delta. As I checked out, the salesclerk told me something about identity and authorship that I have never forgotten. He was highly critical of the book I was buying because it was, he told me, written by one more outsider who came to the Delta to write about the racial sins of other people without giving back to the community. This haunts me. I too am an outsider—a white man from Kansas—who visits Mississippi to write about race. The story told here is part of a larger story about my slowly developed friendship and collaboration with the Emmett Till Memorial Commission of Tallahatchie County. That friendship has not made me an insider or a southerner. But it has shown me that giving back to the community and writing as an outsider are not always competing goods.[1]

On July 28, 2015, I found myself standing in a gravel parking lot in front of a metal building. The gravel lot was in the heart of the Mississippi Delta, 150 miles south of Memphis. I had left the main highway (and paved road) in Glendora and had not seen anyone for miles. Surrounded by pancake-flat cotton fields as far as the eye could see, I felt a long way from anything familiar. Some say that the Delta is so flat you can see the curvature of the earth (Rubin 2002, 47; Moye 2004, 27). Although I've never been able to see the earth falling away, the unbroken expanses of cotton are of such a scale as to induce feelings of dislocation. The metal building itself was plain by comparison. Although it was large, it had only one door and very few windows. It was not what I expected. I checked the address, I checked my GPS location, and I opened the door.

I was trying to find the recorded minutes of the Emmett Till Memorial Commission of Tallahatchie County, Inc. (ETMC). The ETMC is a nonprofit in the Mississippi Delta committed to using the memory of Emmett Till's murder to pursue racial justice in the twenty-first century. By practice if not always by design, the eighteen members of the biracial commission are *memory activists*.[2] From their perspective, investments in public memory are, at the same time, investments in public health.[3] For twelve years, the ETMC had been meeting, all the while keeping detailed minutes. By the time I arrived, the collected minutes had grown into a three-volume archive of memory in the making. The minutes preserved debates over just how Till should be remembered, and to whose benefit. They documented the struggles of everyday citizens trying to figure out exactly what happened to Emmett Till, where it happened, and who was at fault. They recorded the grant-writing, bookkeeping, and political negotiation that are an indispensable—if often invisible—part of commemorative labor. Month by month, the minutes chronicled both the contentious and the quotidian efforts of the commission to remember a civil rights murder. But no one outside the small circle of commissioners had ever seen these core documents.[4]

When the ETMC was incorporated in 2006, Emmett Till commemoration was in its infancy. At the time, the state of Mississippi had only two blue road signs commemorating the murder. Just months before the ETMC held its first meeting, the signs had been installed fifty miles apart from each other on Highway 49E near the towns of Greenwood and Clarksdale, rechristening the intervening stretch of pavement the "Emmett Till Memorial Highway" (Mitchell 2005). In the forty-nine years and eleven months between the murder in August 1955 and the dedication of the blue signs in July 2005, there was not a single commemorative marker in the state of Mississippi dedicated to the murder of Emmett Till.

This commemorative silence was particularly pronounced in Tallahatchie County. Once the site of the trial of two of the men who killed Emmett Till, the "first great media event of the Civil Rights Movement" (Dewan 2005), the county's history of race and resistance had been all but forgotten. By the mid-1990s, the civil rights legacies of scores of Mississippi counties had been chronicled: Sunflower County, Leflore County, Amite County, Bolivar County, Hinds County, Yazoo County, Coahoma County, and of course Neshoba County. Surrounded by well-chronicled stories, Tallahatchie County remained a blank. Even *Local People*, John Dittmer's exhaustive account of on-the-ground organizing in Mississippi, could not identify a single "center of Civil Rights activity" in Tallahatchie County. Ironically, his map suggests that Tallahatchie County was most notable for its absence of civil rights history (Dittmer 1994, 130).

For the eighteen members of the ETMC, this absence was intolerable. On June 20, 2006, at one their earliest meetings, member after member, both white and Black, spoke against the long silence that had prevailed in the Delta on the subject of Till's murder (Minutes). One claimed that the silence was enforced by the White Citizens' Council; another suggested that the "Klan had a hold on [the] county" and "harassed" those who broke the silence; another complained that children in the Delta didn't know the story; and still another complained that he had to "bite his tongue." By the end of the meeting, there was a palpable sense that the commission's "1st order of business" was simply to "acknowledge what happened" (Tell 2018a).

It has now been thirteen years since the ETMC broke the silence that prevailed in Tallahatchie County. It is no exaggeration to say that the commission transformed the local commemorative landscape and, with it, the meaning of Tallahatchie County. In 2005, the commission was formed in a county that had two blue signs. By the time I arrived in the Delta in the summer of 2014, it had created a Civil Rights Driving Tour composed of eight additional signs, obtained official state recognition of the Till murder from the Department of Archives and History, created an interpretive center, offered regularly scheduled tours, and—at the center of it all—overseen a multimillion-dollar renovation to the county courthouse designed to return the building to its 1955 appearance (Tell 2019). The transformation of Tallahatchie County was so remarkable that, in 2007, members of the Till family traveled from Chicago to participate in a solemn ceremony held on the steps of the about-to-be-restored courthouse. As the family looked on, the Black and white cochairs of the commission took turns reading the ETMC's formal commitment to "begin an honest investigation of our history" in order to ensure "equal justice for all our citizens" (Minutes). When the commission had pledged to pursue memory for the sake of justice, the first-ever state-sponsored historical marker dedicated to the Till murder was unveiled on the courthouse lawn.

While the memory work of the commission has been widely celebrated, its investigation of racial history and its construction of permanent commemorative infrastructure is only half the story. From the perspective of the commission, its members' efforts to remember the Till murder are inextricable from their efforts to remake the meaning of Tallahatchie County. Memory making and region making are two sides of the same coin. While I have explored the commemorative aspects of place making and the spatial commitments of memory at length in *Remembering Emmett Till*, here I want to stress one part of the larger story. When the ETMC transformed the commemorative landscape of Tallahatchie County, it also gave the county a new racial history. From a county that had no civil rights history, a blank spot on the maps of 1990s historians, the commission turned Tallahatchie County into ground zero of the civil rights movement.

The inextricability of memory work and region making are perfectly captured by the state-sponsored marker unveiled in 2007 on the courthouse lawn in

Sumner. After briefly reviewing the facts of the case, the sign concludes: "Till's murder, coupled with the trial and acquittal of [murderers Roy Bryant and J. W. Milam], drew international attention and galvanized the Civil Rights Movement in Mississippi and the nation."[5] Once an unmarked spot on Dittmer's civil rights map, Tallahatchie County was now the origin of the civil rights movement. Memory worked by rewriting the meaning of Tallahatchie County, and the meaning of Tallahatchie County shifted with the remembrance of Till's murder.

By the time I made my first trip to Mississippi in the summer of 2014, the commission had been pursuing Till commemoration for eight years. Although its members' accomplishments were easy to document, they had encountered an intractable problem: vandalism. Two roadside markers had been stolen, two others were filled with bullet holes, and one of the blue signs had been spray-painted with the letters "KKK" (Tell 2016; Eubanks and Tell, 2016). In August 2014, in the context of increasing vandalism, Davis Houck invited me to the Mississippi Delta to consult with the commission about the future of Till commemoration. It was a life-changing trip. Alongside members of the Till family (Simeon Wright and Devante Wiley), the director of the commission (Patrick Weems), the FBI special agent in charge of the case from 2004 to 2006 (Dale Killinger), and two other Emmett Till scholars (Davis Houck and Devery Anderson), I spent two days talking about the murder and how to best commemorate it.

It was on this trip that the Emmett Till Memory Project (ETMP) was born. Originally a collaboration among Davis Houck, Chris Spielvogel, myself, and the ETMC, the ETMP is a public, transmedia, vandal-proof project that provides resources with which students, tourists, and the public can learn about Till's murder and its enduring legacy.[6] Funded with grants from the Institute for Museum and Library Services (IMLS) and the University of Kansas, and built in cooperation with the Till family, the ETMP uses a GPS-enabled mobile application to take visitors to ten sites related to Till's murder in Chicago and the Mississippi Delta. At each site, the ETMP provides historical and contemporary photographs; narrative explanations; digital access to archival documents; social media check-ins; and GPS directions to the next site. In the fall of 2014, through the networking of Chris Spielvogel, Google agreed to publish a prototype of the ETMP on its Field Trip app.[7] There was only one catch: Google required us to include *fifty* sites.

Thus it was that in July 2015, Patrick Weems and I (joined for part of the time by Houck and Spielvogel and photographer Pablo Correa) spent ten days in a rental car driving the back roads of the Delta to collect the GPS coordinates of fifty sites related to the Till murder. It was in the car with Weems that I realized

I needed to see the minutes of the ETMC. Driving across the Delta to build the ETMP, I discovered that there was far more to Emmett Till commemoration than meets the eye. Behind the vandalized signs, homegrown museums, and much-publicized renovation projects were gripping stories of memory in the making. As far as I could tell, every instance of Till commemoration was the end result of conflict, interpersonal drama, and competing political investments. At times, the drama was the result of a lingering uncertainty about what precisely happened the night Till was killed. More often, the drama was a function of the fact that the competing theories of Till's death were intimately connected to the possibility of obtaining grant money—a pathway to rural and regional development. No one knew this better than Glendora Mayor Johnny B. Thomas, who has had multiple grant applications rejected simply because the state does not believe his basic claim that Till was killed in Glendora.

Mayor Thomas's experience was hardly unique. The grant money that flowed from the Department of Archives and History to some Till sites and not others gave otherwise-academic debates over the minutiae of Till's murder high-stakes consequences. For example, simply moving the murder site thirty miles east, as Thomas tried to do, had the potential to redirect thousands of dollars in grant money. In the context of the economic devastation of the Delta, such money was often the only thing standing between sustainability and ruin.[8] Because stories of Till's death are one of the few commodities in the region not controlled by agribusiness, the Delta's desperate pursuit of revenue has fueled an even more desperate creativity with Till's story. More often than not, the drive to commemorate Till's murder was a last-ditch, back-against-the-wall effort to spark economic development in the poorest region of the poorest state in the union. In such circumstances, historical fidelity often seemed less important than plausible fundability.

As I spent time with Patrick Weems from 2014 to 2017, the behind-the-scenes stories of how the Delta's commemorative infrastructure was built became, for me, almost as compelling as the 1955 tragedy. While there was no shortage of books and documentaries focused on the events of 1955, the stories of Tallahatchie County's commemorative transformation remained untold. In the space of just a few years, a small band of private citizens crossed racial barriers and created the greatest density of Till memorials anywhere in the world. Just as the commission had foregrounded Till's story, I wanted to foreground the commission's story. Moreover, *I believed the commission's story was part of Till's story.* After all, the commission's commemorative work was not simply preserving or amplifying stories of 1955 that had long been passed down in the county's oral tradition. Rather, they were rewriting the narrative of Till's death and, at the same time, rewriting the narrative of their own county. As the commission put up memorial after memorial, the county gradually

became something it had never been before: the origin of the civil rights
movement. By putting up signs and renovating a courthouse, the commission
was simultaneously involved in memory making and region making.

This is why I needed to see the minutes of the ETMC. In order to tell the
behind-the-scenes stories of Tallahatchie County's transformation, I needed
to do more than read published accounts, visit museums, and photograph
memorial sites. I needed to get behind the scenes. The easiest way to get
behind the scenes was to track down grant applications at the Department of
Archives and History, the Mississippi Development Authority, and the other
public institutions that had funded the transformations (commemorative and
otherwise) of Tallahatchie County. It was much harder to gain access to the
minutes of the ETMC.

On July 27, 2015, one day before I found myself in a lonely Delta parking
lot, I spent the day on the bustling town square of Sumner, Tallahatchie
County's second county seat and the site of the 1955 trial of the men accused
of murdering Till. My first appointment was with Martha Ann Clark, the
long-time secretary of the commission. Since its inception in 2005, Clark had
dutifully kept minutes at every meeting. Thinking she was the guardian of
the minutes, I offered to buy her lunch in one of the county's nicest (and only
Black- and woman-owned) restaurants, the Sumner Grille. It was the perfect
place to talk about the memory of Emmett Till. From our booth along the
front wall of the restaurant, we had an unobstructed view of the courthouse,
which, since 1973, had become a symbol of intentional forgetfulness. In that
year, the county hired the Yale-trained preservationist Jack DeCell to renovate
the storied courthouse. DeCell completely ignored the building's history. He
tore out the historic wooden chairs and replaced them with church-style pews.
He installed a drop ceiling, added hallways on three sides of the courtroom,
and shrank the usable space by 854 square feet (Tell 2019, 99). The impact of
the DeCell renovation was so dramatic that, in 2011, the Board of Supervisors
complained that DeCell was "hiding many reminders of the past." Another local
resident confided that DeCell was hired to "take the curse off the building"
(Dickson 2016). As Martha Ann Clark recounted the work of the commission,
I couldn't shake the feeling that the ETMC was undoing DeCell's work. While
he used the courthouse to bury the past, the commission was using the same
courthouse (renovated yet again) to pull Till's story into the present.

But Clark wouldn't let me see the minutes. She told me I needed to visit the
office of Frank Mitchener, cochair of the commission. Mitchener was one of the
wealthiest plantation owners in the county and the most prominent member
of the commission (MacLean 2009, 89; Anderson 2015, 351). His spacious
office was the quintessential expression of the self-image of the Delta's white
aristocracy (Cobb 1992, 324). Until the 1970s, the riverfront property on which

his office stood was known as "backstreet"; it was home to Black Sumner, a space of refuge for the Black press during the trial of Till's killers (Anderson 2015, 100). Razed in the early 1980s, "backstreet" became the fashionable Walnut Street and the home office of Mitchener Planting. Inside Mitchener's office, the vaulted ceiling was held in place by magnificent wooden beams, and an entire wall was made of glass, overlooking the lush but slow-moving Cassidy Bayou. The walls were white, and the office was filled with art from around the world, relics of Mitchener's time with President Ronald Reagan, and memorabilia of his tenure on the National Cotton Council. There was not a computer (or even a typewriter) anywhere to be found. Framed by magnificent cypress trees rising from the Bayou, it was tempting to think of the gracious office as a place where time stood still, but I knew better. While the location exuded the timeless charm of rural authenticity, it was made possible by the forcible razing of a once-thriving Black business district. White luxury ignoring its debts to forgotten Black labor—the office was the perfect site from which to run a cotton operation.

With a natural interest in (some) history and a soft spot for academic credentials, Mitchener was delighted to sit in the air-conditioned comfort of his office and regale me with stories of days gone by. When I asked to see the minutes, however, he balked. No one had ever seen them, he said, and, besides, he'd need to obtain the permission of the commission's Black cochair, John Wilchie. He promised to call on my behalf and, if Wilchie assented, call me back. I left his office depressed, convinced that I would never see the minutes.

In retrospect, I had no reason to be pessimistic. Mitchener was deeply committed to the preservation of the Walnut Street version of Sumner. He recognized that Till commemoration was good for business and a lifeline for the still-charmed town. When the *Atlanta Journal Constitution* asked him about local commemorative efforts, he replied, "I'm interested in our little town surviving" (Drew 2007). Mitchener understood that commemoration and region making were deeply entwined and that commemorative energy was Sumner's last hope. His gamble paid off. Till commemoration saved the courthouse, which kept the legal industry alive in Sumner, which has, in turn, preserved an entire micro-economy. The town now boasts art museums, a bank, an upscale restaurant, and an array of legal officers. A first-time visitor to the town square will instantly notice an unusual level of flourishing in this small Delta town.

I was halfway back to my hotel when Mitchener called. Because Tallahatchie County does not have a single hotel, I had booked a room in Greenwood— thirty miles south of Sumner in Leflore County. Mitchener gave me an address and told me to be there early the next morning (I think the time stipulated was 8:30). In my excitement I forgot ask any follow-up questions: Where was this address? Who (and what) was there? And why did I need to drive so far into the country? If these questions didn't occur to me as I drove back to Greenwood, they seemed painfully obvious as I stood in the gravel parking lot the next morning.

From the parking lot, I stepped through the unmarked door and into a different world. From the outside, the windowless metal building looked like an agricultural warehouse. On this inside, it looked like a plush corporate headquarters. It was. I had stepped into the unassuming headquarters of the Sturdivant Plantation. I knew portions of the Sturdivant story well. In 1955, Till had been killed in a barn on a Sturdivant farm outside the town of Drew in Sunflower County. At the time, the "manager of farming operations" was Leslie Milam, who made the seed barn available to the murder party. Although the Sturdivant family had no involvement in or knowledge of what was happening on their property (they did not even live on the property), Till was tortured for hours in the north end of the family's barn. For reasons that I explore elsewhere, the role of the Sturdivant barn in Till's murder was all but forgotten in the second half of the twentieth century (Tell 2019). As the barn was pushed out of public memory, the Sturdivant fortunes grew exponentially. In addition to its cotton revenue, the family owned a crop-dusting business and a profitable hotel management company. Although the family started with Holiday Inns in 1956, they eventually managed resort properties on the Gulf coast. In 1983 and 1987, Mike Sturdivant competed in the Democratic gubernatorial primaries, running his campaigns from the same unassuming metal building. Despite being branded as an old-fashioned plantation owner, Sturdivant had an admirable record on civil rights (Salter 2012). His Holiday Inn in Meridian was the state's second hotel to integrate. Mike's son Sykes Sturdivant lives to this day in Glendora and is a long-standing member of the Emmett Till Memorial Commission. Sykes is a rarity in the Delta: a widely respected white planter who speaks up for racial justice.

As I stepped into the nerve center of the Sturdivant empire, the first person I saw was Martha Ann Clark. She was expecting me. After a few minutes of small talk, she retrieved three black, three-inch, three-ring binders from a closet. After giving me a tour of the building and introducing me to Sykes, she took me (and the binders) to the conference room. The gracious oak table was twenty feet long, surrounded by plush chairs and wild game mounted on the walls. As I set up my tripod and camera, Clark explained that John Wilchie was on his way, and I would not be able to look at the minutes until he gave his consent.

Wilchie arrived fifteen minutes later. In a rural southern accent so pronounced I had to struggle to understand, he asked why I wanted to see the minutes of the commission. While he had no problem with my telling the story of the commission in book form, he was anxious to know how my labor would benefit the commission. The timing was perfect. The previous fall I had ghostwritten the narrative of an IMLS grant application submitted by the commission. Funded at $72,670, the grant was helping the commission keep its doors open. When Wilchie learned that I helped to write the grant, whatever reservations he may have had about my seeing the minutes vanished. It was a perfect example of Catalina M. de Onís's call for scholars to engage in practical ways with local communities (de Onís 2016). In the case at hand, my willingness to help the ETMC write grants to do its own work ended up being a key part of the commission's willingness to provide me access to the minutes.

The minutes contained no smoking guns. Perhaps because I had pursued them for so long, I opened the black binders half expecting to find dramatic stories of race-fueled fights over the legacy of the Till murder. There was nothing of the sort. The minutes were filled with receipts, attendance sheets, records of official motions, and vote tallies. I often learned which topics were discussed at which meetings, but I seldom learned the substance of these conversations. The most fascinating item in the minutes was a production history of the Tallahatchie Civil Rights Driving Tour, a collection of nine roadside markers erected by the commission on the west side of Tallahatchie County in the spring of 2008. The tour is the ETMC's most visible mechanism for shaping the story of Emmett Till's murder. As the commission members put it at their October 24, 2006, meeting (Minutes), the driving tour was their chance to "write the story and write it right."

I conclude this essay with a brief and partial analysis of the Tallahatchie Civil Rights Driving Tour, seen through the lens of the ETMC minutes. Although a full analysis can be found in *Remembering Emmett Till*, I foreground a small portion of the tour here. It is a perfect example of how memory making and region making are often intertwined. Indeed, when one looks at the minutes, it sometimes seems that the creation of the driving tour was driven by an imperative to remake the meaning of the Tallahatchie County: by remembering the murder, the commission members saw the chance to make their own county ground zero of the civil rights movement.

Making Tallahatchie County ground zero of the movement necessitated playing a bit loose with history. The first evidence of such looseness is that all nine stops on the commission's driving tour are in Tallahatchie County. It was not always intended to be so. The first time the ETMC discussed a historical trail, on March 23, 2006, its members circulated among themselves a list of ten potential sites, four of which were not in the county (Minutes). In Sunflower County, they proposed a marker near the barn outside the town of Drew, where Till was most likely killed. In Leflore County, they proposed markers at Bryant's Grocery and Meat Market (the site of the infamous whistle), the Greenwood County Courthouse (where Milam and Bryant were initially detained), and the home of Till's uncle Mose Wright (the site of the abduction). Although the minutes do not say definitively why these sites were not pursued, it is likely a product of the fact that the ETMC was commissioned by Tallahatchie County. The formal name of the nonprofit is telling: The Emmett Till Memorial Commission *of Tallahatchie County*, Inc. Even at the level of the nonprofit's governing documents, its mission was to use the memory of Emmett Till for the good of the county (Minutes). It seems likely, then, that the driving tour was crafted by the twin desires of memory making and region making. If the tour had simply been about memory making, there would really be no explanation for eliminating the sites in Sunflower and Leflore counties. These sites are, by virtually every account, critical to the story of Till's murder. But the tour was not simply about the past. It was also about region making, and the commissioners felt obligated to focus exclusively on Tallahatchie County.

The issue of site selection is important. By confining itself to Tallahatchie County, the commission has created a tour that, from the perspective of Till's murder, is oddly incomplete. It leaves out major sites (e.g., Bryant's Grocery and the murder site) but includes sites of marginal significance. For example, the tour contains a roadside marker commemorating the murder of Clinton Melton, an African American gas station attendant killed shortly after the trial of Till's murderers in Tallahatchie County. The Melton murder is important in its own right, but it has little to do with the Till murder (other than proximity in time and place). With the Melton murder site included and Bryant's Grocery excluded, it is clear that the boundaries of the county are of greater importance to the commission than historical fidelity to Till's story.

Nothing reveals the all-consuming importance of county lines with as much clarity as the composition history of the Emmett Till signs themselves. Indeed, the composition history of the signs is, from a rhetorical point of view, the most interesting item in the entire collection of ETMC minutes. For the purposes of this essay, I will focus only on the sign marking the site of J. W. Milam's home, near the eastern end of Thomas Street in Glendora, Mississippi. The final text of the sign notes that Milam's backyard shed was the site of Till's torture, which is not true. Unsurprisingly, when the ETMC prepared to submit the text of this sign for approval by the Mississippi Department of Archives and History in April 2007, they included photocopies of William Bradford Huie's 1956 *Look* magazine account. As I have written at length elsewhere, Huie's account is one of the *most influential but least trustworthy* accounts of Till's murder ever written (Tell 2018b). But it was a useful version of the story for the commission because it moved the torture and murder site from Sunflower County to the shed behind Milam's home, in Tallahatchie County.

It is worth noting that, of the nine original ETMC signs, two of them are justified with recourse to Huie's *Look* article, and another four are justified with recourse to Stephen Whitaker, whose 1963 master's thesis leans almost exclusively on Huie's account. The commission's reliance on Huie is so complete that its first draft of text for the sign that now stands in front of the Glendora cotton gin misidentified the gin as the "Progressive Ginning Company"—a mistake that was corrected by historian Plater Robinson but which could only have originated with Huie's account (Minutes). Another early draft even claims that the "Glendora gin" was "in Boyle," a distant town mentioned only by Huie. While this is obviously false (the Glendora gin is in Glendora), it reveals the extent to which the ETMC uncritically leaned on Huie's Tallahatchie County tale, even when they knew it was not trustworthy. Time and again, historical accuracy was subservient to the needs of regional definition.

The commission had to know that Huie was an untrustworthy source. In its members' efforts to validate another sign, they cited page 154 in Christopher Metress's *The Lynching of Emmett Till: A Documentary Narrative* (Minutes). Although they were trying to preserve another item of interest on the page, they also captured Metress's calling into question the veracity of Huie. Thus it was that the very page they used to document the veracity of one of their signs undercut their reliance on Huie for the sign in front of Milam's homesite.

Even had the commission's members missed the lesson from Metress, however, they were still without excuse. Their preferred historical authority was Plater Robinson, a public historian living in New Orleans. For years, Robinson had driven the backroads of the Delta, talking to anyone he could find, collecting stories, and taking pictures. On a fortuitous 1994 trip, he talked himself into the living room of a still-defiant Roy Bryant. At the time, Byron De La Beckwith's belated conviction for the murder of Medgar Evers was in the news, and Bryant was concerned that he was next. Robinson captured Bryant on tape: "So to hell with them. I'm sick of it," he said. "Forty years old; they need to let that stuff go." Bryant's only regret, he claimed, was that "he ain't never made a damn nickel" (Robinson and Williams 1996). After Robinson left Bryant's home, he continued meandering through the Delta, eventually stumbling across a group of Black and white children playing together. Struck by this (not uncommon) site, Robinson stopped for pictures and conversation. The white children belonged to Delta photographer (and Sumner resident) Maude Schuyler Clay, who was so captivated by Robinson's stories that when, years later, the commission needed a historian, she introduced its members to Plater Robinson.

The minutes of the ETMC are filled with correspondence to and from Plater Robinson, who, by 2008, had become the commission's most trusted historical authority. It was on Robinson's advice that the commission removed the reference to the "Progressive Ginning Company" from the sign in front of the Glendora gin. Robinson also told the commission, explicitly, that the sign in front of Milam's Glendora home was wrong: "Milam told Huie that he and Roy Bryant whipped Emmett at the shed behind Milam's house in Glendora. This is a lie" (Minutes). Robinson then explained the actual relevance of Milam's home. After Till was murdered and his body discarded, "Milam's employees" were made to wash out his truck, which was parked at his home. This is all true; the reference is to Henry Lee Loggins and Levi Collins, Black accomplices in the torture, murder, and cover-up of Till's murder. On this count, the commission chose to follow Robinson's advice, inserting his euphemistic language of "employees" into the final text of the sign.

The sign that now stands in front of Milam's home site thus points to two historical sources, which cannot be reconciled with each other. The sign claims that Till was beaten in the backyard shed, which the commission knew was false because of Robinson's input. But the sign also claims that the Milam house was the scene of the truck's washing, which the commission knew to be true because of Robinson's advice. The commission members thus waivered on which historical authority they chose to trust. When they wrote about the torture and the beating, they followed Huie's account, which they knew to be untrustworthy (via Metress) and wrong (via Robinson). On the matter of the truck washing, however, they followed the advice of Plater Robinson. Through it all, the only consistent principle seems to be an attempt to site the story of Till's murder in Tallahatchie County by whatever means possible. The differential value of Robinson's advice (which was correct) and Huie's advice (which was not) mattered less than county lines. By following Robinson on the truck washing and Huie on the torture, they were able to place both events in Tallahatchie County. The fact that, until the ETMC's driving tour, the two events were considered mutually exclusive and never appeared in the same text is further evidence that the ETMC's most important criterion was geographical location: if an event could be traced to Tallahatchie County, it merited inclusion on the tour.

Memory making is region making. If Tallahatchie County now boasts the greatest density of Emmett Till memorials anywhere in the world, this is partly because commemoration was driven by a commission intent on dramatizing the history of its own county. The end result was that Tallahatchie County became something it had never been before: as the sign that now stands on the Sumner lawn proclaims, the county has become the origin of the civil rights movement. Once this was done, the county found it far easier to fund commemorative work. Indeed, from 2009 forward, every grant application from the ETMC to the Mississippi Department of Archives and History contained the same typo-riddled paragraph, cut and pasted from one application to the next, that proclaimed the county the origin of the movement: "The courthouse is the site of the Emmett Till murder trial, which has received national and international attention as the 'spark that started the Civil Rights Movement in America'" (Tell 2019, 136).

It is easy—perhaps too easy—to criticize the commission for the extent to which its members allowed county lines to influence their telling of Till's story. In Tallahatchie County, however, this was the cost of doing business. Had they not committed to region making, they may not have been able to do any commemorative work at all. One county west of Tallahatchie County is Sunflower County, the site where Till was killed on the Sturdivant plantation. To this day, Sunflower County does not have a single commemorative marker about Till's murder. The murder site sits unmarked, on the private, hard-to-find property of a local dentist. The only reason that Tallahatchie County now boasts a commemorative infrastructure is that a group of local citizens committed themselves to the intertwined pursuits of region making and memory making. As the comparison of Sunflower County and Tallahatchie County suggests, sometimes (if not always) the pure pursuit of commemoration is not a live option.

As I look back now, it occurs to me that my long search for the minutes of the ETMC is entangled with the commission's commitment to Tallahatchie County. After all, I only saw the minutes because I worked on the IMLS grant that helped the commission keep its doors open to the public. The condition of my memory making was that I first joined with the commission members in their region making. If the minutes ultimately revealed the deep, inextricable entanglement of regionalism and commemoration, perhaps it was fitting that I wrote *Remembering Emmett Till* by helping Tallahatchie County become what it needed to be.

NOTES

1. Dave Tell would like to thank Patrick Weems and the Emmett Till Memorial Commission of Tallahatchie County, without whom none of this story would have been possible.

2. Susan Glisson and I debate the origin of the term. I think I first learned it from her; she thinks she learned it from me. Glisson may be the single most important person in Mississippi's racial politics in the last twenty years.

3. Although this point was contentious, and although some members of the commission were involved for personal gain, the perspective of Betty Pearson is telling. In an undated letter to Susan Glisson in the William Winter Institute for Racial Reconciliation Collection, she wrote that her "primary intent in the work of the Emmett Till Commission is not tourism, or marking a 'trail,' or remodeling the courthouse, but in the opportunity it gives us to develop a new kind of bi-racial community here."

4. Sociologists Alan Barton and Sarah J. Leonard (2010) had seen the first two years, through 2008.

5. Although J. W. Milam and Roy Bryant were guilty, they were acquitted by an all-white jury.

6. Download the ETMP at https://tillapp.emmett-till.org/.

7. Field Trip is produced by Niantic Labs. At the time we contracted with them, however, Niantic Labs was a Google subsidiary and not yet an independent company.

8. In 2010, the Mississippi Development Authority sent a team of economic development experts to Glendora, Mississippi. The goal was to rescue the town from poverty. The team's only recommendation was to invest in Emmett Till tourism.

REFERENCES

Anderson, Devery. 2015. *Emmett Till: The Murder That Shocked the World and Propelled the Civil Rights Movement*. Jackson: University Press of Mississippi.

Barton, Alan W., and Sarah J. Leonard. 2010. "Incorporating Social Justice Tourism in Planning: Racial Reconciliation and Sustainable Development in the Deep South." *Community Development* 41, no. 3: 298–332.

Cobb, James C. 1992. *The Most Southern Place on Earth: The Mississippi Delta and the Roots of Regional Identity*. New York: Oxford University Press.

de Onís, Catalina M. 2016. "'Pa' que tú lo sepas': Experiences with Co-Presence in Puerto Rico." In *Text + Field: Innovations in Rhetorical Method,* edited by Sara L. McKinnon, Robert Asen, Karma R. Chávez, and Glenn Howard, 101–116. University Park: Penn State Press.

Dewan, Shaila. 2005. "How Photos Became Icon of Civil Rights Movement." *New York Times*, August 28, 2005. https://www.nytimes.com/2005/08/28/us/how-photos-became-icon -of-civil-rights-movement.html.

Dickson, Richard. 2016. Conversation with author. Clarksdale, MS, October 5.

Dittmer, John. 1994. *Local People: The Struggle for Civil Rights in Mississippi*. Urbana: University of Illinois Press.

Drew, Jubera. 2007. "Decades Later, an Apology." *Atlanta Journal Constitution*, October 2, 2007. https://www.africanamerica.org/topic/decades-later-an-apology-for-emmett -till-slaying.

Eubanks, W. Ralph, and Dave Tell. 2016. "For Better or Worse, How Mississippi Remembers Emmett Till." *Literary Hub.* November 2. https://lithub.com/for-better-or-worse-how -mississippi-remembers-emmett-till/.

MacLean, Harry N. 2009. *The Past Is Never Dead: The Trial of James Ford Seale and Mississippi's Struggle for Redemption*. New York: Basic Civitas Books.

Minutes of the Emmett Till Memorial Commission. Glendora, Mississippi.

Mississippi Development Authority. 2010. "Glendora, Mississippi Asset Mapping." Jackson, Mississippi.

Mitchell, Jerry. 2005. "Highways Renamed for Martyrs." *Jackson Clarion Ledger*, March 22, 2005.

Moye, Todd. 2004. *Let the People Decide: Black Freedom and White Resistance Movements in Sunflower County, 1945–1986*. Chapel Hill: University of North Carolina Press.

Pearson, Betty. Letter to Susan Glisson [Undated]. William Winter Institute for Racial Reconciliation Collection, University of Mississippi Archives and Special Collections. Box 3, Folder: Tallahatchie County.

Robinson, Plater, and Loretta Williams. 1996. "The Murder of Emmett Till." Audio file. Laurel, MD: Soundprint Media.

Rubin, Richard. 2002. *Confederacy of Silence: The True Tale of New Old South*. New York: Atria Books.

Salter, Sid. 2012. "Sturdivant Was One of the Best Men Never Elected Governor." *De Soto Times-Tribune*, May 7, 2012. http://www.desototimes.com/opinion/editorials/sturdivant-was-one-of-the-best-men-never-elected-governor/article_738aee4b-ec46-5d34-be1f-42c0fa29035d.html.

Tell, Dave. 2016. "A Brief Visual History of the Bullet-Riddled Emmett Till Memorial." *Reading the Pictures*. November 16, 2016. https://www.readingthepictures.org/2016/11/emmett-till-bullet-riddled-memorial-sign/.

Tell, Dave. 2018a. "Letter: The Long-Delayed Pursuit of Justice." *The Atlantic Monthly*, July 26, 2018. https://www.theatlantic.com/letters/archive/2018/07/letter-reopening-the-emmett-till-case-is-a-cynical-play/565625/.

Tell, Dave. 2018b. "Emmett Till Never Feared His Killers? No, He Died in Agony." *Jackson Clarion-Ledger*, August 27, 2018. https://www.clarionledger.com/story/opinion/columnists/2018/08/27/emmett-till-never-feared-his-killers-no-he-died-agony/1030485002/.

Tell, Dave. 2019. *Remembering Emmett Till*. Chicago: University of Chicago Press.

Young, James. 2016. *The Stages of Memory: Reflections on Memorial Art, Loss, and the Spaces Between*. Amherst: University of Massachusetts Press.

Chapter 3

COUNTERPUBLICITY
AND REGIONAL NOSTALGIA

Stax, Sun Studio, and Critical Regionalism in Memphis

JONATHAN M. SMITH

I grew up and spent the first thirty years of my life in Corvallis, Oregon. As a West Coast native, I would normally consider myself an "outsider" to the South. I moved to Memphis, Tennessee, in the summer of 2016 as a white man with little experience living in richly diverse areas. However, through my immersion into southern culture these past few years and my academic focus on race, class, gender, and the empowerment of underprivileged communities, I feel more connected than ever. While I may not have the full breadth of experience enjoyed by native southerners, I constantly strive to find ways to bolster my knowledge and contribute productively to scholarship focusing on critical regionalism.[1]

> For the last twenty-five years, more or less, I've been walking the streets of Memphis looking for ghosts, listening for echoes, trying to construct a vision in my mind of what it must have been like. . . . I was prompted by the lure of history (Sun, Stax, and Beyond).
>
> —PETER GURALNICK

Stax Museum of American Soul and Sun Studio are perhaps the two most well-known sites of musical commemoration in the city of Memphis. Positioned just two miles from one another, the two museums represent a studio rivalry that helped the city gain international fame. The Stax museum, located at 926 East McLemore Avenue, occupies the razed ground of the former Stax Records Studio and celebrates American soul artists in the Stax family and beyond. Stax Records launched the careers of a number of legendary artists including Otis

Redding, Isaac Hayes, Booker T & the MGs, Sam & Dave, Rufus and Carla Thomas, and many others (Stax Records n.d.). Located at 706 Union Avenue, Sun Studio was founded by Sam Phillips, a pioneer in the music industry who discovered artists such as Elvis Presley, Johnny Cash, Jerry Lee Lewis, Carl Perkins, B. B. King, Howlin' Wolf, Ike Turner, and Roy Orbison (McPherson 2002, 36).

The Stax museum and Sun Studio help to commemorate the music, culture, and social context present in Memphis during the mid- to late twentieth century. During their musical primes, both studios pushed existing musical boundaries in interesting and innovative ways and thus, I argue, conceived counterpublics in American music. Stax Records and Sun Studio provided an avenue for southern music—largely underappreciated on a national level at the time—to establish relevance and break into the greater American consciousness. Perhaps due to the unprecedented success of Elvis and the so-called Million Dollar Quartet (Elvis, Carl Perkins, Johnny Cash, and Jerry Lee Lewis), the sounds of Sun Studio were quickly accepted by the dominant American culture. Stax Records had a more difficult time gaining acceptance among the white public. The Stax museum website notes that the company's eventual success was largely predicated first on its ability to stimulate interest in Europe: "European fans went crazy for Stax in the same way that American teenagers had when the Beatles first came to America. In Europe, skin color didn't matter—audiences saw the music as authentic and the people who made it as stars" (Stax Museum n.d.). In contrast to country and rockabilly music in nearby Nashville or the pop rock sounds of contemporaries like the Beatles, the Stax label helped to popularize blues, soul, R&B, and other unique forms of African American music.

Coinciding with the civil rights struggle, each studio rose to prominence amidst the significant racial and social tension persistent in the region. Sun Studio appropriated musical innovations originating in the Black community and used them to gain widespread success among members of the dominant white public. Conversely, Stax Records offered racially progressive music that promoted integration in the city and challenged American conceptions of what popular music could be (*Soundbreaking* 2016). The Stax museum website recounts that, "Though racial tension was brewing in Memphis and around the country, the studio had always been integrated, a group of like-minded people creating music and growing a business through community, collaboration and skill, regardless of skin color." Thus, while Stax Records and Sun Studio are iconic music labels, they are also representative of musical and sociocultural tensions that permeated the South and the greater US. The sounds emanating from each studio fell in line with music popular among southern whites and African American southerners. While these different musical styles undoubtedly influenced one another, they are notable for being tied to specific forms of regional identity.

This chapter explores how the Stax museum and Sun Studio perpetuate regional nostalgia through their musical commemorations, thus guiding visitors toward specific understandings of regional identity. As active conduits of present-day public memory, they select and display content in a way that legitimates and interprets the past for visitors (Radley 1991, 67). I follow Douglas Reichert Powell's (2012) assertion that regions should be conceptualized "not about a stable, boundaried, autonomous place," but rather as a cultural history represented by "the cumulative, generative effect of the interplay among the various, competing definitions of that region" (5). Museums have the capacity to influence regional identity through the sense of nostalgia they produce. Regional nostalgia is an affection for distinct, eccentric, and/or anomalous periods in a region's history that tie it to its past. These moments are often held in high regard and encourage individuals in a given geographical place to continually look backward. Regional nostalgia can become problematic when more rigorous interrogations of the point of reference—by a museum, for instance—reveal ideals that are disturbing, violent, or offensive (Powell 2012, 13). Regional nostalgia affects present-day identities when publics use aspects of the past to shape their modern positionalities. Members of distinct regions may be inclined to hold on to aspects of and/or time periods in history because they provide a sense of significance or regional "worth."

Today, the Stax museum and Sun Studio reproduce regional nostalgia in an effort to maintain musical, institutional, and ultimately regional and national significance. The museums generate revenue, bolster the city's tourism, and help provide the region with a sense of musical prestige. However, my analysis reveals that they do so in largely disparate ways. While neither institution provides a perfectly accurate portrait of the race, culture, and music of the time period, the strategic commemorative choices of each are distinct and consequential. Both studios began from a place of musical and cultural counterpublic resistance, but the commemoration of this time period in each museum sends starkly different messages about the race relations that facilitated their respective musical movements.

The Sun Studio site suppresses the significance of its diverse beginnings in order to highlight the rise of Elvis and other white men who were largely appropriating a sound born out of African American culture. This museum adopts the hegemonic Old South perspective that Blacks provided whites with the seeds of something great that required perfecting. It downplays the notion that white artists commandeered or appropriated Black music and instead positions its history as the struggle of a southern counterpublic of poor whites who rose to prominence with the help of Black artists. As expressed in four prominent themes—white male representation, musical specificity, ethnocentrism, and nostalgic hegemony—the Sun Studio site offers a limited, biased, and whitewashed historical narrative.

Conversely, the Stax museum adopts the New South idea that Blacks and whites worked together to produce something great. This concept channels Booker T. Washington's advocacy for cooperation in his 1895 "Atlanta Exposition" speech, in which he encouraged African Americans to pursue the respect of white society through hard work, diligence, and continued education, thus promoting participation in the ongoing economic development of the New South. The Stax museum portrays Blacks and poor whites as part of parallel, cooperative counterpublics that faced opposition from a national public of elite, hierarchical music. In an era not too far removed from extreme forms of segregation and racism, the museum's narrative suggests that Stax Records created a studio environment that promoted racial healing and biracial integration. The studio acted as a counterpublic force that challenged both a resistant white public in the city of Memphis and a greater US public. The Stax museum ultimately adopts this New South myth to avoid addressing how whiteness silenced Black voices and appropriated Black musical styles at all recording houses. By highlighting music's potential for racial healing, the museum offers a reference point for visitors to feel good about the historical connection between race and music in Memphis and the surrounding region. My analysis focuses on four prominent themes of this museum: religious influence, musical diversity, cultural richness, and counterhegemony. While both museums clearly seek to maintain relevance by protecting the musical reputation of the region, they promote differing racially charged narratives, therefore establishing themselves as touchstones for regional identity in contrasting ways.

To support these claims, this study unfolds in four moves. First, I ground my discussion in context with a survey of Memphis's musical, social, and cultural progression. I then review rhetorical scholarship focusing on museums and their connection to public memory and critical regionalism. Third, I perform a critical analysis of the Stax and Sun Studio museums to contextualize their ideological expressions. In my conclusion, I reflect on the capacity of music museums to continue to stimulate progress or resist change within the context of the ever-evolving culture of a given region.

STAX, SUN STUDIO, AND THE LEGACY OF MEMPHIS MUSIC

Music is an integral component of Memphis's history, culture, and regional identity. "Memphis is music," the Memphis Music Hall of Fame proclaims.

For David Dawson (1997), Memphis music is "the sound track to our lives, the tempo of our culture" (36). In Charles Reagan Wilson's "An Introduction to Memphis" (2002), he writes that much of Memphis's overall culture was born out of creative expressions like music (6). Music remains one of Memphis's flagship attractions, and sites of musical commemoration are ubiquitous in the city. Among the more than four hundred music labels that have graced the streets of Memphis in the past century, Stax Records and Sun Studio are two of the city's most important musical institutions (Raichelson and West 2006, 23). In many ways, these companies deserve the lion's share of the credit for Memphis's status as a musical mecca because they were the city's most well-known and successful promoters of music. Today, they are iconic institutions and prominent contributors to the Memphis tourism. Sun Studio's website states: "If music was a religion then Memphis would be Jerusalem and Sun Studio its most holy shrine" (Sun Studio n.d., "Plan Your Tour"). The historical marker outside of the Stax museum boasts of a similarly significant history: "On this site stood Stax Records, Inc. which boasted such stars as Otis Redding, Rufus and Carla Thomas, Isaac Hayes, the Staple Singers, Albert King, the Bar-Kays, and many others. It relied upon its deep soul roots to carry it through, struggling from a back-street garage in 1957 to become a multi-million-dollar organization" (Stax Museum n.d.). In a city full of historical musical innovation and recognition, Stax Records and Sun Studio stand out among the rest.

During the mid- to late twentieth century, the music scene in Memphis helped to influence and shape the ever-evolving sociopolitical and economic landscape of the city. In the early twentieth century, the city contained upwards of ten thousand Ku Klux Klan members. In the 1950s and '60s, Memphis remained largely segregated, and the ongoing and residual effects of Jim Crow and school segregation placed strong divides between Black and white people in the city (Hawes 2016). Even with the US Supreme Court decision in *Brown vs. Board of Education*, Memphis high schools resisted reform and remained segregated. Robert Gordon's (1994) *It Came from Memphis* describes Memphis music as an approach to life and the soundtrack to cultural confrontations among "[B]lack and white, rural and urban, poor and rich" (9). Gordon's book notes that a racial and cultural collision was taking place as the popularity of Memphis music grew. "The forces of cultural collision stuck thrice in the Memphis area," he writes, "first with the Delta blues, then with Sun, then Stax" (6). Stax Records founder Jim Stewart (2007) recalls that "there was nowhere we could meet. You couldn't go to a restaurant with a Black person. You couldn't check them into a hotel. You couldn't be seen in the street, practically, with a Black person." Stewart goes on to say that the company was a pioneering institution for its promotion of integration. African Americans were given equal creative responsibility and compensation, and, to his knowledge, "there was no other company doing that at the time." Sun Studio took a far different approach. Rather than highlighting and celebrating Black artistry, Sun Studio founder and owner Sam Phillips took traditionally Black music and recorded and distributed it via white artists. As musician Jeff Beck remembers, Phillips "was so smitten with Black music and Black blues, but he knew that he'd need a white guy to put it out there. And he found a guy called Elvis Presley" (*Soundbreaking* 2016). This collision of music and race took place during a period that Charles L. Hughes (2015) terms the "country-soul triangle," an "interconnected recording economy" featuring Memphis, Nashville, and Shoals, Alabama, indicative of cross-racial sound, integrated studios, and symbolism suggesting "southern economic renaissance and progress" (2).

As rhetorical expressions, the Stax and Sun Studio museums offer an avenue to understand how racial tensions and ongoing biases are still present in the city of Memphis. The symbolic power of landmarks, museums, and monuments should be considered in conjunction with the more explicit displays of racial unrest that are ongoing in the city. In recent years, the I-40 bridge was shut down due to Black Lives Matter protests, Confederate statues have sparked controversy and been removed from the city, and racially charged protests have erupted at iconic Memphis landmarks like Graceland. In late 2019, Tami Sawyer unsuccessfully campaigned to become the first Black woman mayor in the history of the city.

Analyzing the two museums in conjunction with each other provides a nuanced look at the way long-standing institutions in Memphis continue to affect perspectives and contribute to personal identity. According to Olson, Finnegan, and Hope (2008), scholars should not "study images or artifacts in isolation from larger textual or performative contexts in which an audience might encounter them, but rather in precise relation to those contexts that give them shape and meaning" (2). Juxtaposed with one another, the museums reveal disparate conceptions of how one might conceive of Memphis music, history, and culture.

CRITICAL REGIONALISM
AND THE RHETORIC OF MEMORY PLACES

As popular tourist destinations with musical and cultural significance, the Stax and Sun Studio museums affect individual and group identities beyond just those present in the city of Memphis. While they exist as single entities housed within the city, they have the power to impact greater regional perceptions. Regions are densely saturated spaces marked by relations among people, places, histories, identities, cultures, and the interactions among them (Rice 2012,

206). Rather than being stable and fixed, they contain interrelated, overlapping, and competing identities that house a given space. An analysis of the Stax and Sun Studio museums requires a nuanced analytical lens that takes into account their capacities to affect regional identity. A critical regional approach provides an avenue to critique the way landmarks and entities within regional spaces facilitate regional identity formation. A critical regional approach assesses present relationships and envisions better alternatives (Powell 2012, 10). Powell explains,

> [Critical regionalism] is about being aware that writing about a region creates and sustains a definition of that region and, in so doing, deliberately defines the region to create new, potentially revelatory perspectives on it. It is about being aware of the fact that one's own work participates in that broader constellation of discourse about the region. The path that the practice of critical regionalism draws across the intellectual landscape is designed to lead toward a view of the best possible version of the region from among all the versions that are out there. (7)

Music has been a key factor in the way identities have been shaped in the city of Memphis, but few studies have rhetorically critiqued musical commemoration in ways that might allow us to reframe our perceptions and create better understandings.

Music museums are selectively constructed portraits of history with representations capable of shaping visitor identities and positioning them as subjects within the larger community (Woods, Ewalt, and Baker 343). As Marion Leonard (2007) suggests, the "inclusion of popular music within museum exhibitions provokes a number of debates about historiography, representation and the ascription of value" (147). Music collections provide powerful insights into the history and culture of a community—they, according to Leonard, "inform us about the consumption, operation, sociality and histories of popular musics and the cultures with which they are connected" (162). From a critical regional approach, scholars ought to assess the way music museums in certain regions privilege certain perspectives at the expense of others.

In some cases, such as that of Sun Studio, regional representation can fall into problematic states of nostalgia that limit disruption and the potential for counterpublic resistance (Woods, Ewalt, and Baker 2013, 345). Nostalgia often acts as an insidious force in regional representation because it promotes an uncritical lens that "inscribe[s] a sense of place rooted in the 'good ole days' of the past" (Powell 2012, 27). Communities become locked into a particular vision of the past that promotes a singular and problematic conception of the present. Critical regionalism as a method of study disrupts these problematic narratives and rejects the "traps of nostalgia" (Rice 2012, 203). Critical regionalism is therefore an interventionist mode of critique that exploits narrow rhetorical constructions and promotes the voices of traditionally disadvantaged groups. Woods, Ewalt, and Baker (2013) argue that sites of commemoration like museums have the capacity to articulate "a disruptive critical regionalism and/or fall into a problematic rhetoric of state nostalgia" (345). The Stax and Sun Studio museums operate on opposite ends of a critical regional binary. The Stax museum displays the philosophy of a studio that actively worked to engage in racial healing. Its displayed content represents this historical journey and asks visitors to contemplate past and present efforts to promote integration through music. The Sun Studio site characterizes a problematic time period that was insensitive to oppression and racial dynamics within the city; its specific representations provide a subjective snapshot of this era, thus propelling visitors toward a specific vision and understanding.

A critical regional approach lends itself to an exploration of the way the Stax and Sun Studio museums operate as memory places that shape public understandings of history and culture. Memory places including national parks, city skylines, museums, and other landmarks constitute material rhetorics that facilitate the construction of collective public identity (Woods, Ewalt, and Baker 2013, 343). These sites of commemoration promote cultural understandings and collective senses of the community (Zagacki and Gallagher 2009, 172). Memory places thus possess a synecdochic capacity as the objects, visuals, and narratives commemorated facilitate understandings of the larger region or "imagined community" (Woods, Ewalt, and Baker 2013, 343). Scholars can problematize memory places because they inevitably provide limited conceptions of the complex histories they represent. Bernard Armada (1998) writes that museum displays "can only cue us in to segments of history—they can never represent 'the' past in all of its social, cultural, and political complexity" (236). Similarly, Susan Pearce (1993) suggests we view museums' representations of history as "works of imagination operating within an understood tradition of knowledge and interpretation, and contributing their share towards both the maintenance and the development of this tradition" (141). Museums like Stax's and Sun's are subjective constructions of the past and must be treated as such.

The subjective representations promoted by memory places help to solidify and place in tension the collective identities of the community. Especially in music museums like those of Stax Records and Sun Studio—where many different items and narratives are on display—creating cohesion while simultaneously representing all voices can be an arduous task. This is particularly so when representation of a culture or group is on display (Karp and Lavine 1991, 4). Museums construct some narratives at the expense of others—they take "discourses, events, objects, and practices to be activities of a partisan character, embracing some notions and despising others, willfully or not" (Dickinson, Blair, and Ott 2010, 4). Armada (1998) suggests museums "invite us to see ourselves and others in particular ways by virtue of the narratives told and the evidence selected as 'important.' By privileging certain narratives and artifacts over others, museums implicitly communicate who/what is central and who/what is peripheral; who/what we must remember and who/what it is okay to forget" (236). Inevitably these choices have important implications for understanding racial and cultural dynamics within a community. Aspects of "class, ethnicity, race, regionalism, and a desire for social stability" drive displays in museum culture that ultimately inform communities about "which traditions are dominant and which subordinate" (Kammen qtd. in Browne 1995, 242). Museums have the power to guide visitors toward understandings that may be rooted along a spectrum progressing from popular conceptions of the dominant public to perspectives that highlight the voices of the marginalized.

CONSTITUTIVE AND CRITICAL RHETORICS OF RACE

As a method of analysis, I offer a constitutive-driven framework that views museums as fragmented pieces of ideological strains with inherently raced qualities. By collating fragmented rhetorical expressions into a series of themes, I offer a means to loosely classify each museum in terms of its cultural positionality and regional influence. I follow a number of scholars studying the connection between race and the commemoration of southern landmarks. I work to extend Victoria Gallagher's (2006) argument that regional landmarks can embody "raced" and "de-raced" qualities. Gallagher suggests that viewing memory places in conjunction with one another can "provide very different means for shaping visitors' sense of racial and cultural identity, past, present, and future" (177). According to Stephen A. King (2006), museums are often strategically constructed based on racial motivation. History museums may cater to more prominent mythic narratives that satisfy white tourists who may identify with the commemorative depictions. Consequently, King explains, marginalized groups are then framed inaccurately and positioned in ways that promote a cohesive narrative (247–48). Referring to Memphis specifically, Mark Vail argues that we must work to explicate latent ideologies that are embedded within commemorative sites like museums in order to reveal hegemonic structures and subsequently promote alternative narratives that empower people of color (2012, 431). As an ideologically contested space with a rich history of racial tension, the city of Memphis is full of landmarks, monuments, and commemorative spaces that have racial-ideological leanings.

Scholars and curators who exploit inequality and demonstrate a propensity to feature historically silenced voices have tangible impacts. As Patricia Davis (2013) writes, museums resistant to hegemonic nostalgia make real sociopolitical differences within ideologically contested communities. We can now observe trends toward revisionist versions of regional history that privilege the voices of those typically marginalized, according to Davis:

> The politics of memory, race, and place in southern cityscapes have inspired new areas of inquiry as two interrelated phenomena have conspired to change the urban fabric. First, the white southern hegemony that aided in the construction of an idealized past and dominated the landscape throughout the twentieth century is gradually giving way to revisionist, racially and geographically inclusive narratives. Secondly, the urban public sphere has been subject to increased contestation by groups traditionally blocked from claiming public space. (107)

The Stax and Sun Studio museums produce regional nostalgia in different ways and show stark differences in the way race is integrated into their commemorative tactics; they are representative of the way tensions can form among commemorative styles in ideologically contested spaces.

The integration of racial politics with museum curation promotes the formation of publics and counterpublics. Upon viewing museums, visitors formulate positionalities that align them with other visitors who connect in certain ways with the content on display. Counterpublics are distinguishable because "members are understood to be not merely a subset of the public, but constituted through a conflictual relation to the dominant public" (Warner 2002, 423). While each studio may have begun this way, Sun Studio's whiteness allowed it to transition more quickly into a subset of the dominant public, whereas Stax was perhaps always left to feel as if it were fighting to break through. According to Warner,

> A counterpublic maintains at some level, conscious or not, an awareness of its subordinate status. The cultural horizon against which it marks itself off is not just a general or wider public but a dominant one. And the conflict extends not just to ideas or policy questions, but to the speech genres and modes of address that constitute the public, or to the hierarchy among media. The discourse that constitutes it is not merely a different or alternative idiom, but one that in other contexts would be regarded with hostility, or with a sense of indecorousness. (423–24)

General American racism and an aversion to Black music at the time hindered Stax while propelling Sun Studio. Sun Studio used the innovative sounds in the Black community and projected them through Elvis to worldwide success.

Today, the Stax and Sun Studio museums are fragmented atmospheres containing an amalgam of sites, sounds, and narratives that speak to present-day Memphis identities. The narratives they embody reach beyond the physical confines of the museum and into the larger mythos of the region. The exploration of these narratives requires a method of criticism that lends itself to the process with which they solidify and influence visitors. Thus, the diverse array of rhetorics used in the two museums act constitutively, encouraging the production of subjects with specific conceptions of Memphis history and present-day personhood; they hold the power to establish new types of perceptions, effectively situating visitors into specific ideological positionalities (Charland 1987, 384). Visitors to the two museums experience these fragmented rhetorics as components of narratives that ask them to take on preferred perspectives.

Inevitably, a comparative analysis reveals the way some voices in these institutions are promoted and others are suppressed. I follow Dexter Gordon's (2003) assertion that rhetoricians can theorize rhetorically constructed ideologies latent in African American rhetoric via constitutive, critical, and "rhetorical-material" ideological criticism. Gordon suggests focusing on "both the description of the historic role of discourse in the Black struggle for freedom and justice and the critical rhetorical reconstruction of the past to establish points of intersection with the present" (xv). Building on the work of scholars theorizing fragmentation theory, Gordon argues that critics can assess collections of singular Black voices in order to characterize collective ideological perspectives (198). Such a style of critique allows scholars to embrace the possibility of change and do their part in enacting a better and more inclusive future.

As institutions, the Stax and Sun Studio museums hold both physical and cognitive importance for Memphis and its surrounding region. My critical analysis targets collective artifacts housed within each museum and draws conclusions about how they guide visitors toward specific conceptions of race relations, historically and presently. From this perspective, we can better explore how race can be heard, seen, and bounded in the context of commemorative sites like museums. Memory places are perhaps best studied when we consider the way that words, images, and other rhetorical expressions intersect and contribute to grander interrelated expressions (Olson, Finnegan, and Hope 2008, 2).

FRAGMENTARY IDEOLOGICAL RECONSTRUCTIONS
OF THE STAX AND SUN STUDIO MUSEUMS

As museums with a diverse array of artifacts, the Stax and Sun Studio museums do not offer singular cohesive narratives that can be analyzed simplistically. It would be narrow and reductionist to suggest that the Sun Studio site is comprised of fragments that all speak to a "de-raced" ideology while the Stax museum's exhibits all funnel toward appreciation for racial diversity and inclusivity. However, one can examine the choices made by each museum and argue that there is enough material evidence to warrant some umbrella-level assertions about each museum's narratives. Both museums feature a mixture of artifacts that demonstrate their preferred positionalities aided by signage, visual images, textual dialogue, video content, and section themes.

SUN STUDIO

The Sun Studio experience includes a short tour and three distinct sections: the lobby and gift shop area, the upstairs commemorative area, and the downstairs studio. The tour features a live tour guide, and visitors are limited in the time they can spend in each area by the duration of the thirty-minute tour. The lobby and gift shop area features a café, gifts, and photos and memorabilia covering the walls. The most prominent aspects of this area are a sign that reads "Sun Studio Recording Shop" and a large picture of the Million Dollar Quartet.

The upstairs commemorative area features glass cases with items related to executives, artists, disc jockeys, and other people central to Sun Studio. Pictures, signs, dialogue explanations, musical instruments, records, speakers, and other commemorative items lie behind the glass for viewers to peruse. The most prominent individuals featured are disc jockey Dewey Phillips, Sun Studio founder Sam Phillips, and Elvis Presley. The live tour tells the story of Phillips, who began the "Memphis Recording Studio," which would later become Sun Studio. The tour guide explains that Elvis was moved by the sound of the Prisonaires, and their sound had a profound influence on the nature of his music. The tour then shifts to the downstairs studio where Elvis, Carl Perkins, Johnny Cash, and Jerry Lee Lewis—the musicians comprising the Million Dollar Quartet—are prominently featured. The narrative of the live tour discusses Elvis's beginnings with the recording of "That's All Right," Jerry Lee Lewis's breakout, and other artists central to Sun Studio's success before it was shut down and eventually reopened as a museum and recording studio hybrid in 1987.

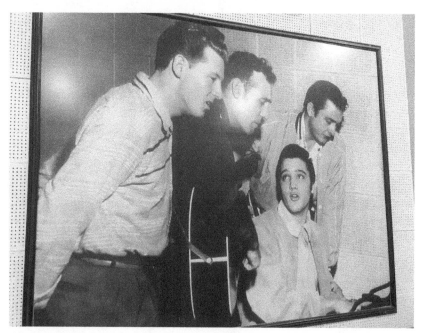

Million Dollar Quartet photo at Sun Studio. Photo by Jonathan M. Smith.

The Sun Studio site is limited in terms of its displays of sociocultural themes; there are few representations outside of the music, musicians, and executives at the studio. From the fragmentary artifacts and narratives present, I identified four themes to demonstrate its expression of whitewashed regional nostalgia: white male representation, musical specificity, ethnocentrism, and nostalgic hegemony.

The narrative theme of *white male representation* is present all over the museum. A large amount of time and energy from the live tour and commemorative areas focuses on Sam Phillips, Dewey Phillips, Elvis Presley, and the Million Dollar Quartet. Sam Phillips is recognized as discovering the majority of the talent that came through Sun Studio. The live tour focuses on his musical tastes and life as the business's owner. He is credited with housing the studio known today as "the birthplace of rock 'n' roll" and discovering Elvis. Dewey Phillips is discussed at length in the tour, and the museum features a recreated radio broadcast studio that symbolizes his broadcasting of Sun Studio music. Elvis is perhaps the most prominent feature of the museum, tour, and Sun Studio overall. Much of the museum's narrative tracks his beginnings and eventual success. His picture and memorabilia tied to him can be found in great quantity in all three sections of Sun Studio (lobby and gift shop, upstairs commemorative area, and downstairs studio). A large photo of the Million

Sam Phillips photo at Sun Studio. Photo by Jonathan M. Smith.

Dollar Quartet appears in two of the museum's sections as a highly visible and prominent feature. Noticeably underrepresented in the museum is B. B. King, a Black musical icon in Memphis who recorded at Sun Studio and has a tribute restaurant and bar on the corner of the internationally known Beale Street in downtown Memphis. Instead, the white artists are granted preferential commemorative treatment.

Another prominent feature of the Sun Studio narrative is its *musical specificity*. Guitars, drum sets, rock 'n' roll records, and musicians positioned as rock 'n' roll pioneers—Carl Perkins, Jerry Lee Lewis, Johnny Cash, among others—feature prominently in visual, textual, and tour-based information. The beginning of the live tour mentions that Sam Phillips sought to record Blues music because he disliked pop music and easy listening, but this is used as a segue to highlight the first use of guitar distortion in the song "Rocket 88" by Jackie Brenston and his Delta Cats—recognized as the first rock 'n' roll song. Part of the live tour also features a demonstration of a Johnny Cash guitar technique that gave him a unique sound.

Finally, the site exhibits *ethnocentrism* and *nostalgic hegemony*. Sam Phillips has said in interviews that his vision for the type of music Sun would go on to produce was inspired by the African American music of the era. Phillips sought to bring Black musicians into his studio to capture their sound but realized a need for white musicians to gain popularity. However, the history, background, and representation of this Black influence is sparsely commemorated at Sun Studio. Black musicians—B. B. King, Chester Burnett, Ike Turner, and the Prisonaires—are featured, but are mainly used to help demonstrate the rise of Elvis. Instead, white male musicians and executives dominate the commemoration. Sun's coverage reflects almost exclusively the dominant white male actors in the historical narrative and thus is not representative of the diverse history of the southern region or of its culture, especially its music. As a result, in terms of the larger US public, tourists may read the museum as accurately depicting the musical history they expect and reflecting the continuing white domination of many areas of endeavor. The museum can thus be read as a nostalgic attempt to retain a power dynamic based on a historically dominant white, hegemonic American culture even though we have, over the last seventy-five years, come to understand that these past periods were, in fact, racially and ethnically diverse.

THE STAX MUSEUM OF AMERICAN SOUL

The Stax museum tour is self-guided. Visitors are free to roam throughout with no time limit during the museum's operating hours. The museum is quite large and has diverse and expansive sections. Visitors begin in a movie theater where a video titled "Soulsville" is shown, before moving into the fourteen other sections in the main portion of the museum, many of which are themed.

The first section has a religious theme. The section contains a re-created church building with an open wall to allow visitors to enter and explore the pews, piano, and wall décor including a reproduction of the Last Supper. A sign

Chapel at Stax Museum of American Soul. Photo by Jonathan M. Smith.

reads "Hooper Chapel AME Church." The church was disassembled and moved to be rebuilt within the museum. Quotes and pictures of houses and graves also grace the exhibit. Visitors then step through a door out of this section into one that blends representation of religion with music. From there, visitors enter a section with a large sign that reads "Discover Our Neighborhood, Soulsville USA." Blues, soul, jazz, country music, and other musical forms are represented. This section demonstrates an intersection of culture, music, history, and tradition that led to the music produced by Stax Records. From there, visitors move through displays commemorating people central to musical development in the 1960s and '70s, before stepping into a ballroom section with a dance floor and disco ball. A sign invites visitors to "Express Yourself" in large letters, and the *Soul Train* television show is commemorated. Visitors next step off the dance floor and into a section featuring specific Stax artists with pictures and text displayed on pieces of soundboard. "Studio A" is displayed in large letters on a sign as visitors enter a re-created recording studio featuring a tape library, waiting area, soundboard, and window into the studio. Inside the studio, instruments of Stax artists are displayed in clear glass cases. Record sleeves and records adorn the following section, with a sign reading "The Stax Family of Labels."

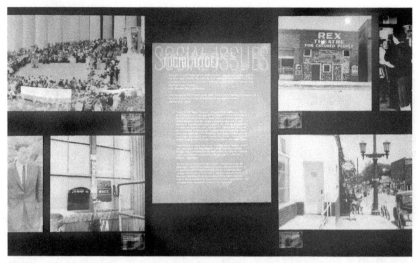

Social Issues display at Stax Museum of American Soul. Photo by Jonathan M. Smith.

As visitors continue through the museum, they enter an area commemorating the intersection of civil rights and music. Signs reading "Issues" and "Social Issues" introduce text discussing the civil rights movement and music in conjunction. This section progresses into an area paying tribute to Isaac Hayes and including his blue and gold Cadillac. The final sections of the museum feature a "Stax Artists List" and a sign titled "Soul Collections." These sections celebrate various soul and other musicians who recorded at Stax and non-Stax artists such as the Supremes and Stevie Wonder and include a photo booth area. The final part of the museum is the gift shop.

The Stax museum contains exhibits that celebrate the intersection of religion, civil rights, and gender and presents a racially diverse body of musicians both within Memphis and the greater southern region. From the artifacts and narratives presented there, I identified four aspects that demonstrate this museum's culturally rich counterpublicity: religious influence, musical diversity, cultural richness, and counterhegemony.

First, signs guiding visitors to an appreciation of *religious influence* include "Gospels of church in the lives of African Americans," "Religion," and "A person's soul." Soul music is demonstrated as evolving from religious beginnings. Additional signs read "Spirituals," "1930s the Birth of Gospel and Gospel Composures," "Gospel Quartet Tradition," "Church Civil Rights and Soul," "The Development of the Gospel Choir." Second, the theme of *musical diversity* is expressed through signs, commemorative cases, and dialogue explaining that many different types of music were central to the birth of soul. Signs read "Birth of soul," "Chicago blues," "White pop," "Country music,"

"Jazz," "Memphis Music Clubs," "The Black Vocal Group Tradition," and "Jump Blues." Ray Charles is quoted in the "Soulsville" video as describing the Stax sound as an intersection of "church, blues, and country music." Textual explanations provide information about the history and influence of these distinct music types. Stax artists are quoted connecting themselves to the influence of diverse musical forms.

Third, the *cultural richness* inherent in the narrative presented by the Stax museum comes through in the video, the civil rights commemorative section, and the variety of artists represented. The video discusses the success and cultural importance of the Stax Record Studio. There is emphasis on the cross-cultural appeal the company offered with African American music appealing to a white audience, thus blurring racial lines. One of the most powerful revelations of the video is the stress on the intersection of Stax's music and the civil rights movement. The narrator of the video says that the company would likely not have closed down if Martin Luther King Jr. had not been shot in Memphis.

Fourth, the *counterhegemony* theme comes through in the museum's overall representation of many traditionally disadvantaged groups that help drive the studio's musical narrative. The narrative does not prominently feature the dominant white male of America hegemonic culture; rather, it puts subordinate groups at the forefront and represents their influence in the studio's success and acclaim. This museum represents Black artists, religion, musical diversity, political struggles, and the revolutionary nature of the civil rights movement. The diversity of representation and influence expressed gives the museum a counterhegemonic quality.

Compared to the Sun Studio site, the Stax museum resonates far more successfully in terms of its relation to racial and cultural progression in the South. Whereas Sun Studio actively resists highlighting these historical maturations through its displays, the Stax museum embraces its diverse roots and arguably features a culture of racial healing just as prominently as did its music. The Stax museum may still hold counterpublic significance on a nationwide level, but its narrative represents a path toward integration that rings true for an increasingly dominant subset of the southern region. Therefore, the museum represents a beacon of progress with continued influence on the tourists and local visitors that pass through its doors.

MEMORY PLACES IN TENSION: CULTURAL IMPLICATIONS

In many ways, the Stax and Sun Studio museums must both engage in the production of nostalgia to maintain relevance, drive tourism, remain profitable, and protect the musical legacy in the city. They must both rely on the narratives of artists who had their roots at their respective studios and went on to achieve international fame. In essence, they share in the same ideals as many museums, tourist attractions, and landmarks across the US. For the greater southern region, the two museums act as windows into history where visitors can come and immerse themselves in the sights and sounds of a bygone period that is still revered. Subsequently, the choices made within the walls of each museum will affect public perceptions regarding the music, history, and culture of the region.

The Stax and Sun Studio museums each use the production of nostalgia via commemoration to send different messages about racial dynamics. Neither museum provides a wholly accurate portrayal of race, music, and the time period. For instance, both actively avoid exploring and exploiting the insidiousness of the racial dynamic—white theft, appropriation, racist studio politics, etc.—that likely helped to facilitate their musical successes. When they do address race, they do so in differing and tempered ways. The Stax museum embraces the cultural and racial turmoil present in the city during its heyday and uses this context to enrich its commemoration through displays of racial cooperation. The Sun Studio site significantly downplays the sociocultural conditions of the era and provides a narrative suggesting that Black artists willingly helped propel white artists to international stardom. From a critical regional perspective—one that attempts to disrupt unrepresentative narratives and reject problematic nostalgia—analyzing the two museums reveals the effects of problematic nostalgia. The Sun Studio site bases its racial approach on the Old South myth, promoting ascription with a regressive view of race relations and regional identity. The Stax museum employs a New South approach that actively avoids featuring the effect of whiteness on the process of musical production. In essence, this museum engages in a sort of rhetoric of nostalgic disruption that produces a future-oriented portrait of racial dynamics that encourages present-day empowerment and racial healing. The Sun Studio narrative embraces a more insidious form of nostalgia that largely shields the studio from critiques and promotes a problematic conception of racial history. Each museum thus promotes adherence to differing conceptions of music, race, culture, and what it means to be a Memphian.

As institutions and historical representations, the Stax and Sun Studio museums hold the power to either facilitate or instill resistance toward present-day racial healing. According to Dickinson, Blair, and Ott (2010), "a memory place proposes a specific kind of relationship between past and present that may offer a sense of sustained and sustaining communal identification. By bringing the visitor into contact with a significant past, the visitor may be led to understand the present as part of an enduring, stable tradition" (27). By providing a more culturally rich and comprehensive view of the connection between Memphis music and race relations, the Stax museum uses its experience as a force for progress, whereas the Sun Studio site downplays the contributions of the Black community and characterizes the Memphis music of the mid-twentieth century as very much a white endeavor. The implications of these choices are further explicated through consideration of Sun Studio's role in a supposedly postracial era. Michael Lacy and Kent Ono (2011) suggest that a critical rhetoric of race allows scholars to productively engage the contradictory and silencing messages of the supposedly postracial era, in which "stories of racialized victims claiming institutional racism are routinely followed by white and Black conservatives charging 'reverse racism,' 'playing the race card,' or 'political correctness'" (1–2).

Regional landmarks like the Stax museum and Sun Studio form dialects of progress and resistance in the regions where they reside. As many regions in the US progress toward improved inclusivity and diversity, commemorative sites can either facilitate these developments or hide behind the guise of postracialism and subjectively recount histories in ways that promote identification with regressive regional identities. The lens of critical regionalism reveals that many of Memphis's present-day landmarks and memory places carry with them an inherent raced and/or deraced quality. These symbols matter immensely given the present sociopolitical climate within the city. Although the Sun Studio site is not as explicitly harmful toward the Black community as are the Confederate statues that still stand, it holds a subtle capacity to indoctrinate visitors with a conception of Memphis music that is directly related to how one might understand the sociocultural atmosphere of the region. Future studies in the city of Memphis should use the critical regional approach to understand the way memory places in the city encourage visitors toward identities that hold these raced and deraced qualities. In the supposedly postracial era, racial discrimination and influence often embody forms that are implicit and thus require critical examinations to uncover the nuanced ways that they extend dominant perspectives and hinder racial cooperation.

NOTE

1. Jonathan Smith would like to dedicate this chapter to the memory of the late Robert Iltis.

REFERENCES

Armada, Bernard J. 1998. "Memorial Agon: An Interpretive Tour of the National Civil Rights Museum." *Southern Communication Journal* 63, no. 3 (Spring): 235–44.

Browne, Stephen H. 1995. "Reading, Rhetoric, and the Texture of Public Memory." *Quarterly Journal of Speech* 81, no. 2 (May): 237–51.

Charland, Maurice. 2016. "Constitutive Rhetoric: The Case of the *People Cuebecois*." In *Contemporary Rhetorical Theory: A Reader*, edited by Mark Porrovecchio and Celeste Michelle Condit, 382–95. New York: Guilford Press.

Davis, Patricia. 2013. "Memoryscapes in Transition: Black History Museums, New South Narratives, and Urban Regeneration." *Southern Communication Journal* 78, no. 2 (April): 107–127.

Dawson, David B. 1997. *Memphis: New Visions, New Horizons*. Memphis: Towery Pub.

Dickinson, Greg, Carole Blair, and Brian L. Ott. 2010. *Places of Public Memory: The Rhetoric of Museums and Memorials*. Tuscaloosa: University of Alabama Press.

Gallagher, Victoria. 2006. "Displaying Race: Cultural Projection and Commemoration." In *Rhetorics of Display*, edited by Lawrence J. Prelli, 177–96. Columbia: University of South Carolina Press.

Gordon, Dexter. 2003. *Black Identity: Rhetoric, Ideology, and Nineteenth-Century Black Nationalism*. Carbondale: Southern Illinois University Press.

Gordon, Robert. 1994. *It Came from Memphis*. Boston: Faber and Faber.

Guralnick, Peter. 1994. "Forward." In *It Came from Memphis*, by Robert Gordon, xi–xii. Boston: Faber and Faber.

Hawes, Jennifer Berry. 2016. "Exposing the Invisible Empire." *Columbia Journalism Review*, Spring 2016, https://www.cjr.org/the_feature/exposing_the_invisible_empire.php.

Hughes, Charles L. 2015. *Country Soul: Making Music and Making Race in the American South*. Chapel Hill: University of North Carolina Press.

Karp, Ivan, and Steven Lavine. 1991. "Introduction: Museums and Multiculturalism." In *Exhibiting Cultures: The Poetics and Politics of Museum Display*, edited by Ivan Karp and Steven Lavine, 11–24. Washington, DC: Smithsonian Institution Press.

King, Stephen A. 2006. "Memory, Mythmaking, and Museums: Constructive Authenticity and the Primitive Blues Subject." *Southern Communication Journal* 71, no. 3 (September): 235–50.

Lacy, Michael G., and Kent A. Ono. 2011. *Critical Rhetoric of Race*. New York: New York University Press.

Leonard, Marion. 2007. "Constructing Histories Through Material Culture: Popular Music, Museums and Collecting." *Popular Music History* 2, no. 2 (August): 147–67.

McPherson, Larry E. 2002. *Memphis*. Santa Fe, NM: Center for American Places.

Memphis Music Hall of Fame. n.d. "Learn: More About Us." Accessed November 1, 2016. http://memphismusichalloffame.com/about/.

Olson, Lester C., Cara A. Finnegan, and Diane S. Hope. 2008. *Visual Rhetoric: A Reader in Communication and American Culture*. Los Angeles: Sage.

Pearce, Susan M. 1993. *Museums, Objects, and Collections: A Cultural Study*. Washington, DC: Smithsonian Institution Press.

Powell, Douglas Reichert. 2012. *Critical Regionalism: Connecting Politics and Culture in the American Landscape*. Chapel Hill: University of North Carolina Press.

Radley, Alan. 1991. "Boredom, Fascination and Mortality: Reflections upon the Experience of Museum Visiting." In *Museum Languages: Objects and Texts*, edited by Gaynor Kavanagh, 65–82. London: Leicester University Press.

Raichelson, Richard M., and Donna West. 2006. *Memphis Innovations: People, Ideas, and Innovations That Changed Our World*. Overland Park, KS: Power House.

Rice, Jenny. 2012. "From Architectonic to Tectonics: Introducing Regional Rhetorics." *Rhetoric Society Quarterly* 42, no. 3 (June): 201–213.

Stax Museum of American Soul Music. n.d. "Story of Stax." Accessed July 2, 2019, https://staxmuseum.com/.

Stax Records. n.d. "Stax History." Accessed November 1, 2016, https://staxrecords.com/history/.

Stewart, Jim. 2007. "Racial Integration at Stax." *Teachrock*, 2007. http://teachrock.org/video/jim-stewart-racial-integration-at-stax-2007/.

Soundbreaking: The Art of Recording. 2016. PBS. Aired November 14, 2016. Television.

Sun Studio. n.d. "About." Accessed November 1, 2016, https://www.sunstudio.com/about.

Sun Studio. n.d. "Plan Your Tour." Accessed November 1, 2016, https://www.sunstudio.com/planyourtour.

Vail, Mark T. 2012. "Reconstructing the Lost Cause in the Memphis City Parks Renaming Controversy." *Western Journal of Communication* 76, no. 4 (July): 417–37.

Warner, Michael. 2002. "Publics and Counterpublics." *Quarterly Journal of Speech* 88, no. 4 (November): 413–25.

Washington, Booker T. 1895. "Atlanta Compromise." Speech, Atlanta, GA, September 18, 1895. *History Matters.* http://historymatters.gmu.edu/d/39/.

Wilson, Charles Reagan. 2002. "An Introduction to Memphis." In *Memphis*, edited by Larry E. McPherson. Santa Fe, NM: Center for American Places.

Woods, Carly, Joshua Ewalt, and Sara Baker. 2013. "A Matter of Regionalism: Remembering Brandon Teena and Willa Cather at the Nebraska History Museum." *Quarterly Journal of Speech* 99, no. 3 (August): 341–63.

Zagacki, Kenneth S., and Victoria J. Gallagher. 2009. "Rhetoric and Materiality in the Museum Park at the North Carolina Museum of Art." *Quarterly Journal of Speech* 95, no. 2 (May): 171–91.

Chapter 4

STYLES AND SPACES OF WHITENESS IN HGTV'S *FIXER UPPER*

JULIA M. MEDHURST

When I meet people for the first time, I often tell them I have lived my entire life within a ninety-mile radius of College Station, Texas (with the exception of a six-month stint in Washington, DC). Raised by my mother and grandmother, a white, middle-class Texan and a white middle-class Floridian, respectively, I have always been fascinated by the ways that southern white women express their collective identity through homemaking/decorating practices. Through formal education and self-study, I have become attuned to how seemingly banal habits of taste invoke whiteness to occlude the rich, diverse cultures of the South, especially given how southern capital was built on Black suffering. It is my hope that critically analyzing these habits will open the door to more authentic, inclusive portraits of southern material culture and challenge southern white women to interrogate and remake their meaning-making practices.[1]

In Waco, Texas, inside the home décor superstore Magnolia Market, long stems of cotton are gathered into bundles, sitting proudly inside large white ceramic vases. Alongside dozens of silk flowers, the fluffy white cotton balls were also long available on the store's website for purchase—for fourteen dollars a stem ("Harvest Cotton Stem" 2019). Magnolia Market's style defines a recent major trend in southern home décor: the return to the southern farm. Oversized sliding barn doors, giant cream-colored candlesticks, white ruffle-edged napkins, galvanized milk cans, white shiplap walls, and reclaimed barnwood tables—these adornments have become commonplace in stores and homes throughout the American South and across the United States.[2]

The source of Magnolia Market's rise to style fame lies in the television sensation that is HGTV's *Fixer Upper*. Market owners Chip and Joanna Gaines made their mark on American audiences with the introduction of their home improvement reality show, in which the couple "fixes up" dilapidated homes and transforms them into sparkling new abodes for ostensibly deserving—often wealthy and white—clients. Racial identity of the show's hosts is immediately foregrounded in the presence of Chip's whiteness, which overcodes the rhetorical moves of the show's narrative arcs. On the other hand, Joanna's seemingly invisible biracial identity (white Lebanese and Korean) is eclipsed, such that the episodes posit her as a monolithically white character with culturally white southern tastes. The combination of these identities works as a template for the show to offer an ideology of whiteness that is reinscribed by the couple's decorating expertise.

Reaching no fewer than twenty-five million viewers during its run of original shows from 2013 to 2017, *Fixer Upper* became HGTV's most successful program and has been syndicated on Netflix (Jones 2016). The show also chronicled the expansion of Joanna's tiny home goods shop, Magnolia, into a thriving behemoth featuring a new shopping and dining complex that attracts tens of thousands of visitors by the month. Since 2014, tourism to Waco has tripled, and some business owners are feeling the effects. A *New York Times* profile confirmed the phenomenon with David Ridley, whose short stint on the show as a featured home buyer allowed him to leverage his celebrity into a lucrative Waco tours business (Skinner 2018).

With success comes controversy—in this case, controversy in both style (located primarily in the symbolic, as seen through the show's preferred décor) and place (located primarily in the material, as seen through the show's promotion of gentrification). The style that *Fixer Upper* models—colloquially known as farmhouse chic—has emerged as a matter of public debate. A 2017 article in the *Washington Post* reported on a university president's choice to host a dinner for Black students where the table centerpieces featured cotton stems (Bever 2017). Critics interpreted the décor as signaling a radical occlusion of the history of slavery in America or a complete insensitivity to the Black communities who carry this traumatic history. Such critiques have a curious resonance with the historical uses of material items to signify race and class hierarchies. As scholars have shown, choices in decoration—from the use of antiques in living room configurations to the color of dinnerware—have a storied history of use by white Americans looking to solidify their rank in US society (Greenfield 2009; Heneghan 2003). The commercialization of these home décor choices, too, is documented by William Brundage (2009), who argues that southern white women of the nineteenth century used their decorating prowess to construct a nostalgic image of white upper-class southern heritage. Moreover, Grace E. Hale (1998) observes that wealthy white southerners sought to control consumption and production as a means of codifying white supremacy in the region. Indeed, home décor has always signified wealth, race, and status in American culture, as elsewhere.

Controversy in terms of the material abounds as well. *Fixer Upper* has been an economic boon to the mid-sized city of Waco, but the influx of wealthy home buyers has made purchasing a house in town unaffordable for low-income workers. As one housing nonprofit administrator put it, "clients are increasingly feeling the pinch as rents rise, wages stagnate, housing assistance wait lists grow, and the stock of affordable housing grows thin" (qtd. in Dodd 2018). Indeed, "affordable housing" is precisely what *Fixer Upper* deals in, as wealthy home buyers are shown a series of "affordable" (old, dilapidated) houses, often located in low-income neighborhoods, that the buyers see as needing a great deal of work to be made worthy of purchase. On the show, the client buys the house for the lowest price possible; then, tens of thousands of dollars are poured into the renovation to convert it into the client's dream home. As this process takes place, the economic effects on the neighborhood are drastic, with residents in low-income neighborhoods witnessing a property tax spike anywhere from 10 to 40 percent of the original cost, leading some to call the Chip and Joanna sensation "*Fixer Upper* gone bad" (Petersen 2019). Displacement of long-time residents due to tax increases is one concern posed by the show's critics, and it is connected to issues of race. Gentrification along racial lines continues to put stress on Black and Brown communities, whose members end up having to divert their attention from the weaving of the neighborhood's social fabric to mounting a defense of the spaces that make up the lifeblood of the community (Bentacur 2011).

Regarding issues of racial representation on television, HGTV, as a network, provides an interesting case study in its own right. Shawn Shimpach (2012) has convincingly argued that even though the network leads others in numbers of racially diverse bodies featured on the screen, the messaging does not reflect diversity in tastes or values. Specifically, he suggests that increased diversity in featured home buyers does not correlate with increased diversity in décor choice. Rather, as noted in an NPR story, "in spite of all this great diversity on HGTV, everybody ends up wanting exactly the same things . . . granite and stainless steel" (Holmes 2011). The homogenizing effect of home improvement reality, Shimpach argues, serves a neoliberal agenda that uses diversity as a tool to further consumerist logics rooted in "the dismantling of government assistance" (525).

In this essay, I argue that *Fixer Upper* and Magnolia Market owe many of their successes to the constitution and commodification of a distinctly white southern subjectivity, operationalized through the physical space of the house and the decorations placed within it. With many of the show's houses having been built between the 1910s and 1960s, the charm in *Fixer Upper* lies in the Gaineses' ability to "restore" these houses to their alleged former glory and repurpose them for modern life in Waco, Texas. Inside the homes, Joanna

Gaines's designs rely on the use of rustic, farmhouse antiques and white ceramics and paint to form a coherent aesthetic that envisions a distinct spirit for southern residents. Taken together, the exterior and interior transformations visited upon these houses produce distinctive spaces that make normative judgments about home living in the South today.

These aesthetic choices—put into practice through the symbolic and material—are structured by the logic of whiteness as an organizing principle, inflected through regionality. Whiteness, defined by Ashley Doane and Eduardo Bonilla-Silva (2003) as a "historically contingent social identity" (9), functions as a system of power relations that reproduce its racial hegemony. Such identity, as well as the racial hegemony that structures it, is affected by regions. Moving beyond nostalgia, kitsch, or pastiche as described by Rice (2012), a critical regional viewpoint means that these ongoing power relations and identities are shaped by contested pasts and presents of a region, its inhabitants, and their everyday meaning-making practices.

Magnolia's home transformations, as I will show, rely upon historically contingent racialized understandings of style and space reminiscent of the aesthetic claims made by antique decorating practices of the nineteenth and twentieth centuries (Greenfield 2009). *Fixer Upper*'s fascination with southern antiques and white décorations announces a relatively recent historical and cultural shift in which members of the elite white public use home objects to constitute a nostalgic past. This aesthetic vision of the home inaugurates a dispute of the local and regional through its claims to the practices that constitute "southern" subjects and life.

Conversations regarding the multiple contested meanings of space are of central concern to the project of critical regionalism, the purpose of which is to explore "the processes by which ideas about regions come into being and become influential," with the understanding that this kind of scholarship should interrogate "whose interests are served by a given version of a region" (Powell 2007, 7). Taking a critical regional perspective, this essay argues that the vision of the South and southern subjectivity put forth by *Fixer Upper* positions whiteness and wealth as the aesthetic of Waco to the exclusion of Black and Brown bodies in these spaces (Nakayama and Krizek 1995; Shabazz 2009). Specifically, the renovation and decoration practices offer a view of the home as a heterotopia that invites a claiming of the communal and regional through individual style. These consumptive choices operate according to the logics of whiteness as an aesthetic particular to one version of central Texas's regional identity. The apex of this citizen-consumer subject is realized in the on-screen moment in which clients view their newly renovated dream home, replete with Magnolia's brand of charm and adornment.

Fixer Upper constructs subjects not only on the symbolic level, but also on the material. As data from the city support, homes featured on the show are often the site of gentrification at work in low-income and diverse neighborhoods of Waco. As legal scholars John Powell and Marguerite Spencer (2002) explain, gentrification "is neither good for cities nor the poor . . . *unless* we disrupt the market in pursuit of a more egalitarian goal: the creation of integrated life opportunities for all people in all places" (434). If we understand the call of critical regionalism as one that requires us to "self-consciously shape an understanding of the spatial dimensions of cultural politics in order to support projects of change" (Powell 2007, 8), then this essay offers one such solution. In examining how discourses of gentrification harm local citizens through the social and economic impact on people of color (in this case, Black and Brown people) and low-income people, this work provides a starting point for community reconciliation by calling for a deeper examination of how the aesthetic and material values of whiteness are deployed in service of maintaining segregated spaces.

UNDERSTANDING STYLE THROUGH
AN EXAMINATION OF SPACE

Fixer Upper's use of style functions rhetorically as it is deployed through the space of the home. That space can productively be considered what Michel Foucault (1984) terms a heterotopia, a material space that functions to enact a utopia (an illusory space). Though the nature of this enactment may take differing forms, the one that is illustrative of the space of the home in *Fixer Upper* is the compensating heterotopia. When a heterotopia compensates, Foucault writes, it creates a location that is "as perfect, as meticulous, as well arranged as ours is messy, ill constructed, and jumbled" (8). Enacting the symbolic through the constitution of a physical space and the material practices that accompany it, the heterotopia provides the subject an opportunity to inhabit modes of being that are impossible in any other locale. For example, a massive, distressed barn door could signify an escape from a cramped urban dwelling to an expansive, idealized farm. In this way, subjects can put utopian elements into practice in the real world. By nature, those utopian elements invite certain thoughts, practices, and bodies and exclude others. The need to exclude thus forces the compensating heterotopia to respond to some crisis or way of being that we are compelled to remedy by the enactment of a more perfect form.

One way we build heterotopias is through the enactment of style, which Barry Brummett (2008) defines as a system of signifying which objects, for example, "are used to create aesthetically charged rhetorical outcomes in the self and others" (2). In this view, style collapses the dichotomy between substance and signs to reveal that our symbolic understandings of the material world constitute our lived realities (12). Particular styles—like farmhouse chic—are unified sign systems that audiences recognize as having an identifiable cultural significance or connotation (14). Wrought iron, shiplap (horizontal wooden slats on interior or exterior walls), weathered creams and greys, wicker, and cozy pillows create a semiotic code. Though the recognizability of a particular style may be evident, it is neither necessarily coherent or fixed. The ability of style to shift "signs and their meanings from contexts that originally gave them meaning" (9) is what gives style its unique power to construct systems of signifying. Removing one of those elements (wicker, let's say) and adding a different one (grandmother's antique wooden chair) shift and individualize the style, giving the user the feeling of agency. All the while, these shifts replicate the code. This workable definition of style allows us to explain how objects, language, and images organize mass culture and how mass culture bears on questions of identity and regionality.

Mass culture draws upon aesthetics in its building of signifying systems. Aesthetics, the dimensions of experience tied to the senses, calls for a "systematic mode of appreciation" (Brummett 2008, 17). Here, aesthetics is not synonymous with beauty *per se*, but with the sensory experiences that tap into the subject's appreciative faculties. As a mode of appreciation, aesthetics can be thought of as a particular communication form that conjures certain associations. When Brummett speaks of the "aestheticized life," he calls attention to the "impulse to stylize" found in popular culture (17). In television about home decorating, aestheticizing is akin to strategizing because the audience is called to purposefully select the elements of style that suit their tastes, which are governed by imagined membership in various rhetorical communities. Viewers imagine themselves as the farmhouse chic clients on the show, picking and choosing their own interior and exterior designs and thus being coached into a particular regional aesthetic. Those who identify today with the moniker of "southern" are called to enact that identity by styling their homes—here, seen as extensions of themselves—in the décor that television imagines for them.

In *Fixer Upper*, the notion of imagined rhetorical communities is implicated in the examination of the space of the home. The show positions the home as a "Lost Cause" heterotopia. Following Reconstruction, the myth of the Lost Cause created "a postwar rhetorical apologia absolving the abrogated antebellum decorum that valued hierarchy, paternalism, and racialized nobility and liberty for Whites" (Vail 2012, 419). The myth worked to ameliorate white southerners' crisis of racial hierarchy following the end of Reconstruction. It reasserted the racial dominance of white culture by valorizing the manners and styles of the white aristocracy. Thus, the narrative offered an alternative mode of imaging life in the South (and the identities of white and Black southerners within those imaginations). Similar to the rhetorical work that the Lost Cause accomplished at the beginning of the twentieth century, *Fixer Upper* invites the audience to understand the space of the home as an alternative, preferred mode of living in the new South. It is a place of nobility and white freedom that hearkens back to agrarian gentility—the spaces for leisure and tea-drinking, as well as a farm that always appears clean and orderly (through invisible and uncompensated labor).

Fixer Upper's use of farmhouse chic makes no explicit reference to Confederate valor or forgotten heroism; rather, bolls of cotton, plantation-faded paints, and reclaimed wood function as subtle allusions. The constellation of such elements works on the audience's impulses to aestheticize, to purposefully select each adornment of the home—from the restoring of the transom, to the fresh coat of white paint, to the magnolia wreath on the front door. This selection functions rhetorically as a means of constituting community membership. As the following analysis contends, such membership is structured by a logic of whiteness—both symbolic and material.

NEW WACO: LOST CAUSE SUBJECTIVITY IN *FIXER UPPER* EPISODES

Like most of the home improvement reality series on HGTV, *Fixer Upper* follows a diegetic formula for each of its episodes, following a fairly standard narrative path. Viewers of the series expect to see a certain progression of scenes and plot devices each time they watch the show. Plot motifs contribute to *Fixer Upper*'s production of white southern subjectivity through the process of neighborhood and house selection, which includes attention to existing architectural elements of the home as well as consideration of farmhouse chic style and farmhouse antiques to decorate the new spaces. Identification occurs within these motifs when, first, white southern charm and politeness are exhibited when the buyer is confronted with the daunting task of selecting a house (demonstrating the luxury to "take everything in stride"); and, second, nostalgic satisfaction is exemplified as Joanna journeys to discover the perfect antique décor pieces to fit the clients' new home. The southern white past is felt as completely congruent with contemporary life needs, as old washstands or rustic shelves from the farm are repurposed to fit the client's new cell phone holder or laptop. Episode six of season one contains these plot motifs and moments for regional identification.

In that episode, "Craftsmen Crave Urban Feel" (*Fixer Upper* 2014), Chip and Joanna are tasked with finding a new home for Clint and Kelly Harp and their three young children. The Gaines's search for the right house takes the Harps first to a three-bedroom abode built in 1915, nicknamed the "Charmer House." Upon entering the house, the Harps are struck by the original details, from the hardwood floors to the solid wood sliding doors. Clint notes approvingly that the fixtures on the door also appear to be original to the home. The bathroom garners equal praise from Kelly, who approves of the hexagonal floor tile. Following the tour of the "Charmer House," the Harps say they are impressed with its style and beauty but have reservations about the small number of bedrooms.

They eagerly move to the next contender, nicknamed the "Catastrophe House," built in 1913. This house elicits a very different reaction from the Harps. As they approach the front door, Clint laments, "This is horrible. It's so bad. We are lost. This is not the right house" (*Fixer Upper* 2014). Indeed, the house appears to be in a terrible state of disrepair. Abandoned trash dots what is left of the rotting front porch. The white painted exterior is peeling around boarded-up windows. The roof appears to be caving in. The front lawn is overgrown and neglected. Clint remarks that "what really struck me at first were the bullet holes." The foursome enter the home to discover an equally unsightly living room space, cluttered with trash, rotting wood, and abandoned furniture. Nonplussed by the mess, Joanna gets to work explaining her renovation and design ideas for the room. She says, "If you guys can just get some vision for this room: new windows, new sheet rock, crown molding. . . . make this room be this grand thing that it once was in 1913." At the end of the tour, the Harps praise the space of the large, five-bedroom house and note that it is located in their preferred neighborhood of Brook Oaks, near Clint's carpentry shop. However, they express deep concerns about the extensiveness of work the house requires.

Moving to the last stop on the tour, the group visits the "Purple House," built in 1915 (*Fixer Upper* 2014). Their initial reaction to the home is positive, save for the purple trim on the eaves. On the inside, the Harps praise the craftsmanship of the doors, the transom, and the original flooring. They especially approve of the original wood-burning fireplaces in several of the bedrooms. From a design standpoint, Joanna suggests a simple coat of paint in addition to kitchen and bathroom renovations to modernize the space. Again, the Harps praise the "character" of the home.

The home selection process for the Harps reveals a concern primarily for the style and character of the house (*Fixer Upper* 2014); however, both of these factors belie some relevant contextual matters. Each of the houses was built in the early 1900s, providing each space with the turn-of-the-century southern style the couple appreciates. The Harps and Gaineses highlight the importance of elements like original wood flooring, intricately carved fireplaces, solid wood doors, large windows, large white columns, and other features indicative of plantation architecture in the US South. While these features may be aesthetically pleasing, they nonetheless serve to rearticulate the class and race logics of the past.

Catherine Bishir (1993), a scholar of the histories of homes built at the turn of the twentieth century in the South, argues that postwar southern architecture was crafted with the intent to glorify the antebellum period, when times were better economically and socially for members of the southern aristocracy. These homes appealed not only to white pride in the old southern order but specifically to racialized logics of white supremacy. To live in one of these houses was a marker of inclusion in white upper-class society, as well as a method for white property owners to reassert their dominance in the changing landscape of the new South. Similarly, Tara McPherson (2003) observes that the emergence of homes built in this style was important to the myth-writing process that wealthy white southerners undertook in order to construct an "escape scenario, simultaneously underwriting and disavowing the early twentieth century's fierce lynching campaigns, insisting on a more perfect past, where paternalistic race relations ensured the good behavior of loyal servants" (45). Southern homes of this era thus worked to produce the space of the house and the spaces surrounding it by reaffirming the supremacy of the planter class, constructing a physical landscape of intimidation.

A similar kind of rhetorical production is at work in the presentation of these homes through what they exclude. In "Craftsmen Crave Urban Feel," the "Catastrophe House" is ruled out at first (*Fixer Upper* 2014). *Fixer Upper* encodes this house as an embodiment of dishonor regarding the history of regionally specific, white upper-class style. Architectural elements, exterior and interior paint colors, and décor will need to be brought in line with a nostalgia for white Old South taste beyond the dilapidation. In this way, subjects who identify with whiteness as a historically contingent social identity are called forth by the promise of a return to a former time. They are invited to restore early twentieth-century grandeur, which refashioned the architectural iconography of the elite Old South. When brought back to life, this heterotopia—a compensating, material space—enacts logics of race and class to compose a new landscape.

Homes built in the era and style that *Fixer Upper* valorizes bring with them a storied history of racism operationalized through the physical and symbolic exclusion of Black and Brown bodies. James Loewen (2005) examines Sundown towns—jurisdictions that prohibited Black Americans from taking up residence within their borders. He describes the early twentieth century as an era defined by *de facto* building and insurance standards that resulted in extreme racial apartheid, even though those standards were not articulated in explicit policy.

Indeed, *Fixer Upper* constructs the space of the home as the embodiment of timeless style and chic aesthetic, thereby suggesting that a return to the lived practices of yesteryear is desirable for contemporary community members. This notion becomes most evident when Joanna speaks of restoring the "Catastrophe House" to its former glory of 1913 (*Fixer Upper* 2014). Persuaded by Joanna's words, the Harps select the bullet-riddled house to become their beloved "fixer upper." One of the reasons the Harps give for selecting the house is its prime location, in the Brook Oaks neighborhood, a noteworthy choice given its rates of reported criminal activity.

That the "Catastrophe House" is described at various points in the episode as the "bullet-ridden" home or the "drug dealer's house" (*Fixer Upper* 2014) is illustrative of the more recent history of the home and its location in the Brook Oaks neighborhood. According to a Waco Police Department Neighborhood Crimes Report for May 2014, when the "Craftsmen" episode first aired, residents of Brook Oaks called in 110 reports of criminal activity in the neighborhood, with ten of those related to narcotics offenses, and eleven related to assaults ("Waco Crime Statistics" 2014). These numbers stand out among the crime statistics for various Waco neighborhoods, as the reports show the amount of criminal activity in the area to be relatively high, especially compared to wealthier neighborhoods like North Lake Waco, which in the same month reported only thirty-five incidents, none related to drug offenses and only two related to charges of assault.

The Brook Oaks neighborhood also has a high level of poverty. In 2013, the median income for a family living in the neighborhood was $26,421, and 37 percent of families there were living below the poverty level ("Brook Oaks Neighborhood" 2016). Brook Oaks was known, too, as an area primed to received state dollars for low-income housing projects, according to the *Waco Tribune-Herald* ("Editorial" 2014). The condition of the neighborhood was further underscored by Chip's evaluation of the home post-renovation. He evaluated the new worth of the house using a fifty-dollar per square foot metric, which he called "offensive," saying that he would refuse to sell such a beautiful home for such a low price (*Fixer Upper* 2014).

In addition to the widespread poverty and crime that occurred in Brook Oaks, the plurality of the neighborhood's residents identified as nonwhite ("Brook Oaks Neighborhood" 2016). The demographics information is suggestive given the claims made in *Fixer Upper*'s opening credits. The Gaineses proudly affirm that they specialize in taking "the worst house in the best neighborhood and turn[ing] it into our clients' dream home" (*Fixer Upper* 2014). In some cases, however, the reality of *Fixer Upper* is marked by taking the worst house in a poor neighborhood and transforming it into a white upper-middle class home among nonwhite, low-income homes. Thus, the material exclusion of particular subjectivities is operationalized through these heterotopic spaces. While the case of the "Catastrophe House" is not representative of every home transformation featured on the show, it does serve as a prime exemplar of how the styling of whiteness works to alter the domestic landscapes of the South. The show discursively discards the lived histories of previous residents and communities and replaces them with a hegemonic style that reproduces particular race and class hierarchies—a process akin to that of gentrification.

FIXER UPPER AND THE GENTRIFICATION OF WACO

As the "Catastrophe House" demonstrates, the purchase and renovation of turn-of-the-twentieth-century homes located in predominantly nonwhite, low-income neighborhoods contribute to gentrification. In its most positive definition, gentrification means repairing and rebuilding, which can lead to economic and environmental rewards. However, it is often accompanied by an influx of middle-class or affluent people into a region, resulting in the displacement of the original (usually poorer) residents. With displacement of low-income residents comes a shift in taste that changes the aesthetic character of the space to conform to middle- and upper-class preferences. Such stylistic differences then reify extreme racial wealth gaps; not only are Black residents more likely not to be able to afford the new tax and insurance rates, but their styles are coopted or destroyed to create a new sense of community in place of the old.

Indeed, when the Harps and Gaineses go on their initial walk-through of the so-called "drug-dealer's house," no attention or concern is paid to what became of the home's previous residents (*Fixer Upper* 2014). The displacement of those residents is elided for a focus instead on the glory of the home decades earlier, when wealthy inhabitants lived there. When Joanna speaks of restoring the character of the space, she does so with an eye toward reclaiming the essence of white wealth. The fate of the home's most recent residents is positioned as antithetical to the future lives the home buyers will be living. In fact, the supposition that the "Catastrophe House" was perhaps the scene of a crime becomes a point of laughter throughout the episode because the notion that anyone with a choice about their living circumstances would consider purchasing a house in such a state is preposterous.

The argument that gentrification is ultimately productive for a community because it increases affluence and levels of education in a neighborhood or expands economic opportunities for residents is challenged by scholars who attend to the multilayered impacts that the practice has on people of color and low-income residents. Daniel Makagon (2010) argues gentrification is not just about the tangible process of displacement. Specifically, his analysis of news articles about white artists' gentrifying an urban neighborhood found that reporters constructed "the city as a frontier and artists as pioneers" coming to tame it. Such rhetoric stigmatized the neighborhood's long-time residents, who were positioned as "dirty" or in need of cleaning up by the artists who came to claim space in the neighborhood (38). Mary Triece (2017) sees gentrification as a tool of white supremacy in its capacity to position the city as a fearsome wasteland in need of a white, "civilized" savior. She explains that it "is a notably White understanding of the urban that ironically turns the tables on the very real history of White violence against Black residents and the city-backed demolition of Black neighborhoods" (258). Referring to the discriminatory practices of redlining and urban "renewal" projects in Black urban neighborhoods of Detroit, Triece reminds us that many communities were sliced apart and decimated at the hands of the federal government (259).

From a policy standpoint, Powell and Spencer (2002) contend that glowing assessments of gentrification ignore the mitigating factors of race and class to the detriment of both the long-time inhabitants of the community and to the gentrifiers. Gentrification, they argue, is not a boon for cities or for low-income residents unless it accompanies a purposeful disruption of the market to allow for the building of integrated life for *all* community residents (437). Achieving integrated life, they explain, requires that the building of new spaces be conducted in such a way as to eliminate the displacement of long-time residents. Planned changes in infrastructure (such as free or low-cost public transportation) that will support the needs of working-class inhabitants are vital to sustaining the lifeblood of the community. These changes require that city officials and gentrifiers take seriously the needs of the community by acknowledging that the presence of long-time residents is equally valuable to the future prosperity of the region.

THE WHITENESS OF STYLE THROUGH THE USE OF ANTIQUES

In the realm of the symbolic, Joanna's selection of southern antiques also works to build the heterotopia. In season two, the search for specific antiques to furnish client homes becomes a major element of the show and is presented as an integral motif of the storyline. What, then, is the significance of purposefully selecting antique items to furnish newly renovated homes? Antiques are items imbued with arbitrary cultural value tied historically to matters of region, class, and race. Three episodes, "Young Couple Chooses Old Home," "Homebuilders Seek *Fixer Upper*," and "High School Friend Seeks Fixer," demonstrate the centrality of the antique search and selection process.

In "Young Couple Chooses Old Home" (*Fixer Upper* 2015a), Chip and Joanna make their way to a local antique shop that specializes in sales of repainted and restained furniture to channel a farmhouse aesthetic. The shop contains items that evoke farmhouse chic, including mason jars, retro make-up vanities, and white floral throw pillows. For the Gaineses, the mission is to locate an antique dresser that can be repurposed into a vanity for the clients' bathroom. Upon entering the store, Chip remarks, "I can sink my teeth into this place, Jo; this is fun." Indeed, the couple enjoys bouncing around the shop, searching for the perfect piece. Joanna finally locates a French antique-style dresser and exclaims, "This is cute!" She promptly purchases the item for her clients' home.

Antique hunting is featured again in "Homebuilders Seek *Fixer Upper*" (*Fixer Upper* 2015b) when the entire Gaines family visits an auction house down the road from their farm. Chip announces his excitement for the visit when he says, "It literally is like walking into the gates of Heaven." Joanna adds, "I'm always decorating these houses and I'm always looking for really unique pieces. . . . there are a lot of good antiques [here]." The family walks away with several items from the auction, including a pair of antique candlesticks that will be used in their current clients' home, as well as several objects that Joanna will clean up and sell at Magnolia Market.

As the mothership of the central Texas antiquing community, the semiannual fair at Round Top houses antiques vendors from across the state, featured in the episode "High School Friend Seeks Fixer" (*Fixer Upper* 2015c). Turning the shopping expedition into a family excursion, the Gaineses load up their vehicle and make for the small town. The excitement and expectations for the trip are palpable. Speaking to her children in the car, Joanna says, "You know when you are in a toy store or a candy store and you feel like you're in heaven? That's what Round Top is for mommy." Joanna and the family spend considerable time weaving through the various vendors and selecting unique finds for *Fixer Upper* clients. The frequent allusions to heaven cement the utopian aspirations of these old pieces. Rather than just pragmatic or restorative, antique sales that fit the farmhouse chic standard are transcendently meaningful for tapping into a "better time" for the Gaineses.

Using antiques in home décor is a fairly recent trend in American culture. It was not until the end of the nineteenth century that large numbers of Americans began to decorate purposefully with antique items. Houses built in styles reminiscent of the antebellum period were constructed rhetorically and materially as a means to codify white supremacy in the built environment, and antiques were used with a similar purpose. Briann Greenfield (2009) demonstrates how this change in aesthetic value occurred when she writes:

> In the decades following the Revolution, Americans defined their country by its newness. History was a yoke to be discarded, a force to overcome. In such an atmosphere, old furniture did not have much meaning, let alone value. By the nation's centennial in 1876, that attitude had begun to change. Faced with the uncertainties of a world marked by rapid urbanization, industrialization, and immigration, many sought refuge in the perceived simplicity of the colonial era. . . . Adherents formed genealogical societies and family associations, restored old houses, staged historical pageants . . . and manufactured colonial-inspired furniture. Antiquing and the appreciation for antiques grew slowly out of this new interest in history, as middle- and upper-class white Americans started to bring antiques into their homes to use as props in their décor. (5)

This transition to a culture that values old items as a means of idolizing the past was not a change embraced uniformly by all middle- and upper-class white Americans—it was also a phenomenon linked to regional values and identity-building (Greenfield 13). These practices were evident not only in the lives of nineteenth-century white New Englanders, but also in the lives of white southerners. *Fixer Upper*'s fascination with southern antiques and décor points more to a relatively recent cultural shift in which members of the elite white public use objects to constitute a nostalgic past that is remembered as superior to the current reality. In the episodes detailed above, the items that Joanna selects for a home's decoration serve the purpose not only of making the house appear aesthetically pleasing, but of giving a room "character," a word that Joanna repeats frequently. In terms of antiques, "character" is measured by an item's ability to conjure a sense of a sentimental past. *Fixer Upper* portrays not only the heralding of antique décor, evinced in the Gaineses' excitement about antique hunting, but also the very practice of searching out these pieces. The appeal of making these discoveries reveals a concern for the aesthetic value that such items bestow on material spaces. For example, the antique dresser that Joanna finds in "Young Couple Chooses Old Home" (*Fixer Upper* 2015a) works well in the renovation design plan not simply because it is pleasing to the eye, but because it infuses "character" into the home.

The constitutive uses of material items like antiques are linked historically to the specified set of relations among white aristocrats, white laborers, and Black laborers, and these linkages have implications for understanding race and class in the South. As W. E. B. Du Bois (1935) shows, the maintenance of white supremacy in the early twentieth century required laboring whites to view themselves as superior to Blacks. For laboring whites, ambition was realized in the hope that, one day, they might become members of the planter class. One method of determining who belonged to that class was the evaluation of the material items the person possessed—from the home itself to the objects within it. The ownership of white items provided one measure of accomplishing class mobility by visually marking who belonged to the aristocracy and who did not.

Such visual marking is evident in *Fixer Upper*'s featuring of white paint (as seen in Joanna's love of white-painted shiplap), white household items, and white dinnerware. Literal whitewashing, as Bridget Heneghan (2003) explains, in which the home itself and objects in it are painted white or selected because of their whiteness, was used beginning in the early nineteenth century to determine which people counted as white or as members of the elite (52). She writes that "class, race, and gender, at base, were constructed by one's relationship to material things . . . and one's Blackness or whiteness depended on access to white goods. Only upper- and middle-class white citizens were entitled to a racial 'whiteness,' therefore, since they could possess and maintain refined white things" (45–46). White ceramics, like those featured in *Fixer Upper*, were used to organize racialized spaces within the home. Heneghan explains that "the whiter the dish and the more ornate its design, the more organized and specialized the meal, and the higher the exhibited class of the family" (60). Conversely, those who lacked access to white paint or white dinnerware were considered members of the lower, nonwhite class. For example, "people who could not afford refined white things settled instead for less expensive, out of fashion or home-made items—creamware dishes, fieldstone grave markers, unpainted or dark-colored houses—unspecialized and nonwhite material markers. Their things and their use of things reflected back upon their skins to create racially liminal, off-white citizens" (46–47). Thus, white material items were used to constitute racial and class identity in the symbolic domain.

In *Fixer Upper*, raced and classed identity is implicated in the farmhouse chic style that Joanna imposes on homes. The notion that antiques and white-painted shiplap are uniquely desirable because they infuse character into a space resonates with a historical version of whiteness. Joanna's use of plain cream ceramic vases, for example, recalls a classed version of the poor southern farm wife who had to "make do" with the decorations available. The deployment of farmhouse chic thus turns on the mythic aesthetic—the sensory experience associated with a particular connotation—of the modest farm family who build a creative masterpiece out of the surrounding objects. This building is done by searching out white things that one's ancestors would have used for decorating. The idea of simplicity in decoration by recycling and repurposing items, too, is instructive for unpacking these meaning-making practices. The act of selecting items because of their plainness becomes a rhetorical one that can be juxtaposed to the act of seeking ornateness as a marker of beauty. In this way, seeking simplicity in the style of one's home mirrors the seeking of simple agrarian life and virtues.

Regionality as a framework is critical to understanding the uses of *Fixer Upper* decorations specifically because they allow lower- or middle-income viewers to purchase symbolic materials associated with movement toward membership in a new version of the southern upper class. The whiteness of the decorations used and the architecture valorized is unique to white subjectivity of the American South because such material items constructed the heterotopia of the prosperous white home. For example, Magnolia style uses the white cotton stem as a stand-in for the flower. For the southern citizen-consumer, this stand-in is valuable because it recalls a version of history that understands cotton as the cash crop that fed struggling farmers and amassed great wealth for the planter class. This nostalgia produces cotton as a symbol of white prosperity *and* disidentifies cotton's association with slavery and Black labor by directing attention to the aesthetic potential of the stem as an adornment for the home. Magnolia's use of cotton in this way provides middle- and lower-class viewers the opportunity to gain access to the white privilege of seeing cotton as white, regional, and floral.

CONCLUSION

Resisting the process of aestheticizing is no small task. The impulse to stylize, to enact subjectivity through the practice of consumption, is a strong motivating force, one that requires resistance through self-reflexivity and action. As Brummett (2008) contends, we must strive to encourage "self-consciousness, an awareness of how one could change the world, how one [is] perceived by others, and, most important, how such perceptions [can] be managed to bring about desired results" (173). The management of perceptions is one area in which *Fixer Upper*'s successors might improve. For example, Black purchasers were occasionally featured on the show, suggesting that racial diversity in cast could reduce the systemic problem of gentrification. It remains to be seen whether a cast featuring more Black and Brown bodies could push the white aesthetics of shows like this into incorporating more regionally representative styles and viewpoints. Because *Fixer Upper*'s success relied so heavily upon farmhouse chic, any meaningful changes to that formula will require audiences and home goods shoppers to open their minds to alternative stories about life in the South—stories that invite audiences to grapple with the history of white supremacy understood through the practices of decorating and homemaking.

Engaging this paradigm shift requires viewers to contend with Black subjects' relationships to these practices. For example, Magnolia's casual use of cotton as decoration elides the material history of enslaved peoples' hands that toiled in cotton fields. As many rhetoricians attest, the materiality of rhetoric has real effects on the audiences who produce and consume it (Kiewe and Houck 2015). In *Fixer Upper*, one effect of deploying whiteness as an aesthetic of the local is the submergence of southern Blacks' unique histories, particularly in relation to the aesthetics of home living. When *Fixer Upper* features no artifacts of southern Black life as paragons of style, it becomes difficult for audience members to understand southern subjectivity as anything other than synonymous with white bodies and white tastes. Moreover, this lack of recognition underscores the problematic assumption that white aesthetics will materially improve Black lives—through gentrification's increasing of property values, for example.

Magnolia's whiteness, with raced and classed decorating and home buying practices, is intelligible in the broader international viewership. Gentrification, a nostalgic fascination with the past, and utopian glorification of antiques are all hallmarks of whiteness more broadly construed. Yet, *Fixer Upper* is strongly place-based, addressing regional style and identity-work in its themes. Without the image of Waco, Texas, as its guiding point, *Fixer Upper* loses a critical part of the charm or "character" that renders its aesthetic desirable to viewers. Indeed, as a journalist for *Country Living* argues, viewing the show makes audiences "pretty much ready to move to Waco, Texas, just so [Chip and Joanna] can find [them] a home" (Shinners 2015). *Fixer Upper*'s deployment of whiteness is regionally inflected by plantation architecture, Lost Cause mythology that "redeemed" white elitism in turn-of-the-twentieth-century homes, and a focus on values of charm, politeness, and simplicity. Yet in doing so, it suggests, incorrectly, that southern style, aesthetic, and subjectivity are a monolith. The real crisis of *Fixer Upper* is an opportunity missed, a chance to tell a story about central Texas that places the stylized space of the home and its aesthetics in conversation with the multiracial, multivocal histories of the region. Such histories may require us to attend to cotton not simply as a pleasant table centerpiece, but as representative of a racialized symbolic thinking that resonates with the decorating practices of centuries past.

Critical regionalism asks us to find opportunities for self-awareness, subversion, or self-aware appropriation. Shows like *Fixer Upper* are prime sites for nostalgia that link the material and symbolic, the landscape and its style. Such television programming is consumed as innocent entertainment, but its reproduction through syndication gives way to a seemingly endless chain of whiteness as practice and style, the embodiment of which is found in the material goods of home decorating. While the ubiquity of the resulting styles may initially render nonthreatening the accompanying symbolism, I see such choices as effecting the opposite: whiteness gleans power from uninitiated viewers' identification with lingering hegemonic stories and styles. Racial understanding and dialogue can begin with the unpacking of innocent-seeming texts as a way to explore deeply interlaced dynamics. Importantly, critics and media can also find ways for monolithic presentations of the South as a white heterotopia to give way to more robust exchanges of prior residents' and communities' viewpoints.

NOTES

1. Julia Medhurst thanks Scott Varda for encouraging her to think through the particulars of this piece. Thanks to Leslie Hahner for her consultation on all things theory, and to Nathan Crick for his advice, encouragement, and support.

2. See, for example, Joanna's home goods line with Target, Pier 1 Imports, and Anthropologie.

REFERENCES

Betancur, John. 2011. "Gentrification and Community Fabric in Chicago." *Urban Studies* 48: 383–406. https://doi.org/10.1177/0042098009360680.

Bever, Lindsey. 2017. "A University President Held a Dinner for Black Students—and Set the Table with Cotton Stalks and Collard Greens." *Washington Post*, September 19, 2017. https://www.washingtonpost.com/news/grade-point/wp/2017/09/19/a-university -president-held-a-dinner-for-black-students-and-set-the-table-with-cotton-stalks-and -collard-greens/?utm_term=.50d34f1ad346.

Bishir, Catherine W. 1993. "Landmarks of Power: Building a Southern Past, 1885–1915." *Southern Cultures* 1: 5–45. https://doi.org/10.1353/scu.1993.0003.

"Brook Oaks Neighborhood in Waco, Texas (TX), 76707, 76708 Subdivision Profile—Real Estate, Apartments, Condos, Homes, Community, Population, Jobs, Income, Streets." 2016. City Data. Accessed July 1, 2019. http://www.city-data.com/neighborhood/Brook -Oaks-Waco-TX.html.

Brummett, Barry. 2008. *A Rhetoric of Style*. Carbondale: Southern Illinois University Press.

Brundage, William F. 2009. *The Southern Past: A Clash of Race and Memory*. Cambridge, MA: Harvard University Press.

Doane, Ashley, and Eduardo Bonilla-Silva. 2003. *White Out: The Continuing Significance of Racism*. New York: Routledge.

Dodd, Lauren. 2018. "Poor Priced Out of Waco's Hot Housing Market, Nonprofit Officials Say." *Waco Tribune-Herald*, December 25, 2018. https://www.wacotrib.com/news/city _of_waco/poor-priced-out-of-waco-s-hot-housing-market-nonprofit/article_e19ccd34

-a128-5739-801f-1fce25407398.html?fbclid=IwAR1d1p0kkyvoJm5m2DDAwppf
_sGrPckfIMsLJunybwwCt3f9CP0U6HO7VUI/.

Du Bois, W. E. B. 1935. *Black Reconstruction: An Essay Toward a History of the Part Which
Black Folk Played in the Attempt to Reconstruct Democracy in America, 1860–1880*. New
York: Harcourt, Brace, and Company.

"Editorial: Let's Hope State Officials Share Vision of Brook Oaks Neighborhood Residents."
2014. *Waco Tribune-Herald*, February 20, 2014. http://www.wacotrib.com/opinion
/editorials/editorial-let-s-hope-state-officials-share-vision-of-brook/article_b9385ffe
-35d1-5916-8320-61556553ef95.html.

Fixer Upper. 2014. Season 1, Episode 6, "Craftsmen Crave Urban Feel," first broadcast May 22
by HGTV.

Fixer Upper. 2015a. Season 2, Episode 2, "Young Couple Chooses Old Home," first broadcast
January 13 by HGTV.

Fixer Upper. 2015b. Season 2, Episode 3, "Homebuilders Seek *Fixer Upper*," first broadcast
January 20 by HGTV.

Fixer Upper. 2015c. Season 2, Episode 6, "High School Friend Seeks Fixer," first broadcast
February 10 by HGTV.

Foucault, Michel. 1984. "Of Other Spaces: Utopias and Heterotopias." *Architecture/Mouvement/
Continuité*, October 1984. Translated by Jay Miskowiec. http://web.mit.edu/allanmc
/www/foucault1.pdf.

Greenfield, Briann G. 2009. *Out of the Attic: Inventing Antiques in Twentieth-Century New
England*. Amherst: University of Massachusetts Press.

Hale, Grace E. 1998. *Making Whiteness: The Culture of Segregation in the South, 1890–1940*.
New York: Random House.

"Harvest Cotton Stem." 2019. Magnolia. Accessed July 1, 2019. https://shop.magnolia.com
/products/harvest-cotton-stem/.

Heneghan, Bridget T. 2003. *Whitewashing America: Material Culture and Race in the
Antebellum Imagination*. Jackson: University Press of Mississippi.

Holmes, Linda. 2011. "If You're Looking for a Little Diversity on Television, Try HGTV."
WBUR News, NPR, April 13. www.wbur.org/npr/135353192/if-youre-looking-for-a
-little-diversity-on-television-try-hgtv.

Jones, Rachel. 2016. "HGTV Finishes 2015 with Highest-Rated Year Ever." Scripps, January 4.
http://www.scrippsnetworksinteractive.com/newsroom/company-news/HGTV-Finishes
-2015-With-Highest-Rated-Year-Ever/.

Kiewe, Amos, and Davis W. Houck, eds. 2015. *The Effects of Rhetoric and the Rhetoric of
Effects: Past, Present, Future*. Columbia: University of South Carolina Press.

Loewen, James W. 2005. *Sundown Towns: A Hidden Dimension of American Racism*. New
York: The New Press.

Makagon, Daniel. 2010. "Bring on the Shock Troops: Artists and Gentrification in the
Popular Press." *Communication and Critical/Cultural Studies* 7: 26–52. https://doi.org
/10.1080/14791420903527772.

McPherson, Tara. 2003. *Reconstructing Dixie: Race, Gender, and Nostalgia in the Imagined
South*. Durham, NC: Duke University Press.

Nakayama, Thomas K., and Robert L. Krizek. 1995. "Whiteness: A Strategic Rhetoric."
Quarterly Journal of Speech 81: 291–309. https://doi.org/10.1080/00335639509384117.

Petersen, Anne Helen. 2019. "'Fixer Upper' Is Over, But Waco's Transformation Is Just Beginning." *Buzzfeed*, April 20. https://www.buzzfeednews.com/article /annehelenpetersen/waco-texas-magnolia-fixer-upper-antioch-chip-joanna-gaines.

Powell, Douglass R. 2007. *Critical Regionalism: Connecting Politics and Culture in the American Landscape.* Chapel Hill: University of North Carolina Press.

Powell, John A., and Marguerite L. Spencer. 2002. "Giving Them the Old One-Two: Gentrification and the KO of Impoverished Urban Dwellers of Color." *Howard Law Journal* 46: 433–90.

Rice, Jenny. 2012. "From Architectonic to Tectonics: Introducing Regional Rhetorics." *Rhetoric and Society Quarterly* 42: 201–213. https://doi.org/10.1080/02773945.2012.682831.

Shabazz, Rasha. 2009. "So High You Can't Get over It, So Low You Can't Get under It": Carceral Spatiality and Black Masculinities in the United States and South Africa." *Souls: A Critical Journal of Black Politics, Culture, and Society* 11: 276–94. https://doi.org/10 .1080/10999940903088309.

Shimpach, Shawn. 2012. "Realty Reality: HGTV and the Subprime Crisis." *American Quarterly* 64: 515–42.

Shinners, Rebecca. 2015. "16 Reasons Why 'Fixer Upper' Is the Best Show on HGTV." *Country Living*, July 27, 2015. http://www.countryliving.com/life/a36015/fixer-upper-hgtv-facts/.

Skinner, Paige. 2018. "Waco, Reborn: A Home-Makeover Show Based in This Central Texas Town Has Created a Tourism Boom." *New York Times*, December 10, 2018. https://www .nytimes.com/2018/12/10/style/waco-gaines-chip-joanna-fixer-upper.html.

Triece, Mary E. 2017. "Whitewashing City Spaces: Personalization and Strategic Forgetting in News Accounts of Urban Crisis and Renewal." *Journal of Communication Inquiry* 41: 250–67. https://doi.org/10.1177/0196859917690693.

Vail, Mark T. 2012. "Reconstructing the Lost Cause in the Memphis City Parks Renaming Controversy." *Western Journal of Communication* 76: 417–37. https://doi.org/10.1080 /10570314.2011.651257.

"Waco Crime Statistics, May." 2014. Waco Police Department Neighborhood Crimes Report. http://www.waco-texas.com/police/pdf/crime-stats/neighborhoodcrimeswlistmay2014.pdf.

Part II

Reconstructing the South in Relational Identity: Decentering the White Victim

Chapter 5

SOUTHERN ENTANGLEMENTS

The Rhetoric of the Dixiecrats and the Evolution of the Southern Strategy

RYAN NEVILLE-SHEPARD

I teach classes in rhetorical criticism, argumentation, and political communication. I was raised in New England but have spent significant parts of my adult life in southern Indiana, South Carolina, and Fayetteville, Arkansas. As a white northerner, I have dedicated much of my research to understanding the ways national political narratives have been influenced by southern identity.

When Republican Tim Scott became the fifth African American to be elected to the United States Senate in 2014, the first in South Carolina history, his election was immediately met with high expectations that he would challenge his party's record of racial divisiveness. At first, Scott was a disappointment. As Nia-Malika Henderson (2014) wrote in the *Washington Post*, Scott lashed out at Democrats for resorting to "fear and race-baiting," pointing to the elections of Indian Americans Nikki Haley and Bobby Jindal as signs of racial progress on the Right. Like other Republicans who refused to acknowledge their party's ugly history, Henderson argued, Scott's strategy "has been to ignore it and tout the progress instead," relying on "the language of race neutrality" in the process.

However, Scott has emerged as a vocal critic of Republicans in the Trump era. When Donald Trump blamed "both sides" at a violent protest organized by the alt-right in Charlottesville, Virginia, in 2017, Scott called the response unacceptable, suggesting the president was affirming "hate groups who over three centuries of this country have made it their mission to create upheaval for minority communities" (Summers 2017). In December 2018, Scott joined Republican Senator Jeff Flake to oppose the nomination of Judge Thomas Farr to a federal district court, contending that the one-time aid to Jesse Helms had a questionable track record on issues of race (Coasten 2018). And when United

States Representative Steve King wondered why the terms "white nationalist, white supremacist, [and] Western civilization" were considered so offensive, it was Scott who said he lacked "some pretty common knowledge" (T. Scott 2019). Chastising his colleagues for their silence on King's racist behavior over the years, Scott claimed that the Iowan was hardly a "lonely [voice] in the wilderness," and that Republicans "cannot let these intolerant and hateful views hold us back."

Despite his growing confidence in challenging his party, Senator Scott has confessed there is only so much he can accomplish. After meeting with Trump regarding his botched response to the violence in Charlottesville, Scott announced, "Anyone who walks into a room with someone . . . and assumed they are going to change the person's mind just because you are present and had a 30-minute conversation—I think you have an unrealistic expectation" (Summers 2017). At best, he added, one could aim for "measurable progress in reasonable time." Wondering why so many Republicans were reluctant to join Scott's rebuke of King, Eugene Scott (2019) summarized that Republicans were silent because they either "do not think racist rhetoric is worth addressing" or they are simply "ignorant about how racist ideas impact black Americans on a daily basis."

This chapter proposes an alternative answer: criticizing overt racism is difficult for conservatives because white supremacy has purposefully become entangled with most conservative vernacular. When George Wallace declared, "The whole United States is Southern" (Carter 2000, 344), his statement may not have applied only to beliefs about white supremacy in the 1960s, but to the coded language used thereafter by conservatives to express those beliefs. The vernacular is so coded, and the words are so common to conservative politics, that one cannot easily disentangle legitimate conservative language from racist ideology. An honest critique of those like Steve King would require greater reflection about what it means to be conservative, think conservatively, and even speak as a Republican. Moreover, understanding the racist discourse of someone like Steve King, an Iowan, requires communication and political scholars to move past rooting racist demagoguery in the regional South, as Brandon Inabinet and Christina Moss (2019) have recently argued, and revise the notion that American public rhetoric at large is inevitably good and somehow different.

Rather than tracing the rhetorical entanglement of racist ideology and conservative vernacular to the GOP's Southern Strategy of the 1960s and beyond, this chapter relates that entanglement to the rhetoric of what I call the *proto-Southern Strategy* led by Strom Thurmond and the National States Rights Party in 1948. Even though Thurmond is said to have "never been the chief strategist nor the most astute tactician for the white southern cause"

(Cohodas 1994, 12), his influence over the Goldwater campaign in 1964 and the Nixon campaign in 1968 showed that his playbook of inferential racism had found its footing nearly two decades after leading the Dixiecrat revolt. Arguing for the need to understand Thurmond's influence in the rhetoric of the Southern Strategy and how his archaic vision of southern life became a broader national appeal, this chapter first explains the history of the plan to break up the Democrats' Solid South, and specifically the rhetorical program of coded racism behind those efforts. Second, the chapter moves to describe Thurmond's proto-Southern Strategy, particularly the Dixiecrats' effort to develop a series of racist dog whistles to disrupt desegregation efforts by the major parties. Finally, through a close reading of Thurmond's campaign speeches from the 1948 campaign, the chapter highlights how he replaced the language of white supremacy with a discourse about constitutionalism, states' rights, and local control, as well as liberty and free market capitalism.

Distinguishing between the proto-Southern Strategy, the Southern Strategy, and the racist dog whistles of contemporary political rhetoric serves an important purpose for this particular book. Referring to inferential racism loosely with the term "Southern Strategy" implies that such language works best in the regional South. While the coded racism sharpened in the Dixiecrats' regional campaign, it actually took more than forty years and a new generation of political leaders to master a "southern" appeal, but by that point the GOP's white rural targets had spread across the nation. The rhetorical "Southern Strategy" is no longer regional, which might explain why a South Carolinian attempting to exorcise racism from the GOP would butt heads with someone from midwestern Iowa who oddly resembles a neo-Dixiecrat.

THE EMERGENCE OF THE SOUTHERN STRATEGY

Most historians trace the Southern Strategy to the Barry Goldwater campaign of 1964. Goldwater saw an opportunity to turn white southerners against the Democratic Party, especially after Nixon "paradoxically lost both the Black vote and that of 'Dixiecrat-segregationalists'" in 1960 (Kalk 1994, 86). While he was not immediately successful, "more whites have voted Republican than Democratic in every single presidential election" since 1964 (Black and Black 2002, 205). By 1968, Richard Nixon followed Goldwater and announced what he explicitly called a "Southern Strategy," which became a way of talking to what he called a "silent majority" of white voters across the country who shared with white southerners a disdain for "urban rioting, anti-war-protest, and countercultural youth style of the 1960s" (Graham 1996, 93–94). Kevin Phillips, who crafted the strategy for Nixon in 1968, explained that they saw the

Democrats' Solid South crumbling, as the party became more associated "with centralized government, welfare clients, militant minorities, radical youth, and intellectual and media elites" (qtd. in Graham 1996, 94). As Phillips explained to the GOP, "Not only did they not need African American votes, they positively did not want them, for whites would continue to defect to the GOP so long as the Democrats were associated with Black interests" (qtd. in Olson 2008, 712). The strategy proved successful for Nixon, as he went on to receive fifty-seven out of eighty-eight electoral votes in the South, a full twenty-four more than he received in 1960 (Kalk 1994, 93). Republicans after Nixon followed the same strategy, and the region eventually flipped completely. By 1980, "Reagan won all of the Southern states, except Carter's home state of Georgia," and by 1984 he won all eleven states in the South (Aistrup 1996, 6).

Beyond the pragmatics of winning GOP support in the South, the Southern Strategy is a national rhetorical program of exploiting racial resentment. Historian Glenn Feldman explained that thanks to those who imagined the Southern Strategy, the Democratic decline and Republican ascendance in the South "would be culturally seamless and already have a language and ideology all its own" (Feldman 2015, 106). This language developed out of the difficult balancing act of Republicans addressing the nation, while also adapting to their new mission in the South. Nixon attempted, in one scholar's words, to "become all things to all people," trying to "slow the pace of integration and avoid busing," but also avoiding the "overtly segregationalist line" that would lose him support elsewhere in the country (Sanders 2002, 338). Appealing to the "majority of the middle," Nixon mastered "ambivalence and equivocation" (338). Explaining this coded discourse, political scientist Joseph Aistrup (1996) noted, "Many of the public words and deeds of the Southern Strategy have hidden meanings to adherents. Seemingly ambiguous political language has important, specific connotations for various groups in society" (19). As Aistrup argued, "It was during Nixon's tenure that the Southern Strategy became an explicit plan to use a web of social and racial issues to win the South" (33).

At first, the code of the Southern Strategy under Nixon was about policy. His position of opposing busing meant that he could pin anyone who backed the policy as "dangerously liberal" (Murphy and Gulliver 1971, 94). He took up the vague issue of "law and order" to propose "getting tough on criminals through stiffer prison sentences, the death penalty, and limiting the rights of accused" (Aistrup 1996, 36). He also began speaking more about the "welfare issue," implying that it was unfair to make blue-collar white Americans "pay the costs of liberal programs to help poor blacks" (36). Of course, Nixon and those who followed him likely knew that Roosevelt's New Deal had excluded many African Americans and attempted to exploit contempt concerning their inclusion in Great Society programs to spread the myth that welfare recipients were disproportionately Black. Ronald Reagan later mastered Nixon's strategy of tapping into racial resentment through ambiguity. Attacking Democrats' "wasteful spending," according to Aistrup, Reagan would portray welfare recipients as greedy and unworthy of help, at times drawing an image of the recipients of these programs as the presumably Black "welfare queen with multiple children, large house, and a Cadillac" (44). Further, Reagan's notion of hard work and the need to cut back social welfare programs played to white people who "feel that Black people are impoverished because of personal reasons rather than because they have a true need" (45). That Reagan's appeals were racially motivated was hardly a secret. After all, he even spoke about his passion for states' rights in Philadelphia, Mississippi, adding that if elected he would emphasize local and state control of governments. As Aistrup noted, "in the South states' rights means local control of race relations" (48).

The coded racism that formed the Southern Strategy moved from the rather concrete policy position to the more abstract. Long-time GOP political consultant Lee Atwater explained this evolution to political scientist Alexander Lamis in a 1981 interview. While overt racism was acceptable in the 1950s, Atwater noted, "By 1968 you can't say 'n****'—that hurts you, backfires. So you say stuff like, uh, forced busing, states' rights, and all that stuff, and you're getting so abstract. Now you're talking about cutting taxes" (qtd. in Perlstein 2012). More recent research has indicated that current iterations of the Southern Strategy have gotten even more abstract. Thomas Edge (2010), for instance, argued that the election of Barack Obama gave rise to the "Southern Strategy 2.0," leading conservatives to suggest the country was free of racism and portray white Americans as victims of continued efforts to address racial discord, while adopting the same coded racism as before. More recently, Ryan Neville-Shepard (2018) described a second-generation Southern Strategy characterized by the rhetoric of post-racialism, neoliberalism, and a selective amnesia about historical racism.

In summary, the history of the Southern Strategy, as it is often told, is pretty straightforward: the Republican Party flipped the South by tapping into coded racism, and that coded racism has gotten even more coded over time. That history may be too simplistic, however. Sharp divisions between Goldwater's Southern Strategy and the tactics of those before him are frequently drawn. Goldwater is often described as making the "anti-civil rights, anticommunist, anti-welfare state perspective" of conservatives before him more palatable to moderate white voters, and Nixon is usually credited with turning segregationist perspectives into an electable policy platform (Olson 2008, 710). This narrative of the Southern Strategy intriguingly describes only a small role for Strom Thurmond, who led the Dixiecrat revolt in 1948. Thurmond is often described in these accounts as a convert to the Republican Party in 1964. As historian

Bruce Kalk (1994) recounted, "Thurmond left the Democratic fold entirely and switched to the GOP out of enthusiasm for Senator Goldwater's presidential bid" (89). By 1968, this narrative suggests, Thurmond offered Nixon "invaluable assistance" in outmaneuvering his opponents in the South (89). As Nixon was quoted praising Thurmond as "no racist," but instead "a man of courage and integrity" (Sweeney 1998, 168), these stories about the emergence of the Southern Strategy regard Thurmond as someone in political purgatory who was suddenly forgiven by more powerful Republicans. What this narrative ignores is that Goldwater's tactics, and even Nixon's success in disrupting Southern politics, were built on Thurmond's efforts. As historian Glenn Feldman (2015) argued, even the Dixiecrats developed coded racism, more out of the need to distinguish their racial politics after World War II from Hitler's concept of Aryan supremacy. The rhetoric of coded racism that developed under the Dixecrats allowed "southerners to speak a general, more benign and respectable, language in which it was understood that white supremacy was the cornerstone of the regional agenda" (107). In the section that follows, I describe Thurmond's proto-Southern Strategy and describe the code that he helped develop for other southern leaders. The strategy was so simplistic yet slippery, I suggest, because it reduced racist politics to empty signifiers that were synonymous with conservative ideology, making white supremacy indistinguishable from the language of conservativism.

STROM THURMOND AND
THE PROTO-SOUTHERN STRATEGY

After President Harry Truman announced a civil rights platform for the 1948 election, southern leaders immediately pushed back against the Democrats, particularly against proposed legislation dealing with lynching, poll taxes, ending racial segregation, and establishing a commission to target racial discrimination in employment. In early 1948, the plan was disorganized, as some southern congressmen hoped to simply convince a candidate like Virginia's Harry Byrd to challenge Truman for the Democratic Party's nomination (Alsop and Alsop 1948). By February, according to Alsop and Alsop, the plan was to send to the Democratic convention uncommitted delegates from South Carolina, North Carolina, Alabama, Virginia, Georgia, Mississippi, Tennessee, and Louisiana, all in an effort to "wrest a weasel declaration on the civil rights and human rights issue" (21). By March, the Conference of Southern Governors published a manifesto, declaring they would prevent the nomination of any candidate who threatened state sovereignty, seek alternative nominees if necessary, and make the civil rights program the key issue in that year's election. After a failed last-minute effort to convince Dwight Eisenhower to run against Truman, South Carolina Governor Strom Thurmond accepted the new splinter party's nomination, formally coined the National States' Rights Party but generally known as the Dixiecrats. Thurmond's explicit goal was to make sure no major party candidate received enough electoral votes in order to throw the election to the United States House of Representatives.

In reality, the Dixiecrats knew they had very little chance of winning in 1948. Instead, their objective was to trigger significant change within the major parties, much like Goldwater and Nixon proposed almost twenty years later. As Thurmond restated throughout the late stages of the campaign, his hope was to punish the Democratic Party, make its leaders realize the importance of the sovereignty of southern states, and force its commitment to tolerate and perhaps even defend segregationist policy. At stake for these Democrats was an entire region's worth of electoral votes. According to Thurmond, the South was a bloc to be won. By summer, he explained "the South, with clocklike regularity, has furnished the Democratic party approximately 50 per cent of the votes necessary to nominate a President every four years for nearly a century" (Howard 1948, 1). Withholding that support would guarantee special attention. Estimating that he would receive at least a hundred electoral votes, Thurmond declared it was a "strong possibility that the election will then be thrown into the House of Representatives," where he ultimately thought he had a chance of winning (Thurmond 1948h, 12–13). However, even losing meant winning. As Thurmond told the *New York Times* (1948b), disrupting party politics meant "We will have crystallized sentiment against the so-called civil rights program and made its passage improbable" (3). At the very least, he added, "We will have brought about recognition for the South in the political affairs of the nation which it has not fully enjoyed since the war between the States" (3). Thus, Thurmond's proto-Southern Strategy was about resetting party politics. If the Southern Strategy adopted by Goldwater and Nixon aimed to flip the Democrats' Solid South to the Republicans through coded racial appeals, Thurmond's version aimed to prime the South for that flip.

The once-blatantly racist positions of the Dixiecrats gave way to more coded forms of expressing their positions. As early as March, Thurmond (1948c) claimed the Dixiecrats would adapt to a national audience, announcing they should "sell our sound case to the people of the Nation, Republican and Democrat alike, so that we shall not fight along in resisting encroachments upon our rights by power-seeking Federal bureaucrats" (6). By the summer, Thurmond cracked down on calls to protect "white supremacy," insisting that he was a "'progressive Southerner' interested in bettering conditions for the Negro" (Popham 1948b, 1). The white supremacy talk reportedly made Thurmond eager to show "the rest of the country . . . that we have some pretty good guys down here" (1). As he began campaigning, Thurmond pivoted to a code of his own. "We are not running on a white supremacy, racial hatred or class prejudice platform," he announced. Instead, he suggested he was "running primarily on the issue of state rights" (*Chicago Daily Tribune* 1948a, 2).

THE RHETORIC OF THURMOND'S PROTO-SOUTHERN STRATEGY

Thurmond's proto-Southern Strategy was about finding the alternative framing for a southern way of life that might unify white voters across the region, while also convincing the national party that a southern ideology could have broader appeal. At times, he struggled to stay on point. In versions of the stump speech he delivered across the South during the summer of 1948, Thurmond concluded, "I did not risk my life on the beaches of Normandy to come back to this country, and sit idly by, while a bunch of politicians whittles away your heritage and mine" (*New York Times* 1948c, 44). Speaking of southern pride, Thurmond (1948e) told an audience in Cherryville, North Carolina, that "The South would not be worthy of its heritage, if it lay down and took this whipping any longer" (5). Discussions of heritage, while protesting subordinate roles that were akin to taking a "whipping," were clear signs that Thurmond did not want southern whites to be "enslaved" by federal desegregation policy. Thus, even as he hoped to move away from this language of white supremacy, he often had trouble escaping it. He had an especially difficult time controlling his team, for instance. His running mate, Mississippi Governor Fielding Wright, told Black voters in his state just as the Dixiecrat campaign launched that if they "envisioned social equality with whites in schools and restaurants it would be better for them to leave the state" (Popham 1948a, 1). However, much of Thurmond's discourse was based on representing these ideas more abstractly, notably through appeals to a strict interpretation of the US Constitution and calls for local control and states' rights, in addition to a protection of free markets and individual liberty.

STRICT CONSTITUTIONALISM

Shortly after Truman declared a civil rights platform for his reelection campaign, Thurmond led other southern governors in drafting a list of questions directed to the Democratic National Committee articulating their protest. The first question on the list asked whether the national party agreed that the reforms mentioned "would be unconstitutional invasions of the field of government belonging to the states under the Bill of Rights in the Constitution of the United States" (Thurmond 1948a, 1). For Thurmond and others, policies targeting white supremacy were illegal based on principle alone. If the Constitution did not allow federal action on the matter, it was simply wrong. Perhaps racial issues brought up by Truman mattered, Thurmond contended, but they were secondary to the more important legal questions of the Constitution. As Thurmond (1948l) argued, "We have taken the position that the racial questions involved are secondary to the broad principles of constitutional government that are under attack. For these principles guarantee the American way of life in every state" (52). Thurmond stated elsewhere that in "plain language" the Constitution granted only eighteen specific powers to the federal government, suggesting the document was "sacred" and guaranteed all other rights to the states "for all time by [including] Article X of the Bill of Rights, which is the crowning glory of the Constitution" (Thurmond 1948e, 3). No negotiation is permitted with these principles, Thurmond argued. "Those are the words of the Constitution," he noted, continuing, "There is no plainer way to say it" (3).

While he maintained an identity as a progressive, Thurmond was actually crafting a definition of "conservative" based on a return to this strict interpretation of the Constitution. This argument from principle surfaced throughout the campaign. When he accepted the nomination of the Dixiecrats in August, Thurmond called for "a return to constitutional government in America" (*Chicago Daily Tribune* 1948b, 3). This "return," which is inherently a conservative mission to restore a certain approach to governance, called for federal action in limited situations. Just before the election, Thurmond (1948l) declared that federal action required voter consent in the states, arguing the Constitution "says that such measures may only be enacted within the states, by the vote of the people of those states" (52). The language of "returning" to constitutional forms of government was an argument about nostalgia. A return to strict readings of the Constitution would preserve an "American" way of life that preserved white hegemony. This white supremacy, now coded as a "traditional" way of life dictated by the Constitution, was further portrayed as necessary for preventing chaos, and preventing chaos was good for minority groups. As Thurmond (1948j) summarized, "Let me say now to the people of those minority groups, that if the United States Constitution is not preserved to the letter, the minorities of this country will be the first to suffer" (5). Only through the benevolence of conservative values and strict constitutional interpretation could minorities (like the maligned southerner) avoid persecution by the federal government. Reading through his arguments in light of the consistent white supremacy of his campaign suggests he was saying that African Americans should love white supremacy because at least their constitutional rights were protected. This argument would later open the possibility for Republicans like Tim Scott to enter a party that so often dog-whistles white control—racism could be forgiven if it at least ensures sufficient federal power to suspicious conservatives, to ensure federal power is not misused by others.

LOCAL CONTROL AND STATES' RIGHTS

Transforming white supremacy into coded appeals, Thurmond moved beyond constitutional principle to advocate instead for "states' rights" and a notion of local control. According to the Dixiecrat, the United States was composed of local governments. Thurmond (1948e) told one audience in North Carolina, "Remember, the original colonies came together to form 'a more perfect union.' The original colonies or States once had all the power of government" (2). Those powers were still relevant, he argued, stating, "They chose to surrender *certain* of these powers only in order to form a Union" (2). In party politics, the Democrats were committed to state sovereignty since the party's very first platform in 1840. As the States' Rights Resolution (1948) noted, that platform stated that "Congress has no power under the Constitution to interfere with or control the domestic institutions of the several states, and that such States are the sole and proper judges of everything appertaining to their own affairs not prohibited by the Constitution" (4). The sovereignty of the states was always meant to be protected, Thurmond suggested, especially to make the Union perfect by providing a system of checks and balances. During a campaign appearance in Arkansas, Thurmond (1948f) stated, "The genius of our government is the sovereignty of the States—a system of checks and balances which guard the individual's freedom from government encroachment" (3). In this sense, "local government and home rule" were "just as important to individual liberty as the right of free speech, the right of trial by jury, and freedom of religion" (3). Quoting Thomas Jefferson in a speech to Democrats in Columbia, South Carolina, Thurmond (1948b) stated, "When all government, domestic and foreign, in little as in great things, shall be drawn to Washington as the center of all power, it will . . . become as venal and oppressive as the government from which we separated" (13).

Because local rule and states' rights were considered important to protecting individual rights, allowing the federal government to infringe on local control was seen as the greatest danger of all. The Southern Governors' Conference was clear during the early stages of the campaign that local control was more important than the federal government's desire to protect marginalized people. The organization declared, "there is no Federal suffrage" and that it was the states' "function and prerogative alone to deal with that right" ("Committee

Report" 1948, 2). Ultimately, "the ability of a Federal administration to perpetuate itself in power through Federal control of the ballot boxes of the Nation" was the greater threat (2).

Describing white supremacy instead as a defense of local control, Thurmond also crafted a narrative of the enemies of states' rights. The labels for these enemies became code for identifying the opposition to white supremacy in the South and beyond. Describing the rebuilding of Germany, Thurmond (1948l) said, "We are now engaged in an effort to restore the German people to a kind of democracy which will make it impossible for another Hitler to take them over" (52). In order to protect individual Germans, he said, "We are making it certain that the power of government be decentralized, for we know that Hitler came to power by centralizing all powers in Berlin" (52). Those who favored a strong federal system, then, were akin to German Nazis. While preventing something like Nazism at home was an important mission, Thurmond described federalists as *actual* communists seeking to overthrow the American way of governing. "Under the guise of antilynching," he argued, "the Reds, pinks and subversives are making use of the horror which the American people have for lynching to change our form of government" (*Washington Post* 1948a, 4). Thurmond was certain the communists were responsible. In the final days of the campaign, he warned, "Communists are working through the racial minority machine to get the kind of centralized power they must have if they are to be successful" (Thurmond, 1948l, 52). These communists were allegedly in control of the Wallace, Truman, and Dewey campaigns and were making a "powerful weapon out of the machine-controlled minority blocs in the big-city states" (Thurmond, 1948i, 14). Communists were synonymous with other labels, too. During a rally in Jackson, Thurmond (1948d) announced, "These big city machine bosses and their puppets in office, as well as those who think everything can be done by a law from Washington" should realize they crossed the line when they advocated "social intermingling of the race of our people" (19). Thus, federalists were referred to as "Nazis," "Communists," "big city" types, and referred to simply as "Washington." The labels became a way of talking about outsiders as oppressors, without focusing so directly on issues of race.

INDIVIDUAL LIBERTY AND FREE MARKETS

Attempting to move away from segregationist language, Thurmond embraced instead the language of "individual liberty" and "free markets." Building from the argument that local control protects the individual, Thurmond warned that violating state sovereignty would mean "the liberty of the individual will perish" (*Washington Post* 1948b, 6). Violating local control, he argued, would be an attack on "the personal liberties of the citizens of California and Maine, as well as the liberties of the people of South Carolina and Virginia" (6). Individualism was the heart of the American experiment, he declared. While speaking in Texas, Thurmond (1948g) stated, "In America the individual became supreme, and the government became the servant of the people, instead of the people's master or disciplinarian" (4). Under that ideology, he argued, "there is more freedom in America than anywhere else in the world" (4). An opposite system was posing grave danger, he argued. This system meant "the people become insignificant cogs in the great wheel of government. Individuality is destroyed so that everyone can conform to standards prescribed by a few men in power" (4). For Thurmond, individualism was about choice, and taking a stand against federal intervention in all of its forms meant liberating the individual. Personalizing the issue, Thurmond (1948k) told an audience in Knoxville, Tennessee, that the "issues of which I speak are deeply concerned with the way you as an individual live" (8). Thurmond elaborated, "I am talking about your freedom to move around this city without hindrance, to choose your own friends, to choose your own work, to hold meetings when you please and how you please, to worship God as you choose" (8). Thus, every aspect of an antiracist agenda was coded as compulsory collectivism, coding federal policy as the antithesis of individualism.

Federal overreach stemming from Truman's civil rights proposals was described not only as a violation of individual rights, but a destruction of free enterprise. In this sense, Thurmond's framing was not far from modern Libertarian language that puts the rights of the business owner above all others. This pivot was seen in the States' Rights Resolution (1948) released by the Dixiecrats in May. The group claimed to believe in "private enterprise and the profit and loss system as opposed to totalitarian idealogies [sic]," in the "fullest encouragement to individual initiative and self-reliance—that the citizen should depend upon his own efforts for existence and security rather than upon the Government" (5). Moreover, the Dixiecrats declared they believed in "freedom to work; to till one's land, do one's job, ply one's trade, conduct one's business" (5). Attacking efforts to curb employment discrimination, Thurmond claimed that private enterprise was being threatened, cautioning, "No man could any longer call his private business his own. He would lose the right to hire whom he pleases, whom he finds best suited to carry on his work and to get along with his other employees" (Washington Post 1948a, 4). For Thurmond, building a bridge between white segregationists and other conservatives meant highlighting the threat to individualism and enterprise. A threat against one became a threat against the other, thus functioning as a code that made the ideas interchangeable.

CONCLUSION

While the Southern Strategy pursued by Republicans in the 1960s sought to find wedge issues and coded ways of tapping into white resentment, the proto-Southern Strategy described in this chapter sought to reduce racist ideology to the simplest of conservative values. The coded appeals took time to develop and were not natural to the Dixiecrats at first. After all, even the party's Declaration of Principles explicitly called for the "segregation of the races and the racial integrity of each race" ("Declaration of Principles" 1948, 5). During the National States' Rights Party convention in Birmingham, Alabama, Thurmond himself broke character, stating in his acceptance speech, "We have just begun to fight," adding, "There are not enough troops in the army to break down segregation and admit the Negroes into our theaters, swimming pools, schools and homes" (Howard 1948, 1). Asked about that specific statement more than forty years later, Senator Thurmond cringed and confessed, "If I had to run that race again, some of the wording I used would not be used. I would word it differently" (qtd. in Cohodas 1994, 177). As Nadine Cohodas (1994) suggested, Thurmond's "observation seemed to be more about semantics than substance" (177). After all, he appeared to have little problem with the ideas of segregation, but simply suggested he should have expressed those ideas differently. It was essentially an admission that his commitment to the coded racism was sloppy, but that the code he helped develop was successful at changing American political culture.

While Strom Thurmond's coded racism might have worked over the long run, especially when formally adopted by the Republican Party twenty years later, it is important to note that the Southern Strategy and the strategy that preceded it did not necessarily reflect the South as a region. The editorial board of the *New York Times* was quick to point this out after Thurmond lost in 1948. The National States' Rights Party accomplished one thing that year, the newspaper's staff argued, and that was showing "how great a majority of Southern voters disagree with the antediluvian attitude that it represents" (*New York Times* 1948a, E10). Pointing out that President Truman received almost two million more votes than Thurmond in the fifteen southern states where the Dixiecrat made a showing, the newspaper summarized, "it doesn't seem to us [that the States' Rights Party's candidates] represent the real attitude of our Southern neighbors" (E10). Although the observation was perhaps a bit too optimistic, Thurmond's loss did serve a valuable lesson. As one tradition of southern communication criticism has historically "denoted white male political orators as demagogues" (Inabinet and Moss, 2019, 165), Thurmond embodied this tradition, but his limited influence points to competing traditions of rhetorical practice in the region that also deserve attention.

When conservative vernacular is loaded with double meaning, implying traditional conservative ideas and racist ideology at the same time, modern conservatives find themselves constantly trapped and unable to escape a system of meaning that their own party created. The power of this trap is perhaps felt most by Black Republicans. As Senator Tim Scott was hailed by some conservatives for having "both the desire and the capacity to rebrand conservatism for a new age" (Desanctis 2018), the Black man who first won national office by defeating Strom Thurmond's own son in a GOP primary in 2010 has faced a tougher challenge in beating the rhetorical legacy of the original Dixiecrat. Describing the partisan paradox of Black Republicans, *The Atlantic*'s Theodore Johnson (2015) wrote that such candidates succeed only when they "harbor the principles often associated with conservatism: race-neutral frames, individualism, respectability, and hard work." Following the implications of those linguistic choices, Black Republicans typically "espouse the party platform *and* accept the party's view that structural racism does not play a role in denying Black America access to today's meritocratic society." While such leaders maintain a commitment to civil rights protections, Johnson wrote, this is ultimately "the genesis of their loneliness," leaving them to at best hope for what Senator Scott has described as "measurable progress in reasonable time." As Thurmond's hope in designing the proto-Southern Strategy was always about slowing federal intervention in matters of racial discrimination, this waiting game is exactly what the Democrat-turned-Republican originally planned by entangling racist ideology and conservative vernacular, forever intertwining his version of the South with national politics.

REFERENCES

Aistrup, Joseph A. 1996. *The Southern Strategy Revisited*. Lexington: University Press of Kentucky.

Alsop, Joseph, and Steward Alsop. 1948. "Matter of Fact: For Southern Rights They Are." *Washington Post*, February 13, 1948, 21.

Black, Earl, and Merle Black. 2002. *The Rise of Southern Republicans*. Boston: Harvard University Press.

Chicago Daily Tribune. 1948a. "Rebels to Try to Put Ticket in All States." July 25, 1948, 2.

Chicago Daily Tribune. 1948b. "Gov. Thurmond Rips Truman on Rights Plan." August 12, 1948, 3.

Coasten, Jane. 2018. "GOP Sen. Tim Scott: 'Stop Bringing Candidates with Questionable Track Records on Race Before the Full Senate.'" *VOX*, December 7, 2018. https://www .vox.com/policy-and-politics/2018/12/7/18130510/tim-scott-gop-racism-wall-street -journal-thomas-farr.

Cohodas, Nadine. 1994. *Strom Thurmond & the Politics of Southern Change*. Macon, GA: Mercer University Press.

"Committee Report Adopted by Southern Governors' Conference." 1948, March 13. States' Rights Papers, Strom Thurmond Institute, Clemson University.

"Declaration of Principles; Birmingham, Alabama Convention of States' Rights Democrats." 1948, July 17. States' Rights Papers, Strom Thurmond Institute, Clemson University.

Desanctis, Alexandria. 2018. "The Republican Party's Joyful Warrior." *National Review*, July 2, 2018. https://www.nationalreview.com/2018/07/senator-tim-scott-could-reunify-republican-party-and-nation/.

Edge, Thomas. 2010. "Southern Strategy 2.0: Conservatives, White Voters, and the Election of Barack Obama." *Journal of Black Studies* 40, no. 3: 426–44.

Feldman, Glenn. 2015. *The Great Melding: War, the Dixiecrat Rebellion, and the Southern Model for America's New Conservatism.* Tuscaloosa: University of Alabama Press.

Graham, Hugh Davis. 1996. "Richard Nixon and Civil Rights: Explaining an Enigma." *Presidential Studies Quarterly* 25, no. 1: 93–106.

Henderson, Nia-Malika. 2014. "Tim Scott Doesn't Want to Talk about the Past When It Comes to the GOP and Race. He Should." *Washington Post*, November 7, 2014. https://www.washingtonpost.com/news/the-fix/wp/2014/11/07/tim-scott-doesnt-want-to-talk-about-past-when-it-comes-to-the-gop-and-race-he-should/?noredirect=on&utm_term=.cf0baa81f9d7.

Howard, Robert. 1948. "Dixie Chooses Thurmond." *Chicago Daily Tribune*, July 18, 1948, 1.

Inabinet, Brandon, and Christina Moss. 2019. "Complicit in Victimage: Imagined Marginality in Southern Communication Criticism." *Rhetoric Review* 38, no. 2: 160–72.

Johnson, Theodore. 2015. "The Partisan Paradox of Black Republicans." *The Atlantic*, February 5, 2015. https://www.theatlantic.com/politics/archive/2015/02/the-partisan-paradox-of-black-republicans/385187/.

Kalk, Bruce H. 1994. "Wormley's Hotel Revisited: Richard Nixon's Southern Strategy and the End of the Second Reconstruction." *The North Carolina Historical Review* 71, no. 1: 85–105.

Murphy, Reg, and Hal Gulliver. 1971. *The Southern Strategy.* New York: Charles Scribner's Sons.

Neville-Shepard, Ryan. 2018. "Rand Paul at Howard University and the Rhetoric of the New Southern Strategy." *Western Journal of Communication* 82, no. 1: 20–39.

New York Times. 1948a. "The Dixiecrat Vote." November 7, 1948, E10.

New York Times. 1948b. "Thurmond Scores Truman on Rights." November 2, 1948, 3.

New York Times. 1948c. "Thurmond Warns of Rights Strife." August 1, 1948, 44.

Olson, Joel. 2008. "Whiteness and the Polarization of American Politics." *Political Research Quarterly* 61, no. 4: 704–718.

Perlstein, Rick. 2012. "Exclusive: Lee Atwater's Infamous 1981 Interview on the Southern Strategy." *The Nation*, November 13, 2012. https://www.thenation.com/article/exclusive-lee-atwaters-infamous-1981-interview-southern-strategy/.

Popham, John. 1948a. "Southerners Name Thurmond to Lead Anti-Truman Fight." *New York Times*, July 18, 1948, 1.

Popham, John. 1948b. "Thurmond, Candidate of Rebels, Decries 'White Supremacy' Idea." *New York Times*, July 20, 1948, 1.

Sanders, Randy. 2002. "Rassling a Governor: Defiance, Desegregation, Claude Kirk, and the Politics of Nixon's Southern Strategy." *The Florida Historical Quarterly* 80, no. 3: 332–59.

Scott, Eugene. 2019. "Once Again, Republicans Rely on Sen. Tim Scott to Speak Against Racism." *Washington Post*, January 11, 2019. https://www.washingtonpost.com/

politics/2019/01/11/once-again-republicans-outsource-work-explaining-racism-sen-tim
-scott/?noredirect=on&utm_term=.3ef2d6c8978b.

Scott, Tim. 2019. "Why Are Republicans Accused of Racism? Because We're Silent on Things like This." *Washington Post*, January 11, 2019. https://www.washingtonpost.com/opinions /2019/01/11/tim-scott-republicans-can-no-longer-be-silent-bigotry/?noredirect=on &utm_term=.d9e03282631a.

"States' Rights Resolution." 1948, May 10. States' Rights Papers, Strom Thurmond Institute, Clemson University.

Summers, Juanna. 2017. "Scott: Trump Tried to Convey His Intent in Post-Charlottesville Remarks." *CNN.com*, September 13, 2017. https://www.cnn.com/2017/09/13/politics /donald-trump-tim-scott-race-america/index.html.

Sweeney, James R. 1998. "Southern Strategies: The 1970 Election for the United States Senate in Virginia." *The Virginia Magazine of History and Biography* 106, no. 2: 165–200.

Thurmond, Strom. 1948a, February 23. "Statement by the Southern Governors Committee to J. Howard McGrath, Democratic National Committee." States' Rights Papers, Strom Thurmond Institute, Clemson University.

Thurmond, Strom. 1948b, March 17. "Address of J. Strom Thurmond, Governor of South Carolina, at Columbia Democratic Party Rally, Statewide Radio Broadcast." States' Rights Papers, Strom Thurmond Institute, Clemson University.

Thurmond, Strom. 1948c, March 31. "Statement of J. Strom Thurmond, Governor of South Carolina, Prepared for the Dixie Democrat, Pell City, Alabama." States' Rights Papers, Strom Thurmond Institute, Clemson University.

Thurmond, Strom. 1948d, May 19. "Address of J. Strom Thurmond, Governor of South Carolina, Before Democratic Party Rally, Jackson, Mississippi." States' Rights Papers, Strom Thurmond Institute, Clemson University.

Thurmond, Strom. 1948e, July 31. "Address of J. Strom Thurmond, Governor of South Carolina, and Presidential Candidate of States' Rights Democrats, at the Watermelon Festival, Cherryville, North Carolina." States' Rights Papers, Strom Thurmond Institute, Clemson University.

Thurmond, Strom. 1948f, August 26. "Address of J. Strom Thurmond, Governor of South Carolina and States' Rights Democratic Candidate for President, at Mariana, Arkansas." States' Rights Papers, Strom Thurmond Institute, Clemson University.

Thurmond, Strom. 1948g, September 7. "An Address by J. Strom Thurmond, Prepared for Broadcast over the Liberty Network, Radio Station KLIF, Dallas, Texas." States' Rights Papers, Strom Thurmond Institute, Clemson University.

Thurmond, Strom. 1948h, September 23. "Address of J. Strom Thurmond, Governor of South Carolina, and States' Rights Democratic Candidate for President, at Augusta, Georgia." States' Rights Papers, Strom Thurmond Institute, Clemson University.

Thurmond, Strom. 1948i, September 25. "Address of J. Strom Thurmond, Governor of South Carolina, and States' Rights Presidential Candidate, at Madisonville, Kentucky." States' Rights Papers, Strom Thurmond Institute, Clemson University.

Thurmond, Strom. 1948j, October 4. "Address of J. Strom Thurmond, Governor of South Carolina, and States' Rights Democratic Candidate for President of the United States, at Asheville, North Carolina." States' Rights Papers, Strom Thurmond Institute, Clemson University.

Thurmond, Strom. 1948k, October 23. "Address by J. Strom Thurmond, Governor of South Carolina, and States' Rights Democratic Candidate for President of the United States, at Knoxville, Tenn." States' Rights Papers, Strom Thurmond Institute, Clemson University.

Thurmond, Strom. 1948l, October 31. "Address by Governor Thurmond, States' Rights Candidate, in Texas." *New York Times*, October 31, 1948, 52.

Washington Post. 1948a. "Threat to Liberty: FEPC Called Un-American by Thurmond." August 23, 1948, 4.

Washington Post. 1948b. "Thurmond Hits Racial Appeals." October 12, 1948, 6.

Chapter 6

TAKE 'EM DOWN

Rhetorical Temporality and Critical Regionalism in the Struggle to Remove Confederate Monuments in New Orleans

JEREMY R. GROSSMAN

I have spent most of my adult life living in various parts of the South, but I was reared in the western United States. My own physical movement as a white man from, in broadly descriptive terms, a region marked by nominal tolerance but also by structural and representational adherence to the history of white supremacy (including the fetishization of indigenous cultures) to a region steeped explicitly in symbols of the violence of that history situates my work as a personal lesson from both: I have felt neither conflicted about the destruction of Confederate memory objects nor a psychic investment in the identificatory logics of white supremacy, but at the same time have cultivated a deep skepticism for proceduralist and incrementalist approaches to racial injustice that substitute nominal justice for structural justice, or else conflate the two as a declaration of political victory.[1]

After a years-long process involving all branches of the Louisiana state and New Orleans city governments, in 2017 New Orleans Mayor Mitch Landrieu (2017b) took to the podium to announce the removal of four prominent Confederate monuments in the city. "So for those self-appointed defenders of history and the monuments," he said, "they are eerily silent on what amounts to this historical malfeasance, a lie by omission. There is a difference between remembrance of history and reverence of it." The speech was an impassioned, unapologetic, and systematic denouncement of the memory politics of the Lost Cause of the Confederacy, and it drew both immense praise and criticism across the nation. As Cynthia Mills (2003) has noted, "to the descendants of former slaves, these sculptures appear to be hurtful remnants of a biased history, not appropriate models for emulation" (xxiv). Neo-Confederates and some others argue that the statues maintain regional—and sometimes familial—history and their removal would amount to history's erasure, a claim that elides the fact that most of the monuments were installed as part of a coordinated effort to glorify the Confederacy and displace its motivations for secession.

Landrieu (2017a) later said he was surprised to see the speech go viral, contending that it was addressed solely to the citizens of the city of New Orleans: "Evidently it's an issue that people across the country are dealing with," he told *Meet the Press*'s Chuck Todd the following week, "and I hope they do it in a forthright, honest manner with each other." Of course, Landrieu knew well that the removal of Confederate monuments had become a contentious national issue. Like other mayors across the country, his initiative on the subject had begun amidst the growing national concern that, in the wake of the Charleston, South Carolina, shooting, avowed neo-Confederate memory was the banner under which white nationalists were carrying out violence and murder against people of color and against those who stood in support of the removal of the public memory objects of the Confederacy from public places of commemoration.

Early that same fall, however, mere days after the far-right violence in Charlottesville, Virginia, over its own memory objects, protesters swelled onto the streets of New Orleans in a march from Congo Square to Jackson Square, chanting in unison, "We won't get no satisfaction till we take down Andrew Jackson!" (McWilliams 2017). Organized by Take 'Em Down NOLA (TEDN)—a local organization committed to removing all white supremacist monuments in New Orleans, from statues to street and school names—the protest organized in solidarity with those in Charlottesville, rearticulated TEDN's demands for complete removal of white supremacist iconography in the city, and addressed the mayor directly to demand that the statue of Andrew Jackson at the center of Jackson Square also be removed. As Malcolm Stuber (2017), long-time New Orleans activist and spokesperson for TEDN, said in a press conference two days before the march, "Four is not enough. From the very beginning, Take 'Em Down NOLA has taken the position that we want to see all of the Confederate monuments, all of the slave-owner monuments, in our statues, in the streets, on the public schools, we want all of that gone." The tenuous and sometimes antagonistic relationship that TEDN had with Mitch Landrieu, whom they often saw as co-opting decades of local activism on this issue for his own political visibility, can be felt in Stuber's and his compatriots' speech, even as they approved of Landrieu's persistence in taking down the four. As anthropologist Bailey Duhé (2018) notes, "Landrieu's successful removal of the monuments (thanks to a 6–1 City Council vote) is but a *fraction* of a long line of locally led initiatives addressing public symbols of white supremacy" (123).

This contestation between pro-removal positions (rather than with monument defenders) should be understood as the symptom not of a difference of a mathematical type (how many monuments and which ones), but rather as the product of two rhetorical disjuncts. The first concerns the rhetorical function of monument removal. On the one hand, for Landrieu the reverence of "bad history" is a public wrong that must be reversed. Akin to arguments lamenting roads not taken and wrong turns made, the justificatory logic of Landrieu's speech is organized around the notion of revision, of going back and making things right. On the other hand, TEDN's demand for total removal involves not so much *revision* as it does *reconstruction*, a complete remaking of the city's social symbology, which absolutely requires a positive act of destruction. At a practical level, this first disjunct truly manifests only at the mathematical level. Whether one chooses to see removal as revision or reconstruction does not necessarily determine how many or which memory objects one should remove, and the end goal may be the same. However, taken at a formal discursive level, the conceptual distance between revision and reconstruction reveals itself through each discourse's rhetorical temporality.

Megan Foley's (2015) re-examination of *epideixis* provides a clear exposition of the analytic reading strategy opened by considering temporality at this level. As a response to Martin Medhurst's (2015) diagnosis of rhetorical studies on the occasion of the centennial issue of the *Quarterly Journal of Speech*, Foley argues that Medhurst's own "roads not taken" lamentation about the field of rhetoric has, as it were, mis-genred itself at a temporal level: epideictic, she argues, "marks a point of no return. . . . The past—that which has already come into being—is the domain not of *epideiktikon*, epideictic rhetoric, but of *dikanikon*, judicial or forensic rhetoric" (209). Moreover, the temporality of the epideictic "is simultaneously progressive and perfect. Progressive action is action that is under way; perfect action is action that has been completed. [This tense] hangs between the as-yet and the already" (210). The clear parsing at work in Foley's analysis helps to distinguish between temporality of content—that both Medhurst and Landrieu are envisioning a time to come is not in question—and temporality of form. One need not take the word of the rhetor advocating a way forward on the basis of shared values when the temporality of their speech closes up both the past and the possible.

Positioning epideictic in this way also enables the critic to examine removal with the same complexity with which one might read the shapes and figures and texts of a proposed or existent public memory object or speech. Just as monument-making functions epideictically in the constitution of various place-invested collective identities, so too do the heterogeneous claims for and the very act of removal. This is to say: pro-removal, ostensibly a politically coherent position, only appears coherent to the degree that removal itself is theorized as non- or anti-epideictic, and that different political and rhetorical demands for removal can therefore be consolidated. As a result, different pro-removal challenges to the white supremacist nostalgia of Lost Cause *epideixis* become recoded as uniformly anti-nostalgic *per se* when, in reality, some pro-removal rhetoric enacts its own revised nostalgia under the banner of pure history. As I will argue in this chapter, while Landrieu's speech disrupts the nostalgic narrative of the Lost Cause directly through regional appeals, it offers a separate, revisionary nostalgic history and then closes that interpretation off, delimiting in advance political possibility; by contrast, TEDN deploys an epideictic regional rhetoric that affirms the history of its struggle while leaving open the as-yet of the future of New Orleans and the South. These two positions are thus completely heterogeneous in their re-construction of Southern regional identity. As Bradford Vivian (2006) notes, "whether in somber elegies or celebratory tributes, epideictic organizes the terms of public remembrance in order to shape perceptions of shared values and commitments serviceable to future deliberative agendas" (2). The systematic, concerted destruction of those objects of memory can function likewise. Indeed, Antonio de Velasco's (2019) examination of "Take 'Em Down 901," a Memphis-based pro-removal coalition, diagnoses the institutional conflation of the "ends" and the "means" of removal as a failure to acknowledge that the movement "was, in fact, less about the *means* of removal, than about the *meanings* of removal" (234). Removal, in fact, is one of today's most visible appeals to the reconstruction of regional identity in the South, its manifest memory work hung inexorably between the as-yet and the already.

As I detail below, the tendency to treat monumentality through primarily spatial/material theoretical lenses has overdetermined the methodological assumptions about analyzing memory objects such that the language for removal papers too broadly over incoherent political positions within calls for removal, setting removers as monolithically opposed to defenders. More specifically, while a focus on spatiality has tended to privilege the extant, temporality concerns the possible and the as-yet. Indeed, as Duhé (2018) makes clear, what is at stake in the debate is primarily symbolic in the sense that public memory objects participate in the constitution and legitimization of narrative history. As James Young (1994) argues, "both the reasons for memory and the forms memory takes are always socially mandated, part of a socializing system whereby fellow citizens gain common history through the vicarious memory of their forebears' experiences" (6). What is at stake in the fight over the material, constitutive symbols of regional and national identity is thus as temporal as it is spatial, and the primary theoretical aim of this chapter will be to argue for the centrality of rhetorical temporalities within critical regionalism, both in its theorization and its praxis.

CRITICAL REGIONALISM, NOSTALGIA, AND UTOPIA

Conceptually amenable to the question of temporality, critical regionalism itself is also often characterized by a strong focus on space and place. Jenny Rice (2012), for example, argues that regionalism is a "strategic interface" between the global and the local, both at the level of the material site and that of the abstracted region, a place-based activity that produces, challenges, and (re)defines modes of belonging (210). Douglas Reichert Powell (2007) contends that "region is always a relational term" that refers "not to a specific site but to a larger network of sites" that escapes the institutional divisions of other spatial concepts like nation, city, or state (4). Dave Tell (2012) thickens this further by arguing for the existence of "counter regions," or spaces of resistance within region-making rhetorical practices, that demand a cartographic reading strategy capable of mapping the sometimes-competing articulations between locality and the abstractions of regional identity.

These theorists and others have crafted theories of regionalism attentive to the complicated relationship between space and the sociorhetorical imaginary, as well as the means by which that relationship produces region itself as an idea, as a mode of belonging, and as an identity. This focus on material place should come as no surprise, given that critical regionalism's theoretical lineage leads ultimately to Lewis Mumford (1927) and his examinations of architecture and region. For Mumford, regionalism was a technical rationality grounded in the material properties of physical place—land, climate, resources, and other broadly geographic divisions. "Not merely is the region a fact," he contends; "its individuality is also a fact" (284). He argues that any given region ignores the technics that humans impose on it, including but not limited to the cartographical, the economic, the architectural, the juridical, the political, the environmental, and the agricultural.

Yet, the question of time and memory in the construction of region is also present in the literature from Mumford onward. On an aesthetic–political level, Mumford's prescient meditations on the technics of region involved distinguishing between, on the one hand, both the reductive regionalism that reflected "revivalist pastiche and cheap nostalgia" and the "blood and soil" lockstep regionalism of Nazism (Eggener 2002, 228) and, on the other hand, a self-conscious, self-reflexive regionalism that rebuffed the architectural universalism of modernity. In other words, it sought a critical architectural mode that avoided the modernist, utopian production of placelessness, but that also avoided a pastoral nostalgia that attempted to recoup such lost sense of place (see also Frampton 1998).

Cheryl Temple Herr (1996) derives from critical regionalism—as simul-taneously an academic protocol of critical judgment and a critical praxis—a cultural studies methodology that she argues remains open to a wide range of theoretical approaches and avoids both the utopian promise of modernity and the nostalgia of uncritical regionalism (18). Liane Lefaivre (2008) sums up this dual opposition by arguing that Mumford's lasting influence includes a view of regionalism "critical of an outside power wishing to impose an international, globalizing, universalizing architecture against the particular local identity" but which is "also critical of regionalism" itself (51–52). Indeed, as Carly Woods, Joshua Ewalt, and Sara Baker (2013) confirm, critical regionalism is concerned with "larger networks of spatial, *temporal*, and political relationships" (342, my emphasis), and the literature on critical regionalism consistently stages the temporal opposition of nostalgia and utopia as the dual threats one must avoid in "doing" regionalism well. Insofar as these threats are figured within the imaginary, Rice's (2012) assertion insists, "what is critical in critical regionalism is exactly what prevents it from bleeding into a kitschy or nostalgic regionalism: a disruption of narrative" (203).

But, as Keith Eggener (2002) observes, while proponents of critical regionalism acknowledge the sometimes contradictory logic that accompanies its pretenses (i.e., how does one resist universalism without reproducing it in the nostalgic rhetorical construction of the local?), "in stressing place, identity, and resistance over all other architectural and extra-architectural considerations, critical regionalist rhetoric exemplifies a 'revisionary form of imperialist nostalgia'" (234; quote from Jane Jacobs 1996, 14). The mandate of critical regionalism is to transcend that spatial dilemma through disruption of the universal sense of place. This transcendence therefore must come with the emphatic promise that it does not operate within nostalgic *or* utopian temporalities and that it rejects the idealization at root in each. The problem, though, is that the spatiotemporal binary that organizes critical regionalism involves already in the United States a colonial-turned-postcolonial logic. That is to say, critical regionalism seems always *set against* the modernist fantasy of the universal in the sense that it remains both organized and antagonized by this preoccupation with the universality of place. Critical regionalism's resistance to this universality is a promise made impossible by its very premise, a project whose logic, like that of architectural gentrification, involves reviving deteriorated concepts while abjecting the conditions that produced them. In being thus required to cast off the pretense of a nostalgia of bad history, the task of reconsolidating something like "regional identity" risks becoming the substitution of a revisionary nostalgia that disrupts old narratives but, in addition, internalizes, rather than works through, the utopia–nostalgia binary. What results is often less critical than it is contradictory, a disavowal resulting in revision more than an interruption or disruption.

Taking on the question of temporality and critical regionalism head-on thus assists the study of the South in two ways. First, it provides a language for describing the relationship between the nostalgia set into the heart of southern Lost Cause mythology and the revisionary nostalgia that characterizes Landrieu's speech. Second, it makes possible a careful parsing of different calls for removal that possess radically different rhetorical and political temporalities and thus rhetorically reconstruct very different Souths.

FIGURING THE SOUTH AND NEW ORLEANS

The post-Reconstruction US South developed its mythology in the context of the historical articulation of regional identity and public memory particular to the region. This is likely true of regional mythology generally, but for the South it involves a particularly tricky negotiation of the relationship between region and nation. First, as Klaus Lösch and Heike Paul (2016) note, the South has often been depicted as representing what the nation is not, a regional anathema too often at odds with national ethos. This rejection of synecdoche as the proper figuration of the South troubles even the more moderated descriptions of such an interface. Not only are the local and the global nonconcentric; here they are in direct antithesis. And yet, Tara McPherson (2003) argues, this relation is constitutive: "an isolated and 'pure' South never existed. . . . if one is to understand the many versions of the South that circulate throughout U.S. history and culture, one has always to see them as fundamentally connected to, and defined in relation to, the non-South" (2). Second, the debate over Confederate monuments should be read as a symptom of a larger dilemma over the function of public space in the production of regional memory. How does one understand the relations among place, region, and identity, for instance, in a postcolonial southern city whose regional imaginary remains multiplied along and across the various historical layers of colonialism, slavery, Jim Crow, modernity, and late stage capitalism, to name only a few? This amplified historical stratification of the so-called local in the South threatens the very concept of the regional altogether (rooted as it is in the spatial), and the public struggle for authority over narrative and memory is but a symptom of that fact. As W. Stuart Towns (2012) has argued in his extensive account of the rhetoric of the Lost Cause, the emergence of that narrative served the function for post-Confederates of making "their region . . . whole again" (xi). And as Towns's work demonstrates, the possessive "their" remains part of a mnemic politics that displaces the region-making rhetorical practice of African Americans, Native Americans, and others excluded from that post-Confederate narrative of greatness. "The communication goals of these Lost Cause speakers," he notes, "involved creating a unified front in the white South regarding the region—an 'us against them' mentality that created its own set of heroes and myths" (xi).

Nowhere is this displacement more complicated than New Orleans, which, on the one hand, has often been depicted (both from within and from without) as especially diverse and tolerant, a melting pot more regionally metaphorized by generations of commentators as a cultural gumbo. "Travel writers were already thinking themselves witty in the nineteenth century for calling New Orleans culture a gumbo," Ned Sublette (2009, 116) notes. John Burrison (2007) argues that "while the salad-bowl paradigm may be useful in describing America's ethnic diversity, it doesn't go far to explain the country's regional diversity—geocultural differences so significant as to have ignited a civil war." Burrison prefers the metaphor "gumbo" because it reflects the principle of creolization, a metaphor of cohabiting that abstracts the dish's French, African, and Native American influences into a "blending of ideas from different groups occupying the same area to create something new" (84–85). As Louise McKinney (2006) confirms, "Creole cuisine offers up particularly apt figures of speech because form fits content: Creole cuisine, with its blending of French, Spanish, African, Native American, Caribbean and Acadian elements, expresses the very make-up of New Orleans' present-day population" (11–12).

Yet, on the other hand, much scholarship confirms that New Orleans must also be considered resolutely "southern" inasmuch as it conforms to the historically popular figuration of the South. Justin Nystrom (2010) contends that, from an historical perspective, "critics miss the point when distracted by the presence of Catholicism or Creole culture or when they suggest that, as the region's largest city, New Orleans was anomalous in the overwhelmingly rural South. It was the most valuable jewel in the crown of the former Confederacy. . . . What happened in New Orleans . . . mattered both regionally and nationally" (3). In addition to this strictly historical argument, as Shannon Lee Dawdy (2009) reflects, referring to Louisiana culture as creole gumbo indicates "the temptation to exoticize cultures by singling them out as hybrid, both because of the racial connotations and the colonial histories of inequality that seem always to lurk beneath the surface" (255). Indeed, Lynnell Thomas's (2014) incisive critiques of New Orleans's tourist industries roundly demonstrate that such exoticization, framed as both dangerous and desirous, has long been exploited financially and culturally: "For many whites, this idea of New Orleans provides a safe, sanctioned space to indulge in black culture and unite with black bodies, if only vicariously" (14). In other words, for all its diversity, in the context of Confederate memory, New Orleans evinces all the traits of what has popularly been figured as the typical southern city and its monuments.

"It took [the Confederacy's] defeat in 1865 as bitterly as the rest of the South," explains Gerald Capers (1965), "and it has contributed its share to the southern legend and the southern postmortem" (232). That the South in general, and New Orleans in particular, "remains at once the site of the trauma of slavery and also the mythic location of a vast nostalgia industry" (McPherson 2003, 3) definitively articulates the organizing binaries of space and time, of region and the politics of memory.

At the heart of this southern postmortem is what came to be known as the Lost Cause, a movement that sought to redefine the parameters of Confederate memory through its rhetorical objects, thus redefining the very meaning of the war. Towns (2012) argues that "twentieth-century white southerners learned much of how they were going to think about race, about the North, about the Civil War and Reconstruction, and about themselves from the rhetoric of the Lost Cause" (x). Mills (2003) has defined the Lost Cause as a "whole body of writings, speeches, performances, prints, and other visual imagery" (including monuments and memorials) that reshaped the history of the Confederacy from a southern perspective (xvii). "All had a common goal of controlling the revision of history," she writes; "their programs included textbook and school curriculum campaigns as well as lectures, entertainments such as tableaux vivants, and veterans reunions" (xviii). The Lost Cause mythos is generally understood by historians to have inaugurated with the death of Robert E. Lee in 1870, but it gained greater momentum around the turn of the twentieth century in the period during which the United States more generally was engaged in what Erika Doss (2012) has labeled "statue mania" (27). The vast majority of these public monuments to the Confederacy were built between 1899 and 1918 (Winberry 2015, 23; see also Cobb 2005; Foster 1988; and Goldfield 2013).

The Robert E. Lee statue in Lee Circle in New Orleans was among the earlier ones, unveiled and dedicated on the eighteenth of February—George Washington's birthday—in 1884. While the dedication speech written by Confederate political leader and later Louisiana Supreme Court Justice Charles E. Fenner was never formally delivered owing to a severe rainstorm on the day of the dedication, it was widely disseminated in print (Towns 2012, 79). (Unsurprisingly, Fenner would later pen the *ex parte* decision upholding the constitutionality of "separate but equal" that sent *Plessy v Ferguson* to the US Supreme Court [*Ex Parte Plessy* 1892]). In both argument and form, Fenner's (1884) speech shares much with many other speeches given at such unveiling ceremonies for the memory objects of the post-Confederacy—a valorization of Lee and a constitutional defense of the Confederacy under the banner of states' rights. In short, the Lee monument in New Orleans was installed with as typically southern pretense as any other in the South, with the notable exception that he did not mention slavery.

DE-STRUCTING THE "SOUTH"

It is to this narrative that Mitch Landrieu's May 2017 speech issues a corrective. More accurately, his speech issues a call for a narrative corrective: throughout it, Landrieu (2017b) makes clear that the aim of removal is to "make straight a wrong turn we made many years ago," to take a crooked, nostalgic history and make it straight. These calls are echoed in his memoir (Landrieu 2018, 4, 222) and in interviews as well (Landrieu 2017b). "They are not just innocent remembrances of a benign history," he explains. "These monuments purposefully celebrate a fictional, sanitized Confederacy; ignoring the death, ignoring the enslavement, and the terror that it actually stood for" (Landrieu 2017b). He then makes two quick, sharp points meant to challenge this sanitization. First, he lays out historical evidence by way of citation. Landrieu invokes Confederate Vice President Alexander Stephens's certainty of the "natural and normal" superiority of "the white man" in the defense of slavery, thereby securing the certainty of the historical record. Second, he then references President Barack Obama's speech (2016) at the opening ceremony of the National Museum of African American History and Culture, in which Obama reflects upon an auction block, where "men and women were torn from their spouse or their child, shackled and bound and bought and sold and bid like cattle," and on which an engraving honoring Andrew Jackson and Henry Clay was subsequently placed. "For a long time," said the president, "the only thing we considered important, the singular thing we once chose to commemorate as history with a plaque were the unmemorable speeches of two powerful men." By way of analogical appropriation, Landrieu draws equivalence between this and the situation in New Orleans through an almost mathematical appeal to the politics of history and memory: "One story told. One story forgotten" (Landrieu 2017b). In this way, Landrieu's rejection of Confederate memorialization in favor of the "searing truth" brings to mind Marcos Piason Natali's (2004) characterization of nostalgia-as-bad-history. By itself, however, this fails to justify the act of removal because it shares a certain logic with those who decry the "erasure" of history, many of whom argue for addition rather than subtraction.

Layered into and alongside this "lie by omission," then, is an extended metaphor of regional healing by way of a diversity that contains within it a contradiction. "Centuries old wounds are still raw because they never healed right in the first place," Landrieu (2017b) says. Specifically, Landrieu begins the speech by defining the national motto of the United States—*e pluribus unum*, out of many, one—not as a consensual cry of unity among and between individual states, as proponents of the Lost Cause would have, but rather as an assertion that the diversity of people in the United States and the city of New Orleans is what makes us "better together than we are apart." Drawing on the long-standing idealization of New Orleans's diversity, Landrieu enumerates a series of diverse peoples, from the indigenous to the colonized to the colonizers, and then draws out the lesson: "New Orleans is truly a city of many nations, a melting pot, a bubbling cauldron of many cultures." Therein lies the contradiction: to what extent is New Orleans exceptional, and to what extent is it synecdochal of the diversity of the United States? The question is never answered, and cannot be, for the same revisionary mythology that instituted "gumbo" as a master metaphor that exoticizes and depoliticizes racial and cultural difference in New Orleans—all the while enacting white supremacy with the same force as the rest of the South—also posits "diversity" as both a quality that city has always possessed and a road unfortunately not taken. Insofar as this contradiction remains suspended in the speech, Landrieu's own nostalgia, his own deployment of the revisionary imperialist form, is reflected in this longing for the perfect figuration of a diverse New Orleans that should have been. The rhetorical gestures of the post-Confederacy reflect merely an injustice of memory and commemoration, an exaltation of a moral lie that, once corrected, secures the city's inherent, wayward ethos.

Thus, the limitation of Landrieu's (2017b) regional disruption of the narrative of the Confederacy lies in the fact that he accedes to the neo-Confederate pretension that the rhetorical gesture is primarily forensic rather than epideictic in its temporality. "History cannot be changed," he relates. "It cannot be moved like a statue." The nostalgia for what should have been, articulated to the commitment to a "recitation of our full past," thus fails to escape the forensic temporality onto which defenders of the monuments hold so tightly. As one such detractor argued at the time, "Everyone involved needs to put down their personal prejudices and let the magnificent memorials of real history remain" (qtd. in McCausland 2017). A "full" or "more complete" past is conceptually heterogeneous to the epideictic, which instead "points toward a moment of movement [and] toward the promise of change" (Foley 2015, 211).

This promise of change is one of the central points of grievance with Landrieu among the members of TEDN. Landrieu and the city council, perhaps out of a sense of political expediency in the era of the Donald Trump presidency or perhaps out of the necessity of political compromise (it matters not which), named four monuments to be removed: the aforementioned statue of Lee, one of P. G. T. Beauregard, one of Jefferson Davis, and one statue commemorating the so-called "Battle of Liberty Place," during which the Crescent City White League violently took over the Reconstruction-era Louisiana state government for three days. The removal of these monuments, TEDN organizers have said, is but the beginning of what should be the systematic removal of all symbols of white supremacy in the city (Smith 2017). Instead, it appears to them to have been the end of the city's attempts. "The mayor and city council of New Orleans ought to publicly denounce ALL symbols of white supremacy AND REMOVE THEM," declares Angela Kinlaw (*Roots Rising* 2019, 8), cofounder of TEDN. It is from this premise that we begin to detect a different kind of temporality in TEDN's discourse. For them, removal is not based merely on the corrective gestures of a flawed history, pointed towards an abstract romanticism of New Orleans's diversity and presumed in advance to result in some sort of collective healing. Rather, they position the removal of (all) Confederate monuments and symbols of white supremacy in New Orleans as an act of constant struggle, a fight that has been and will continue to be. This, I contend, is the critical temporal gesture of TEDN's regional rhetoric.

Consider first the inaugural issue of *Roots Rising* (2019), a zine that details the origins, purpose, and political philosophy of the movement. From the start, the zine's name evinces the temporal liminality of the movement: a movement grounded in activism against white supremacist monumentalism in the city dating as far back as the 1950s, using these foundations as the basis for demanding social change for the future. The zine includes poetry, essays, interviews, and artwork from a wide range of activists involved in TEDN and its predecessors. It begins with a Letter from the Editor, who remains without name, which in form is less a letter and more an enumerated response to "those who still question why we do what we do," each beginning with the conjunction "because." Unlike Landrieu's recounting of historical facts that seek to sediment the record, TEDN's enumeration of motive holds open the "as-yet" as it details past injustice: "Because the future generations will be systematically inclined to aspire for the bare minimum / Because of the artificial courage it gives to those who abuse their privilege / Because our visuals influence reality / Because a city with a sorrowful past must aspire for a brighter future." The letter's finale bears the organization's signature in proclaiming, "We say Take 'Em Down NOLA / Remove the centuries old decay / Make room for new growth our roots are rising. . . ." The ellipses at the end of this statement embrace the possible variegations of this growth, and while the demand is concrete, the specificities of its effects are not.

The zine also articulates the removal of monuments to other political causes by including essays written by Latin Americans, indigenous peoples, teachers, and children. It links the ideals of white supremacy not just to the Confederacy proper as a matter of historical record, but also to past and current systems of oppression and exploitation that, as essayist Fernando López argues, "are working as intended" (*Roots Rising*). Such issues include raids by US Immigration and Customs Enforcement (ICE), the aversion to activism around the issue within schools, and the removal of similar monuments around the country. These essays, poems, and letters quite clearly demand the recognition that Confederate and white supremacist monuments are not at all a matter dealing with the historical record, but are rather symbols that function rhetorically and politically in the present and that articulate the values that constitute the possible.

The other central issue that TEDN takes with Landrieu and the larger national narrative of the issue of removal is the centering of the Confederate narrative. As Bailey Duhé (2018) argues, "While the riots and busses of Klansmen and Klanswomen made for interesting news coverage, we need to consider what happens when national news outlets come into town and sensationalize the ugliest, messiest parts of a debate, leaving before they address the years of work community activists have been doing" (122–23). NPR, for instance, reported that "Landrieu began pushing for the monuments' removal in 2015" (Gonzales and Held 2017), while Christopher Mathias (2017) wrote in the *Huffington Post* (2017) that "Landrieu has led the campaign" and affirms that "death threats won't stop us from taking down Confederate monuments." What results is the sort of erasure that Landrieu in other contexts calls a "lie by omission." Even he, bastion of history, mentions TEDN only twice in the main text of his memoir, and with devastating metonymy:

> A racially diverse group called Take 'Em Down NOLA, which wanted every street name, park, or statue associated with slave owning removed or renamed, was marching and mounting protests. Many of their principals had been involved in the movement for several decades.
>
> In early May, vandals spray-painted slogans on the base of the Lee monument: *Memory never dies . . . White Supremacy is a lie . . . Take it down now.* (Landrieu 2018, 192)

And a few pages later, he notes, "As we made plans to dismantle the Jefferson Davis statue, the site became a magnet for both white power advocates and for Take 'Em Down NOLA activists" (196). The metonymic articulation in the first passage, that is, the linking of TEDN and vandals reinforced by the language of the demand—"Take it down"—presents the relations necessary for the second passage to be intelligible as if it were neutral historical record. The "we" in the second passage, then, does not include TEDN or others advocating for removal. Instead, TEDN shows up as merely one half of a rowdy and passionate public existing outside of the institutional advocacy of Landrieu's government.

What is most properly epideictic about TEDN's rhetoric is the refusal of this erasure. Throughout *Roots Rising*, within the structure of the movement, and in the content of its demands, TEDN consistently pays homage to the people and values that it places within its history. *Roots Rising* (2019), for instance, directly after Kinlaw expounds on the political demands of the movement, features an essay entitled "Ancestors in the Struggle" that tallies the important legacy of Avery Caesar Alexander, who fought alongside Martin Luther King Jr. and opposed the monuments publicly. "In 1993," it recounts, "an 82-year-old Alexander would be choked and restrained by police for interrupting the re-dedication of the so-called 'Liberty Place Monument'" (12). The statue of Alexander erected in front of City Hall in 2002 was removed after Hurricane Katrina and then relocated to a nonpublic space on the campus of the University Medical Center in 2015. After this profile in *Roots Rising* appears an interview with Reverend Marie Galatas, who has been fighting against the monuments since Alexander's involvement, followed by an essay by Malcolm Stuber, who likewise has been organizing in New Orleans since 1978. Through these interviews and profiles, through its examination of organizing against white supremacist public ceremonies since the 1950s, and by linking the symbols of the Confederacy to the ideals against which generations of New Orleanians have consistently fought, the inaugural issue of *Roots Rising* praises its roots while simultaneously tying those roots to the political demands of the present.

The regional epideictic rhetoric of TEDN concerns itself not with a flattening, universal vision of the future—no romanticized *e pluribus unum*— nor is it grounded in the nostalgic lament of the past, either as the glory days or in an absence of its full account. What Landrieu fails to find is the rhetorical temporality that would define a radical or revolutionary *epideixis*, and that is because he remains too firmly in the position of the critic. The consistent and forceful use of epideictic temporality by TEDN indicates that its members are not critics of nostalgic productions of region, but, rather, theorists of regional potentiality. As Foley (2015) explains, "While forensic rhetoric addresses a *kritēs*, the addressee of epideictic is a *theōros*. While the *kritēs* judges that which has already come to be, the *theōros* envisions the potential for becoming. The *theōros* is the one who looks *peri tēs dunameōs*, who sees the double possibility of generation. . . . While the *kritēs* sees what is and what was, the *theōros* sees what could be" (211).

Taking closely into account the issue of temporality alongside the spatiality of region in this case removes altogether the specters of nostalgia and utopia, undercutting the revisionary nostalgia that the dominant focus on space and place has always risked in critical regionalism. Moreover, it assists in further specifying those rhetorical redresses that challenge and disrupt a failed mnemic temporality at work in region-making rhetoric. Whereas Landrieu's speech indicates that full history represents an end unto itself but presents nothing outside of that end, and thus firmly aligns his critique of the Confederacy with a closed history of the past, TEDN finds in epideictic that which organizes a potentiality, one grounded in a regional political imaginary, unrevised but re-remembered, and thus produces an alternate temporal means towards the possible, towards an articulation of a different South that defies a monolithic identitarian mythos without reinstating another.

In addition to these theoretical implications, of course, this chapter has attempted to parse an important and understated political dynamic across the South, which concerns the sometimes radically heterogeneous calls for removal that are often consolidated into a politically coherent position, particularly by popular media. These appeals to removal, insofar as they are understood as epideictic, are also arguments for various futures of the South and southern regional identity/ies. When we talk of removal in too broad terms, the motive structure across various appeals remains enthymematic, which allows for analyses like this, from Brentin Mock (2017) of *The Atlantic Cities*: "Take 'Em Down NOLA gave Landrieu the cover, and the mandate, to join a healing and cleansing process that has been many decades in the making. And they have no intention of letting the city stop at just the four monuments brought down this month." Mock makes the important point that TEDN was instrumental to Landrieu's administrative method, both as public cover and as public pressure, and softly chides Landrieu for not acknowledging the group in his speech. But, as I hope to have demonstrated, each appeal to the reconstruction of the South aims towards a different political articulation expressed through a different rhetorical temporality, not a different number of monuments removed. The appeals serve as the foundation for a new South, one that hides not in a new mythology of an elusive yet transcendent (national or regional) diversity, but rather in the de-struction of all that forecloses political possibility.

NOTE

1. Jeremy Grossman would like to thank Roseann Mandziuk, Aya Farhat, and Jason Williamson for invaluable feedback on the various drafts and iterations of this chapter as well as the editors of this volume for their careful and patient interventions. Previous versions were presented at the Southern States Communication Association Convention in 2018 in Nashville, Tennessee, and the National Communication Association Convention in 2019 in Baltimore, Maryland. Correspondence: jeremy.r.grossman@gmail.com.

REFERENCES

Burrison, John A. 2007. *Roots of a Region: Southern Folk Culture*. Jackson: University Press of Mississippi.

Capers, Gerald M. 1965. *Occupied City: New Orleans under the Federals 1862–1865*. Lexington: University of Kentucky Press.

Cobb, James C. 2005. *Away Down South: A History of Southern Identity*. Oxford, UK: Oxford University Press.

Dawdy, Shannon Lee. 2009. *Building the Devil's Empire: French Colonial New Orleans*. Chicago: University of Chicago Press.

de Velasco, Antonio. 2019. "'I'm a Southerner, Too': Confederate Monuments and Black Southern Counterpublics in Memphis, Tennessee." *Southern Communication Journal* 84, no. 4: 233–45.

Doss, Erika. 2012. *Memorial Mania: Public Feeling in America*. Chicago: University of Chicago Press.

Duhé, Bailey J. 2018. "Decentering Whiteness and Refocusing on the Local: Reframing Debates on Confederate Monument Removal in New Orleans." *Museum Anthropology* 41, no. 2: 120–25.

Eggener, Keith L. 2002. "Placing Resistance: A Critique of Critical Regionalism." *Journal of Architectural Education* 55, no. 4: 228–37.

Ex Parte Plessy, 11 So. 948 (La. 1892), http://louisianadigitallibrary.org/islandora/object/uno-p16313coll86%3A65.

Fenner, Charles E. 1884. "Ceremonies Connected with the Unveiling of the Statues of General Robert E. Lee." Speech, New Orleans, LA, February 22, 1884. *Lee Family Archives*. https://leefamilyarchive.org/reference/books/fenner/index.html.

Foley, Megan. 2015. "Time for Epideictic." *Quarterly Journal of Speech* 101, no. 1: 209–212.

Foster, Gaines M. 1988. *Ghosts of the Confederacy: Defeat, the Lost Cause, and the Emergence of the New South, 1865–1913*. Oxford, UK: Oxford University Press.

Frampton, Kenneth. 1998. "Towards a Critical Regionalism: Six Points for an Architecture of Resistance." In *The Anti-Aesthetic: Essays on Postmodern Culture*, edited by Hal Foster, 17–34. New York: The New Press.

Goldfield, David. 2013. *Still Fighting the Civil War: The American South and Southern History*. Baton Rouge: Louisiana State University Press.

Gonzales, Richard, and Amy Held. 2017. "New Orleans Prepares to Take Down Statue of Gen. Robert E. Lee." *NPR, The Two-Way*. May 19, 2017. https://www.npr.org/sections/thetwo-way/2017/05/19/529130606/new-orleans-prepares-to-take-down-statue-of-gen-robert-e-lee.

Herr, Cheryl Temple. 1996. *Critical Regionalism and Cultural Studies: From Ireland to the American Midwest*. Gainesville: University Press of Florida.

Jacobs, Jane M. 1996. *Edge of Empire: Postcolonialism and the City*. New York: Routledge.

Landrieu, Mitch. 2017a. "Full Interview: Mitch Landrieu on Removing Confederate Monuments." *Meet the Press with Chuck Todd*. Aired May 27, 2017, on NBC. https://www.nbcnews.com/meet-the-press/video/full-interview-mitch-landrieu-on-removing-confederate-monuments-954886211962.

Landrieu, Mitch. 2017b. "Mitch Landrieu's Speech on the Removal of Confederate Monuments in New Orleans" (speech). *New York Times*, May 23, 2017. https://www.nytimes.com/2017/05/23/opinion/mitch-landrieus-speech-transcript.html.

Landrieu, Mitch. 2018. *In the Shadow of Statues: A White Southerner Confronts History*. New York: Viking.

Lefaivre, Liane. 2008. "How Lewis Mumford Rethought Regionalist Precedents." In *Understanding Meaningful Environments: Architectural Precedents and the Question of Identity in Creative Design*, edited by Karina Morales Zarzar and Ali Guney, 51–60. Amsterdam: IOS Press.

Lösch, Klaus, and Heike Paul. 2016. "Critical Regionalism: An Introduction." In *Critical Regionalism*, edited by Klaus Lösch, Heike Paul, and Meike Zwingenberger. Heidelberg: Universitaetsverlag.

Mathias, Christopher. 2017. "New Orleans Mayor: Death Threats Won't Stop Us from Taking Down Confederate Monuments." *Huffington Post*, May 7, 2017. https://www.huffpost.com /entry/new-orleans-confederate-monuments-white-supremacist-threats-mitch-landrieu _n_590c9b70e4b0104c734e7b5d.

McCausland, Phil. 2017. "Defenders, Detractors of New Orleans Confederate Statue Turn Out in Force." *NBC News*. May 7, 2017. https://www.nbcnews.com/news/us-news /defenders-detractors-new-orleans-confederate-statue-turn-out-force-n756106.

McKinney, Louise. 2006. *New Orleans: A Cultural History*. London: Oxford University Press.

McPherson, Tara. 2003. *Reconstructing Dixie: Race, Gender, and Nostalgia in the Imagined South*. Durham, NC: Duke University Press.

McWilliams, James. 2017. "Take 'Em Down." *The Virginia Quarterly Review* Fall. https://www .vqronline.org/essays-articles/2017/09/take-em-down.

Medhurst, Martin J. 2015. "Looking Back on Our Scholarship: Some Paths Now Abandoned." *Quarterly Journal of Speech* 101, no. 1: 186–96.

Mills, Cynthia. 2003. "Introduction." In *Monuments to the Lost Cause: Women, Art, and the Landscapes of Southern Memory*, edited by Cynthia Mills and Pamela H. Simpson. Knoxville: University of Tennessee Press.

Mock, Brentin. 2017. "How Robert E. Lee Got Knocked Off His Pedestal." *The Atlantic Cities*. May 29, 2017. https://www.citylab.com/equity/2017/05/how-robert-e-lee-got-knocked -off-his-pedestal/528378.

Mumford, Lewis. 1927. "Regionalism and Irregionalism." *The Sociological Review* 19, no. 4: 277–88.

Natali, Marcos Piason. 2004. "History and the Politics of Nostalgia." *Iowa Journal of Cultural Studies* 5: 10–25.

Nystrom, Justin A. 2010. *New Orleans after the Civil War: Race, Politics, and a New Birth of Freedom*. Baltimore: The Johns Hopkins University Press.

Obama, Barack. 2016. "Remarks by the President at the Dedication of the National Museum of African American History and Culture." Speech, Washington, DC, September 24, 2016. https://obamawhitehouse.archives.gov/the-press-office/2016/09/24/remarks -president-dedication-national-museum-african-american-history.

Reichert Powell, Douglass. 2007. *Critical Regionalism: Connecting Politics and Culture in the American Landscape*. Chapel Hill: University of North Carolina Press.

Rice, Jenny. 2012. "From Architectonic to Tectonics: Introducing Regional Rhetorics." *Rhetoric Society Quarterly* 42, no. 3: 201–213.

Roots Rising: The Take 'Em Down NOLA Zine. 2019.

Smith, Clint. 2017. "The Young Black Activists Targeting New Orleans's Confederate Monuments." *New Republic*, May 18, 2017. https://newrepublic.com/article/142757 /young-black-activists-targeting-new-orleanss-confederate-monuments.

Stuber, Malcolm. 2017. "Live Updates: Take Em Down NOLA Wants More Monuments Removed" (speech). *Nola.com*. August 17, 2017. https://www.nola.com/politics/index .ssf/2017/08/confederate_monuments_city_cou.html.

Sublette, Ned. 2009. *The World That Made New Orleans: From Spanish Silver to Congo Square.* Chicago: Chicago Review Press.

Tell, Dave. 2012. "The Meanings of Kansas: Rhetoric, Regions, and Counter Regions." *Rhetoric Society Quarterly* 42, no. 3: 214–32.

Thomas, Lynnell L. 2014. *Desire and Disaster in New Orleans: Tourism, Race, and Historical Memory.* Durham, NC: Duke University Press.

Towns, W. Stuart. 2012. *Enduring Legacy: Rhetoric and Ritual of the Lost Cause.* Tuscaloosa: University of Alabama Press.

Vivian, Bradford. 2006. "Neoliberal Epideictic: Rhetorical Form and Commemorative Politics on September 11, 2002." *Quarterly Journal of Speech* 92, no. 1: 1–26.

Winberry, John J. 2015. "'Lest We Forget': The Confederate Monument and the Southern Townscape." *Southeastern Geographer* 55, no. 1: 19–31. First published 1983.

Woods, Carly S., Joshua P. Ewalt, and Sara J. Baker. 2013. "A Matter of Regionalism: Remembering Brandon Teena and Willa Cather at the Nebraska History Museum." *Quarterly Journal of Speech* 99, no. 3: 341–63.

Young, James E. 1994. *The Texture of Memory: Holocaust Memorials and Meaning.* New Haven, CT: Yale University Press.

Chapter 7

MARY CHURCH TERRELL AND MULTIPLE CONSCIOUSNESS

A New Regional Paradigm

CYNTHIA P. KING

I am a middle-aged, African American, southern woman who is fully aware of the power this positionality imbues. Far too long has one image of southern identity held sway over the nation's imagination of the South's character. And while this image and the realities it represents demand interrogation, on behalf of my mother, who like our enslaved ancestors, tirelessly served southern food to white families, I declare that we are now insiders. I marginalize the voices of those who seek to deny the contribution and sacrifices Black women like my mother made in building the South. Grounded in and empowered by this new positionality, I seek to work with others to constitute a new southern identity, diverse in its composition, inclusive in its orientation, and progressive in its vision of community.

At the turn of the twentieth century, the successful move to enshrine Jim Crow laws and customs across southern states and the District of Columbia formed a chasm between Black and white citizens (Woodward 1974). Vigilante violence and myths about Black people's racial incapacity and unsuitability for citizenship sustained a color line that established separate but patently unequal institutions, public facilities, schools, and housing. The frustration and humiliation African Americans faced daily in their efforts to work and live compelled them to fight their circumscribed existence. At the forefront of this fight were "race activists," high-achieving, socially prominent African American women and men imbued with a sense of responsibility to elevate their race from a subordinated status in society (Mitchell 2004, xix). Mary Church Terrell was among this group of elite activists who used their personal status, social resources, and access to interracial and international audiences to call for racial equality.

We need to understand figures like Mary Church Terrell, with their complicated consciousness employing multiple identities, not as an exception or counterargument to southern discourse, but as an ideal embodiment of it. Church Terrell herself was born in Memphis and lived in Washington, DC. Her essay "What It Means to Be Colored in the Capital of the United States" demonstrates this multiple consciousness that coheres regionally, as she brings together (converges) and separates (diverges) aspects of her identity to persuade, while remaining firmly rooted in a liminal, difficult place: Washington, DC. The regionalist view of consciousness being posited here expands our understanding of Robert Terrill's use of "double consciousness" (a W. E. B. Du Bois coinage) because it moves beyond Barack Obama's presidential rhetoric to a woman, African American, speaking at a spatial margin between North and South. It suggests that the tools of convergence and divergence are used to navigate multiple displacements, not only of intersectional identity but also of marginal and liminal spaces. Further, it connects our work in rhetoric to Black feminist study and the work of sociologist Deborah K. King, who highlights "multiple consciousness" as the chief insight to bringing visibility back to the body of African American women.

What also makes Church Terrell's essay interesting is that like texts of so many marginalized voices in the South, it is a "fugitive text."[1] Supposedly delivered as a speech October 10, 1906, to the United Women's Club in Washington, DC, it exists in newsprint and proliferates online, but cannot be found as a primary document: neither the event at which she supposedly spoke nor the artifacts from her life have proven definitely that she gave this speech at this time and to this audience. All we know is that, beyond that moment, the speech has had strong significance as a meaningful mode of speaking by a person of multiple subjectivities, converging and diverging in space and time. Despite all these mysteries and complications of consciousness and identity, we also know the "realness" of Church Terrell and her scathing critique of racial hypocrisy in the United States. Her resilience and scorching tone strike a reader as stridently placed—she is not going anywhere, despite being "between." Her divergent and convergent consciousness sits at the heart of belonging that ought to constitute "southern" identity in local, national, or international senses.

Since the early nineteenth century, African American women have recognized the significance and challenges of their interconnected social identities. Dr. Anna Julia Cooper, a former slave and later race activist and educator, asserted this interconnectivity succinctly when she pronounced that Black women are "confronted by a woman question and a race problem" (Lerner 1974, 57). Mary Church Terrell also encapsulated this challenge when she wrote in the *Progress of Colored Women* in 1904 that "not only are colored women handicapped on account of their sex, they are almost everywhere baffled and mocked because of their race" (9). Twentieth- and twenty-first-century Black activists and scholars have continued to recognize the unique challenges that circumscribe Black women's lives, especially in the American South (Gilmore 1996; Hunter 1997). Activist Frances Beale, founding member of the Women's Liberation Committee of the Student Nonviolent Coordinating Committee (SNCC), introduced the term "double jeopardy" in the "Black Women's Manifesto" to describe the dual discrimination of racism and sexism that subjugates Black women (cited in King 1988), while Deborah K. King contends that "racism multiplied by sexism multiplied by classism" equals a "multiplicative effect" (1988, 47). And finally, Kimberle Crenshaw's (1989) seminal piece on intersectionality theorizes about the compounded marginalization that results from Black women's intersecting social identities. Crenshaw's concept of intersectionality explicitly invites an understanding of identity as complex and multifaceted.

Although African American women's unique intersectional identities compound their oppression, their identity intersections have also been the basis for collective agency and empowerment. This work follows from Campbell and Huxman's (2003) study of Sojourner Truth and the protean nature of agency. This agency, they write, has propelled Black women through a hostile terrain of derogatory rhetoric and social subordination to demand equality for themselves and for their community. This agency, they explain, is communal and individual; is invented by authors; emerges in artistry; and is affected through form (4). Black women thus constitute paradigms for "the ways in which individuals accept, negotiate, and resist the subject positions available to them" (4).

The analysis in this chapter illustrates how collective frames of reference associated with the intersections of race, gender, or class can create tensions and contradictions within a single text, and it argues that Church Terrell's speech witnesses such tensions. On the one hand, her rhetorical maneuvers to indict Jim Crow practices in the nation's capital in the first part of her text advances her rhetorical agency by daring to center her voice and the experiences of African Americans to declare her race respectable. But on the other hand, implicit biases of classism combined with colorism inhere to create the tensions that could impede her agency with members of her community who might not see themselves represented in the image of "respectability" she presents.

However, despite its internal tensions, her rhetoric reflects a powerful indictment against those whose racism contradicts the nation's ideals. And thus, she better embodies a southern relational identity than do the white male demagogic orators of her day, from Huey Long to Benjamin "Pitchfork" Tillman. If we center Church Terrell, then we begin to better situate these demagogues not as uniquely "southern," but instead as uniquely progressivist (especially in the case of Long) or white supremacist (especially in the case of Tillman). Like so many other Black southern women who have been made invisible, even by their liberation within the women's suffrage and civil rights movements, Church Terrell helps us reveal and reclaim visibility for Black women as truly and iconically "southern." They, in fact, embody the regional marginality that white demagogues have so frequently wanted to project onto their own bodies and experiences, while still existing and thriving in the US South.

CHURCH TERRELL'S CONSCIOUS MANEUVERING

Church Terrell and her elite peers had ascended to a unique place by living on the margins of their marginal identity. Washington, DC, was less than ten miles from the Jim Crow South and the extreme poverty for African Americans it fostered. Church Terrell and the upper-middle-class Black community of DC appointed themselves the arbiters of Black respectability, deeming themselves representatives of what was possible when the rule of law made economic opportunity possible. Black elites conceded that some members of their race were an embarrassment and might not be entitled to all the privileges of equality, and they were angered that whites did not differentiate between "respectable" African Americans and the lower masses. Black elites believed that most members of the Black lower classes needed to improve themselves, and the race's reputation would follow suit (Gatewood 1990, 185–86). Washington, DC's community of elite African Americans was uniquely qualified to foster this improvement, at the doorsteps of the former Confederacy (Moore 1999, 187–214).

Known as "Black uplift," respectability was a "master value" and political weapon (Rael 2002, 130–31). It also made social agitation possible, as this Black elite frequently felt the resentment of the poorest members of the white majority population, who needed all African Americans to remain at the bottom rung of the socioeconomic ladder in order to retain their own position just above that. Since respectability could be derived from race, gender, class, or religious identities, it often provided a platform for identification and persuasion. Black elites drew their ideas about respectability from "the philosophy of racial self-help, Victorian ideology, and the democratic principles of the Constitution" (Higginbotham 1993, 186). Black elites could pivot between scolding lower social strata in the Black community and identifying with dominant white values to make the case against Jim Crow segregation.

Although censuring racial discrimination is the obvious goal of Church Terrell's "What It Means to Be Colored in the Capital of the United States," the speech can also be read as an index of class-biased sensibilities about the view of respectability held by elite African American "race" leaders at the beginning of the twentieth century. The quest for respectability in the larger society by African American elites mirrored the values of the white middle class at the time and was the *raison d'être* of their political activism. Although Church Terrell did not address it explicitly in the speech, class-based uplift constitutes a subtext of her indictments of discrimination in the nation's capital.

In 1895, when James W. Jacks, a white newspaper editor and president of the Missouri Press Association, wrote a letter to a female member of the international reform community defending lynching and denigrating the character of African American women, he unknowingly provided the catalyst for the founding of the National Association of Colored Women (NACW), one of the most important organizing events for African American women in the nineteenth century (Cash 2001, 37–38). Not only did the organization unify local Black women's clubs into a powerful national network of female resistance, but it also launched the lifelong career of Mary Church Terrell as a vocal spokesperson of the movement and prolific racial activist. For Church Terrell, cofounder of the NACW, and a new generation of African American female activists, Jacks's disparagements validated the goals of their vigorous rhetorical offensive: repudiate racial oppression and defend their character as Black women.

Mary Church Terrell's political agency was grounded in these goals and the women who advanced them, but her privileged background distinguished her even among them (Shaw 1996, 15). The daughter of the South's first Black millionaire, she was primed almost from birth to become a "race woman." According to her autobiography (1940), both of Church Terrell's parents were offsprings of enslaved mothers and their masters who paved the way for her mother and father's economic and social prominence.[2] Measured support from her father's white parent gave him the business sense to become a wealthy Memphis property owner. A successful businesswoman in her own right, Church Terrell's mother also benefited from her white parent (8–9). Her parents' wealth gave her educational and cultural opportunities that developed her leadership skill and talent, cultivated her activist voice, and imbued her with the confidence and will to fight racial injustice.

Her biracial bloodline also gave her the added social advantage of bearing physical traits associated with her white ancestry. When coupled with economic advantages, the ideology of race that alleged Blacks' inherent inferiority to whites also placed the highest premiums for outward beauty on European features, notably light skin and straight hair. African Americans with these features possessed a type of social capital that improved their chances for success. This is borne out by the fact that although the majority of light-skinned biracial Black people were not economically privileged, a disproportionate number of elites at the turn of the twentieth century evinced physical evidence of their white ancestry (Gatewood 1990, 152–53). The hegemonic politics of beauty that privileged their white features created a "colorism" (a term coined by Alice Walker) among African Americans that bred practices of exclusivity by lighter-skinned elite Black people, even among the club women of the NACW (T. Jones 2000, 1489). Darker-skinned Black people envied their lighter-skinned counterparts for the advantages their physical features provided, and they also resented segregation practiced in the community (Gatewood 1990, 152). Although Church Terrell was subject to some of the colorist and elitist attitudes of her class, those prejudices did not deter her from fighting for the advancement of all members of her race. This ambivalence reflects the complex identity position of African American elites at the turn of the twentieth century.

Church Terrell's pedigree alone, however, did not guarantee her ascendance to race leadership. An extraordinary education, which began with attending predominantly white liberal educational institutions from age six, was equally important (Gatewood 1990, 265–66). At the first of these, a model school associated with Antioch College in Ohio, she saw the initial "signs" of her talent for public speaking, developed an interest in politics, and learned German (Church Terrell 1940, 25–26). Unintentionally perhaps, her race pride was nurtured while at Antioch when she learned that she was the descendant of enslaved persons, but quickly realized that so too had most other groups in the world been enslaved; therefore, she wrote, her race should not be shamed or stigmatized (21–22).

The character and philosophy that would shape her activism in later years began to evolve at the Oberlin College institutions she attended for almost a decade (Gatewood 1990, 251–53). In an early sign of her later inclination to push conventional boundaries for race and gender, she chose the "Classical Course" of study, a rigorous curriculum generally taken by men (Waite 2001). Even after her classmates warned that it was "unwomanly" and "might ruin [her] chances of getting a husband," she persevered through the curriculum (Church Terrell 1940, 32). The racial liberalism at Oberlin also convinced Church Terrell of the "advantages of a mixed school" (33). Her interactions with white classmates persuaded her that members of their race were wholly ignorant about African Americans and the impact of racial oppression.

Their antipathy toward Black people, she reasoned, could be remedied by associating with members whose "standards of conduct were similar to their own," and she concluded that such encounters would compel white people to reject "blanket charges . . . against the whole race" (Church Terrell 1940, 33).

This view undergirded the philosophy of interracial cooperation that defined her early activism. During the first three decades of her career, Church Terrell "adopted and redefined" polarizing ideas about the "race problem." Notably, she took pieces from the opposing theories of Booker T. Washington and W. E. B. Du Bois, the pair of which "dominated the [B]lack world of the last decade of the nineteenth century and the first two decades of the twentieth century" (B. Jones 1990, 31). This philosophy and her access to interracial audiences positioned her as a bridge—between the races and between different strains of Black thought—and an orator with convergent and divergent identities beyond race.

Presumably, Church Terrell maintained that optimistic outlook in 1884, when she became the third African American woman to graduate from Oberlin College. After graduating, Church Terrell taught school at Wilberforce College, the first African American institution of higher learning. In 1888, at her father's urging, she took an extended trip to Europe where she explored the continent's history and culture unencumbered by the violence and racism of Jim Crow. Although Europe's racial liberalism tempted her to stay, she decided she would be happiest "working hard" to promote the welfare of her race in her own country, so she returned home (Church Terrell 1940, 99).

When Church Terrell began her public career in the late 1880s, post-Civil War racism had crystallized into a coherent and virulent ideology that justified systematic oppression of Black people. Passage of the Thirteenth, Fourteenth, and Fifteenth Amendments to the US Constitution had elevated African Americans' legal status in theory, but the passage of stringent Jim Crow laws mandating segregation ensured that they remained subordinated. White supremacists' successful schemes to deny African Americans any rights in law and society hurt the pride and status of Black aristocrats most. Jim Crow laws derailed their plans post-slavery to assimilate and continue their upward trajectory and forced them to retreat into their own communities. Though limited in access to a culture protected by whiteness, accomplished African Americans like Church Terrell found outlets for their skills in the Black community. Resistive community building in the form of frustration and indignation over racial proscriptions gave purpose to the circulation of texts and individual ethos. Despite their negative assessments of the Black masses—a damper on their passion and an incentive to ambivalence—middle-class and elite Black women pooled their passions and forged a movement. Working within established Black self-help organizations like the NACW to cultivate their own sociopolitical agency, African American women created networks to contest racist ideologies on the one hand and to address what they perceived as substandard domestic conduct among African Americans on the other (Giddings 1984; White 2004, 21–109). They enacted their agency despite the structures of racism and sexism that conspired to deprive them of a sense of their own power to promote and realize change.

Perhaps sensing the coming Black "women's era," as Frances Ellen Watkins Harper (1995), cofounder of the NACW, called it in 1893, Church Terrell returned home from Europe (Church Terrell 1940, 43). She began her career as "race advocate" while transitioning into the role of wife to Robert Church, a Harvard honors graduate who was later appointed judge in the District of Columbia Municipal Court, and mother to their two daughters. Their lineage, affluence, and accomplishments placed Church Terrell and her husband at the pinnacle of Black Washington society. Viewed widely as "the Athens of colored America," the nation's capital was the center of the Black aristocracy during the early twentieth century (Moore 1999, 9). Wealthy Black families socialized and worshipped with those similar "in origins, culture, color, aspirations and life roles" (Gatewood 1990, 19). Their exclusivity and what some viewed as "pomposity" attracted criticism from some classes and intellectual groups among the city's Black population (Moore 1999, 10). This insular lifestyle put elite activists like Church Terrell in a conundrum. They positioned themselves as intermediaries and advocates for the Black masses, but separated themselves ideologically, socially, and geographically from the very people they sought to represent.

Church Terrell's entrance into activist circles coincided with a groundswell of resistance among elite Black Washingtonians outraged by underfunding of their schools, poor public facilities in their communities, and exclusion from the city's social life (Green 1967, 155–83). They were especially insulted by the wholesale nature of Jim Crow discrimination, especially in the states to the immediate South. Their education, money, achievement, and community status as elites made little difference in the way white people treated them. In Church Terrell's own words, white people "insist[ed] on gauging the Negro's worth by his most illegitimate and vicious representatives rather than by the more intelligent and worthy classes" (qtd. in B. Jones 1990, 154). This indignation along with alarm over shrinking Black rights was especially painful for educated African American women who were subjected to both racism and sexism. Church Terrell was among the educated female activists intent on using every part of her identity to fight multiple forms of discrimination (Shaw 1996; Harley 1982).

A central vehicle for Church Terrell's activism was her role in the NACW, of which she was a founding member and the first president (Berkeley 2001; Davis 1996; Neverdon-Morton 1989; Scott 1990). The largest national organization of African American club women at the time, the NACW waged an aggressive campaign of respectability in the 1890s to countervail pejorative stereotypes about African American women as immoral and poor homemakers (Clark-Lewis 1994). These sentiments fueled Black women's desire to create what theorist Patricia Hill Collins describes as a "sphere of influence, power and authority which produced a worldview markedly different from that advanced by the dominant group" (1990, 147).

Under Church Terrell's leadership, the NACW began to forge a symbolic space for Black women to defend the character of their race and their gender. She led the organization through its formative years as it drafted its first constitution, established nationwide monthly newsletters, and organized biennial conventions (B. Jones 1990, 21–29). She also coordinated the activities of local members as they performed a variety of social welfare, healthcare, and educational services. She and other determined women were committed to the higher purpose of "saving the race through its women" and, in the process, making liars out of those who defamed their character (White 2004, 35–38). She was explicit about the connections between community service, racial uplift, and the collective image of African American women when she declared that the "amelioration of discrimination is contingent upon the 'elevation of black womanhood, thus both struggles are the same'" (B. Jones 1990, 21).

The NACW was problematic, however, when it sought to impose its expectations and standards of conduct on the broader community (White 2004, 53–60). The Whiggish idea that personal reform, focused on the individual, was the root of structural reform could be powerful when the discourse of respectability "emphasized traditional forms of protest such as petitions, boycotts, and verbal appeals to justice" (Higginbotham 1993, 187). But too often it came with browbeating. The NACW's motto, "lifting as we climb," was both inspirational and aspirational; simultaneously, it indicated its members' view of their mission and position in the community relative to the Black masses (Kerr 2006; Moore 1999). Club women often viewed the masses of impoverished Black people with distaste and tried to insulate their own lives from the poor; however, pragmatism as well as a sense of *noblesse oblige* fueled their activism. The NACW assiduously developed a variety of educational programs to support working-class Black women, including childcare, work training, home improvement, night schools, clean-up campaigns, and help for senior citizens, while also pushing the organization to take political stances on issues affecting African Americans such as lynching, the convict lease system, and Jim Crow laws (B. Jones 1990, 21–29).

As president of the most powerful organization of African American women in the nation, Church Terrell had access to interracial and international platforms of reform-minded women. In these cross-cultural venues, she assumed the role of racial protagonist who bemoaned the perils of being African American in a segregated society and extolled the history and progress of her previously enslaved people. Among the most notable platforms was her lecture on the Chautauqua circuit between 1895 and 1910, as well as her speeches to the National American Woman Suffrage Association (B. Jones 1990, 34–42). On these platforms, Church Terrell walked the line between outright confrontation and accommodation. She carried her message about race to the International Congress of Women in Berlin in 1904, where she aroused so much interest in "the Race Problem of the United States that requests for articles on the subject came from newspapers and magazines in German, France, Austria . . . and other lands" (Church Terrell 1940, 205). Terrell had proudly ascended to the top, leveraging race and class as convergent (i.e., a Black woman behaves well to white sensibilities when wealthy Black activism goes alongside bourgeois domestic happiness) and divergent (i.e., she was most non-Black when she was wealthy and not part of the poor Black masses who did little and could do little to improve). Thus, Church Terrell's own consciousness is grounded in the contradiction between the freedom promised in the nation's creed, indeed in the spaces of the nation's capital, and the exclusion and domination reified in Jim Crow practices. Jim Crow laws in an egalitarian democracy created an incongruity between her racial and national identities, which precluded convergence. Nevertheless, Church Terrell's activism offered a way to negotiate her identity, both regionally and globally.

LEVERAGING ELITE MERITOCRACY
FOR THE BLACK RACE

By 1906, the year she delivered the Washington, DC, speech, conditions had been worsening for African Americans throughout the United States over two decades, but especially in the American South, where Jim Crow became most entrenched (Loewen 2005, 33–36). A few months before she delivered her speech, a race riot started in September 1906 in Atlanta when angry white men viciously attacked Black homes and businesses (Mixon 2005). These conditions might explain why, though still gracious, Church Terrell's critique in the speech was censorious and sarcastic. Her tone showed both frustration and an epiphany that precipitated a shift in attitude among Black elites in the nation's capital. Jacqueline Moore (1999) argues that the collapse of Reconstruction and the rise of Jim Crow racism had created a general sense of solidarity among the lower classes, while reinforcing elites' commitment to uplift and race leadership. But this commitment was tempered by class and self-interested ambivalence on the part of elites. Rejection from white institutions, Moore explains, had driven Black elites further into their own communities. They needed the support and approval of the masses to sustain the businesses and institutions they built, and, Moore writes, "to get this approval they had to demonstrate genuine concern for the race" (3).

Early in the twentieth century, Black adults were attracted to the nation's capital over other US cities, with government jobs more likely to offer equal opportunity and the public school system for Black children surpassing those of other cities. Black Washingtonians were thought to be more educated than "typical urban blacks and more cosmopolitan and sophisticated than their Southern contemporaries" (Kerr 2006, 49). Positioned so close to the American South, the elitism of a middle class would be far more obvious. But in the opening lines of her speech, Church Terrell bristled at the idea that Washington, DC, was the "Colored Man's Paradise," seeing "colored people walking about like freemen, minus the overseer and his whip" (2012, 3). Clearly puzzled and offended by this rosy image, for the remainder of the speech she painted a bleak picture of a city "doing its level best to make conditions for [African Americans] intolerable."

Church Terrell was reputed to have a compelling rhetorical style. Dean Benjamin Brawley of Morehouse College wrote that she earned endless compliments for "the eloquence, the grace, the culture, the tact, and the poise" she exhibited (1919, 91). Her physical comportment and polish served as an added refutation against the wholesale claim that African Americans were inherently disreputable (Campbell and Huxman 2003, 107). Near the outset of the speech, she argued:

> As a colored woman I might enter Washington any night, a stranger in a strange land, and walk miles without finding a place to lay my head. . . .
> As a colored woman I may walk from the Capitol to the White House, ravenously hungry and abundantly supplied with money with which to purchase a meal, without finding a single restaurant in which I would be permitted to take a morsel of food. (Church Terrell 2012, 2–3)

She continued in the same rhetorical vein, but this time pointed out the bitter irony that "As a colored woman I cannot visit the tomb of the Father of this country, which owes its very existence to the love of freedom in the human heart. . . . As a colored woman I may enter more than one white church in Washington without receiving welcome which as a human being I have the right to expect" (4–5).

The anaphoric phrase "as a colored woman" emphasized race and gender in the regional position of Washington, DC, but her class enactment should not be missed. High-styled diction, oratorical finesse in repetition, and appeal to sacred national principle implicitly rebutted her poor social treatment. The incongruity between the physical reality of her person and her treatment as an outcast in the nation's capital make salient the indignities of Jim Crow in this between-space in DC—not under "the slave's whip," but vividly far from "paradise."

The remainder of the speech is composed of representative anecdotes of this placed consciousness as it affects Terrell's multiple consciousness. Given its target audience, moderate whites, her appeal regarding the usefulness and productivity of the Black body is key and follows the respectability politics of Black elites. For example, Church Terrell describes how Black people often applied for positions for which they were infinitely overqualified, as was the case with a "young woman" who had already attracted some attention in the literary world by her volume of short stories," but who, nevertheless, sought employment as a "stenographer and expert typist" (2012, 10). Church Terrell editorialized that it was "unnecessary to state the reasons why" a woman so talented should "seek to earn money in this way" (10). If by some chance, African Americans were fortunate enough to gain employment in the profession of their training, a new layer of setbacks awaited, she continued. For example, Jim Crow laws mandated that the "colored" public school superintendent and directorships were removed and replaced by whites. Discouragingly, "no matter how competent or superior the colored teachers in our public schools may be, they know . . . they can never rise to height of a directorship, can never hope to be more than an assistant" (16).

Church Terrell also described the resilience of an aspiring Black artist whose ability to move up north made possible opportunities not available in a liminally southern DC. The young woman had planned to refine her artistic talent at the Corcoran Art School in Washington, but her plan was derailed when the school "discovered that the young woman was colored" (2012, 8). The artist's request for admission was rejected even though "she possessed great talent." But undeterred, the young artist "incur[red] the expense" of attending "the Women's Art School of Cooper Union in New York," where she "graduated with honor, and then went to Paris to continue her studies where she achieved signal success."

While countering the image of the lazy unskilled Black worker suited only for low-paying jobs, Church Terrell's account of talented, hardworking, opportunity-seeking Black people is tinged with racial elitism. The majority of her speech recounted specific incidents of discrimination against more professional and privileged African Americans: a nurse (2012, 6), an artist (7), a writer (9), a sales clerk and head saleswoman in a white department store (10, 11), a government clerk (12), a government worker and educator (17), skilled laborers (18, 19), and teachers (12, 13). These positions required levels of education, training, or social refinement that most African Americans did not have and stood little chance of gaining. Holding even the slightest hope of getting these jobs not only required formal training, but called for personal gumption to challenge the strict color line of the regionalized spaces. Three distinct social classes and living areas existed in Washington. A small number of wealthy Black people like Church Terrell and other leaders of the NACW owned their own homes, but then there were the middle-class Black people (most of whom were employed as government clerks) and the "poor black majority" (Kerr 2006, 42). Such stratification in such strong numbers by definition rendered the District implicitly distinct. It was a place to challenge Jim Crow, facing the American South across its border. It was also a place to truly see multiple consciousness at work as Black women sought to be a part of the respectable class as well as being proudly resistant to regional suppression.

LEVERAGING HER WHITENESS IN SKIN COLORISM

This mission of racial improvement was complicated by the elite desire to be separated from what one leader called the disgrace generated by the "crimes of the lower millions" (White 2004, 70). Church Terrell clearly represented this ambivalence while president of the NACW when she acknowledged that, "even though we wish to shun [the poor masses], and hold ourselves entirely aloof from them, we cannot escape the consequences of their acts" (qtd. in B. Jones 1990, 26). With practical resolve, she asserted that "self preservation would demand we go down among the lowly, the illiterate, and even the vicious to whom we are bound by the ties of race and sex" (26). Church Terrell clearly saw it to be her mission to make the "lowly" masses respectable.

Most telling of her bias is the fact that the professionally talented and ambitious individuals portrayed by Church Terrell typically had light skin, the second way class is marked in her speech. Complexion bias created tension even within the ranks of NACW and between members and the working-class women their programs were designed to help (White 2004, 79). For instance, Church Terrell argues for the "colored school teacher . . . whose relation to her African progenitors is so remote as scarcely to be discernible to the naked eye" (2012, 12). Even this woman, she says, was humiliated and denied service in a white restaurant. Church Terrell used similar language when she described the skin color of a "colored clerk" who "look[ed] more like his paternal ancestors who fought for the lost cause than his grandmothers who were victims of the peculiar institution" (13). A subtle but unmistakable reference was made to the skin color of a "skilled stenographer" for whom "there was some doubt . . . concerning her racial pedigree," but when asked "point-blank whether she was colored or white," she confessed the truth about her race and was fired (10).

The higher premium Church Terrell placed on light skin is even more evident in her reverential description of the physical features of the light-skinned Black victims rejected or fired by white employers. The stenographer was "very fair and attractive indeed" (2012, 10) but was never given a chance to work when her race was revealed. Suffering the same fate was the "head saleswoman," who was as "fair as a lily and beautiful as a Madonna" (11), but who was terminated nevertheless when the proprietor "accidentally discovered that a fatal drop of African blood was percolating somewhere thru her veins" (11). When combined with "attractive" and "beautiful," the adjective "fair," though a descriptor for light skin, also became an integral property of beauty and attractiveness. These references contrast the terse descriptors to the darker skin tones Church Terrell used; for example, the complexion of the clerk's mother, who was "a bit swarthy" (13), was refused admission to the theatre. The same can be assumed about the darker-skinned "teacher at the Colored High School" who received similar treatment (13). It certainly was true for the little girl who was "a bit brown" and tried to enter the theatre with her lighter-skin siblings but was denied admission (14). Church Terrell does not speak ill of darker skin, but neither does she tout it as she does light complexions.

Clearly her intent is to illustrate the irrationality of color line practices. As her anecdotes show, white people were so obsessed with race that even when Black people could pass for white, the whites still refused to employ them or grant them access to public facilities. Also, rejecting the most skilled and respectable members of the race who were also the most qualified for the job illuminated the structural flaws of Jim Crow. But when read against the aims, philosophies, and biases of the elite, her references index a class-conscious idea about respectability. Black elites at the turn of the century had light skin and were exclusive, facts that afforded them social capital but also engendered envy and resentment from other Black people. In the white community, the function of complexion as social capital was more complex. Rhetorically, representing the victims as possessing a Eurocentric form of attractiveness possibly generated sympathy from the audience and even identification with them. Black people passing for white could gain the privileges of whiteness temporarily, but if "discovered," they were rejected and resented.

Church Terrell's multiple references to skin color suggested that, in some ways, she was as concerned about complexion as Jim Crow-minded white people were about race. While she did not expressly devalue the impoverished darker-skin masses, she evinced a clear preference. Light skin may not have been essential to the image of respectability held by Church Terrell, but her politic of beauty made it a factor in her assessments of it.

Juxtaposing the image of respectability projected in Church Terrell's own embodiment and enactment of the value itself with the ill treatment and disrespect received by the poorer, darker masses makes her descriptions of them seem outrageous; however, her preoccupation with the Black upper classes and skilled labor along with her biased descriptions of skin color reflects a view of character and potential limited by class ideology. The beginning of the twentieth century saw a shift in the intracial mindsets of Church Terrell and her peers. Her speech in fact indexes that shift. Elite Black people began to understand that their fates were intertwined with their darker peers, even when visible evidence of Blackness was not present. Put in terms of Church Terrell's complex consciousness, race converged with class, though her own bias made this convergence uneasy. Though privileged, she and her peers would continue to face some of the same indignities as poorer and darker members of her race.

Church Terrell continued her activism until a few years before her death of cancer in 1954. In addition to her work with the NACW, she helped found, along with W. E. B. Du Bois and others, the National Association for the Advancement of Colored People (NAACP) in 1909, and she served on numerous boards, including the District of Columbia Board of Education and the board of the American Association of University Women (AAUW). She worked with white suffragists to get the Nineteenth Amendment passed, even though she was often disappointed in the racist policies and stances adopted by white suffrage organizations (Terborg-Penn 1998).

In the 1920s and 1930s, she worked closely with the Republican National Committee on political campaigns and remained a lifelong member of the party. In high demand as a speaker, she frequently addressed white and international audiences about race in the United States. In 1949, she wrote her autobiography, themed around her experiences as a member of group that faced what she termed as the dual "handicaps" of race and gender. Even in 1949, the dual consciousness experienced by Black women was still laced with colorism and classism. Still, Church Terrell's performance itself, especially in its focus on belonging and place, gave truth to the possibility of convergence and divergence as the practices of situated rhetorical agency. In 1906, this militancy was only nascent in her strident attacks on an unfair system.

IMPLICATIONS

Mary Church Terrell needs to be thought of as a leading voice in southern history and a primary leader in a South that was inherently liminal and contested. Too often, "southern" is taken to mean "white" (especially prior to Martin Luther King Jr.'s activism, beginning around 1960), whereas Church Terrell (like Septima Clarke and so many others) was a southern leader giving speeches about southern practices that would feed the roots of the civil rights movement—the most iconic rhetoric and advocacy movement of the American South. Over a hundred years later, we still miss the ironic point of Church Terrell's speech, especially when we fail to think of her as an insider to southern history, whose organizing would help spur the South's greatest social movement. The place of Washington, DC, and her accusatory rhetoric to the white women of the city—between two worlds—made her multiple consciousness evident.

Church Terrell better embodies a southern identity and consciousness than the demagogic male orators often studied as southern orators because she embodied agency promiscuous and protean—the way individuals navigate difficult spaces of life that are not solidly one world or the other, but relational and in-between. Her performance manifests her agency as convergent and divergent, as embattled relationship as region intersects with race, race with gender, and gender with class. Not only does her performance in the "What It Means to Be Colored" speech, through those rhetorical moves, better embody the experience of most identities in the South (intersectional and complicatedly nondominant), but it also functions as a more persuasive text—pioneering identity from the margins in her ironic call-out.

The turn of the twentieth century was simultaneously the era of Jim Crow and the era of African American female empowerment. Using her resources and rhetorical skill, Mary Church Terrell led an army of community-focused women in the fight against racial oppression that would explode as the twentieth century progressed. Church Terrell's intersectional identities converged to paint a class-based version of Black respectability. Her condemnation of the irrationality of color-line prohibitions against well-qualified, upstanding, and, in her view, "fair" and attractive Black people also converged to embody a politic of class and physical aesthetics which divided the African American community.

Perhaps not lost on her audience was the fact that the individuals and situations she highlighted were clearly exceptions rather than the rule in the African American community. Yet, the performed divergences between region and class, region and race, and color and class showed the problem of "place" that was DC. Women like Church Terrell, light-skinned and wealthy, could not really "make it" as a fully articulated agent. Thus, the cultural chasm between elite race leaders like Church Terrell and the poor Black majority did not prevent African Americans from forming interclass resistance to oppression. Washington, DC, on the border of the American South, created again and again a space for such cruel, self-traumatizing divergence and convergence as society attempted to churn itself out of misogynist and white supremacist hierarchies. It is the story not just of Church Terrell, but of many millions rendered invisible in a South that demands radical rethinking in terms of what bodies and performances we center.

NOTES

1. Multiple versions of the speech exist, but after an exhaustive search, I have been unable to find the original, even in the Mary Church Terrell Papers at the Library of Congress. The speech was published as an essay on July 14, 1904, in the *Independent* magazine, though Church Terrell's name was not given. Whether the piece is a speech or essay is less important for this chapter since it analyzes her ideas rather than her performance of those ideas. Ultimately, I chose a version included in an anthology published by a university press and edited by two rhetorical scholars who vetted it before including it in their volume.

2. In her autobiography, Church Terrell confirmed explicitly that her father was a former slave and the offspring of his white master who seemed to embrace her father as his son; "he raised [him] from a baby" (1940, 2) and also gave him employment (5). She is not explicit about her mother's bloodline, although she attests to unusual kindness and generosity by her mother's slave master, who seemed to take a personal interest in her development and well-being: he "had not only taught her to read and write, but had given her French lessons," purchased her "wedding trousseau," and given her a "nice wedding at which a delicious repast had been served" (10).

REFERENCES

Brawley, Benjamin. 1919. *Women of Achievement*. Chicago: Women's American Baptist Home Mission Society.

Cash, Floris Loretta Barnett. 2001. *African American Women and Social Action: The Club Women and Volunteerism from Jim Crow to the New Deal, 1896–1936*. Westport, CT: Praeger.

Collins, Patricia Hill. 1990. *Black Feminist Thought: Knowledge, Consciousness, and the Politics of Empowerment*. Boston: Unwin Hyman.

Campbell, Karlyn Kohrs, and Susan Schultz Huxman. 2003. *The Rhetorical Act: Thinking, Speaking, and Writing Critically*, 3rd ed. Belmont, CA: Wadsworth Thomson Learning.

Church Terrell, Mary. 1940. *A Colored Woman in a White World*. Ayer, NH: Ayer Company.

Church Terrell, Mary. 2012. "What It Means to Be Colored in the Capital of the United States" (1906). In *The Will of a People: A Critical Anthology of Great African American Speeches*, edited by Richard Leeman and Bernard K. Duffy, 196–204. Carbondale: Southern Illinois University Press.

Clark-Lewis, Elizabeth. 1994. *Living In, Living Out: African American Domestics in Washington, D.C., 1910–1941*. Washington, DC: Smithsonian Institution Press.

Crenshaw, Kimberle. 1989. "Mapping the Margins: Intersectionality, Identity Politics, and Violence against Women of Color." *Stanford Law Review* 43, no. 6 (July): 1241–99.

Davis, Elizabeth Lindsey, ed. 1996. *Lifting as They Climb*. New York: G. K. Hall and Company.

Gatewood, William B. 1990. *Aristocrats of Color: The Black Elite, 1880–1920*. Bloomington: Indiana University Press.

Giddings, Paula. 1984. *When and Where I Enter: The Impact of Black Women on Race and Sex in America*. New York: William Morrow and Company.

Gilmore, Glenda Elizabeth. 1996. *Gender and Jim Crow: Women and the Politics of White Supremacy in North Carolina, 1989–1920*. Chapel Hill: University of North Carolina Press.

Green, Constance McLaughlin. 1967. *The Secret City: The History of Race Relations in the Nation's Capital.* Princeton, NJ: Princeton University Press.

Harley, Sharon. 1982. "Beyond the Classroom: The Organizational Lives of Black Female Educators in the District of Columbia, 1890–1930." *Journal of Negro Education* 51: 254–67.

Harper, Frances Watkins. 1995. "Woman's Political Future." In *With Pen and Voice: A Critical Anthology of Nineteenth-Century African-American Women,* edited by Shirley Logan. Carbondale: University of Southern Illinois Press.

Higginbotham, Evelyn Brooks. 1993. *Righteous Discontent: The Women's Movement in the Black Baptist Church, 1880–1920.* Cambridge, MA: Harvard University Press.

Hunter, Tera W. 1997. *To "Joy My Freedom": Southern Black Women's Lives and Labor After the Civil War.* Cambridge, MA: Harvard University Press.

Jones, Beverly Washington. 1990. *Quest for Equality: The Life and Writings of Mary Eliza Church Terrell, 1863–1954.* Brooklyn, NY: Carlson Publishing.

Jones, Trina. 2000. "Shades of Brown: The Law of Skin Color." *Duke Law Journal* 40.

Kerr, Audrey Elisa. 2006. *The Paper Bag Principle: Class, Colorism, and Rumor and the Case of Black Washington, D.C.* Knoxville: University of Tennessee Press.

Lerner, Gerda. 1974. "Early Community Work of Black Club Women." *The Journal of Negro History* 59: 158–67.

Mitchell, Michelle. 2004. *Righteous Propagation: African Americans and the Politics of Racial Destiny After Reconstruction.* Chapel Hill: University of North Carolina Press.

Mixon, Gregory. 2005. *The Atlanta Riots: Race, Class and Violence in a New South City.* Gainesville: University Press of Florida.

Moore, Jacqueline M. 1999. *Leading the Race: The Transformation of the Black Elite in the Nation's Capital, 1880–1920.* Charlottesville: University Press of Virginia.

Neverdon-Morton, Cynthia. 1989. *Afro-American Women of the South and the Advancement of the Race, 1895–1925.* Knoxville: University of Tennessee Press.

Rael, Patrick. 2002. *Black Identity and Black Protest in the Antebellum North.* Chapel Hill: University of North Carolina Press.

Scott, Anne Firor. 1990. "Most Invisible of All: Black Women's Voluntary Associations." *The Journal of Southern History* 56: 3–22.

Shaw, Stephanie J. 1996. *What a Woman Ought to Be and Do: Black Professional Women Workers during the Jim Crow Era.* Chicago: University of Chicago Press.

Terborg-Penn, Rosalyn. 1998. *African American Women in the Struggle for the Vote, 1850–1920.* Bloomington: Indiana University Press.

Waite, Cally F. 2001. "The Segregation of Black Students at Oberlin College After Reconstruction." *History of Education Quarterly* 41: 344–64.

White, Deborah Gray. 2004. *Too Heavy a Load: Black Women in Dense of Themselves, 1894–1994.* New York: W. W Norton and Company.

Woodward, C. Vann. 1974. *The Strange Career of Jim Crow.* 3rd ed. New York: Oxford University Press.

Chapter 8

SONGS OF THE SOUTH

Embodying the Crossroads of Southern Narrative Inheritances

CASSIDY D. ELLIS AND MICHAEL L. FORST

Growing up working-class in rural Alabama ensured I internalized all the stereo-typic southern white feminine norms and had a lot of the stereotypic southern white experiences. In many ways, I know the South like the palm of my hand. My "insider" status is easy to see. But when my PhD program took me out of the South for the first time ever, things began to change. My time away from all my southern comforts has now constituted me an "outsider" to the South. My southern white identity is now characterized by this "insider–outsider" status, requiring me to occupy a liminal space that's "southernish." I'm finding ways to balance this slippery status made up of elements that often seem incommensurable—things like being a sweet-tea-lovin', football-watchin', country-music-singin', left-leanin', whiteness-criticizin', highly educated feminist, reproductive justice advocate, and scholar. Like a true southerner, I tell stories to make sense of experience.
—Cassidy D. Ellis

As a queer young person who moved to the South from outside the region, claiming and defending my southern identity constituted a challenging yet hard-pursued project. Hoping to pass as an accepted southerner, I internalized the performances of white southern masculinity that I observed in east Texas and Alabama's River Region. I characterize my experience in the South as a sort of "insider–outsider" relationship. Now living outside the South, I feel more like a southern "insider" than ever before. Often asked to speak for the region, I am challenged to story the South in a way that accurately depicts the complex historical and contemporary characteristic of my home. The American South I experience is a contradictory space, best understood through stories that resist singular narratives of southern identity.
—Michael L. Forst[1]

SWEET HOME ALABAMA

It's game day at the University of Alabama (UA). Packed into the student section of Bryant-Denny Stadium in Tuscaloosa, Alabama, we are surrounded by approximately 100,000 of our closest friends. There are few empty seats for this game. Between sneaking sips out of mini bottles of Smirnoff vodka and Fireball that we stuffed into our boots and bras and stealthily smuggled inside the stadium (a process perfected and passed down by generations of students before us), we chat with those sitting near us about the prospect of one of our players winning another Heisman Trophy. Soon, a familiar guitar riff interrupts our conversation, and the crowd erupts in applause, shouting the lyrics that follow. Along with everyone else in the stadium, we scream-sing Lynyrd Skynyrd's lyrics with a UA twist, "Sweet home Alabama [Roll Tide Roll] / Where the skies are so blue / Sweet home Alabama [Roll Tide Roll] / Lord, I'm comin' home to you" (1974). Singing "Sweet Home Alabama" in Bryant-Denny Stadium before a big Alabama football game is a tradition meant to elevate our shared identity as Alabama football fans (Borucki 2003). We sing to celebrate southernness and southern pride, but more specifically state pride.

Even though the excitement brought on by Lynyrd Skynyrd's 1974 hit, "Sweet Home Alabama," is not confined to the Heart of Dixie, I (Cassidy) was surprised the first time I heard it playing in a bar in Denver, Colorado. I was even more surprised to see those around me singing all the lyrics—even my friend from Spain knew the words to this song about my homeplace. As I sang along outside of the South for the first time, the lyrics began to take on a different meaning. "Singin' songs about the Southland" (Lynyrd Skynyrd 1974) in Denver, where I was confronted by people's stereotypes of southerners, complicated my relationship to my own southernness. Unexpectedly reminiscing about home in a random bar with new friends from my PhD program, I sang alongside Lynyrd Skynyrd's Ronnie Van Zant, "I miss Alabamy once again, and I think it's a sin, yes" (1974). Some of my new friends would ask me why I missed such a conservative place and would question why I would ever want to go back there. Others would ask if southern academics were more racist than those "out here" in the West. Through singing songs of the South like "Sweet Home Alabama" alongside non-southerners, I began to realize that communicating about Alabama and about the South is difficult, complex, and contradictory. I also began to realize how my embodiment of southernness (particularly through my accent) marked me as an outsider in spaces outside the South. This led me to become more reflective of how southernness is read, constructed, and complicated through my interactions with non-southern colleagues.

SOUTHERN EXCEPTIONALISM

Mainstream narratives of the South are often rife with stereotypes that characterize the region as an atemporal, backwards space, doomed to forever be the antithesis of a "true" progressive United States. These popular narratives are generally disembodied and rarely center the lived experience of those who call the South home and who call themselves southern. Despite this exclusion, these narratives permeate discourse on regionalism in the United States and contribute to the "myth of southern exceptionalism" or the idea that a "retrograde South" exists inside a monolithic "progressive" United States (Lassiter and Crespino 2010). Many seek to wash their hands of the region entirely, arguing for the South to secede from the United States to benefit the rest of the country. This characterization of the region results in oversimplifications and overgeneralizations.

The myth of southern exceptionalism has long held sway in studies of the South. For instance, Griffin identifies the South as the most "distinctive" region in the United States, a region so exceptional in its racism and conservativism that it "historically has been so profound as to provoke repeated changes in the nation's laws governing citizenship rights" (2006, 7). Similarly, Steven White, a political scientist, analyzes southern voting data to argue that the South is a "uniquely Evangelical region" (2014, 553) and "that the white South remains distinct in the 21st century, but the Deep South still especially so" (552). Griffin and Hargis (2008) also discuss regional differences between the northern and southern US, focusing on perceptions of racial opinions. They found white survey respondents "below the Mason–Dixon Line expressed more conservative views, including, on some questions, more laissez-faire racist views" (121) and argue that there is "a distinctive, pervasive white Southern racial attitudinal pattern."

While the southern exceptionalism thesis still underlies much of the scholarship on the South, scholars like Lassiter and Crespino (2010) help to illuminate the theoretical and practical shortcomings inherent within narratives that reinforce southern exceptionalism. For instance, the ways in which oppressive politics function throughout the entire United States are rendered invisible by southern exceptionalism. Racism, conservatism, and religious extremism, which exist from Selma to Seattle, become impossible to see if these issues are supposedly unique to only those states below the Mason–Dixon Line. Additionally, southern exceptionalism narratives erase the complexity of living in the South and identifying as southern, for those living both within and outside the region. Constructing the South as a regional "other" (Burton 2013) is an intentional stance, which sits differently when done by southerners or folks outside of the region. Nuancing insider–outsider status is a useful step toward a more complex read of the South.

It is essential to recognize how, "in common parlance, *Southerners* often refers to white Southerners—specifically, those white Southerners who proudly identify themselves as such" (Watts 2008, 2–3). Southern identity and race are braided in nuanced (and often problematic) ways. The history of the South and the concept of southern heritage is based in antebellum nostalgia and is noticeably whitewashed. We account for the ways we are implicated by this history and heritage, and we, as embodiments of southern white hegemony, use this space to own this embodiment while simultaneously challenging it.

MASTER NARRATIVES AND NARRATIVE INHERITANCES

Effectively, southern exceptionalism is a "master narrative," defined as "the ongoing ideology passed from generation to generation by way of the stories we tell" (Corey 1998, 250). In this chapter, we push back against these master narratives of the South, depicting the southern "impulse" to story experience (Berry 2000). Berry writes that "Southern personal narrative is a conversation, often heated, within the self, between the self and the community, between the South and the country, and with those outsiders within, the other race" (13–14). Our narratives illustrate this impulse to use story to analyze experience.

Goodall defines narrative inheritance as "stories given to children by and about family members" (2005, 492) and argues "what we inherit narratively from our forebears provides us with a framework for understanding our identity through theirs" (497). Through our stories, we demonstrate the ways in which narratives are not only inherited from family, but from larger cultural institutions, such as schools, the media, and the social spaces we inhabit. We make visible the narratives we inherited about our identity as white southerners that contribute to how we understand ourselves today. Narrative inheritances, we argue, construct our identities as white southerners, and more specifically as Alabamians. For instance, we learned what it means to call Alabama home from the stories of (often white) Alabamians with deep roots in the region. While we certainly inherited these narratives from larger institutions, more often we have learned through stories, through the land and the music and the nice old ladies at church. We inherit through the mundane and everyday experiences of life in the South.

THRESHOLD PERFORMANCE

Our southern narrative inheritances almost always conflict with the progressive ideologies and worldviews we now hold. Thus, we write as born and/or bred white southerners, who, through our progressive politics and intersecting (concurrently privileged and marginalized) identities, exist at and embody a threshold of cultural change in the South. To interrogate these identities, we articulate threshold identity performance as progressive/transgressive Alabamians and consider the ways we are implicated by southern narrative inheritances. Thus, this chapter centers these tensions to illustrate how threshold identities composed of competing narrative inheritances are managed on a quotidian basis. Our narratives reflect our co-concurrent contributions to and learning from cultural narrative inheritances.

Our chapter advances the theorization and application of Keating's notion of threshold performance (1996). Her articulation of threshold theory primarily draws from the work of scholars of color and anticolonial thinkers: for example, Mignolo's border thinking (2000), Anzaldúa's *nepantleras* (1987), and Lorde's Black feminism (1982). The impetus for Keating's theorizing is inextricably tied to the experiences of persons of color in Western, white-centric society. Expanding from this locus, we embrace Keating's (1996, 2013) encouragement for academics/writers/activists of all backgrounds and identities to cultivate scholarship that moves beyond dichotomous, oppositional discourse toward nuanced, relational thinking. Keating weaves personal narrative with theoretical analysis to illustrate that thresholds "represent complex interconnections among a variety of sometimes contradictory worlds" (1996, 10), making them often difficult to embody and socially navigate. Engaging in threshold theorizing requires that we move "betwixt and between" (a term borrowed from anthropologist Victor Turner) our marginalized and dominant identity markers to draw connections between seemingly siloed cultural spaces. We find this movement particularly useful for challenging the myth of southern exceptionalism and the idea of a monolithic southern identity.

* * *

Situated in this literature, we offer three main arguments. First, southern exceptionalism narratives erase the complexity of living in the South and/ or identifying as southern by flattening experiences of southernness into stereotypes like rednecks and hillbillies (Holladay 2018) or genteel belles and beaus (Lewis and Page 2012). We push back against this flattening by identifying the tensions we experience as a part of our southern identities. Second, we consider the embodiment of our southern identities alongside experiences and values that conflict with our southernness (such as queerness and progressive politics). This embodiment exemplifies an insider–outsider identity and demonstrates the complexity of southern identity. We blend rhetorical criticism and autoethnography to further theorize Keating's (1996) threshold performance and to demonstrate the concept's usefulness for understanding the embodiment of cultural change. Finally, we argue that a successfully nuanced articulation of threshold identity reflects the inherent tensions experienced between our narrative inheritances and lived experiences. Rhetorically analyzing these narratives illustrates southern identity outside of and in conversation with the hegemonic norm with which we are all most familiar.

BLENDING PERFORMATIVE
AND RHETORICAL AUTOETHNOGRAPHY

We use a collection of texts—three songs of the South—as entry points for our discussion; yet the narratives we share are themselves the central text under analysis. Enacting thresholds is an embodied experience, so autoethnography and performative writing are appropriate for the theoretical work in which we are engaged. Autoethnography is particularly useful in rhetorical studies because, as Lunceford notes, "The truth of the matter is that we already tell stories within criticism. . . . [Autoethnography] reminds us that the individuals we write about are actually living, breathing human beings" (2015, 7–8). Thus, we utilize performative autoethnography as our method, as "it is a method that calls upon the body as a site of scholarly awareness" (Spry 2016, 727). The *performative* in the autoethnographic denotes particular attention to the body in the story. In this way, we foreground our (oftentimes nonhegemonic) bodies in (oftentimes hegemonic) southern spaces in order to highlight the ways in which we (in)appropriately perform, and thus (re)construct, southern identity.

Our performative approach to autoethnography in this chapter centers and implicates the body in experience. Langellier (1999) writes that performance asks us to attend to the "so what" of our personal narratives, to consider how our bodies are read and experienced by others in space. As insiders to the white South, we can use our "specialized knowledge . . . to translate and unveil extant philosophical systems to those who (without this knowledge) are unable to locate them" (Madison 1993, 215). We expose our insider knowledge throughout this chapter in ways that highlight how our performances of southernness often render us outsiders in our home spaces.

In composing our narratives, we turn to performative writing. As a method, performative writing is (much like our own enactments of southernness) resistant and disidentificatory and challenges hegemony. Additionally, because of the attention to our own bodies and embodiments of southern identity through performative autoethnography, we ground this chapter in a performance paradigm, which "flourishes in the liminal, contested, and recreative space between deconstruction and reconstruction, crisis and redress, the breaking down and the building up of the workshop-rehearsal process" (Conquergood 2013, 57). In this way, as a theoretical paradigm, performance calls attention to the way identity is embodied and then performed and the way identity is consistently in flux. Thus, when we discuss ways we *perform* southern identity, we refer to how we embody and enact the narrative inheritances that taught us what it means to *be* southern, as well as the way our performances are a space for "deconstruction and reconstruction" of southern identity. Threshold performances are especially generative spaces for this work.

Autoethnography and performative writing push back against the way rhetorical criticism (like many academic disciplines) demands disembodied and "objective" authorship. We ground our chapter in the everyday lives of southern folks that we exemplify with our narratives of seemingly mundane southern experiences. Centering these narratives of the everyday through autoethnographic and performative methodologies allows us to "meet texts on their own terms" (Calafell 2014, 115). As demonstrated by Calafell, one way to accomplish this is by blending performative methodologies with critical rhetoric. In this way, we move throughout this chapter to write *through* our positionalities as queer white southerners in order to analyze performances at the intersection of sexuality, race, class, and regional identity.

The narratives in this chapter are temporally bound, historically situated, and carefully crafted with attention to language use, word choice, and dialogic embodiment. The meaning we make from them is contextual (Pollock 1998, 79). Thus, this rhetorical duo/autoethnography is both a rhetorical text and a rhetorical critique. Rhetorical autoethnography has the same goal as any other method of rhetorical criticism, "to help us more fully understand the rhetorical artifact under consideration" (Lunceford 2015, 10). Communicating about Alabama and about the South can be difficult, so our narratives take the form of a layered account (Ronai 1995) to demonstrate this tension and complexity. Ultimately, this chapter (literally) layers and contrasts our experiences to generate collective narratives that explore evolving cultural stereotypes, place-based memories, insider–outsider regional identity, and the way(s) we come to know ourselves as southern.

In what follows, we use songs about the South as entry points to auto-ethnographically articulate our experiences as Alabamians and discuss conflicts and challenges that result from embodying cultural crossroads. We consider how our articulation of Alabama/ness (to outsiders, insiders, and ourselves) reflects the narratives we have inherited, while simultaneously articulating future potentials for our home space. Our narratives articulate struggles around race, sexuality, class, and politics, and they challenge white hegemony of southern identity. We invite readers to join us in complicating the notion of "home" and in imagining what it might mean to embody the crossroads of cultural change.

Thus, our duo/autoethnography of place and lived experience contributes to a "reconstruction" of the South by highlighting these tensions and threshold identity performances.

REVISITING SWEET HOME

I (Michael) moved to Alabama from east Texas as a high school junior. My new home was familiarly southern, but the sounds were different. Alabama was brought to life by the noise of water rushing through creeks after summer thunderstorms and crickets humming in the backyard at night and folks singing songs about the Southland. I learned what it meant to be an Alabamian through these songs of the South and from older white men in my neighborhood who taught me to sing along. In their slow, River Region drawls, which became more characteristically Alabamian with each Bud Light they downed, they first taught me the words to "Sweet Home Alabama." Tackling this song first was presented as an obvious choice. As one friend said, "Bama's fight song is important, but Sweet Home is kin to gospel." So, I learned the words, and I preached the gospel, just as I was taught.

Now, if scream-singing "Sweet Home Alabama" during football games fosters shared identity as a Crimson Tide fan, then talking shit about Neil Young communicates your identity as a true Alabamian. In the second verse of the song, Ronnie Van Zant sings, "Well I heard Mister Young sing about her / Well I heard ol' Neil put her down / Well, I hope Neil Young will remember / A southern man don't need him around anyhow" (Lynyrd Skynyrd 1974). Cue a quick guitar riff, followed by the world-famous chorus, and the song continues without ever bringing Neil Young back into conversation. I wasn't familiar with Neil Young, but I knew he had done something to mess up, and I knew we didn't like him.

After shit-talking Neil for at least a year, I finally got up the nerve to wonder out loud about why he was hated in the South. I asked one of my neighborhood mentors what "ol' Neil" had done, hoping to gain some clarity. I was told, "That man is arrogant, entitled, a damned Yankee, and stickin' his nose in shit that don't belong to him." As I had come to learn, singing "Sweet Home Alabama" wasn't just about collective belonging, but it was also a way to proclaim the values and ideals that are important to folks in Alabama. Humility, hard work, self-reliance, and not being a "damned Yankee" were at the top of the list provided by my neighbor. I learned that if I wanted to fit in, I would have to make sure people knew I was the opposite of "ol' Neil." From that moment on, each time I heard this verse my body swelled with disgust for Neil Y**ng and his self-righteous affront to my adopted home. He was an unwanted Other who (apparently) didn't share our values. He was an outsider that could be opposed to prove my belonging as an Alabamian.

Young's song is an address to southern men. As a white man from the South, I am implicated by his lyrics and invoked anytime his song is played. When I moved to Alabama as a sixteen-year-old, I had yet to fully understand and publicly name my bisexual identity. As such, I experienced an unnamed and not-entirely-understood fear that my attraction to men would be "found out" and that I wouldn't measure up to well-known standards of southern masculinity. My performance of gender and sexuality, combined with the fact that I wasn't born in Alabama, represented barriers to being a true insider in my new home. These threats to belonging terrified me. My visceral reaction to Neil Young's name wasn't *only* about him (assuming my reaction can be attributed to him at all); it was also a manifestation of deeply internalized shame and self-doubt. It reflected the limited scope of masculinity taught and celebrated by the men from whom I was learning.

Music functions as a vehicle for cultural narrative inheritance. Southern values are communicated through the song's lyrics, and my identity as a white Alabamian was informed by the narratives white folks offered me about their memories tied to the classic song. I could cite the stories they shared—and the lessons that are inherited through any *good* southern story—to inform the aspects of my identity that were aligned with white masculine cultural norms. Years later, as a graduate student living in Illinois, I finally looked up the lyrics to Neil Young's "Southern Man" to explore what he had actually said about the South. What I discovered plucked Skynyrd's words out of my mouth and knocked me into silence. Young, a Canadian singer, had written the song about a figurative (though not fictional) white man who exploited Black people across the antebellum and Jim Crow South. Young sings, "I saw cotton and I saw black / Tall white mansions and little shacks / Southern man, when will you pay them back?" (1970). I had never heard these words, as Young's music wasn't allowed where I'm from. Whiteness often moves unmarked in US society (Nakayama and Krizek 1995) and is never explicitly cited in Skynyrd's lyrics; however, speaking out against Neil Young is directly predicated upon disagreement with his antiracist politics and distrust of his non-southern identity.

Young's racially progressive politics are aligned with the progressive political ideas I have cultivated (inherited) through more recent life experiences. This new information causes me to reconsider my orientation to Skynyrd's lyrics about Neil Young: should I remove the song from my playlists and disaffiliate from "Sweet Home Alabama," or can I continue enjoying the song, as if I know nothing new? The decision to strike Skynyrd from my music world feels unproductive (not to mention improbable, given its frequent play in Alabama). However, ignoring the very real negative impact of the song for listeners of color is a privilege only afforded me by my skin tone. Singing "Sweet Home Alabama" from a race- and gender-privileged space, complicated by marginalized aspects of my identity, encourages me to consider how my performance potentially challenges the southern masculinity I was taught by cultural insiders and had worked to embody as a young person.

Ultimately, being a politically progressive queer southerner requires me to strike a balance between these two responses and to chart a third course of performative disidentification. Disidentification pushes back against hegemonic cultural forces in nuanced ways by attempting to "transform a cultural logic from within" (Muñoz 1999, 12). Intentionally disturbing fixed, oppositional, performative binaries challenges our sense of stable collective identity and creates space for nuanced identification, increasing the potential for performative disturbance of hegemonic master narratives (Tlostanova, Thapar-Björkert, and Koobak 2016). In my case, it creates space to challenge hegemonic southern masculinity.

Disidentification implies incomplete identification with (or resistance to) a dominant performative script, while also expressing partial connection to it (Muñoz 1999). Performative disidentification is a well-appointed tool for this work, as embodying a threshold identity is founded upon nuanced, nonunitary choices. Keating (1996) asserts this orientation to identity and challenges us to expand our own understanding of personal identity, to reject modernist notions of unitary identity, and to see the transformative potential inherent in complex intercultural negotiations. As white Alabamians whose antiracist and otherwise progressive political beliefs cause serious conflict with the narratives we culturally inherited, threshold performance represents a meaningful opportunity to challenge master narratives without completely alienating white folks who more closely align with the hegemonic norm. My (Michael) disidentification in this narrative originates from a place of privilege, given the cultural currency of whiteness, which differs for people of color who may embody thresholds as a strategy for survival. Further, disidentification was originally theorized for and by scholars of color. It is important to note that we don't seek to appropriate or whiten this theory. Rather, we seek to complicate the dominant and monolithic way whiteness is often theorized by illustrating often unacknowledged racial tensions.

DIXIELAND DELIGHT

One of my (Michael's) favorite things about being an Alabamian is singing "Dixieland Delight." It doesn't matter where the song plays—Crimson Tide football games, dive bars, expensive weddings, the local Walmart—folks sing along. Participating in this song is part of my southern narrative inheritance: "Rollin' down the backwoods Tennessee by-way / One arm on the wheel / Holdin' my lover with the other / A sweet, soft, southern thrill" (Alabama 1983). This song teaches about the simple joy of driving down winding country roads in the South; however, the folks who shared it with me taught me what the lover who I was holdin' on to should look like. My boyfriend didn't match the expectation. No one ever mentioned that "rollin' down the backwoods Tennessee by-way" feels a whole lot less appealing if you aren't a couple of white straight folks.

I always felt the urge to challenge the song's presumption of straightness through how I perform my sexuality. When my out-of-town boyfriend started going to Tide football games with me, I surprised him by pulling him in close during this part of the song, just like the straight folks around us did. This was my small attempt at a nuanced disidentification, of pushing back against the expectation of southern masculinity. Standing to my right, I looped my arm around his shoulders and pulled him toward me with a tight squeeze. As the stadium sang, "holdin' my lover with the other," I gave him a quick kiss on the cheek and released my hand from his shoulders.

While sharing a version of this story with a colleague a few years after it happened, they asked, "What was your boyfriend's reaction? Was he upset?"

"I'm not sure," I responded, "probably not . . . maybe . . . but probably not . . ."

My fumbling response was followed by a short pause. Looking back, I don't know how he felt in this moment of forced intimacy. I didn't ask his permission. I was already accepted as an insider by the group because of my Crimson Tide allegiance and experienced bi-passing privilege, but he could not rely on either source of social advantage to push back the surprised looks from straight folks around us in the stadium. My intention for this performance of rebellion was to articulate my threshold identity as *both* fully queer *and* fully Alabama football fan—to claim this threshold in an overwhelmingly heteronormative, masculine environment. But when I'm asked about my boyfriend's reaction to the experience, my thoughts become unclear, and I am unsure of the impact of my actions.

Now several years removed from the experience, I question my simplistic rendering of my "Dixieland Delight" mini rebellion. Autoethnography is read as a political/personal project to drive theory building (Adams and Jones 2011). I am reminded of Spry's writings about the ways the Other may be implicated in autoethnographic storytelling. Spry asks us to sit with the ethical considerations of writing Others into our narratives and challenges us to foreground intersubjective worldmaking in our scholarship (2016). The narrative shared above demonstrates a nonhegemonic relationship between southernness and sexuality, which contributes to the visibility of queer-identified folks and their experiences in Alabama. However, the story also demonstrates the importance of self-reflexively considering the Other in lived experience and in our performances of disidentification.

Reading my threshold performance through an intersectional lens produces a generative analysis. Southern masculinity is nuanced at the threshold of both/ and southern queer identity, thus uncoupling masculinity from an assumption of straightness and creating space for future performative potentialities. Yet, my ability to safely and boldly transgress performative expectations was based on my insider status. My class privilege afforded trendy (and expensive) Alabama "gameday" outfits, and my white skin allowed me to move unmarked around UA's racially steeped campus. As such, disidentification is rendered a relatively nonrisky performance. I undoubtedly embodied the crossroads of cultural change in this narrative; however, the implications for reimagining my southern home place are limited in scope.

* * *

I (Cassidy) am in a class on race, gender, and communication when a professor, who is a Black woman from the rural South, asks me, "Do you think your family would be more upset if you came home in a queer relationship or an interracial relationship?" My gut instinct is to definitively reply, "A queer relationship." But I know it's more complicated than that. The memories of conversations had with my momma quickly come to mind, and I pause . . .

I never directly came out to my mom before she died. At the time of her death, I was in the early stages of figuring out what my sexuality meant for me. I felt as if I was something else—something not quite straight, but not quite gay—and I didn't know how to say that then. But I knew I needed to test the water to see how she might respond if I were to figure it out. I was in Tallahassee visiting her over spring break when I decided to dip a toe in to see where she stood.

I drove out of the Dollar General parking lot. We sat in silence at a red light, waiting on our turn to go left. The silence was thick as I felt the words bubbling inside my throat, wanting to escape but being held back by all kinds of internalized shame and stigma. Just as the light turned green, I blurted out, "Mom, what would you do if I liked guys *and* girls?" And I held my breath waiting for her to respond.

"I love you and that don't matter to me," she replied. It was so nonchalant that I don't even know if she looked at me when she said it. It was as if I asked her what the weather was going to be tomorrow—it just was.

My momma was one of those kinds of southerners who "wasn't racist" 'cause she was friends with Black folks. She loved my childhood best friend (who was Black), and she was close with Black people in the community. So, if you asked her if she was racist, she would surely answer "no" emphatically. I knew this about her. She used the N-word and other racially derogatory language every now and then, but her racism never manifested in "outright" discrimination, so she could easily brush off any comments about her microaggressions and oppressive language. Because of this, I was surprised by her comments when I showed her a photo of a friend from high school who was in an interracial relationship. She sneered. "If God wanted the races to mix," she said, "He'd've made everybody the same color!"

   . . . I blink and the memories fade. I'm back in the classroom, and my peers and professor are waiting on my response to her question. "Honestly, I'm not sure," I say. "I think they'd be displeased with either. Certainly they'd be the most unhappy if I was in a queer interracial relationship though." But the more I think about it, the murkier my thoughts become. Could there ever be a type of "nonnormative" (i.e., a nonmonoracially white, heterosexual, and Christian) relationship that my incredibly southern and religious family would find acceptable?

＊ ＊ ＊

Both stories shared in this section utilize conversational pause as a narrative tool to articulate the challenges connected to threshold identity performance in the South. As Keating (1996) cautions, thresholds can be dangerous and/ or unsettling precisely because they mark sites of potential conflict between dissimilar identity groups' values and beliefs. These stories overtly identify probable sites of conflict between people based on their oppositional identities, value systems, and social beliefs. These conflicts are easy to identify and relatively simple to navigate in the moment, both because they're external to ourselves and because of the significant privileges we embody (race, familial support, straight/bi-passing privilege), which protect us from many social repercussions. However, our narrative pause points to the internal conflict experienced as a result of threshold negotiation. Again, thresholds unsettle modern notions of exclusionary identity categories and force us to confront difference in complex, nonreductive ways, while also requiring us to balance potential backlash from our communities. By identifying and textually engaging these moments of threshold negotiation, we have demonstrated struggles around sexuality and place, and complicate the notion of a monolithic southern "home."

FREE BIRD

My (Cassidy's) momma once told me that "we're just poor ole country folks." She and my daddy grew up in the rural Florida panhandle, and while my daddy's family was lower-middle class, my momma's was working class. With her alcoholic father bouncing from job to job around Jackson County, she often told me how her family barely got by while she was growing up. After my parents got married in 1979, my daddy worked on tugboats traveling the Southeast undertaking the dangerous task of repairing parts of the boats that were underwater. He'd be gone for six weeks at a time and then would come home for two weeks. When he was home, my parents would ride motorcycles around the county visiting friends, selling drugs, and causing trouble. When I listen to songs like Lynyrd Skynyrd's "Free Bird," I can see them cruising in my daddy's deep red 1975 Corvette. The t-top is off, and my momma's long blond locks blow around in the wind. Taking sharp turns on dirt roads too fast, I see my momma close her eyes listening to my daddy's voice carry over the loud music as he sings "'Cause I'm as free as a bird now, and this bird you cannot change" (Lynyrd Skynyrd 1973). The cotton and soybean fields that line the dirt roads blur as they speed by.

From the narratives I've inherited from family about my parents, I understand the first thirteen years of their marriage to have been characterized by poverty, drugs, and fighting. Despite my daddy's middle-class upbringing, my parents were what many would consider "trailer-park-livin' white trash." My momma worked off and on as a waitress at a truck stop by the interstate, but even with her financial contribution they made just enough to make ends meet. The way my grandma tells it, they blew all their money on drugs. The way my momma told it, they were the most lucrative drug dealers in Jackson County, Florida. Either way, it's clear that they lived life like many impoverished country folks with little social mobility or access to resources, and in such a way that broke southern (white) respectability politics.

* * *

Ken tossed us each another walkin' beer and sent us on our way, saying, "Y'all go look at them sad folks crawlin' 'round in the mud on your way to the concert." His words of encouragement pushed us out of the campsite.

I (Michael) was invited to my first race at the Talladega Superspeedway by my college friend, Chris. His family owned a small construction company in lower Alabama and, from how they acted at Talladega, it seemed as if they were some sort of Wiregrass Region royalty. A nonstop stream of folks visited their private, RV-only campsite that day. Each time a visitor showed up, Ken tossed them a beer and offered to fry up a porkchop or some shrimp if they were hungry. Old friends sat down in the circle of camping chairs and dove into stories about the fun times they all had when they were active in the Masons and the Shriners together. Ken had led each group at one time or another and, as he told it, he was the "the best damn Potentate that Pensacola ever saw."

As Chris and I left the campsite, Ken wanted to be sure we knew that he wasn't the same as those poor folk in the general Talladega camping fields. Those folks were stuck in ankle-deep mud after a day-long thunderstorm; he had a brand-new RV with a private shower and queen-size bed. They might both be country folks, but he wasn't a "poor son-a-bitch" like them. Southern (white) respectability politics is like that—it is simultaneously straightforward and exceptionally complicated, nuanced by factors such as class and family legacy. Ken's class status afforded him (and me) a privileged disidentification with the dominant narrative of poor white folks at Talladega, while the stories I inherited from his friends around the campsite reaffirmed how a respectable southern man should behave.

* * *

It took them thirteen years, but my parents cleaned themselves up before I (Cassidy) was born. The first decade and a half of my life was spent in middle-class bliss. I had the things I needed and the things I wanted, and I didn't think too much about money. For this decade and a half, I had escaped the working-class "white trash" narrative, despite the ways my momma carried that mindset into my life. But after my daddy, our household breadwinner, died, things went downhill quickly. My momma turned back to substance use and, the way my grandma tells it, blew all our money on drugs.

I quickly learned what it meant to be "poor ole country folks" and all about the stereotypes that came with it. I saw the competing emotions of concern and judgement in the eyes of women at church, and I felt the pity of my friend's parents who simultaneously chastised my momma while offering me a place to stay or help with lunch money. I heard the way people lumped my momma and me in with the "trashy" people around town. "Trashy" had a very specific meaning in my southern community. It meant poor and it meant a lack of respectability, not to mention a lack of the "southern values" and "southern morals" that follow respectability. The societally enforced demand to embody southern respectability (like respectability politics more broadly) is, of course, an embodiment of whiteness. This "trashy" living consistently conflicted with my desired performance of respectable white southern femininity (Rennels 2015).

For a while, my momma and daddy tried to instill in me a white middle-class southern respectability, but my momma couldn't escape her own poor country girl upbringing. Trailer park girls can't be southern ladies because "the Southern Lady's code of behavior . . . is handed along directly—via observation and example"

(Tartt 1999, 101), and in my poor, country family I didn't have an example to follow. My momma's, and by extension my, lack of respectability pushed us further away from southern white ideality. I later realized that living as a "poor ole country girl" makes it difficult, if not impossible, to perform respectable southern white femininity. Thus, I was no longer able to identify with narrative inheritances that taught me what it meant to be a (white) southern woman.

* * *

Chris and I (Michael) wandered through the muddy camping fields at Talladega and eventually made it to a large, sloping hill with a small stage where a band from Dothan, Alabama, was playing covers of 1970s and '80s southern rock music. I had never seen so many people double-fisting bottom shelf whiskey and Bud Lights. Folks squeezed closer and closer to one another as the hill filled up with drunk NASCAR fans.

"Y'all want some?" An older woman wearing a cut-off T-shirt held out a repurposed two-liter Sprite bottle and poured moonshine into two blue Solo cups before we had a chance to answer. This performance of southern hospitality served as a bridge across identity markers and welcomed us into the nascent concert-field community. The woman's moonshine symbolized a sense of belonging and reflected the openness that I had seen Ken show to campsite visitors earlier that day. Clearly, southern respectability and hospitality transcended (in some ways) the campsite's class divide. It didn't matter if people were trashy, classy, or Yankees; there was a spirit of social leveling while we listened to the band play at the bottom of the hill. Yet, the crowd was made up almost entirely of white people, and the threshold spanning in which we engaged was based on less-visible markers of social difference—not race. In this way, the crowd maintained a tacit insider–outsider (racial) dichotomy, which no amount of moonshine was likely to shake.

A few minutes after arriving, the band began to play the notoriously long intro to "Free Bird." After the audience's cheers and hollerin' died down, the band leader made a request of the audience. "Y'all join me in holdin' your drinks up in the air right quick," he said. "I wanna say a prayer while we're all here together." As a nonreligious queer person, I hesitated before slowly holding up my Bud Light in my right hand. His prayer began. "It's been a rainy few days here in ole 'dega. They say that rain is a sign for a good race, but, God, I'm a little worried they're gunna cancel tomorrow if things don't clear up. So, Father God, we pray that you let the thunder rolllll tonight, so that we can hear the engines rolllll on the track tomorrow. Amen."

"Amen!" the field congregation shouted in reply. I stayed silent and took a swig of moonshine, followed by a long gulp of beer. The alcohol served as a stand-in for religious affirmation, a performative disidentification from the normative expression. Immediately the song picked up pace, and "Freebird" echoed across the crowd.

My identity as a white Alabamian is informed by the narratives I inherited from friends' family members and songs of the South. Traditionally these inheritances have served to constrain possible constructions of southern identity, limiting transgressive performance like a "bird you cannot change" (Lynyrd Skynyrd 1973). However, as this story demonstrates, it is possible to shift the way we enact our narrative inheritances to support our threshold positionalities. By observing Ken's interactions with his friends and listening to their stories at Talladega's RV-only campsite, I inherited the knowledge necessary to navigate both a stranger's offering of moonshine and a group prayer while "Free Bird" played in the background. Because I knew these social cues, I could select other moments of disidentificatory performance that nuanced my group participation without outright rejecting Talladega's dominant script.

CONCLUDING THOUGHTS

This chapter is intended to contribute to a body of scholarship that elucidates the importance of blending rhetoric with performance and autoethnography. We follow Calafell, who calls for a "privileging of the body as a way of knowing" (2014, 117), as we investigate how the "body houses [our] stories and remembers them sensually. Viscerally" (Boylorn 2014, 312). Like Boylorn, we use our bodies' stories of the South to autoethnographically build bridges towards understanding difference—both our own difference and others'. Autoethnographically investigating our identities and experiences as white queer Alabamians allows us to identify and challenge prejudices that are deeply ingrained, which often manifests subtlety (yet still violently) in ways we are conditioned not to see due to our privileged positionalities. Doing so allows us to articulate the way(s) our embodiment and performances of southern identity transgress southern respectability and contribute to a changing South, or a (re)construction of the South, that is full of promise and potential.

For southerners seeking to complicate master narratives of the South, autoethnography offers a useful rhetorical space of engaging with the self and with Others through our personal narratives. Thus, through analyzing our autoethnographies of transgressive performances of southern identity and through outing/owning our own prejudices, we work to articulate a southern identity capable of reconstructing the South, its stereotypes, and its violent past. Our narratives expose the everyday manifestations of oppression that exist within and beyond the South that are frequently overlooked in scholarship and popular media. We demonstrate the need to look towards rhetoric of the body in order to expose the ways in which identity and experience work together towards a (re)construction of the South. This (re)constructed South is one that is intersectional, complex, and complicated, and it is one in which whiteness is nuanced, deconstructed, and reinterpreted.

We are insider–outsiders of the South. We are "included" for our internalization of southern culture, white skin, and cisgender identities. But we are also outsiders—literally and figuratively. We write from outside the South, our homeplace, and we are outsiders because of the ways we depart from hegemonic southern identity. We are queer and critical (of the South's history, "heritage," and culture), and we violate norms of respectability due to our performances of gender. As our insider–outsider narratives demonstrate, this state of being comes with tension and discomfort. As our autoethnography illuminates, insider stories can be particularly useful because of our ability to implicate ourselves and others who share our identities in ways that are inaccessible by someone who isn't from the South.

It is difficult to write about the South as insider–outsiders. We do not want to contribute to narratives that demean our home region, but we want to represent our experiences honestly. And sometimes what we honestly experience in the South is—for better or worse—stereotypically southern. We want to hold the South accountable for its part in slavery, genocide, and white supremacy and to avoid defensiveness when non-southerners leverage criticism. Admittedly, it's difficult not to be defensive when one colleague after another makes one condescending remark after another about the place you grew up and still love. We also want to hold onto our love and appreciation for the South, but to do so critically and in ways that drive us toward contributing to a more equitable and socially just place.

In this way, the presentation and analysis of whiteness are central to the narratives shared in this chapter. To more fully understand our threshold performances, we honestly engaged aspects of performance that span both/ multiple sides of the metaphorical threshold—including privileged aspects of our identities. The narratives we inherited that inform our identities as white southerners often allowed whiteness to remain untroubled, unchallenged, and unnuanced as the "normative state of existence" (Dyer 1997, 3). However, analyzing whiteness through the lens of threshold theorizing, as we have done using performative autoethnography, highlights potential disidentificatory fractures in our embodiment of southern identity. Narratives of threshold performance are often ignored as mundane lived experiences. We have chosen to highlight them here because "any gesture or event—at minimum, being present in spaces of dominant discourse—can encourage radical, unpredictable personal and political change" (Forst 2017, 15). In this way, threshold performances can be a catalyst for embodiments of cultural change.

Finally, in our critique of southern exceptionalism, we do not seek to argue that all parts of the US are entirely the same. Of course, the South is shaped by its history (of anti-Blackness and slavery), just like the West is shaped by its own history (of anti-indigenousness and forced removal). However, our narratives reveal the ways in which regionalism is complex and necessitates a thick and intersectional analysis that attends to unmarked identities (like regional identification, as well as whiteness) and that is also capable of producing "more nuanced, richer, and more intricate research that captures the embodiments and lived experiences of individuals and groups inhabiting multiple identities" (Yep 2010, 174).

The southern soundscape is vibrant, storied, and instructional. Using songs about the South as entry points for our narratives of southernness, we have demonstrated the ways performative autoethnography can be used to reconstruct southern identity for transgressive and progressive purposes. Specifically, we have exemplified the ways in which our own southernness is performed as a threshold identity through our disidentification with aspects of southern identity that are oppressive and that maintain white supremacy. Focusing on thresholds in our narratives, the spaces where experiences are articulated as both/and, is particularly generative toward the process of reimagining white southern identity. Our narratives demonstrate a deviation from master narratives of southerners as hyperconservative and of the South as an exceptional space of racism and oppression unique to the United States at large. Ultimately, our narratives work to reconstruct discourse about the South in ways that reflect the complexity of southerners' lived experience.

NOTE

1. Portions of this essay were presented at the 2019 Symposium on Autoethnography and Narrative Inquiry. The authors thank those who gave them feedback from that presentation, including Robin Boylorn, Tony Adams, and Carolyn Ellis.

REFERENCES

Adams, Tony E., and Stacy Holman Jones. 2011. "Telling Stories: Reflexivity, Queer Theory, and Autoethnography." *Cultural Studies ↔ Critical Methodologies* 11, no. 2: 108–116. https://doi.org/10.1177/1532708611401329.

Alabama. 1983 "Dixieland Delight." Side B, Track 1 on *The Closer You Get. . . .* RCA Records, vinyl record.

Anzaldúa, Gloria. 1987. *Borderlands/La Frontera: The New Mestiza*. San Francisco: Aunt Lute.

Berry, J. Bill. 2000. "The Southern Autobiographical Impulse." *Southern Cultures* 6, no. 1: 7–22.

Borucki, Wes. 2003. "'You're Dixie's Football Pride': American College Football and the Resurgence of Southern Identity." *Identities: Global Studies in Culture and Power* 10: 477–94. https://doi.org/10.1080/10702890390251544.

Boylorn, Robin M. 2014. "From Here to There: How to Use Auto/Ethnography to Bridge Difference." *International Review of Qualitative Research* 7, no. 3: 312–26.

Burton, Orville Vernon. 2013. "The South as 'Other,' the Southerner as 'Stranger.'" *The Journal of Southern History* 81, no. 1: 7–50.

Calafell, Bernadette M. 2014. "Performance: Keeping Rhetoric Honest." *Text and Performance Quarterly* 34, no. 1: 115–17. https://doi.org/10.1080/10462937.2013.846476.

Conquergood, Dwight. 2013. "Beyond the Text: Toward a Performative Cultural Politics." In *Cultural Struggles: Performance, Ethnography, Praxis*, edited by E. Patrick Johnson, 47–63. Ann Arbor: University of Michigan Press.

Corey, Frederick. 1998. "The Personal: Against the Master Narrative." In *The Future of Performance Studies: Visions and Revisions*, edited by Sheron J. Dailey, 249–53. Washington, DC: National Communication Association.

Dyer, Richard. 1997. *White*. New York: Routledge.

Forst, Michael. 2017. "Kneeling AND Still Singing: Threshold Identity, Disidentification, and Invitation in U.S. American National Anthem Protest." *Kaleidoscope: A Graduate Journal of Qualitative Communication Research* 16, no. 1: 1–18.

Goodall, H. L., Jr. 2005. "Narrative Inheritance: A Nuclear Family with Toxic Secrets." *Qualitative Inquiry* 11, no. 4: 492–513.

Griffin, Larry J. 2006. "The American South and the Self." *Southern Cultures* 12, no. 3: 6–28. https://doi.org/10.1353/scu.2006.0033.

Griffin, Larry J., and Peggy G. Hargis. 2008. "Still Distinctive After All This Time: Trends in Racial Attitudes in and out of the South. *Southern Cultures* Fall: 117–41.

Holladay, Holly Willson. 2018. "Reckoning with the 'Redneck': Duck Dynasty and the Boundaries of Morally Appropriate Whiteness." *Southern Communication Journal* 83, no. 4: 256–66.

Keating, AnaLouise. 1996. *Women Reading, Women Writing: Self-Invention in Paula Gunn Allen, Gloria Anzaldúa, and Audre Lorde*. Philadelphia: Temple University Press.

Keating, AnaLouise. 2013. *Transformation Now! Towards a Post-Oppositional Politics of Change*. Champaign: University of Illinois Press.

Langellier, Kristen M. 1999. "Personal Narrative, Performance, Performativity: Two or Three Things I Know for Sure." *Text and Performance Quarterly* 19, no. 2: 125–44.

Lassiter, Matthew D., and Joseph Crespino. 2010. "Introduction: The End of Southern History." In *The Myth of Southern Exceptionalism*, edited by Matthew D. Lassiter and Joseph Crespino, 3–22. Oxford, UK: Oxford University Press.

Lewis, Cynthia, and Susan Harbage Page. 2012. "Secret Sharing: Debutantes Coming Out in the American South." *Southern Cultures* 18, no. 4: 6–25.

Lorde, Audre. 1982. *The Black Unicorn*. New York: Norton.

Luanceford, Brett. 2015. "Rhetorical Autoethnography." *Journal of Contemporary Rhetoric* 5, no. 1–2: 1–20.

Lynyrd Skynyrd. 1973. "Free Bird." Track 8 on *(Pronounced 'Lĕh-'nérd 'Skin-'nérd)*. MCA Records, compact disc.

Lynyrd Skynyrd. 1974. "Sweet Home Alabama." Track 1 on *Second Helping*. MCA Records, compact disc.

Madison, D. Soyini. 1993. "'That Was My Occupation': Oral Narrative, Performance, and Black Feminist Thought." *Text and Performance Quarterly* 13, no. 3: 213–32.

Mignolo, Walter. 2000. *Local Histories/Global Designs: Coloniality, Subaltern Knowledges, and Border Thinking*. Durham, NC: Duke University Press.

Muñoz, José E. 1999. *Disidentifications*. Minneapolis: University of Minnesota Press.

Nakayama, Thomas K., and Robert L. Krizek. 1995. "Whiteness: A Strategic Rhetoric." *Quarterly Journal of Speech* 81, no. 3: 291–309.

Pollock, Della. 1998. "Performative Writing." In *The Ends of Performance*, edited by Peggy Phelan and Jill Lane, 73–103. New York: New York University Press.

Rennels, Tasha R. 2015. "Taking Out the Trash: Using Critical Autoethnography to Challenge Representations of White Working-Class People in Popular Culture." *The Popular Culture Studies Journal* 3, no. 1 & 2: 349–63.

Ronai, Carol Rambo. 1995. "Multiple Reflections of Child Sex Abuse: An Argument for a Layered Account." *Journal of Contemporary Ethnography* 23, no. 4: 395–426.

Spry, Tami. 2016. *Autoethnography and the Other: Unsettling Power through Utopian Performatives*. New York: Routledge.

Tartt, Donna. 1999. "The Belle and the Lady." *The Oxford American* 26: 94–105.

Tlostanova, Madina, Suruchi Thapar-Björkert, and Redi Koobak. 2016. "Border Thinking and Disidentification: Postcolonial and Postsocialist Feminist Dialogues." *Feminist Theory* 1, no. 2: 211–28.

Watts, Rebecca Bridges. 2008. *Contemporary Southern Identity: Community through Controversy*. Jackson: University Press of Mississippi.

White, Steven. 2014. "The Heterogeneity of Southern White Distinctiveness." *American Politics Research* 42, no. 4: 551–78. https://doi.org/10.1177/1532673X13501855.

Yep, Gust A. 2010. "Toward the De-Subjugation of Racially Marked Knowledges in Communication." *Southern Communication Journal* 75, no. 2: 171–75. https://doi.org/10.1080/10417941003613263.

Young, Neil. 1970. "Southern Man." Side 1, Track 4 on *After the Gold Rush*. Reprise Records, vinyl record.

Chapter 9

INDIAN TRILOGY RHETORIC AND THE *MARSHALLING* OF SOUTHERN AND INDIGENOUS IDENTITIES

JASON EDWARD BLACK

I am a settler-colonial born, raised, and educated on the traditional homelands of Seminole, Miccosukee, Calusa, Tequesta, Timucuan, Chatot, Ocali, Jaega, and Tocobaga peoples (colonially known as Florida). I have lived the majority of my life in what is known as the US South (North Carolina and Alabama), lands stewarded throughout generations of Indigenous peoples from time immemorial. My scholarly, pedagogical, and activist work over two decades has involved reckoning with my privileged colonial position in these spaces, working to respect Indigenous sovereignty and to help decolonize the logics of coloniality. I am committed to labor that centers Indigenous cultures and spaces, spotlights Native agency, and seeks to unsettle colonialism, mostly in the southeastern portion of what Native American and First Nations, Inuit, and Métis people call Turtle Island. This chapter is one such emblem of these efforts.[1]

Two months before future Supreme Court Chief Justice John Marshall was born in Fauquier County, Virginia, the French and Indian War came home to rural Appalachia. The year was 1755, and the lightly settled county in central Virginia had recently caught wind of a hostile Cherokee band quickly approaching from the south. Fauquier's "pioneer inhabitants were nervous and apprehensive that autumn," as news spread from other lower colonies regarding travesties being wrought by the French and their Indigenous allies (Smith 1996, 22). Quickly, the county's chief military leader—twenty-three-year-old George Washington, a captain of the Virginia rangers—called upon the Crown to fortify the towns' boundaries. With little time to spare, the colonial governor sent troops to blindside the Cherokee force along the Monongahela River where they had been crossing. Though Washington counted among his defense some five thousand red-coated regulars ("the largest force the British had ever deployed in the colonies"), the Cherokee band retained the military advantage, having aligned with a stand of French soldiers (Fauquier County Historical Society 1922, 109). The allied force proved too strong for the Virginia rangers and the British brigades; American colonists had lost one of their first battles on the southern frontier.

The defeat presaged the inevitable confrontations colonists would engage vis-à-vis Indigenous people on the frontier.[2] The French and Cherokee ambush and the resultant "panic flight of the few survivors shattered the myth of English invincibility," while also convincing the American colonists that they had to fend for themselves (Smith 1996, 22). Gradually, frontier settler identities were partially defined in opposition to the so-called "savage" Natives who represented the very "animalism" the American colonists hoped to eclipse as they performed, within the frontier, their errand of civilization (Wilkins 1997, 11). As Ian Haney Lopez argues of this period, "race [as well as racism] was not an immanent phenomenon only in our heads, but an injurious material reality that constantly validated the common knowledge of race" (1996, 133). Ostensibly, the British defeat at Monongahela provided their own self-evident proof that Indianness was a racialized threat.

Growing up during this conflict, Marshall experienced what Richard Drinnon deems "Indian hating and empire building" at a young age (1997, 4). Marshall was born on the veritable eve of the French and Cherokee victory at Monongahela. Needless to say, Marshall was steeped in the colonial and racialist principles of frontier Virginia and was educated in its southern mores that championed white superiority.[3] Whether or not he bought into an anti-Indian ideology is difficult to determine. Marshall's papers and correspondence offer little of his views (outside of the Supreme Court) other than an obvious fascination with American Indians. For instance, in an October 29, 1828, letter to fellow Supreme Court Justice Joseph Story about southeastern expansion, Marshall illustrated his interest in a people he would later demarcate as "American wards." He noted in the letter, "I have been still more touched with your notice of the red man than the white" (2002, 94).

There remain paradoxes in Marshall's extant discourse concerning Indigenous populations. On the one hand, he deemed US forebears' military actions against American Indians debilitating and unjust. At the same time, however, he administratively reified the construction of Indigenous communities as ruthless, uncivilized, and in need of colonizing—the very roots of injustice, particularly in the South. These racialized tensions emerged in a series of cases that legal scholar Eric Cheyfitz terms the "Indian Trilogy," a sequence of decisions that produced laws governing "colonial space of Indian country even today" (2001, 14).

The Marshall era is memorialized as the tenure that helped legally "manage" the primary Five Southeastern Tribes (Cherokee, Choctaw, Chickasaw, Creek, and Seminole nations) dwelling in the US South. Interestingly, the Indian Trilogy—*Johnson v. McIntosh* (1823), *Cherokee Nation v. Georgia* (1831), and *Worcester v. State of Georgia* (1832)—partially made American Indians the only ethnicity in the United States guided by a distinct corpus of law (Wald 2000, 59). Together, Marshall's decisions in *Johnson*, *Cherokee Nation*, and *Worcester* defined, in some measure, what it meant to be American Indian.[4] At first judging the Cherokee Nation, as synecdoche for all of Native America, "neither citizens nor aliens," Marshall ensured that Indigenous people would "not be legally representable" (Cheyfitz 2001, 7). A decade later he delivered his opinion that the Cherokee Nation was an "independent," "sovereign," and "nationalist" group (*Worcester*).

Vitally, for this volume, Marshall's court might also be remembered as the one that enacted the largest number of cases supporting US federalism. Indeed, the period between 1801 and 1833 witnessed the championing of federal powers over state rights. Moreover, the period propagated a rise in cases extending the power of the Supreme Court as a legitimate agency in intervening into southern politics.

The Marshall court, thus, deployed constitutive power here within American Indian communities during the early nineteenth century. It also, though, signaled a southern identity predicated on relational conflict with the federal government, one that leveraged American Indian communities and territory as fodder for said conflict. The Indian Trilogy, I argue, moved beyond constructing Indianness alone to achieving political ends by the articulation of southern identities through federal paternalism. As James Boyd White notes, the law retains the function of constituting peoples' identities, but also of creating rhetorical communities and systems. The jurist, for instance, he writes, considers "what kind of community should we be, [we] who are talking the language of law . . . with each other, with our clients, with the rest of the world? What kind of conversation should the law constitute, should constitute law?" (1989, 34). I contend that Marshall treated *Johnson*, *Cherokee Nation*, and *Worcester* as ciphers—empty vessels "that help market" unrelated "things"—through which the court could assert its power over southern states (Ono and Buescher 2001, 26). To this end, Marshall's discourse not only reaffirmed the paternal ties between the US government and Native nations, but also "used" the Cherokee Nation to demonstrate the federal government's power.

This chapter proceeds by outlining the constitutive and paternal functions of US nationalism and its implications for American Indian nations and southern identities in the early nineteenth century. Then, each case of the

Indian Trilogy is examined for its respective role in constituting Indigenous people and southern communities.

PATERNAL NATIONALISM AND AMERICAN FEDERALISM

The constructive power of discourse hearkens to Maurice Charland's conception of constitutive rhetoric, a vital identity-builder that explains how "the people, in general, exist only through an ideological discourse that constitutes them" (1987, 141). Typically, we study constitutive rhetoric internally, as a marginalized or consummatory community scripts itself into existence in apposition to a dominant public and dominant narratives. However, constitutive rhetoric can flow top-down, as well. For instance, the process of constitutive rhetoric broadened with the work of James Jasinski, in which we find constructions of "The American subject . . . resid[ing], ironically enabled by those excluded negative others: the white middle class woman, the American Indian warrior, and the enslaved African-American. This dialectic between self and 'other' functions as a central element in this dimension of discursive constitution" (1998, 76). Constitutive rhetoric, thus, reveals a top layer of Supreme Court rhetoric: the representation of cultural identities through juxtaposition to a dominant power.

A key dynamic of US nationalism involves a heightened sense of family and an insistence on dividing a population along parent–child lines.[5] Implicit in such a division are power dynamics that advantage some and subordinate others—a social mechanism that provides parental control, typically, to white men in privileged positions, while relegating so-called others to the lowly status of childlike dependence. As Benedict Anderson argues, nations are constructed as a natural part of people's lives, and "in everything natural there is always something unchosen . . . just for that reason [nationalism] can ask for sacrifices" (1983, 131). Particularly during the nineteenth century, marginalized groups of "wards" (e.g., women, people of African descent, Indigenous populations, and immigrant enclaves) suffered oppression at the hands of sacrificial notions invoked by an American familial nationalism.

Constructing the "other" as childlike, the nineteenth-century "white father" would "break the child's tie to nature so the child could grow up" but continue an "infantilized dependence upon the white father and his fragmented workings of the liberal marketplace and bureaucracy" (Rogin 1975, 10). For women, this meant supporting the white father in the private sphere by looking after domestic affairs, especially ensuring the posterity of future generations of (even more) republican fathers; for enslaved Africans, the construction of child demanded suffering physical and social death. Similarly, American Indians were forced to sacrifice their lands, cultures, and identities in order to maintain the parent–child relationship.

American paternal nationalism certainly finds its roots in early colonial ideals regarding the United States as a providential and chosen civilization. Paternal nationalism retained increased vigor and rejuvenation, however, in the Jacksonian era as the US nation continued breaking away from Europeanism to create its own national identity. Walter Russell Mead (2002) contends that Andrew Jackson, in particular, insisted on strengthening the nation by elevating family, especially fatherhood, as a means to an end concerning slavery, Indian removal, and the fortification of sectionalism. Mead writes that Jackson's rhetoric was infused with concepts of family: "Jacksonian realism is based on the very sharp distinction in popular feeling between the inside of the folk community and the dark world without it. Jacksonian patriotism is an emotion, like the love of one's family—not a doctrine. The nation is an extension of the family. Members of the American folk are bound together by history, culture, and a common morality" (245). Early providence and paternalism combined to enhance American nationalism by allowing for white control over the continent in the name of Manifest Destiny. As a result, a white identity formed the core of the US nation. Part of this control involved the oppression of Indigenous populations in North America.[6]

Scholars have addressed several categories of paternalism, chief among them the roles of patriarch and frontiersman. Patriarchal representations "include males as 'breadwinners,' 'family protectors,' and 'strong father figures'" (Black 2005, 254). Strong fathers garner respect and authority through the heroic actions of providing for their families and protecting the familial unit from outside influences. Marshall and the Supreme Court met this outside influence on the frontier—what historian Frederick Jackson Turner called the "outer edge of the wave, the meeting point between savagery and civilization" (1894, 200–201). Interestingly, the outside influence for Marshall became southern states (Georgia, Alabama, and North Carolina) that sought control over Indigenous populations; and the frontier manifested along southern state lines versus the far western expanses of the Louisiana Purchase. The frontiersman persona placed Marshall in the role of protector concerning American Indians and the role of conqueror over Jacksonian states' rights proponents. This American frontiersman myth is vital because, as Janice Hocker Rushing contends, it is "a powerful and value-laden embodiment of cultural identity" (1986, 274). The frontier role defined early US identities in the nineteenth century, particularly because it was "the line of most rapid and effective Americanization" of the continent and its Indigenous peoples (Turner 1894, 201).

Of course, the Supreme Court, as the chief legal institution, retains vitality in constituting communities. In a recent historical account of racialized nationalism in the United States, Lopez argued that "Races are social products. It follows that legal institutions and practices, as essential components of our highly legalized society, have had a hand in the construction of race. . . . cases constitute a relatively forthright example of the role law sometimes plays in creating, rather than simply adopting racial definitions" (1996, 111). Notice here that the law is not extrasocial, but rather assists in the creation of the social and political. Seemingly, what is meant by law is "the study of ways in which character and community—and motive, value, reason, social structure, everything, in short, that makes a culture—are defined and made real in performances of languages" (White 1984, x–xi). Law is constructed through language and constitutes cultures. Therefore, we can work to interrogate the ways legal rhetoric punctuates identities.

Civilizing and assimilating American Indians became foundational to the Marshall court. Wilkins contends that "the law is masked as an absolutely essential element in moving Indian persons and tribes from an uncivilized to a civilized state" (1997, 14). These rhetorical moves manifest as the guardian–ward (or parent–child) relationship. And, like Marshall's wavering on the Indian issue, the parent–child dynamic unfolds in two ways: it could be benevolent (viewing Indians as helpless children or incompetent wards), or it could be malevolent (viewing Indian lands, resources, and political rights as commodities to be unilaterally and forcefully taken).

Moreover, the Marshall court codified a strong federalism, particularly through its reliance on Native construction to challenging a rising sense of southern sovereignty. This second layer of constitutive rhetoric illustrates the community-building function White (1989) discusses in noting that court decisions are not solely about the message of law, but also about the experience it offers the community. Part of "communal existence" involves racializing the nation through legal rhetoric, especially as "it is in this capacity to shape and constrain how people think about the world they inhabit" and to "most powerfully affect the construction of race" (Lopez 1996, 123).

It is vital to note that the leaders mentioned above—Andrew Jackson and John Marshall—were both southerners. At the same time that the former interpolated American Indians into savage and childlike roles, he too worked over time to strengthen southern mores and to punctuate southern identities as sovereign. Marshall, on the other hand, viewed Indigenous communities as less savage and more needy, but nonetheless depreciated. And, though a southerner, he championed federal power. In the maelstrom of competing constructions of American Indians and southern communities between Jackson and Marshall (representing southern and federal ethos), we find the influence of judicial law and the insistence of rhetoric as a modulator of identities in the South.

MARSHALLING AMERICAN INDIAN IDENTITIES
AND SOUTHERN COMMUNITIES

At the same time the Marshall court was adjudicating the role of Indigenous people in the United States, Jackson was tackling a dual project of Indian removal and southern strength. In May 1830, Jackson—a self-professed "Indian fighter"—signed the Indian Removal Act, a law that called for the "immediate removal of all Eastern tribes" from the southeastern United States and granted the US government "the same superintendence and care over any tribe or nation in the country to which they may remove . . . that he is now authorized to have over them at their present places of residence" (Indian Removal Act). The act retained a great deal of support from Congress, Jackson's administration, and the numerous southern white squatters ready to pounce on coveted American Indian lands in the South. Not unexpectedly, the act also enraged and mobilized Native nations and white progressives to petition Jackson, the Congress, and the Supreme Court for reconsideration of the blatantly racist legislation.[7] According to Theodore Frelinghuysen (1830), one of the two most outspoken US Senators opposed to the Indian Removal Act, Jackson's plan encouraged aggrandizement at the "expense" of cultures that not only assisted American expansion under the "guise of peace," but also settled North America long before the arrival of European colonists. He exhorted Jacksonian supporters: "[With the] Act, we find a whole people outlawed—laws, customs, rules, government, all, by one short clause, abrogated and declared to be void as if they never had been. . . . by oppressive encroachments upon the sacred privileges of our Indian neighbors, we minister to the agonies of future remorse" (312). Despite Frelinghuysen's rallying rhetoric, Jackson's plan of removal and reservationism ruled the day.

The historical record indicates myriad possibilities for why the Indian Removal Act was passed. Remini argues that "Jackson intervened in Congress to make certain that committees in the House and Senate . . . were staffed with reliable supporters of his policy" (2001, 233). Also, Jackson played the economic card by convincing Congress that removal would yield more land and hence more money for American agriculture. In addition to packing the "Indian Affairs" committee and lauding increased revenue, though, Jackson espoused a southern-centered rhetoric that championed southern interests. Jackson argued that, in "order to preserve union *lands in the South*," a mandate needed to be passed to provide for the alleviation of tensions between American Indians and "Southern citizens" of the United States (Remini 2001, 237; emphasis added). Such a tension, he noted, would eventually tear down the federal government. Ostensibly, Jackson promised a federalist plan, but he also insisted that southern states take the reins of US Indian policy.

For instance, once the Indian Removal Act was passed, Jackson maneuvered his federalist rhetoric to one of southern protection. The Five Civilized Tribes were to be removed by federal mandate, while individual states (particularly southern states) were gently urged to encroach into Indian Country to assist with removal. According to Norman Finkelstein, Jackson wanted to use southern states "to force the tribes to cede their land" more expeditiously in the wake of the Indian Removal Act (1995, 34). The Indian Trilogy involved as a unifying legal theme the questions of southern states' roles in expediting removal. Marshall questioned, in the *Cherokee Nation* case, how "to parcel out the territory of the Cherokees" and to whom the responsibility of fatherly guide would fall: the federal government or state governments (*Cherokee Nation*).

Jackson's elevated notion of southern sovereignty clashed with the strong federalism upheld by the Marshall court. Undoubtedly, Jackson's political influence in support of antifederalism, along with his adversarial relationship with the Supreme Court, affected the ways in which Marshall dealt with constituting Indigenous nations and rethinking US nationalism vis-à-vis Indigenous peoples. At least from Jackson's perspective, there existed divisiveness between his pro-state executive branch and Marshall's federalist court. Jackson worried in a March 6, 1832, letter to Colonel Anthony Butler, "If anything the Court can paralize [*sic*] the course of the executive. . . . they [the court] have never ceased to endeavor to put me down and the supreme court [*sic*] in a late decision declaring the Cherokee an independent nation, have united to embarrass me. *It all will not do*" (Jackson 1832, 415). When Jackson was running for the presidency in 1828, Marshall made the wry remark that "perhaps I should consider the election of Jackson as a virtual dissolution of the government" (2002, 94). There was no love lost between the two public men. The rift was personal, as well as political, and played out across a southern state–federal dynamic.

Marshall, indeed, glossed his readings of the Constitution with principles of federalist politics detrimental to states' rights. He understood the need to protect the federal government and its ability to foment commercial transactions from incursions by local authorities. Specifically, Marshall disagreed with southern states over issues of internal commerce, slavery, state judicial power to abrogate Supreme Court decisions, and state executive power to forge treaties with American Indian nations (Johnson and Hamilton 1995, 1253). By engaging a federalist interpretation of the Constitution, he "further defined the relationship between the Southern states and the federal government" as one of dominance for the latter (Olken 2000, 745). Contextually, the Indian Trilogy was an emblem of this sectional conflict. Most vitally, it was a stentorian signal of—and a surrogate for—southern insistences of sovereignty and territorial authority.

DENIGRATING THE RED CHILD AND BLOCKING
SOUTHERN TERRITORIAL AUTHORITY

The first Cherokee case to come to Marshall's attention was *Johnson v. McIntosh* (1823). Ironically, this case involved neither an American Indian nation or Native person nor a southern state government, but rather two white settler-colonials wrangling over control of previously held American Indian lands. In 1775, a group of British investors, including Thomas Johnson, purchased a tract of land in what is today the state of Virginia from the Piankeshaw Nation. In 1778, during the Revolution, the state of Virginia seized this tract of land. Following suit, in 1783 Virginia ceded the land to the newly created US government. Finally, in 1818, the government sold nearly twelve thousand acres to William McIntosh.[8] The sale to McIntosh provoked a lawsuit by the heirs of Thomas Johnson, who claimed the land was theirs based on trade with the Piankeshaw Nation. Ostensibly, the legal question at stake was whether the Piankeshaw Nation held land rights and subsequently could sell land, or whether the US government's annexation of the land superseded any former Indian title. The Supreme Court "found that such a sale [of the Piankeshaw] was not legal, precisely because, in the opinion of the Court, the United States held absolute title to Indian lands" (Cheyfitz 2001, 4). Thus, McIntosh held title to the land because the US government, and not a Native nation, had sold him the tract.

Marshall's justification for denying the Piankeshaw Nation land rights brings to light an early example of how the court first constituted America's "red children." Marshall codified the rule of law that "the extent of their right of alienation must depend upon the laws of dominion under which they live. . . . They are subject to the sovereignty of the United States" (*Johnson v. McIntosh*). Thereafter, American Indians became characterized as the dependents of the US nation in Supreme Court rhetoric. Moreover, racial stereotypes of the "red child" were fomented with Marshall's insistence that the government treat Indigenous people "as an inferior race of people, without the privileges of citizens, and under the perpetual protection and pupilage of the government" (*Johnson v. McIntosh*). It is precisely this rhetoric of protection and pupilage that drove the continued denigration of American Indians well into both the nineteenth and twentieth centuries. As Joy Porter argues, Marshall's decision "paved the way for further progressive infringement of independent sovereignty" (2000, 183). Casey Ryan Kelly adds that such cases endorsed the Bureau of Indian Affairs' needs over the interests of American Indians, and consequently prompted the Red Power protests of the 1960s that confronted such colonial control (2014, 170–71).

Marshall, in a sense, spoke of American Indians as "red children" through the rhetoric of discovery. He "establishe(d) the boundary" of American Indian "motives and experience" (Charland 1987, 148). In turn, Marshall then reworked and transformed his subjects—actions Charland deems vital to constitutive rhetoric—into a child-like state solely dependent on an American father (148). The doctrine of discovery asserted the idea that European Americans "discovered" North America and thus reigned supreme over not only the land's flora and fauna, but over its human occupants as well. This characterization entailed a civilizing, parental role to indoctrinate the "savages" into Christianity, European cultures, and American economies. Supplanting Indigenous traditions and sovereignty, in this respect, relates to what Todorov calls the "conquest of America" (1992, 51).

Marshall's insistence on the doctrine of discovery as law solidified the European narrative of New World conquest. Furthermore, this narrative was rife with negative identity constructions of American Indians. As Marshall noted:

> Tribes of Indians inhabiting this country were fierce savages, whose occupation was war, and whose subsistence was drawn chiefly from the forest. To leave them in possession of their country, was to leave the country a wilderness; to govern them as a brave distinct people, was impossible, because they were as brave and as high spirited as they were fierce, and were ready to repel by arms every attempt at their independence. (*Johnson v. McIntosh*)

Notice Marshall's rhetorical construction of American Indians as earthly and natural. Their subsistence derived from the "wilds" versus from cultivated land, a "civilized" replacement of the hunter–gatherer mode of survival. If Native nations were to remain in possession of these newly discovered lands—which the US government claimed as its own by divine right and Manifest Destiny—then the land would go to waste. The entire "country" would be a "wilderness," a breeding ground for brutality and godlessness (*Johnson v. McIntosh*). According to Tadd Johnson and James Hamilton, Marshall had to take into account Manifest Destiny: it "could not be ignored. Indian tribes could not be too sovereign" (1995, 1253). Extending too many rights and privileges to too many people, especially those deemed savage, would presumably weaken a strong American nationalism.

Moreover, consider Marshall's insistence on characterizing Natives as violent, war-like, and animalistic. Marshall chose these descriptors despite full knowledge of treaty-making and peace meetings. In fact, Marshall even relied on the Holston Treaty of 1791 to note how, through "civilized" negotiations, "there shall be peace and friendship between all the citizens of the United States and Indians" and how treaties as early as 1791 made it necessary "to remove the causes of war, by ascertaining [Indians'] limits and making other necessary, just, and friendly arrangements" (*Holston Treaty*). (He cited this passage in his majority opinion of the case.) Yet, despite these savage and violent characteristics, Marshall constituted American Indians in a frail, dependent light to justify ceding their lands and extending to the federal government the full right to control, sell, and possess Indigenous territories. He ensured that "Indian inhabitants are to be considered merely as occupants, to be protected," perpetual children needing the guidance and care of their "father the President" (*Johnson v. McIntosh*). All of the savage, earthly/natural, and violent identity frames that Marshall unfurled pointed to Natives as infantile and, thus, dependent on the US government to uplift them.

The primary legal consequence of *Johnson v. McIntosh* for American Indian sovereignty was the transfer of Native land ownership from tribal authority to the US government. Here, southern states were not considered as legitimate governmental parties. The exclusion of southern control over land, or at the least negotiation for it, would lead to complications in the following cases of the Indian Trilogy. The court admitted Natives were "occupants" of land, but with the caveat that "their rights to complete sovereignty, as independent nations, were necessarily diminished, and their power to dispose of the soil at their own will, to whomsoever they pleased, was denied by the fundamental principle of discovery" (Cheyfitz 2001, 1). Marshall's rhetoric pointed to a paternalism that blocked American Indian empowerment and also southern territorial control.

REARING THE RED WARD AND REMOVING SOUTHERN INFLUENCE

The second case of the Indian Trilogy, *Cherokee Nation v. State of Georgia*, strengthened American paternal federalism by confirming Marshall's early constitution of Indigenous peoples in *Johnson* and continuing the proscription of southern connections to Native land. The 1831 case retains importance to American Indian identities in that the Cherokee Nation was an actual party to the case and worried about land grants and their "character" as an independent people (Porter 2000, 91). The case is also vital in couching Marshall's valorization of federalism—though not southern authority—through paternal control over American Indians. The case came in the wake of Jackson's Indian Removal Act of 1830, which provided that the Five Civilized Tribes relocate within five years. The state of Georgia, knowing it had Jackson's support, crafted its own state laws to expedite the removal of the Cherokee Nation, in particular. The Cherokee

Nation, perhaps informed by their savvy leader, Chief John Ross, likewise knew that Marshall was intent on limiting states' rights (Black 2015). Bearing this political clash in mind, the Cherokee Nation hired former US attorney general William Wirt to represent them in challenging the Georgia laws. Here enters a formidable challenge on Marshall's part to southern territorial ethos.

The grievance forwarded by the Cherokee Nation demanded that the Supreme Court enjoin Georgia from forcibly removing them and from allowing the southern white citizens to squat on Cherokee land. Wirt noted in the case, "Cherokees were the occupants of and owners of territory in which they now reside, before the first approach of white men of Europe to the western continent" (*Cherokee Nation*). Considering this, the Cherokee Nation demanded to be recognized, Wirt continued, as "a nation of Indians, a foreign state, not owing allegiance to the United States, nor to any state of this union . . . other than their own." The state of Georgia responded by asking the court to recognize the Indian Removal Act as proof that the newly passed southern state laws were constitutional. Marshall ruled in favor of the Cherokee Nation: that is, the court protected it from any incursions into its land by Georgia. But the Cherokee Nation's victory proved pyrrhic. Marshall's opinion constituted them as "dependent wards," securing the parental rights of American Indian control to the federal government and not to individual southern states.

In order to rule in favor of enjoining Georgia from touching Cherokee land, Marshall then constructed the Cherokee Nation as reliant on the federal government, not southern states, for protection and subsistence. He first argued that they were once independent, but in the present remained subordinate to the fatherly "house" of the US government: "A people once numerous, powerful, and truly independent, found by our ancestors in the quiet and uncontrolled possession of an ample domain, gradually sinking beneath our superior policy, our arts, and our arms, have yielded their lands by successive treaties" (*Cherokee Nation*). Continuing the diminution from the *Johnson* case, Marshall reminded the Cherokee Nation that their lands were "found by our ancestors." Marshall's rhetoric took on the traditional dominating tone of US colonialism. Morris and Wander articulate the consequences of such imperialism: "America found and conquered the Native Americans, and can thus do as they see fit with their discovery" (1990, 180). Marshall also expressed no qualms that, like a child living in a father's "house," the Cherokee Nation were "beneath our superior policy, our arts, and our arms" (*Cherokee Nation*). Superiority took on two dimensions here. First, there existed the judgment that settler-colonial agency was superior to Indigenous cultures. Second, Marshall contended that all of Native America rested beneath the aegis of US political and social systems. This double meaning punctuated the parent–child dynamic. Furthermore, the notion that such political and social systems were manifested in the federal government shut down the sense that southern states were overreaching in their grabs for land.

Marshall next argued that the Cherokee Nation was neither a foreign nation nor a sovereign state, but rather a domestic "case of people" that the US government watched over. He denied the injunction against Georgia, not based on the Cherokee Nation's claim to sovereignty, but on a need for the federal government to protect Indigenous populations from southern states that could not care for the "red children." A code also existed that it was not just southern care that was in question, but also southern control of territory. Here, Marshall reiterated the neediness attached to the Cherokee Nation:

> They may, more correctly, be denominated domestic dependent nations. They occupy a territory to which we assert a title independent of their will, which must take effect in point of possession when their right of possession ceases. Meanwhile, they are in a state of pupilage. Their relation to the United States resembles that of a ward to his guardian. They look to our government for protection; rely upon its kindness and power; appeal to it for relief of their wants; and address the President as their great father. They and their country are considered by foreign nation, as well as by ourselves, as being completely under the sovereignty and domination of the United States, that any attempt to acquire their lands, or to form a political connexion [*sic*] with them, would be considered an invasion of our territory and an act of hostility. (*Cherokee Nation*)

The last sentence presents an inconsistency between Marshall's charge that a nation is neither sovereign nor foreign and his claim that an attack on American Indians would qualify as an attack on the US government. Clearly, Marshall's argument flows from the 1823 Monroe Doctrine, which was designed to protect US interests by dually "preventing European incursion" into American spheres and "defending foreign nations" from outside threats (Monroe 2002). Nevertheless, the Cherokee Nation was not deemed foreign. Moreover, the Cherokee Nation was not constructed as a domestic "state" that the US government would have a right to protect. Thus, one wonders where Marshall's decision left the Cherokee Nation and what consequence the limbo-like status he granted them had on American Indian identities beyond the nineteenth century.

Interestingly, in constituting the Cherokee Nation, Marshall also constructed the US government as a strong federal power versus a confederation of states. Jody Freeman (1991) argues that this constitutive function of the Supreme Court helped embody a federalist system and shut down southern claims to sovereign control of former Indigenous land. She maintains that the emphasis on constitutions was "not aimed solely at winning arguments but at using rhetoric in a self-conscious, community building way" (307). Marshall demonstrated this constitutive rhetoric by cleverly employing the Cherokee Nation as a cipher, a vessel used for larger purposes, in order to trump federalism over southern governance. If he declared the Cherokee Nation a subject-protectorate, the southern states would have the power to exert full control, and thus Indigenous people in general would be at the mercy of southern communities. At the same time, had he acknowledged them as foreign sovereigns, the Cherokee people would have been independent of federal control. Instead, Marshall generated an extraconstitutional political status for American Indians by characterizing them as "domestic dependents." In essence, the "domestic dependent" moniker codified them under the pupilage of the federal government, but freed them from the whims and control of southern states. Hence, Marshall's Cherokee construction allowed for a federally paternalistic hold over American Indians, while outright denying Jackson and his southern state a chance to exert their influence over Indigenous peoples and land.

Apparently to Marshall, it was enough to label the Cherokee Nation "dependent." As the US government's "children," Cherokee people would be protected at all costs—either from foreign invasion or, in the case of Georgia, from southern states wishing to annex tribal land. And Marshall's language made it appear that American Indians chose to become wards: as he contended, we took "control when they *negotiated* away their land rights" and the US government became a parental unit "when their right of possession ceases due to *their own willingness* to trade" land for security (*Cherokee Nation*; emphasis added). Therefore, he elided any imperial guilt or motive on the part of the US government and justified removal by falsely placing the onus on American Indians to decide.

In the end, *Cherokee Nation v. State of Georgia* worked to reconfirm the dominant stance of the US government in controlling and deciding the fate of American Indian territories, sovereignties, and identities.

WRESTING CUSTODY OF THE RED CHILD
FROM THE SOUTHERN STATES

The final episode of the Indian Trilogy involved the transference of American Indian identities from "domestic dependent" to "distinct community." Of course, this distinct community existed in a child-like state, always expecting to hold the hand of its US father in negotiating with states (particularly southern states that demanded "custody" over its "red" inhabitants). In *Worcester v. State of Georgia* (1832) white missionaries, who were previously arrested by Georgia authorities for visiting the Cherokee Nation in the state, brought suit to demand visitation with their Indian friends. Missionary Samuel Worcester and the Cherokee Nation pleaded to the court that they were sovereign and thus not subject to southern state law. Georgia, of course, argued that as a southern governmental body it could indeed control territorial boundaries. Of note, Georgia had recently passed a law to enjoin any white persons from meeting with the Cherokee Nation; the logic behind the law was that antiremoval missionaries might inspire American Indians to buck the Indian Removal Act and stage uprisings against the state. In the process, the fear was that antiremoval activists would diminish southern rights to land, territory being necessary to a people (i.e., "southern" people) with distinct identities and sovereign space.

The rhetorical transformation undertaken from "domestic dependent" to "distinct community" represents Marshall's strongest threat to Jacksonian southern rights. *Worcester* punctuated both the paternal rhetoric inherent in constructing American Indian identities and the constitutive power of the Supreme Court in imbuing the political character of the US government with "federal" superiority. In an inconsistent ruling, per *Johnson* and *Cherokee Nation*, Marshall shifted Native identities to "distinct community" in order to stop Georgia from blocking Cherokee–missionary relations (Olken 2000, 746). The Cherokee Nation, once again, appeared to win the day. However, Marshall's rhetoric pointed to emancipating them from a "dependent" label in order to quell southern authority and, hence, to strengthen a paternal federalism.

Marshall's rhetoric reconstituted American Indianness in order to secure the US government's custody of the Cherokee Nation. And following the familial metaphor, the reconstitution limited Georgia's custody over the nation. Marshall argued:

> The Cherokee Nation, then, is a distinct community occupying its own territory, with boundaries accurately described, in which the laws of Georgia can have no force, and which the citizens of Georgia have no right to enter, but with the assent of the Cherokees themselves, or in conformity with treaties, and with acts of Congress. The whole intercourse between the United States and this nation, is, by our constitution and laws, vested in the government of the United States. (*Worcester*)

Evidenced here is the way that Marshall denied Georgia access to Cherokee lands. Why? Not because the Cherokee Nation was sovereign—Marshall never deemed them independent or self-sufficient, but rather considered them "distinct." Instead, a southern state could not act as surrogate father because "the whole intercourse" between the US government and American Indians was "vested in the government of the United States" (*Worcester*). As a result of *Worcester*, southern "states were excluded from the Federal/Tribal relationship, and the tribes retained a very broad grant of sovereignty" inviolate save by federalist intervention (Johnson and Hamilton 1995, 1253). Allowing southern states custody would only weaken the federalist hold over Native territories.

Most poignantly, the new label of "distinct community" allowed a relationship between Indigenous peoples and the US government, not between Native nations and southern states. Marshall basically replaced the control bequeathed to the federal government by deeming the Cherokee "domestic dependents" with another form of control—a sole possession of American Indian sovereignty. Instead of having two fathers to answer to—a construct in the past that often helped Native nations tactically and wisely play southern states against the federal government—the Cherokee Nation was now to be controlled by one "great white father" (Black 2015, 53–58).

Worcester is generally considered the strongest defense of tribal sovereignty against localized, southern government. But the Cherokee Nation was simply a channel, argues Wilkins, for the case "can more accurately be understood as a defense of federal over state power" (1997, 14). He continues that *Worcester* was "the test case Marshall had been waiting for" to exert the power of federalism via the Supreme Court over the South (14). According to lore, Jackson was so incredibly angered by the Marshall decision to deem the Cherokee Nation a "distinct community" that he is known to have blurted, "'Well, John Marshall has made his decision: *now let's see him try to enforce it!*'" (Remini 2001, 257; emphasis in original). Jackson's ire reflected the obvious reduction of southern authority vis-à-vis Indian Removal and southern states–Indian relations.

Also of interest in the *Worcester* case is the fashion in which Marshall vilified the southern states via Georgia. Notice in the following his insistence on discussing Georgia's encroachment into Cherokee land an inconsistent practice: "The Acts of Georgia are repugnant to the constitution, laws, and treaties of the United States. They interfere forcibly with the relations established between the United States and the Cherokee Nation, the regulation of which, according to the settled principles of our Constitution, are committed solely to the government of the union" (*Worcester*). Again, Marshall pointed the way toward building a strong federal nationalism based on the US government's relationship with the Cherokee Nation to the detriment of southern states that would "interfere forcibly" (*Worcester*).

IMPLICATIONS: THE MULTIPLE FUNCTIONS OF CONSTITUTING PATERNAL FEDERALISM

Amid the meandering course of the Indian Trilogy, I identify the Supreme Court as a powerful agent that deploys discourse characterizing multiple identities (Black 2011). Bearing in mind the constitutive potency of the Marshall era, Priscilla Wald notes that "these cases call attention to the symbolic processes through which the United States constitutes subjects: how Americans are made" (2000, 59). Indeed, we see in these Marshall cases relational constructions among three parties: American Indian nations, the federal government, and, vitally for this book, regional identities by way of southern communities.

This reading of the Indian Trilogy attends to the legal ramifications and the historical significance of the Cherokee cases, but most importantly examines some constitutive results of Marshall's decisions. As I have argued, the Indian Trilogy exemplified a rhetoric of paternal nationalism that unearthed two related ends. To wit, the decisions in *Johnson*, *Cherokee Nation*, and *Worcester* bolstered a heightened sense of American federalism by denigrating American Indian identities to dependent and childlike, while simultaneously limiting southern authority in favor of a strong federal presence.

The first implication of this constitutive power involves the Supreme Court—through its decisions and language defending its positions—in helping to establish the identities and characterizations of cultural groups. By deeming American Indians, for instance, "domestic dependents" or "distinct communities," Marshall otherized Indigenous populations and ensured that America's "white fathers" would act as Native wardens. In this vein, Marshall assisted in constituting how American Indians would live, to what extent Native nations would retain sovereignty, and how they would be viewed as "transhistorical subjects" (Charland 1987, 140). According to Porter, such constitutive moments of Indigenous identity "makes talking about Native peoples collectively as sovereign nations difficult" based, in part, on a hegemonic memory that champions settler-colonial identities over Indigenous communities (2000, 177).

But, by concomitantly deeming southern states unable to control Native territory and to even negotiate with Indigenous nations, the Marshall court also maligned a sovereign southern ethos. Regionalism thus became a contextual factor in the matrix of decision-making regarding a strong federal power and the ascendency of a grander nationalism mandating whose voices mattered in debates over issues connected with states' rights. Clearly, regionalism was used by the Marshall court as a type of cultural currency. We learn through the Indian Trilogy that southern regionalism could be ignored or outright occluded if its presence interfered with a grand national vision. In a way, regional identity was thus *paternalized* as well. One area of further exploration might interrogate how regionalism is subordinated to both federalism and a central national imaginary in similar cases (Anderson 1983, 131). Viewing how southern regionalism and identities were "traded" for federal gains might shed additional light on the constrained spaces of the South particularly during the nineteenth century.

Speaking of the Marshall court, the second implication is that this version of the high court stands as a synecdoche of the Supreme Court as a constructivist institution. The court's incidental role in building and controlling the trajectory of public affairs resonates clearly with Marshall's support of federal powers. At least with regard to the Indian Removal Act and the guiding of American Indian nations, Marshall guaranteed that the federal government would overrule southern community privilege. He "appreciated the need for constitutional restrictions upon arbitrary local authority that jeopardized the security of commercial transactions, particularly those involving property rights and contracts" (Olken 2000, 752). The Indian Trilogy seemed to maintain the battle over federalism and southern governance, a debate that began prior to both the constitution and Constitution of the US nation. Moreover, his unique position as chief justice allowed Marshall to help construct the US government based on his personal interpretation of the Constitution. To James Boyd White's question, "what kind of community should we be, who are talking the language of law . . . ?" (1989, 34), Marshall's decisions might have resounded: a strong, central federal government. Together with his constitution of American Indians, Marshall enacted a partial construction of the US political system grounded in the backlighting of southern ethos.

Third, the Marshall court's insistence on ciphering Native nations to suppress them while concurrently using such identities to reinforce federal power to the detriment of southern states hearkens to what Laurie Whitt (1995) calls the "cultural imperialism of Native America." To Whitt, dominant cultures "enhance [their] political power, social control, and economic profit by declaring the resources of Indigenous culture to be common property" (8). Marshall employed the inventional resource of Native identities to enhance both the fatherly status of the federal government and the political dominance of federal power. Exploiting American Indian statuses (e.g., as child, dependent, and savage) for ideological purposes brings to light a cultural imperialism that works insidiously. That is, Marshall's reliance on cultural imperialism played a "politically diversionary role" that masked his federalist goals in a rhetoric of protection ("domestic dependents") of and benevolence ("distinct communities") toward the Cherokee Nation (Whitt 1995, 20). Simultaneously, Marshall deployed a logic of domination that hinged his subordination of American Indians on the need to bolster federalist power. This dual constitutive function ultimately led to dire consequences for Indigenous populations. For, as Bosmajian writes, "once the Indians were successfully defined as governmental nonentities" to be exploited at the whimsy of the white establishment, "no more justification was needed to drive them off their lands and to force them into migration and eventual death" (1973, 92).

Fourth, this chapter interrogates the role of paternalism in early nineteenth-century US–Native relations. A primary implication of exposing such paternalism, especially championed through US nationalism, is the critique of parent–child relationships. As Shawn Parry-Giles and Trevor Parry-Giles remind us, "conceptions of masculinity are not fixed, or natural, and the critical scrutiny of existing hegemonies of masculinity potentially erodes the oppression and domination that such discourses typically express" (1996, 342). Understandably, eroding Marshall's paternalistic constructions of the federal government and infantile characteristics of American Indians is beyond the scope of present social change and reform, some hundred and eighty years later. But, according to Marouf Hasian (1994), such deconstruction retains importance in understanding how our legal past connects with our legal present. The challenge for criticism in this type of case then is to be deconstructive and reconstructive. Hasian notes, "If effective social change is going to take place, it will be accomplished only by paying attention to the ways in which legal fragments operate in the pragmatic" (51). Hence, change can occur by being mindful of Marshall's rhetoric and comparing it to contemporary rulings that implicate Indigenous identities. Once cognizant of a diminutive rhetoric, such as that located in the Indian Trilogy, we can continue demystifying how the court constructs Indigenous people. Rhetoric's "revenge" on legal discourses involves employing rhetorical criticism of current legal problems while keeping in mind past legal action (Hasian and Croasmun 1996, 384). Basing our critiques on how past Supreme Courts have created, for instance, childlike and oppressed American Indian identities adds credence to criticism of more contemporary cases. Therefore, we do not fall victim to the debunking of the law in the current instant. Instead, we have evidence on which to base our reconstruction, as opposed to our "tearing down" (Lucaites 1990, 435).

Finally, this study points to some early nineteenth-century roots of oppressive treatment of American Indians—and suppressive treatment of southern authority—by way of the legal system. Elite legal bodies—especially the Supreme Court—wield incredible power in establishing and sustaining cultural identities, whether ethnic or sectional. These identities tend to benefit US nationalist interests. For contemporary American Indians who have often become assimilated, and yet sometimes live segregated from a central US nation on reservations, inclusion becomes blurred at best. Morris points out that acculturation has caused Indians to become "both Indian and White, and neither Indian nor White. Everything in their world is now in conflict—particularly their feelings about themselves, which are constituted by what they must not be . . . and what they must be" (1997, 161). S. Elizabeth Bird concurs that "American Indians are permitted only an identity they do not recognize, and which they reject with both humor and anger, making us wonder if their own tales of alternative identity will ever be told" (2001, 121). At the same time, Michael Lee has argued that federal policy sanctioned certain political maneuvers for the South and likewise proscribed others, leaving southern communities in their own version of liminal spaces (2006, 356–58).

This reading of the Indian Trilogy points out the possibility that Native sovereignties and southern identities in the US nation have been manifestly impacted by Marshall's decisions across time. This possibility might motivate future efforts to uproot and decolonize legal decisions about US–Native relations and to uncover ways southern regionalism was impacted by federalist politics.

NOTES

1. Jason Black wishes to thank Shawn Parry-Giles for reading early versions of this chapter. He also acknowledges the Catawba, Waxhaw, Cheraw, and Sugeree peoples, past and present, upon whose land this chapter was written and who are an inspiration to unsettle logics of colonialism.

2. In this article, I refer to Native communities in North America as Native American, American Indian, Indigenous nations, First Peoples, and Natives, per the current trends in American Indian cultural studies. These designations, in particular, are welcome identity signifiers according to Garroutte 2003; Mihesuah 1998; and Thornton 1998. Readers are encouraged to bear two precepts in mind. First, the proper designation of Native communities in North America remains controversial. Differences in labeling divide cultural studies scholars, rhetoricians, sociologists, anthropologists, historians, and—most importantly— Native groups themselves. Second, due to the variant descriptors accepted/rejected, I am dedicated to integrating all five primary labels. Whenever possible, I will designate populations based on their national affiliation (e.g., Cherokee Nation). Also, due to the importance of representing the fulsome context of this project, this essay often employs terms such as "savages," "red children," "tribes," "tribal," "heathen," and "hostiles" among other dubious metonyms to American Indian groups. Such labels arise from the texts of the particular eras under investigation.

3. For more on how the nineteenth-century US government and American communities supported white nationalism to the detriment of American Indian rights and sovereignty, see Bosmajian 1973; Brown 2000; Horseman 1981; Prucha 1984; Stephanson 1995; and Takaki 1990.

4. Marshall, as chief justice during the Indian Removal years, wrote the majority opinions in the *Johnson*, *Cherokee Nation*, and *Worcester* cases. It is for this reason—combined with his hermetic grip over the court at the time—that Marshall's rhetoric is the focus of this article. For more on this argument, see Newmeyer 2000; and Olken 2000.

5. For more on the importance of family to nationalism—particularly US nationalism— see Anderson 1983; Morris 1997; Rogin 1975; and Todorov 1992.

6. For more rhetorical studies on how diminutive constructions of "Indianness" have affected Native identities and how American Indians have challenged these constitutions, see Black 2007; Lake 1983; and Stuckey and Murphy 2001.

7. For more on resistance to removal, see Black 2007; Black 2009; Black 2015; and Kelly and Black 2018.

8. William McIntosh, party to this case, was a Scottish fur trader and not the William McIntosh who was a principal chief of the Creek Nation in the 1830s. The names are coincidental.

REFERENCES

Anderson, Benedict. 1983. *Imagined Communities: Reflections on the Origins and Spread of Nationalism*. London: Verso.

Bird, S. Elizabeth. 2001. "Indians Are like That: Negotiating Identity in a Media World." In *Black Marks: Minority Ethnic Audiences and Media*, edited by Karen Ross and Peter Playdon, 105–122. Aldershot, England: Ashgate Press.

Black, Jason Edward. 2005. "Authoritarian Fatherhood: Andrew Jackson's Early Familial Lectures to America's 'Red Children.'" *Journal of Family History* 30, no. 3: 247–64.

Black, Jason Edward. 2007. "Remembrances of Removal: Native Resistance to Allotment and the Unmasking of Paternal Benevolence." *Southern Communication Journal* 72: 185–203.

Black, Jason Edward. 2009. "Native Resistive Rhetoric and the Decolonization of American Indian Removal Discourse." *Quarterly Journal of Speech* 95, no. 1: 66–88.

Black, Jason Edward. 2011. "Plenary Rhetoric in Indian Country: The Lone Wolf v. Hitchcock Case and the Codification of a Weakened Native America." *Advances in the History of Rhetoric* 11: 59–80.

Black, Jason Edward. 2015. *American Indians and the Rhetoric of Removal and Allotment*. Jackson: University Press of Mississippi.

Bosmajian, Haig. 1973. "Defining the 'American Indian': A Case Study in the Language of Suppression." *The Speech Teacher* 21: 89–99.

Brown, Dee. 2000. *Bury My Heart at Wounded Knee: An Indian History of the American West*. New York: Henry Holt.

Carter, Dan. 2000. *The Politics of Rage: George Wallace, the Origins of the New Conservatism, and the Transformation of American Politics*. Baton Rouge: Louisiana State University Press.

Charland, Maurice. 1987. "Constitutive Rhetoric: The Case of the *Peuple Quebecois*." *Quarterly Journal of Speech* 73: 133–50.

Cherokee Nation v. Georgia, 30 U.S. 1 (1831).

Cheyfitz, Eric. 2001. "Doctrines of Democracy." *Journal of Early American Life* 2, no. 1: 1–14.

Drinnon, Richard. 1997. *Facing West: The Metaphysics of Indian Hating and Empire Building*. Norman: University of Oklahoma Press.

Fauquier County Historical Society. 1922. "The Genesis of the Frontier." *Bulletin of Fauquier County Historical Society* 1: 109–122.

Finkelstein, Norman. 1995. "History's Verdict: The Cherokee Case." *Journal of Palestine Studies* 24: 34–50.

Freeman, Jody. 1991. "Constitutive Rhetoric: Law as a Literary Activity." *Harvard Woman's Law Journal* 14: 307.

Frelinghuysen, Theodore. 1830. "Frelinghuysen's Remarks, April 9, 1830." In *Gales & Seaton's Register of Debates in Congress*, Senate (April 9, 1830), 312.

Garroutte, Eva Marie. 2003. *Real Indians: Identity and the Survival of Native America.* Berkeley: University of California Press.

Hasian, Marouf. 1994. "Critical Legal Rhetorics: The Theory and Practice of Law in a Postmodern World." *Southern Communication Journal* 60: 44–56.

Hasian, Marouf, and Earl Croasmun. 1996. "Rhetoric's Revenge: The Prospect of a Critical Legal Rhetoric." *Philosophy and Rhetoric* 29, no. 4: 384–99.

Holston Treaty with the Cherokee, 7 Stat. 39 (1791).

Horseman, Reginald. 1981. *Race and Manifest Destiny: The Origins of American Racial Anglo-Saxonism.* Cambridge, MA: Harvard University Press.

Indian Removal Act, 1830, *United States Statutes at Large,* 21st Congress, Sess. 1, Ch. 148, 1830.

Jackson, Andrew. 1928. "Letter to Colonel Anthony Butler, March 6, 1832." *The Correspondence of Andrew Jackson,* vol. 4. Edited by John Spencer Bassett. Washington, DC: Carnegie Institution of Washington.

Jasinski, James. 1998. "A Constitutive Framework for Rhetorical Historiography: Toward an Understanding of the Discursive (Re)Constitution of 'Constitution' in The Federalist Papers." *Doing Rhetorical History: Concepts and Cases,* edited by Kathleen J. Turner, 72–94. Tuscaloosa: University of Alabama Press.

Johnson, Tadd M., and James Hamilton. 1995. "Sovereignty and the Native American Nation: Self-Governance for Indian Tribes—From Paternalism to Empowerment." *Connecticut Law Review* 27: 1253.

Johnson v. McIntosh, 21 U.S. 543, 5 L.Ed. 681, 8 Wheat. 543 (1823).

Kelly, Casey Ryan. 2014. "Détournement, Decolonization, and the American Indian Occupation of Alcatraz Island (1969–1971)." *Rhetoric Society Quarterly* 44, no. 2: 168–90.

Kelly, Casey Ryan, and Jason Edward Black. 2018. "Introduction." In *Decolonizing Native American Rhetoric: Communicating Self-Determination,* edited by Casey Ryan Kelly and Jason Edward Black, 1–24. New York: Peter Lang.

Lake, Randall. 1983. "Enacting Red Power: The Consummatory Function in Native American Protest Rhetoric." *Quarterly Journal of Speech* 69: 127–42.

Lee, Michael. 2006. "The Populist Chameleon: The People's Party, Huey Long, George Wallace, and the Populist Argumentative Frame." *Quarterly Journal of Speech* 92, no. 4: 355–78.

Lopez, Ian Haney. 1996. *White by Law: The Legal Construction of Race.* New York: New York University Press.

Lucaites, John Louis. 1990. "Review Essay: Between Rhetoric and the 'Law'—Power, Legitimacy, and Social Change." *Quarterly Journal of Speech* 76: 435–49.

Marshall, John. 2002. "To Joseph Story, May 1, 1828." *Papers of John Marshall,* vol. 11. Edited by Charles F. Hobson, 94. Chapel Hill: University of North Carolina Press.

Mead, Walter Russell. 2002. *Special Providence: American Foreign Policy and How It Changed the World.* London: Routledge.

Mihesuah, Devon. 1998. *Natives and Academics: Writing about American Indians.* Lincoln: University of Nebraska Press.

Monroe, James. 2002. "Monroe Doctrine—Annual Message of 1823." In *A Documentary History of the United States,* 7th ed., edited by Richard D. Heffner, 96–98. New York: Signet.

Morris, Richard. 1997. "Educating Savages." *Quarterly Journal of Speech* 83: 152–71.

Morris, Richard, and Phillip Wander. 1990. "Native American Rhetoric: Dancing in the Shadows of the Ghost Dance." *Quarterly Journal of Speech* 76: 164–91.

Newmeyer, R. Kent. 2000. "Law and Character: John Marshall as an American Original— Some Thoughts on Personality and Judicial Statesmanship." *University of Colorado Law Review* 1365.

Olken, Samuel. 2000. "Chief Justice John Marshall and the Course of American Constitutional History." *John Marshall Law Review* 743 (Summer).

Ono, Kent, and Derek Buescher. 2001. "Deciphering Pocahontas: Unpackaging the Commodification of an American Indian Woman." *Critical Studies in Media Communication* 18: 23–43.

Parry-Giles, Shawn, and Trevor Parry-Giles. 1996. "Gendered Politics and Presidential Image Construction: A Reassessment of the Feminine Style." *Communication Monographs* 63: 337–53.

Porter, Joy. 2000. "Native Americans: The Assertion of Sovereignty and the Negotiation of Citizenship and Identities." In *Federalism, Citizenship, and Collective Identities in U.S. History*, edited by Cornelius A. Van Minnen and Sylvia Hilton, 180–98. Amsterdam: VU Boekhandel University Press.

Prucha, Francis Paul. 1984. *The Great Father: The United States Government and the American Indians*, unabridged. Lincoln: University of Nebraska Press.

Remini, Robert V. 2001. *Andrew Jackson and His Indian Wars*. New York: Viking.

Rogin, Michael Paul. 1975. *Fathers and Children: Andrew Jackson and the Subjugation of the American Indian*. New York: Knopf.

Rushing, Janice Hocker. 1986. "Mythic Evolution of the New Frontier in Mass Mediated Rhetoric." *Critical Studies in Mass Communication* 3: 265–96.

Smith, Jean Edward. 1996. *John Marshall: Definer of a Nation*. New York: Henry Holt and Company.

Stephanson, Anders. 1995. *Manifest Destiny: American Expansionism and the Empire of Right*. New York: Hill and Wang.

Stuckey, Mary E., and John Murphy. 2001. "By Any Other Name: Rhetorical Colonialism in North America." *American Indian Culture and Research Journal* 25: 73–98.

Takaki, Ronald. 1990. *Iron Cages: Race and Culture in 19th Century America*. New York: Oxford University Press.

Thornton, Russell. 1998. *Studying Native America: Problems and Prospects*. Madison: University of Wisconsin Press.

Todorov, Tzvetan. 1992. *The Conquest of America: The Question of the Other*. New York: Harper Perennial.

Turner, Frederick Jackson. 1894. "The Significance of the Frontier in American History." In *Annual Report of the American Historical Association for the Year 1893*, edited by S. P. Langley. Washington, DC: Smithsonian.

Wald, Priscilla. 2000. "Terms of Assimilation: Legislating Subjectivity in the Emerging Nation." In *Cultures of United States Imperialism*, edited by Amy Kaplan and Donald Pease, 59–84. Durham, NC: Duke University Press.

White, James Boyd. 1984. *When Words Lose Their Meaning: Constitutions and Reconstitutions of Language, Character, and Community*. Chicago: University of Chicago Press.

White, James Boyd. 1989. *Heracles' Bow: Essays on the Rhetoric and Poetics of the Law.*
    Madison: University of Wisconsin Press.
Whitt, Laura Anne. 1995. "Cultural Imperialism and the Marketing of Native America."
    American Indian Culture and Research Journal 19: 1–33.
Wilkins, David E. 1997. *American Indian Sovereignty and the Supreme Court: The Masking of
    Justice.* Austin: University of Texas Press.
Worcester v. State of Georgia, 31 U.S. 515 (1832).

Part III

Reconstructing the South in New Locales

Chapter 10

OLD SOUTH RHETORIC RECKONING

The Case of Kappa Alpha's Old South Balls

WHITNEY JORDAN ADAMS

As a native Appalachian growing up in Charleston, West Virginia, I relocated with my family to Aiken, South Carolina, when I was still in high school. After graduation, I first attended a small liberal arts college in Ohio. I then ended up transferring to and graduating from the University of South Carolina, which was followed by earning a master's degree from the College of Charleston in Charleston, South Carolina, and a doctoral degree from Clemson University in Clemson, South Carolina. As a West Virginian, I am certainly an outsider to the South, but obtaining all of my degrees from institutions in South Carolina has given me a closer look at the region. My time at the University of South Carolina, back in 2007, provided, unknowingly at the time, a basis for part of this chapter. I hope that my work in antiracist pedagogy continues to inspire individuals to rethink and examine their relationship with the past, including symbols and events that promote division and racism.[1]

I am from Appalachian West Virginia. There, southern identity is often articulated by a "nothing can be done to change your lot" mentality of ahistorical white poverty, articulated in works like J. D. Vance's highly touted *Hillbilly Elegy* (2016). However, my time in South Carolina afforded me a closer look at "Old South" culture, one my Appalachian background of "learned helplessness" (as Jennifer Senior [2016] termed it) did not specifically revere or celebrate. And yet some of those same common persuasive icons and arguments (or "loci," from the Roman rhetorical tradition) circulated as a means to defend an outsider status. For example, I specifically recall the Confederate flag being sold at a flea market in Milton, West Virginia, a place I frequented with my nana as a child.

The University of South Carolina put me in contact with various layers of racialized memory. On a campus where over 10 percent of undergraduate students identify as African American (University of South Carolina n.d.), I observed another group of students, those affiliated with the all-white Kappa Alpha fraternity, walk around with an image of Confederate General Robert E. Lee over a Confederate flag emblazoned on their T-shirts. The campus is mere blocks from the State Capitol dome where the flag was raised in 1961, a gesture both opposing the civil rights movement and celebrating the one hundredth anniversary of the Civil War. The flag flew on these grounds until it was removed a month after the massacre of nine Black church members at Emanuel AME Church on June 17, 2015 (Kenneally 2015). Perhaps due to the fraternity's ambivalent or ironic relationship to white terror, Lee on the T-shirts was depicted wearing Ray-Ban sunglasses. At the University of South Carolina, the viewer is not supposed to take Lee's violent slaveholding or his treason for the cause of slavery and white supremacy seriously.

The Kappa Alpha Order (KA) has one hundred and fifty chapters in the southern United States and seventeen beyond the region ("Active Chapters" n.d.). With the fraternity's being founded at Washington and Lee University, Lee himself is dubbed the spiritual founder of the organization (a tradition since 1923), and the root organization (Kuklos Adelphon) is shared with the Ku Klux Klan. Although the fraternity was founded in Virginia, the organization is considered one of the most prestigious fraternities at universities in South Carolina, as several alumni have ties to state and national government. For example, the University of South Carolina page on the Kappa Alpha website lists former congressmen Robert W. Hemphill and Floyd Spence as two of its distinguished alumni ("Rho Chapter" n.d.).

KA members today would likely be quick to differentiate Kappa Alpha, with its "gentlemanly" respect for Lee, from the virulent racism of the Klan—a conclusion based on my conversations with past and current members. Yet the preservation of antebellum ritual, frequent reference to racist Lost Cause mythology, and continual racist incidents by individual members and sometimes small groups frustrate such distinctions for its members. In fact, as I was making final edits to this chapter, a group of University of Mississippi KAs shared a photograph of themselves with rifles around the bullet-ridden roadside sign memorializing Emmett Till (Vigdor 2019), a sign described by Dave Tell in another chapter of this book.

This chapter interrogates the preservationist rhetoric that allows such horrific acts of memory vandalism and brotherly defenses of casual or "cool" racism, as seen in the sunglass-wearing Lee. Part of this preservationist discourse is not surprising to scholars of commemoration and communication. As Stuart Towns (2012) suggests in *Enduring Legacy: Rhetoric and Ritual of the Lost Cause*, rituals such as Confederate Memorial Day, Confederate veteran reunions, and the ongoing dedication of Confederate monuments propagate a white southern worldview necessary for a Lost Cause narrative. Yet what is different about KA's deployment of Lee and the flag is its lack of reference to a broader political or social Confederate commemoration or explicit white supremacist politics. In short, it survives as a monologic rhetoric, within the guise of fraternal "tradition," to shut down engagement with marginalized voices in the context of the university. This rhetorical strategy will become clearer in this chapter through the review of forums where KA members and their allies reply to accusations of racism and upholding an ideology of systemic oppression.

Because this phenomenon occurs on university campuses, the KA rhetorical situation provides the opportunity for a pedagogical intervention. This chapter will analyze KA's history and key symbols, as well as a recent forum in reaction to the ending of Old South balls, a traditional practice of the fraternity. From this analysis emerges an interrogation of what I call "frozen loci"—stagnated ideas and ideology that can be fractured and eventually dismantled through pedagogical practices. The essay specifically pulls from Margaret J. Wheatley's (2002) theory of the pedagogical "disturbance" to foreground openness and listening in the classroom, but goes further by presenting concrete practices related to legacies of slavery and antiracist strategy.

Kappa Alpha's frozen loci are distinctive, as the arguments provided by fraternity documents, social events, and social media postings all are ironically detached from a broader antebellum framework. Increasingly, the organization cuts out even more of that context, as with the end of occasional wearing of Confederate uniforms in 2010 ("Kappa Alpha Laws" n.d.) and discouraging chapters from holding Old South balls in 2016 (Ingram 2020), pretending the organization's racist activities can escape media censure just by excising the most obvious Lost Cause connections. In this way, white male students looking for a sense of belonging may find the surrogate features of whiteness sufficient to join—the privilege of a mostly or all-white set of friends, icons, and founding dates from prior centuries, or an occasional gesture toward "the South." This shrouded and piecemeal presentation of history is not unique to KA, but is frequently encountered in fraternities, whose primary function is social and whose exclusive privileges are only fully realized after time in the organization. Reasoning into broader aspects of southern history is mostly lost in the defensive arguments encountered in this study of an online forum.

Issues concerning what happens to unchecked nostalgia have been widely analyzed in literary studies. Rafael Miguel Montes delineates the plight of unchecked nostalgia as it "locks identities in place and . . . [arrests] forward progress in the social and historical arena" (qtd. in Glassman 2006, 224). Similarly, Tara McPherson suggests in *Reconstructing Dixie: Race, Gender, and Nostalgia in the Imagined South* that locations become frozen "in the service of nostalgia" (2003, 129). This stagnation of identity and location is shown in this chapter to be especially fragmentary, nonobvious, and ironically thin in the context of college campuses. Rather than receiving a complete antebellum "world," college students are often happy just to defend white privilege and its icons devoid of a broader context or historical metanarrative. Faculty have an important role to liberate students from stunted ideas about gender, race, and labor contained in the myths of a world that made female and Black labor invisible.

THE "FORGOTTEN" HISTORY OF KA

From its founding to 2010, the Kappa Alpha fraternity had initiated over 150,000 members (Huston 2010). KA's influence on the cultural makeup of some southern college campuses is undeniable, yet scholars of southern history and culture have done little to include them alongside the Klan or Confederate reenactment groups as primary narrators of the Lost Cause. KA is considered one of the most popular fraternities at many southern universities, with 122 active chapters ("Active Chapters" n.d.). The organization's popularity is also partly due to its affiliation with the Lexington Triad (also referred to as the Southern Triad)—a group of fraternities with some of oldest origination dates, in the midst of southern Reconstruction. Historical roots in white brotherhood form a strong bond among white students looking for friendship based on status, gender, and race today. Furthermore, as historian John M. Coski (1996) argues, KA itself exists as a sort of Confederate memorial organization. Yet, given recent moves of the organization to distance itself from use of the Confederate battle flag as an official symbol and from Old South balls as its iconic social event, I argue that such memorialization is incomplete. Rather, iconography forms a bond itself, in circulating frozen loci that breed white resentment of critique.

The first fraternity, Phi Beta Kappa, was founded at the College of William and Mary on December 5, 1776 ("Phi Beta Kappa" n.d.). American fraternities originally began as social clubs and debating groups, bringing together young men with common interests ("Phi Beta Kappa" n.d.). Although fraternity life flourished in American universities, many chapters halted during the Civil War as most young men volunteered for battle. Kappa Alpha was originally founded as Phi Kappa Chi in 1865, at the close of the Civil War, at Washington College (now Washington and Lee University) by James Ward Wood, William Archibald Walsh, and brothers William Nelson Scott and Stanhope McClelland Scott ("Our KA Heritage" n.d.).

Samuel Zenas Ammen is credited as the fraternity's practical founder and is given special credit as shaping the organization in the early days ("Samuel

Zenas Ammen" n.d.). Ammen and founder Wood began to see themselves as an order of Christian knights, with focus also placed on the practices of the ancient Order of Knights Templar. In searching for a leader to center the organization around, Robert E. Lee became an obvious choice. The fraternity's assertion of noble Christian values of white supremacy and battlefield valor led to its choosing Lee as spiritual founder in 1923. Washington College had been renamed Washington and Lee following the death of Lee, considered "the school's most illustrious president" ("Our KA Heritage" n.d.). Kappa Alpha considers Robert E. Lee the embodiment of what it means to be a "southern gentleman," and members therefore not only embrace him as a southern icon but also as a kind of sacred pillar of (white Christian) masculinity.

Lee's connection to the Confederate flag helps us understand how it made its way into KA iconography. Robert E. Bonner's *Colors and Blood: Flag Passions of the Confederate South* describes proposed designs for the first Confederate flag: for example, some hoped the Confederacy would unfurl a banner that would "make clear that the Confederates were establishing a proudly proslavery republic" (2018, 48). A group from employees of the South Carolina Rail Road Company suggested a design that, according to Bonner, "displayed Black slaves picking cotton on one side of its eighteen-foot length and slaves rolling cotton bales on the other" (24). Instead, the original Confederate flag, also known as the Stars and Bars, was used as a more coded form of its inheritance of the American tradition, implicitly claiming that a slaveholder republic was closer to the founders than northern democracy. Yet, its visual proximity to the US flag caused confusion on the battlefield. The design of the Confederate flag we know today, explains Bonner, was adopted from General Lee's northern Virginia army. Due to Lee's position as the inspiration for the fraternity and his role as founder of the flag, members of Kappa Alpha Order developed an enthusiasm for the Confederate battle flag.

KA chapters at the University of Mississippi, Louisiana State University, the University of Alabama, and the University of Georgia served as main forces in reintroducing the flag as a popular symbol in the university culture of the South in the 1940s and 1950s, supporting its rise from that time and into the 1960s to statehouse domes and state flags (Cobb 2007). Coski reports that KA students displayed the flag after delegates returned from the 1948 Dixiecrat Convention at the University of Mississippi (1996, 232–33). Throughout the twentieth century, Coski reports, KA students flew the flag to clearly oppose integration and desegregation, including as a means to terrorize Black athletes on opposing teams. The image of the flag dominated fraternity T-shirts, flasks, and coolers, with the symbol becoming a sort of status symbol of white privilege affiliated with Kappa Alpha. And yet, based on my experience, few students in the organization are likely to know this origin story; rather, students defend the icons *against* being associated with racism or slavery's cause, just as an often-derided icon of a southern fraternity.

Fraternity culture also brings forward the issue of multigenerational ethnic identification. Even more than avowed or explicit white supremacist organizations, in which members make strong ideological choice for entry, plenty of KAs join because of their fathers' legacy in the organization. Herbert J. Gans (1979) argues that symbols become more important from generation to generation. Hegemonic white antebellum memory making in this sense can continue without individual fraternity members having a strong case to make for a return to the "Grand Old South," as well as against strong feedback that the symbol is indeed deeply intertwined with racial terror.

Eighty percent of African Americans polled in 2017 said they saw the flag as a signifier of hate (Jones 2017). Decontextualized from history and without Black friends or relatives, the "heritage not hate" argument becomes the binary logic by which the flag becomes a frozen locus. As Rebecca Watts (2007) has also pointed out, pushback against southern identity continues to cocreate that identity. In this instance, rather than an explicit attack on desegregation, young men are asked to associate themselves with a chain of older men who have been willing to defend the symbol. As Watts explains, when the national organization, with a better understanding of the flag's history and contextual logic (including, we hope, contact with African American individuals), decided to phase out use of the emblem, members affirmed their attachment to this band of brothers and voiced their frustrations with what they saw as white erasure. What is significant here is that the national organization of Kappa Alpha can cancel historical icons in a way that groups like Sons of Confederate Veterans cannot. Rather than Lost Cause metanarratives, white supremacist identification is possible within KA through resentment of change. The continued feeling of being the imagined victim within elite academic institutions maintains brotherhood.

That feeling of being "robbed" of white supremacy's icons is even clearer in the case of KA's social functions. The *Gone with the Wind*-style formal events became an important invented tradition. These events promote what McPherson terms "lenticular" logic, in which "the past is partitioned from the present, black from white, old racism from new" (2003, 28). Adapted as a KA ritual in 1939 at Mercer University, typical balls included period clothing by men and women ("Kappa Alpha Fraternity at Wake Forest" 1964). At Florida State University (FSU), historian Abel Bartley revealed to me, during an interview in 2018, the very pointed and intentional hiring of all African American servers for these events; as an enticement to such humiliating work in the 1980s, the FSU KA chapter offered Black students enough compensation for a semester's tuition. As charity, such wages showed how KAs viewed their position—a graceful remembering of past indignities tied to present paternal "uplift." If Black students were only willing, through such humiliation at the hands of white privilege, they could better themselves—directly recalling Jim Crow arguments of white benevolence.

Ralph Ellison's story about the "battle royal" in *Invisible Man* (1995) demonstrates the cultural humiliation felt by African Americans in this position. As a teenager, the Black narrator is tricked into taking part in the battle as entertainment for white men. He is blindfolded and instructed to pummel other young Black men until a victor is declared. Following the fight, golden coins are thrown on a rug wired with an electrical current, and the young men are shocked as they reach for the coins, much to the amusement and delight of the drunken white men of the town. Ellison notes, "All of the town's big shots were there" (17)—all of the so-called pillars of the town's white community.

In the 2000s, Bartley, also in our interview, revealed how the targeted hiring of African American men for the KA's Old South balls finally stopped or at least was made implicit in the form of integrated staff (even as many private catering companies employed Black staff at low wages). However, the Old South balls continued and became more self-referential, with promotional materials and T-shirts recalling Ellison's "big shots"—men of importance invited to attend to southern tradition. After the battle royal, Ellison's (1995) young narrator is given a scholarship to a Black college, although his white benefactors never allow him to forget that his opportunities are dependent on their charity. In somewhat similar ways, Old South balls continued to promote this dependence on white "charity" in which Black servants could increase their own value only by their service to the white southern elite.

Women invited to Old South KA balls were expected to dress in antebellum-style dresses, complete with lace parasols—an event I observed from afar at the University of South Carolina. This practice relates to the notion in which privileged southern white women, as McPherson (2003) explains, were expected to reproduce plantation culture as delicate flowers dependent on Black servants. By keeping this tradition alive, these young women (whether knowingly or not) were participating in a modern rendering of what McPherson describes as making certain social relations invisible, especially those dealing with race (23). The white southern lady is always racialized, with her existence predicated on the existence of a Black enslaved female who made her dress and lifestyle possible. As I observed at the University of South Carolina, elaborate female dress of the antebellum period became fetishized at the KA balls, with young women paying large sums of money to have taffeta dresses custom-made, complete with hoop skirts. Elizabeth Boyd, author of *Southern Beauty: Race, Ritual, and Memory in the Modern South,* claims that such dress itself delineates a "choreography of exclusion" (qtd. in Makaris 2017). Even if freed Black women claimed some of this fashion as their own, as Makaris writes, too little of today's performances serve that disruption. "European" wealth signified plantation wealth, especially when fraternity members sometimes dressed in Confederate "greys," paying homage to the uniforms of Confederate soldiers.[2]

In light of the Confederate flag removal in South Carolina following the June 2015 massacre at Emanuel Church in Charleston, Kappa Alpha declared in January 2016 that Old South Balls would no longer be condoned (Regester n.d.). According to Regester, Larry Stanton Wiese, the national executive director of KA, sent out an email to the chapters announcing a "Regulations Update." "OLD SOUTH, CHAPTER CANNONS, CONFEDERATE UNIFORMS, AND PARADES," Regulation R-16–113, states in relation to Old South balls that "Chapters shall not sponsor functions with the name Old South or functions with any similar name. All functions and activities must be conducted with restraint and dignity and without trappings and symbols that might be misinterpreted and objectionable to the general public" (qtd. in Regester). Without naming white supremacy or indicting the Lost Cause metanarrative, the national organization gave the possibility of others' discomfort as the reason for change. Such a framing—of changing course to satisfy outsiders' "misinterpretation"—was a perfect cue to set off white resentment rhetoric, posted in online forums.

READING THE FORUM

The official notice from KA's executive director received resentment responses posted on the website Total Frat Move (TFM; https://totalfratmove.com/total -frat-move/), which caters to young, mostly white men in fraternities across the US. A visit to the site's homepage uncovers what one might expect on a platform dedicated to all things "frat." The homepage, at the time of this writing, featured the tag line "COLLEGE IS CRAZY," with a space to "submit your best photos and videos." Photos included a game of beer chess and a young man passed out, presumably from a night of drinking, with Sharpie markings on his face. In a section titled "TFM Girls," "the hottest college girls in the country" are "featured" daily. In addition to these sections, one can also find blog posts and "articles" concerning various facets of fraternity life. After I sought and was denied access to KA's archives and internal conversations, I used the postings on this website about the end of KA Old South balls (Regester n.d.) as a way to analyze discourses within the group. I last accessed these postings on March 6, 2019; they have subsequently become removed from the Total Frat Move website.

Pantomiming states' rights rhetoric, students and KA members disliked the notion of being forced to move forward by the executive branch of their organization (Regester n.d.), perhaps mirroring deeply rooted suspicions of the federal government. In his post that generated others' comments, Dan Regester explains: "Girls get fucking STOKED to get all dolled up in those brightly colored, ridiculously large Victorian dresses with hoop skirts, giant floppy Southern belle hats, and—for the overachievers—those useless lace umbrellas that serve virtually no purpose other than to look more regal. Seriously, they love it." He continues throughout the post to flip his tone between informative reporting and insider racism and sexism: "Overall, it's a typical formal weekend to commemorate KA's principles of courtesy, graciousness, and open hospitality. So essentially a weekend where you get blown while wearing a paisley ascot and top hat." Facetiously complimenting KA's national office for ending the commemoration of the antebellum period, which he calls a "really shitty time period for a certain group of people" (referring to African Americans), he calls on KAs to "squeeze in all your antebellum fetishes" and ends by commenting on all the people who "get offended about get offended [*sic*] over anything related to your organization."

Regester's sophomoric post created an opportunity for even more unfiltered, anonymous commentary. Of the fifty comments, the ones that appear to come from KA members themselves (with "we/our" prepositions or self-identification) are the following:

Dan Regester-edsexoffender: Wow, next they are gonna change our spiritual founder from Robert E. Lee to Martin Luther King

ColonelRebForever: Just another example of the fleecing of the South. The liberals are hard at work to turn our nation inside out. The fight isn't coming–it's here now.

Prex8390: 30 years from now, all public institutions that bear the name of a white man such will be changed to Martin Luther King or Trayvon Martin. Every elementary school in America will indistinguishable

MarkDaniels: Problem number one is KA having our Executive Council meeting in San Francisco.

TM1215: I am a KA alum and fuck those fucking pussies in VA that have fallen to their knees and swallow Obama's brown load. Every chapter should print the largest "LONG LIVE OLD South" banner possible and fly it from airplanes until January 18.

Captain_Decatur1865: Next we'll be giving bids to women and having Tupperware parties.

RustyFlask123: They said you couldn't have Old South but they never said you couldn't have a plantation/slave owner themed party. Loopholes.

VanillaBeanFrat: Should I stop wearing cotton?

Supertank156: I'm a KA alum . . . I'm going to throw a huge "old South" party here in Louisiana. All of you fuckers are invited! Fuck this BS!

(And in response to an African American women who wrote, "KA is actually irrelevant anyways[;] there are many other fraternities that actually have values.") Supertank156: KA does have values! sorry we are pissed Blacks can be racist and whites can't even be proud of our heritage. And I'm not talking about slavery. Maybe you should sign up for TFM-SWAC and leave us be. (Regester n.d.)

Three main themes I have termed "frozen loci" of white southern argument run through these statements. First and most clearly, the fear of a majority nonwhite America (sometimes referred to as majority-minority) runs throughout. Claims that names of the spiritual founder or sacred institutional names for white institutions will be changed to civil rights leaders or victims of racist violence (King and Martin) are examples (Regester n.d.). Second, an imagined liberal or northern antagonist is to blame for "making trouble," as nostalgic, racist traditions are assumed normal and any opponents are breaching a sacred covenant. As ColonelRebForever put it, the "fight" is "here now." Third and relatedly, it is the fault of those outside the KA community claiming change is necessary. A self-identified African American woman is asked to leave the forum and join one better suited to her identity. Gender issues run throughout these comments as well. "San Francisco" symbolizes a replacement of the Old South with openly LGBTQIA+ friendly spaces; meanwhile, the worry that fraternities will be forced to enlist women mirrors concerns at southern military colleges that women's enrollment would ruin what they call southern valor.

The comments in the online forum help demonstrate KA's dominant rhetorical strategy: taking a frozen locus (of the Old South ball, in this case) and expressing resentment of outsiders by offering ironic appeasement strategies. One could still hold "plantation/slave owner" themed parties but change the name, said RustyFlask123 (Regester n.d.). Supertank156 proposes to throw "Old South" parties without the official sanction of the KA national office. VanillaBeanFrat suggests he'll stop wearing cotton so as to avoid "being racist." Strategies such as these, whose primary goal is protection of southern iconography, have no pragmatic goal, but serve to reinforce generational and fraternal connection with insiders. Moreover, each functions to uphold and normalize the white supremacy of its members. The self-identified alumnus in the comments goes the furthest, to say that the change symbolizes a national office kneeling before Black leaders. Echoing centuries of racial antipathy, these posts imply that, without white supremacy, Black men will claim Black supremacy and ban white people from respecting their families or traditions.

None of these posts attempted to articulate coherent principles often identified as "southern principles," nor were they really engaging with the historical record or memory in order to argue for the significance of the Confederate dead (Regester n.d.). Although a limited sample, the self-identified insider statements quoted above can be contrasted with those of a commenter who does not identify himself as a KA brother. His lengthy reply reads as follows:

> TossMeABronson: If the Confederacy was about maintaining white supremacy, why did the 5 civilized tribes (The Nations) not only ally with The South, but send many to fight wearing Confederate uniforms? Interestingly enough, the last Confederate General to surrender was a Cherokee Indian named Stand Watie. Also, why did thousands of Tejanos join the Confederate Army, many serving in Hood's Brigade, and many serving as officers? Or how about the Hispanics from Spanish colonies including Cuba, Puerto Rico, and Mexicans (estimated upwards of 10,000) who came to the South to fight for The Confederacy? Also, let's not forget that the only reason Lincoln emancipated slaves in the rebellious states (slavery was still legal in 5 Federally controlled states and territories) was to insure the Confederacy would not get support from staunchly anti slavery Britain and France. Such support could have changed the outcome, or at least lengthened the war. Lincoln himself said his primary objective was to preserve The Union, not fight to end slavery. And General US Grant, the so-called Great Emancipator, was a slave supervisor and owner. | The fact is less than 10% of Southerners even owned slaves. With that in mind, saying the War for Southern Independence was fought for slavery is the same level of stupidity as saying anyone who enlisted after 9/11 fought for Halliburton.

Loaded with false equivalencies and inverted power hierarchies, as well as historical inaccuracies, this posting suggests this commenter has absorbed many Lost Cause mythologies that are still perpetuated today. KA's elitism, within the protected confines of the university, has it resentfully protecting frozen loci, instead of attempting rational counterargument.

The field of rhetorical studies has long been interested in correcting the teaching of regional history in the South; scholars doing this work include Brandon Inabinet and Christina L. Moss (the editors of this collection), Rebecca Bridges Watts, Abel Bartley, A. D. Carson, and many others. To do so, we might be better off with a Lost Cause mythologist like TossMeABronson in our classrooms. After all, he at least demonstrates an interest in historical reasoning. More generally, the online forum provides a window into those undergraduates' thought processes that the Old South icons need protecting not so much because of their embedded context or historical function, but as symbolic relics of white supremacy. Our classrooms and the texts we assign present opportunities for guiding such students toward understanding the harm caused by those relics and hopefully rejecting them. In the case of Kappa Alpha, additional means are needed. Because my plan to produce an ethnography of the fraternity at my current institution was prohibited by the director of Greek life and denied by the KA national executive director (Wiese never responded to the numerous emails I sent to him), I am curious about the legitimacy of KA's wanting to seriously commit to racial understanding or healing. Instead of starting at the national level, we might begin, first, by forming solidarity with KA members, in the belief that their national office merely wants to avoid negative publicity. Second and most importantly, detached from a coherent nostalgia or ideology, frozen loci are perfect sites for one-class lessons. Rather than convincing students through rational argument that the entire history of Lost Cause organizations is illegitimate, we might instead show students their odd attachments as what they are.

Some signs of change may be coming, as insiders begin to go public with their shame at having been part of the perpetuation of racist iconography and Old South mythology. Mike Ingram, in his 2020 essay, "How I Confronted the Truth about My Fraternity's Racist History," explains how he joined the KA fraternity at James Madison University, where many of his fraternity brothers were from the North. Ingram's chapter of KA did not celebrate Old South, yet they had the "requisite oil painting of Lee" on display in their fraternity house. Ingram also talks of his childhood in Charleston, South Carolina, where he recalls adults around him talking about their time in the "Order." Later, Ingram highlights his actualized distance from the fraternity; at a party in his first year when he returned home on break, a member of the fraternity at another university seemed surprised they were both KAs. "No offense," that member said to Ingram, "but you don't really strike me as the type."

Recognizing the fraternity's members came largely from "old-money Charleston society," Ingram (2020) explains that he knew he was different from what many consider a "typical" KA. He writes candidly about how the fraternity draws on the concept of being a southern gentleman and how, at first, he was attracted to this notion of gentleman-like behavior and what he termed Lee's "quiet dignity." Furthermore, Ingram recalls his schooling in South Carolina: "On school field trips to plantations, we learned the differences between 'good' slave masters and 'bad' ones (curiously, the masters of the plantations we were touring always fell into the 'good' category). My eighth-grade South Carolina History textbook took pains to de-emphasize slavery as the chief cause of the war, instead leaning into a Lost Cause narrative of states' rights and unchecked federal power."

Ingram (2020) recalls how he had to educate himself out of this way of thinking. He then discusses the Unite the Right Rally in Charlottesville, Virginia, centered on the proposed removal of the Robert E. Lee statue in Market Street Park, and notes that Samuel Zenas Ammen, the fraternity's practical founder, openly praised the Klan. As an insider, Ingram knows his fraternity's history, stating that its "elaborate Old South celebrations didn't flourish until the 1950s, when college campuses across the South were facing pressure to integrate." He also tells how, at the University of Alabama in 2010, "a parade of KAs in Confederate uniforms paused their march in front of the Alpha Kappa Alpha house, where members of the historically black sorority and their families were celebrating the chapter's 35th anniversary." In 2016, after the forced discontinuation of Old South balls, he add that "the Ole Miss chapter was still playing antebellum dress-up at its annual formal, which they renamed the Rose Ball."

Ingram's (2020) self-reflection makes important connections between past and present. He concludes, "white supremacy was embedded in the lessons I learned in school, and in the aristocratic power structures of old-money Charleston, and in the willful ignorance I practiced every time I tried to shrug away my fraternity's ugly history." Ingram implicates himself in perpetuating this history and boldly states that he is part of the problem. The question that remains is how faculty members can help lead our students into such self-reflection.

ANTIRACIST PEDAGOGY AND A NEW DIALOGISM

According to Nesari (2015), KA's iconography and white resentment may be considered a form of monologic discourse (built on the theories of Mikhail Bakhtin), made up of objects integrated through a single consciousness. Other people, including African American students, have their own values and icons, but the monologic perspective reduces those people to the status of objects. They are not recognized as another consciousness or as having power. As stated in the posts quoted above, a Black woman can have her own sorority, her own icons of sisterhood, and should not bother white men in their space, as long as white men are able to continue their legacies of privilege uninterrupted. Monologism pretends to have a final word, by disavowing a world of meaningful others.

In my own setting, aiming for more community-based approaches in first-year writing classrooms and beyond seems of prime importance. This approach might be especially helpful in the context of first-year composition classrooms at southern universities. While it is unhelpful to bring up the specific acts of one campus group (targeting certain students in the classroom as *the* racists), this approach makes a turn to broader institutional rhetorics of race even more important, especially as students are just learning the central iconography they will identify with for life.

At Clemson University, those who have tried to rename Tillman Hall (called Old Main first and later renamed for lynching advocate Ben Tillman) have been met with hostility.[3] Tillman was a former governor of South Carolina and a key figure in the creation and development of Clemson University; but, as a domestic terrorist, the nature of his legacy should be made clear. One mode to enact this confrontation with the past is through the investigation of tradition as a conversation starter and an opening for positive change and modification through discourse. At Clemson, tradition and heritage are explicitly connected to Tillman, the same man who stated that "blacks must remain subordinate or be exterminated" (cited in Carson 2015). As a PhD student at Clemson, Carson started the "See the Stripes" campaign to urge administrators to stop "whitewashing" the school's history ("See the Stripes [Clemson]" n.d.). Carson, now assistant professor of hip hop and the global south at the University of Virginia, fought to raise awareness of how racism is embedded deep in Clemson's history. And yet, despite his efforts, Clemson has chosen to keep the name, with markers of context to acknowledge its "unpleasant stones," as Clemson board chairman called Tillman.[4] Despite Tillman's racism, Tillman Hall is emblazoned on much of Clemson's merchandise, including diploma frames, T-shirts, Christmas ornaments, and other commodities. Tillman Hall exists synonymously with tradition at Clemson, and the campus is built around this central point.

Questioning tradition may tend to shut down conversation, but certain academic voices may help keep that space of discussion open. Rasha Diab et al. (2013), in "Making Commitments to Racial Justice Actionable," emphasize the importance of what Margaret J. Wheatley calls the pedagogical "distur-bances" (3). As Diab et al. write, "willingness to listen and to be disturbed makes us develop ways to resist how these micro manifestations of aggressions and inequities recycle their ever-present historical legacies" (2). Wheatley's *Turning to One Another: Simple Conversations to Restore Hope for the Future* (2002) not only addresses the disturbance but describes ways that tasks like listening can be put into action. Wheatley, evoking Friere's thoughts on vocation, ends her book with prompts that promote different ways of thinking and listening. A pedagogical disturbance could, for example, introduce historically marginalized voices regarding racist symbols, like that of the Confederate battle flag, to help students understand why social events like Old South are problematic and why and how they terrorize minorities. It is better when students bring up these student group-specific examples, so that course instructors do not risk creating nonlistening audiences from the outset.

At Clemson University, this notion of the disturbance was begun with the work of Carson. Additionally, Rhondda Robinson Thomas leads the "Call My Name" project on campus, documenting and sharing the stories of African Americans who contributed to the development of Clemson University from 1825 to the present. Through my four years at Clemson, I was able to observe this important project and the impact it has made. Part of the "Call My Name" project involves a tour of Clemson, highlighting and sharing the role of African Americans in its development. The tour presents a dialogic encounter, allowing students and others the ability to experience a history that has been ignored and overlooked. This history includes convict-lease Black labor brutally robbed to build key academic buildings, Black service communities left in disease-ridden and inadequate housing, musicians and "outsiders" who began to break down this racial hierarchy, and finally Harvey Gannt and the desegregation icons who altered this history. These kinds of institution-wide educational programs add to an overall constructive exchange by setting up a positive and successful pedagogical disturbance that affects all students. Professor Thomas has been careful not to end her narrative in the sad mistreatment of her ancestors but to carry the story up to her being a leading intellectual presence in the life of the university.

Abel Bartley, another leading presence at Clemson, also enacts this form of discourse in the courses he teaches. Through conversations with him, I was able to learn of his pedagogical practices. He equates wearing or promoting the Confederate battle flag to that of wearing the emblem or mascot of your favorite sports teams. As an African American professor of history, he tells his students what the flag means to him. To Bartley, the flag is a racist symbol. This process is grounded in Lévinasian ethics, which involves the "right to tell" and the "obligation to listen" (qtd. in Diab et al. 2013, 11). Bartley has the right to tell his students this, and they, therefore, have an obligation to listen. Using the emblems and mascots of sports teams as an easy-to-understand mode of identification, Bartley tells his students that, if he sees them wearing or promoting a shirt, jersey, jacket, or hat of a team, they must identify with or support that team. With a top-ten-ranked football program, this metaphor also offers a strong point of identification to see why partially ironic or casual displays of racism are still racist acts. This is especially important at Clemson, where students in another fraternity (Sigma Alpha Epsilon) went viral for mocking African American culture in "Cripmas" Parties, where they "dressed like Crips and Bloods gang members and posed for pictures" (Roberts 2017). Also problematic is the fraternity's conflation of African Americans with gangs, with an implication that the two are synonymous.

What is significant here is the openness and honesty with which Bartley engages his students. For many of the students entrenched in a heritage-versus-hate understanding of the Confederate flag, they often only hear one group's feelings and attitudes toward the flag. And from the feeling of being misunderstood, they act out in frozen loci of racism without substance. White students may get the joke of a "Cripmas" Party, wherein their resentments of a culture of political correctness or oppressive oversight are expressed in acts of pure racial antipathy. Ironically, of course, many of those white students have never talked to or listened to African Americans or historians who can explain the "hate" made real in this dichotomy.

Diab et al. emphasize the importance of the disturbance in the classroom, noting the "need to appreciate, to challenge, and to be willingly disturbed" (2013, 11). Bartley does just this. By challenging the often-held heritage versus hate ideology, he causes a disturbance in his students. Although a disturbance often carries a negative or problematic connotation, in this case the disturbance focuses on the positive expression of identity through jerseys or other sports items. The obligation to listen, as expressed by Lévinas (2003), is then placed on the student. In *Rhetorical Listening: Identification, Gender, Whiteness*, Krista Ratcliffe defines rhetorical listening as a "stance of openness that a person may choose to assume in relation to any person, text, or culture" (2005, 17). Students hopefully see such listening as a willful opportunity and not a faculty member's forced drive toward a goal of antiracist advocacy.

Of course, a more customary but not insignificant way to practice dialogic pedagogy is to find the voices of traditionally underrepresented groups in a space like the first-year writing classroom. Tina McElroy Ansa begins her short essay on the Confederate flag with her personal identification: "I'm one of those Black folks who identifies herself, along with African American, female, author, womanist, and feminist, as 'Southerner'" (2001, 5). Ansa adds a personal narrative to the ongoing conversation surrounding the flag—she is from Georgia, another state in the Deep South and the former Confederacy. Ansa alerts her readers that she is aware of the history of the region, writing, "A Georgian does not even have to travel one state up to see the image of the Confederacy emblazoned on the state flag. The Georgia flag also bears that image" (5). In short, the flag has been a staple of her environment. Ansa closes her narrative with her refusal to let the racist image of the flag control her or influence her in any way (6). It is significant that she reminds her readers that she is still a Georgian and connects with her home state on a very personal level, even as she explains the flag's racist connotations and racist meaning to her. Like Bartley, she has the "right to tell" her views of the symbol.

Furthermore, Ansa (2001) takes on an important and often contested topic: how to have southern pride and identity when this identity is so connected to the Confederate flag. Here we can see a break in the self-referential notion of Confederate rhetoric. Ansa discusses part of her identity as a southerner, articulating her own role in the tradition of the South. She too has southern heritage. As students read articles like hers, they can begin, from the viewpoint of others, to question the validity of tradition being used as device to perpetuate hate. When this "right to tell" notion of discourse is used in a classroom, students might be able to view frozen loci like emblem arguments differently.

In another commentary on the Confederate flag, Mae Henderson begins with the following quote from an undergraduate student at the University of North Carolina at Chapel Hill: "'Tradition does not make [the flag] right or necessary'" (2001, 85). Henderson blends personal experience and narrative in her interpretation of southern tradition surrounding the flag. Henderson invokes the notion of "interpretive communities," which "read the icon of the confederate flag according to their/our history, background, personal education, and training" (89). She concludes that "the confederate flag, and the confederacy for which it stands, imagines a community—whether past, present, or future—as a community whose citizens—dead, living, and unborn—are defined not by their region so much as by their racialized 'whiteness'" (90).

This distinction between racism and regionalism is important, as too often studies of the South and its icons focus on the region alone, rather than the way such iconography functions as loci for broader white supremacy. Henderson argues that the flag creates an "imagined community," in which rights and privilege rely on both "racial exclusion and privilege" (2001, 90). By reading texts like those of Ansa and Henderson, students can gain new perspectives on tradition and history from Black voices that may have been largely left out of their previous conversations. In terms of pedagogy, this process can open doors for community building outside of regional territorialization, while also providing an environment for themes focusing on social justice and equity to enter into the space of learning.

In his essay on the Confederate battle flag, Guy Davenport (2001) compares the flag to Nazi symbolism and discusses its implications for African Americans. Davenport opens his essay with discussion of the display of the Nazi flag at the Church of Les Invalides in Paris, France, noting that while it is illegal to display the Nazi flag in Germany, the flag hangs in Paris as a "captured flag" (51). He suggests that the flag has a different connotation in this context because it is "captured" and therefore fallen. It gains a new rhetorical force as a captured flag, not able to harness the power it once did. By contrast, South Carolina's use of the flag on its State House dome signifies what he terms "obsolete patriotism."

As Davenport (2001) concludes, he suggests that African Americans might "wittingly" display the flag as a form of reclaiming it, much like the Nazi flag displayed in Paris. Similarly, *NuSouth* clothing line, started by Angel Quintero and Sherman Evans in Charleston, South Carolina, replaces the Confederate colors with the colors of the Marcus Garvey pan-African flag, attempting to reclaim the meaning of the South and resignify it for a Black-inclusive South (Backman 2015). At first, Evans said he felt the Confederate battle flag really "had nothing to do with us," but then realized it "has everything to do with us" (qtd. in Backman 2015). Backman also quotes Charleston African American high school student Shellmira Green saying that she wore a T-shirt with the flag designed by Quintero and Evans as "a rebuttal to white classmates wearing shirts with slogans like '100 percent cotton and you picked it.'" According to Backman, South Carolina artist Leo Twiggs paints the flag in artwork that places it as a tattered, worn relic, often with the death of fellow Black people or the haunting white faces of its bearers.

Unlike texts, which convey a kind of certainty and direction, art can trigger deeper emotional reactions and a multiplicity of opinions. Terrorist Dylann Roof obsessed over Confederate flag imagery alongside other racist symbols like the state flag of Rhodesia on his social media accounts (Beauchamp 2015). A writing assignment might ask students to reflect on why designers like Quintero and Evans or artists like Twiggs might want to reclaim the flag in such a way as to remove its power from white supremacists. On campuses with KA chapters, such art works may allow classmates to question white supremacy in an indirect way. On campuses without a KA chapter, the unpacking of KA traditions as I described above may serve as a resource for organizations to investigate their own ideologically fraught narratives and traditions.

Skirting institutional risk aversion, individual conversations between students in the classroom could be a deeply meaningful way to address the frozen loci of white supremacist and resentment rhetorics. I have suggested that this rhetoric can be dismantled not only through continued scholarship, but also through positive pedagogical disturbance and action in the first-year writing classroom and beyond. The academic and social outcomes of this dismantling might result in a new dialogism that promotes teaching for activism. Teaching for activism and awareness is paramount now that social media has so clearly made visible the white supremacist discourses that were once invisible.

NOTES

1. Whitney Adams would like to extend gratitude to her dissertation chair, Cameron Bushnell, for support and guidance in all areas of her life. Additionally, she would like to thank all who have believed in her scholarship, especially Brian Gaines, David Blakesley, Steven B. Katz, Abel A. Bartley, and Mike Coggeshall. Lastly, she extends love and gratitude to her mom, Catherine Whittington Adams, her aunt, Shelia Whittington, and good friend Dee Dolin. She is fortunate to have so many amazing people believing in what she does.

2. Confederate grey has also recently also been a source of appropriation and disruption, in Childish Gambino [Donald Glover]'s "This Is America" music video. Glover views recent ongoing racial events targeting African Americans as a continuation of the Confederate past and dons grey pants as a nod to the troubling continuation of racist ideals and nostalgia for the Old South.

3. My affiliation moved, as a graduate student, to Clemson University, where a plantation house still centers the campus and campus buildings continue to bear the names of white supremacists Ben Tillman and Strom Thurmond. Additionally, Clemson has a student body with less than 7 percent identifying as Black or African American ("Clemson University Factbook" 2018), which is problematic for a state where the African American population was around 28% in 2019 (University of South Carolina n.d.). Increased need for diversity is not only apparent in the student body, but also when considering faculty diversity, as Clemson's faculty remains predominantly white and male. In 2018, among tenured and tenure-track faculty members, thirty-six were Black, thirty were Hispanic, 145 were Asian, and 693 were white ("Clemson University Factbook" 2018).

4. Clemson board chairman David Wilkins made the following response to the 2015 decision to keep Tillman Hall's name intact: "Every great institution is built by imperfect craftsmen. Stone by stone they add to the foundation so that over many, many generations, we get a variety of stones. And so it is with Clemson. Some of our historical stones are rough and even unpleasant to look at. But they are ours and denying them as part of our history does not make them any less so. For that reason, we will not change the name of our historical buildings. Part of knowledge is to know and understand history so you learn from it. Clemson is a strong, diverse university in which all of us can be proud. That is today and tomorrow's reality and that is where all our energy is focused" (Ross 2016, 188).

REFERENCES

"Active Chapters." n.d. Kappa Alpha Order. Accessed October 24, 2019. https://www.kappa alphaorder.org/ka/active-chapters/.

Ansa, Tina McElroy. 2001. "What's the Confederate Flag Got to Do with It?" *Callaloo* 24, no. 1: 5–7. https://doi.org/10.1353/cal.2001.0003.

Backman, Melvin. 2015. "These Guys Protested the Confederate Flag 20 Years Ago and All They Got Was This Defunct T-Shirt Company." *Quartz*, July 11, 2015. https://qz.com /446005/these-guys-protested-the-confederate-flag-20-years-ago-and-all-they-got-was -this-defunct-t-shirt-company/.

Beauchamp, Zack. 2015. "The Racist Flags on Dylann Roof's Jacket, Explained." *Vox*, June 18, 2015. https://www.vox.com/2015/6/18/8806633/charleston-shooter-flags-dylann-roof.

Bonner, Robert E. 2018. *Colors and Blood: Flag Passions of the Confederate South.* Princeton, NJ: Princeton University Press.

Carson, A. D. 2015. "My South Carolina University Is Whitewashing Its Complex Racial History." *The Guardian*, July 9, 2015. https://www.theguardian.com/commentisfree/2015 /jul/09/clemson-confederate-flag-racist-tillman-hall.

"Clemson University Factbook." 2018. Tableau. https://public.tableau.com/views/Clemson Factbook2017v5/TableofContents?:embed=y&:dispdi_count=yes&:toolbar=no%20 :showVizHome=no&:embed=true.

Cobb, James C. 2007. *Away Down South: A History of Southern Identity.* New York: Oxford University Press.

Coski, John M. 1996. "The Confederate Battle Flag in American History and Culture." *Southern Cultures* 2, no. 2: 195–231. https://doi.org/10.1353/scu.1996.0012.

Davenport, Guy. 2001. "The Confederate Battle Flag." *Callaloo* 24, no. 1 (February): 51–54. https://doi.org/10.1353/cal.2001.0019.

Diab, Rasha, Thomas Ferrel, Beth Godbee, and Neil Simpkins. 2013. "Making Commitments to Racial Justice Actionable." *Across the Disciplines* 10, no. 3 (Special Issue): 1–18.

Ellison, Ralph. 1995. *Invisible Man.* 1952; rpt. New York: Vintage.

Gans, Herbert J. 1979. "Symbolic Ethnicity: The Future of Ethnic Groups and Cultures in America." *Ethnic and Racial Studies* 2, no. 1: 1–20. https://doi.org/10.1080/01419870 .1979.9993248.

Glassman, Steve. 2006. *Florida Studies: Proceedings of the 2005 Annual Meeting of the Florida College English Association.* Newcastle upon Tyne, UK: Cambridge Scholars Publishing.

Henderson, Mae. 2001. "For Which It Stands." *Callaloo* 24, no. 1 (February): 85–90. https:// doi.org/10.1353/cal.2001.0033.

Huston, Andy. 2010. "Kappa Alpha Order Surpasses 150,000 Initiates in Its History." North-American Interfraternity Conference, November 4, 2010. https://web.archive.org/web /20101123200835/http://www.nicindy.org/blog/kappa-alpha-order-surpasses-150000 -initiates-in-its-history/.

Ingram, Mike. 2020. "How I Confronted the Truth about My Fraternity's Racist History." *Medium*, January 6, 2020. https://humanparts.medium.com/how-i-confronted-the-truth -about-my-fraternitys-racist-history-2202e05ec08a.

Jones, Robert D. 2017. "What Does the Confederate Flag Symbolize? Seven in Ten Working-Class Whites Say 'Southern Pride.'" *PRRI*, August 14, 2017. https://www.prri.org/spotlight /white-working-class-americans-confederate-flag-Southern-pride-racism/.

"Kappa Alpha Fraternity at Wake Forest in Celebration of Old South Weekend, 1964." 1964. *Digital Forsyth*. https://www.digitalforsyth.org/photos/8659.

"Kappa Alpha Laws." n.d. Kappa Alpha Order. Accessed March 15, 2021. https://www .kappaalphaorder.org/wp-content/uploads/2011/04/Laws-concerning-Old-South.pdf.

Kenneally, Meghan. 2015. "SC Confederate Flag Taken Down from State Capitol in South Carolina." ABC News, July 10, 2015. https://abcnews.go.com/US/confederate-flag-state -capitol-south-carolina/story?id=32354059.

Lévinas, Emmanuel. 2003. *Humanism of the Other.* Champaign: University of Illinois Press.

Makaris, Skye. 2017. "This Difficult-to-Wear Skirt Helped to Break Down Class Barriers." *Racked*, December 7, 2017. https://www.racked.com/2017/12/7/16717206/cage-crinoline -feminism-class.

McPherson, Tara. 2003. *Reconstructing Dixie: Race, Gender, and Nostalgia in the Imagined South*. Durham, NC: Duke University Press.

Nesari, Ali Jamali. 2015. "Dialogism versus Monologism: A Bakhtinian Approach to Teaching, from the 6th World Conference on Psychology Counseling and Guidance, 14–16 May 2015." *Procedia: Social and Behavioral Sciences* 205 (October): 642–47.

"Our KA Heritage." n.d. Kappa Alpha Order. Accessed August 19, 2019. https://www .kappaalphaorder.org/ka/history/heritage/.

"Phi Beta Kappa." n.d. William & Mary. Accessed March 15, 2021. https://www.wm.edu /offices/fsl/scholarship/phibetakappa/index.php.

Ratcliffe, Krista. 2005. *Rhetorical Listening: Identification, Gender, Whiteness*. Carbondale: Southern Illinois University Press.

Regester, Dan. n.d. "KA Nationals Ban Chapters from Using Traditional 'Old South' Themed Formal." Total Frat Move. Accessed March 6, 2019. http://totalfratmove.com/ka-nationals -bans-chapters-from-using-traditional-old-South-themed-formal/.

"Rho Chapter." n.d. Kappa Alpha Order. Accessed October 24, 2019. https://www .kappaalphaorder.org/chapters/university-of-south-carolina.

Roberts, Nigel. 2017. "'Cripmas Party' Leads to Probation for Clemson's SAE Fraternity Chapter." *The Root*, January 12, 2017. https://www.theroot.com/cripmas-party-leads -to-probation-for-clemson-s-sae-fr-1790859358.

Ross, Lawrence C. 2016. *Blackballed: The Black and White Politics of Race on America's Campuses*. New York: St. Martin's Press.

"Samuel Zenas Ammen." n.d. Kappa Alpha Order. Accessed August 19, 2019. https://www .kappaalphaorder.org/ka/history/ammen/.

"See the Stripes [Clemson]." n.d. *AyDeeTheGreat.com*. Accessed October 24, 2019. https:// aydeethegreat.com/see-the-stripes/.

Senior, Jennifer. 2016. "Review: In 'Hillbilly Elegy,' a Tough Love Analysis of the Poor Who Back Trump." *New York Times*, August 10, 2016. https://www.nytimes.com/2016/08/11/books /review-in-hillbilly-elegy-a-compassionate-analysis-of-the-poor-who-love-trump.html.

Towns, W. Stuart. 2012. *Enduring Legacy: Rhetoric and Ritual of the Lost Cause*. Tuscaloosa: University of Alabama Press.

University of South Carolina, Office of Diversity and Inclusion. n.d. "Demographics." Accessed February 18, 2020. https://sc.edu/about/offices_and_divisions/diversity_and _inclusion/diversity_data/demographics/index.php.

Vance, J. D. 2016. *Hillbilly Elegy: A Memoir of a Family and Culture in Crisis*. New York: HarperCollins.

Vigdor, Neil. 2019. "Emmett Till Sign Photo Leads Ole Miss Fraternity to Suspend Members." *New York Times,* July 25, 2019. https://www.nytimes.com/2019/07/25/us/emmett-till-ole -miss-students-fraternity.html.

Watts, Rebecca Bridges. 2007. *Contemporary Southern Identity: Community through Controversy*. Oxford: University Press of Mississippi.

Wheatley, Margaret J. 2002. *Turning to One Another: Simple Conversations to Restore Hope to the Future*. San Francisco: Berrett-Koehler Publishers.

Chapter 11

THE SOUTHERN SKILLET

Creating Relational Identity to a Changing South through Food

ASHLI QUESINBERRY STOKES AND WENDY ATKINS-SAYRE

As a white, first-generation-college, cisgender woman from the Mountain South, I am of the South while existing on some of its cultural margins. My South is not that of the country club, the private college, or manners polished through cotillion; yet privilege is provided to me in ways that may affirm and reinscribe these exclusionary forms of southern culture. I seek to speak the language of the academy but with a mountain accent, drawing on those outsider elements of my identity to connect with and highlight southerners whose rhetoric and culture have been marginalized.
—Ashli Quesinberry Stokes

I am a white woman who grew up in south Texas, not knowing that many people didn't consider me southern. I was steeped in southern culture from both sides of my family who had been in the South for many generations, but also in the Latinx culture that surrounded me. I ate cornbread dressing for Christmas dinner, but really lived for the tamale and green chile pie at Christmas Eve dinner. That experience may be part of the reason that I fight and write for a more diverse understanding of the South. After living in Georgia, Mississippi, and Tennessee for the past twenty years, I have seen even more evidence of how multilayered the southern experience is and have committed to exploring those layers through my research.
—Wendy Atkins-Sayre

After the devastating flooding that New Orleans experienced following Hurricane Katrina, many displaced residents searched for ways to show their commitment to their hometown. African American New Orleans food writer Lolis Eric Elie (n.d.) explains that some of those Crescent City residents came together to eat at the same table, providing a dish that cut across lines of class and race. In this case, he explains, "Serving red beans and rice was an affirmation of our fidelity to our hometown, our determination to return to our hometown, despite the fact that a lot of people said that New Orleans wasn't worth rebuilding, that New Orleans would never be rebuilt." The food symbolized their commitment, but it also fortified their commitment. That simple dish said more about the city, its resilience, and the determination of its residents than any political speech that was made during that time. Red beans and rice, according to Elie, became a rallying cry for New Orleaneans.

It's not surprising to claim that southern food speaks. Viewing the cuisine rhetorically helps this volume undertake its important project: examining southern rhetoric from a contemporary perspective, building from previous works that primarily examined public address and the way that certain individuals defined the region to challenge what counts as southern discourse. Wisely, this volume seeks to explore beyond the speech, the speaker, and the predictable. In adding to the consideration of southern/regional rhetoric, we must account for a much wider range of rhetorical texts than merely speeches. For example, memorials, symbols, songs, and so forth add to our understanding of the South's rhetorical construction, whether positive or troubling (Black and Harrison 2015; de Velasco 2019; Watts 2008). Further, the lens of critical regionalism suggests ways we might expand our notion of the South and its more contemporary meanings. Indeed, we have argued previously for the central role of food in redefining the region, a contention that seems particularly relevant when considering questions of how people realign and reckon with the South's past as they experience its present (Stokes and Atkins-Sayre 2016).

This chapter examines the way that food helps create a sense of relational identity, specifically allowing individuals to negotiate their relationship to the US South. To fully explore the topic, we approach the question through the metonym of the southern skillet. There is, arguably, no stronger symbol of southern cooking than the cast iron skillet. As Marcie Cohen Ferris writes, "Fried catfish, greens, pork barbecue, and cast-iron skillets are an edible expression of southern identity" (2013, 284–85). Although these instruments did not originate in the South, the ongoing centrality of the skillet in the region's foodways serves as a symbolic vessel of southern realignment that helps counter nostalgia for white-dominant understandings of the South and offer fuller narratives of the region's history and present. In this chapter, we consider the ways that southern food (by way of the skillet) adjusts to a changing region and remains a constant figure in helping to define it. At the same time, southern food highlights the diversity of southerners both historically and today. If the southern rhetorical project is in need of new critique and fresh insight, some might argue the same about its food, as a cast iron skillet might be viewed as a simplistic tool used to create predictable southern dishes. To that, we say, look closer. There is more to the skillet than sentimental stories about Grandma's cast-iron cooking and white southerners buying $40 skillets from Cracker Barrel as badges of their "heritage." A closer look at the role of the skillet as metonym for the South shows that, while imperfect, thinking about the South through this rhetorical device allows us to see how the skillet is a conversation starter about race, class, gender, and belonging in the region. Indeed, the skillet is full of inventional possibilities, allowing southerners of all backgrounds—people of color, white Appalachians, "blue collar" workers, and more—to enrich the stories of the South in order to help forge a more complex and balanced regional dish. We develop this argument by first discussing southern identity and exploring the symbolism of the skillet in a South imbued with nostalgia. We then provide examples of how southern food both reflects and refracts the history of the South and draw conclusions about the rhetorical potential of southern foodways.

THE PROBLEM WITH SOUTHERN IDENTITY

"Southerner" is a problematic identity to claim, given the complexity of the region (Stokes and Atkins-Sayre 2016). As Todd Leopold (2012) writes, "A century and a half after the Civil War—and more than a generation after the presidential election of Jimmy Carter was supposed to herald the awakening of a 'New South'—the lower right-hand portion of the U.S. of A. is often pigeonholed as a tobacco-spittin', Bible-thumpin', gun-totin' (and worse) backwater." According to lingering stereotypes featured in this type of media coverage, white southerners in particular live in the past, oppose all things progressive, live unhealthy lives, are racist, and remain poor. Attempts to redefine the region or, in the words of this volume, to experience regional "realignment," are often thwarted by these stereotypes. Of course, there is also some truth to the images, given the region's tumultuous history. As we have previously written, however, "Struggling with the past is healthy for the region; indeed, it is better to question the past than to ignore it. The [white] South's record of slavery, violence, racism, and discrimination should always be remembered as a part of our defining history" (Stokes and Atkins-Sayre 2016, 51–52). Moreover, many of these problems continue to affect the region, albeit in new forms.

Stereotypes related to Black southerners are more destructive, sometimes connected to oppressive rhetoric historically used to justify slavery, Jim Crow laws, or other types of discrimination and violence (National Museum of

African American History & Culture n.d.). The Great Migration, when Black southerners fled southern states to escape discrimination (often violent) and to seek opportunities in northern cities, meant that around five million rural African Americans left the region between 1915 and 1960 (Harrison 1991, vii). Although some of that migration has reversed, seeing some southern Black families return, the justified rejection of the region is hard to forget for many Black southerners (Jackson 1991, xi–xviii). Most other minority groups such as Latinx and Asian Americans remain largely invisible in southern stereotypes. Consequently, the relationship to the South, for many people of color, but specifically African American southerners, is troubling.

Given the problems that the region has faced and continues to face, it is worth considering how individuals "negotiate their relational identity to a region" (as the volume editors suggest) even as they claim membership. Inabinet and Moss (2019) pointed out previously that these southern claims to identity can be problematic, given the region's past. Despite the South's ongoing struggle with questions of identity as a legacy of a racist, violent, poverty-ridden, and gendered past, scholars contend that perceptions of a "South" persist that still result in regional identification, with three-quarters of its residents identifying as southern (Cooper and Knotts 2013; Hood 2018; Sloan and Thompson 2012; Stokes and Atkins-Sayre 2016). But, as Antonio de Velasco (2019) argues, it is possible to constitute alternative southern identities that are more inclusive and constructive. He writes that "African Americans have worked for centuries to 'own, and own well' regionally centered narratives of belonging" (238). The South has experienced increasing migration, modernization, urbanization, and diversification (Hood 2018), and individuals must negotiate regional identity combining these recent developments with its fraught past. Indeed, scholars argue that questions of regional identification are of particular relevance in the American South (Cooper and Knotts 2013). Whether it is because of feelings of difference from other US regions, a desire for "rootedness in the community," or, problematically, white southern desire to return to its "old order of division," patterns of regional identification persist (Cooper and Knotts 2013; Cooper and Knotts 2017; Hood 2018; Watts 2008, 16). Fights over the Civil War and Confederate or Old South symbols remain polarizing forces in southern identity formation today, for example, but studies continue to show Black and white people in the region both identify with the southern label (Cooper and Knotts 2017).

As a result, examining identification's role in the process of region making through frameworks of critical regionalism is important in the case of the South. Regions become institutionalized symbolically, where region making can be used to "maintain division and exclusion" along with providing possibilities of connection and community (Paasi 2003, 481). Thus, regional identities may be viewed as constitutive or productive forces that not only answer questions regarding belonging and membership but also produce particular institutionalized structures (Paasi 2003; Rice 2012). Not only are the regions themselves rhetorically constructed and maintained, but the regions then influence how individuals see themselves and others. As Dave Tell (2012) explains it, "At the heart of this construction is the building of contingent bridges, the forging of tenuous links, the *articulation* of people, places, institutions, and ideologies that would not otherwise coexist in the same formation" (215). Importantly, the contingent nature of these rhetorical links means that there are constant messages at play in shaping identities, thus attention to the rhetorical nature of region building is important (Powell 2007; Rice 2012).

Indeed, given that parts of the southern region are portrayed as deeply, and often uniquely, dysfunctional, it is important to consider why identifying with the southern label remains compelling, and for whom. If identities are used strategically to unite, divide, and perpetuate societal structures, what identity-building symbols are most important in speaking a contemporary southern image, and how do they help build or break down that identity? (Wood 2012). Previously, we have argued that southern food and foodways help to create and reify an identity with the region by sparking discussion about similarities and differences that help cross racial and class lines, thus providing the opportunity for shared experiences and conversations (Stokes and Atkins-Sayre 2016). Here, we extend the argument that food helps create this sense of relational identity from the vantage point of the southern skillet, where the foodways of the region are diverse, complex, and worthy of exploration. The food traditions are not "stuck in the past," but are instead tied closely to the past in a way that recognizes their painful histories. If a southern African American buys a skillet to reclaim southern cuisine as something more than white American food or a poor white southerner uses a skillet to stretch the week's food budget rather than create a hipster dish, these expressions help show how southern identity is complex and nuanced beyond either moonlight and magnolias or "backward" southern stereotypes. In other words, by creating and consuming the traditional foodways of the region, we are given opportunities to talk about the origins and histories of certain foods, the reasons for inclusion or exclusion of certain ingredients, the adaptation of recipes over time, and the people who were most likely to make them.

SKILLETS, NOSTALGIA, AND THE SOUTH

When it comes to iconic representations of southern cooking, few compare to the image of cornbread in an iron skillet. Google "southern food" images, and you'll find yourself staring at thousands of variations of cornbread and other foods prepared in the iron cookware, but these images cast a long shadow. Skillet cornbread is considered to be one of the core components of southern cuisine. Cast iron care has its own entry in *The Southerner's Handbook*, where skillets are described as the "one common denominator" in the "big place" that is the South (Editors of *Garden & Gun* 2013, 9). Cast iron imagery extends well beyond the kitchen and cornbread, though. For instance, one of the South's first hillbilly bands was called the Skillet Lickers; one of the leading organizations devoted to the study of southern food, the Southern Foodways Alliance, features a skillet on its logo; and Cracker Barrel, one of the most successful southern food chain restaurants, made the skillet central to its menu and country store. The skillet may be a traditional southern cooking instrument, but it also figures into contemporary and diverse expressions of the region's identity.

Skillets not only represent the South, but their use is celebrated for connecting families and enhancing the skills of a cook, despite background, training, and income. As one observer explains skillets' multi-audience appeal: "They're classless: the poorest family and the hippest foodie has one, and cherishes it" (McFee 2016, 94). Indeed, families revere the household item as an irreplaceable cooking instrument that stands outside the times and the trends (Ozersky 2012). As *Southern Living* magazine explains, "A cast iron skillet is a prized possession among Southern cooks. Seasoned with years of cooking and loving care, heirloom cast iron skillets and Dutch ovens are as valued (and fought over) as Grandma's china and sterling silver" (York n.d.). Some writers romanticize how cooks become "acquainted" with their cast iron skillets as they are handed down within families, their multigenerational use creating a "relationship" between cook and object, and their seasoned surfaces adding character and flavor to foods (McFee 2016, 94). It is difficult to think of another cooking tool that gets as much praise among southern cooks (St. George 2014). Cast iron's ongoing legacy suggests that there is more to this kitchen tool than just long-lasting qualities and multifunctionality; we argue that the cast iron skillet acts metonymically to show the face of southern cooking historically and today, in a region where representing identity is a complex rhetorical problem. Indeed, moving beyond praise of the instrument shows how the skillet metonym complicates the dominant narrative of white southern nostalgia that often surrounds southern food.

Problematic nostalgia is easy to call forth when it comes to the skillet. The primary skillet manufacturer, Lodge, is located in the South and embraces its ongoing association with the region. Joseph Lodge opened the Lodge Manufacturing foundry in 1896, and it continues to create some of the most-recognized cast iron skillets in the world, touting its use of southern materials (iron, steel, fire, air, sand, clay, and water), southern labor, and a southern marketing scheme (Lodge n.d.). Customers visiting one of the region's many

Cracker Barrels also encounter celebration and praise of the tool, along with particular visions of the region. It is easy for a traveler, for example, to see the wall of Lodge merchandise in the "country store" part of the restaurant, purchase a skillet, and imagine a connection to what is frequently portrayed as a simpler, easier time. In doing so, however, they participate in the type of white-dominated southern nostalgia that commodifies objects while excluding the complicated histories of those objects and the reality that some southerners remain more likely to be working in, rather than eating in, the restaurant.

While nostalgia can certainly be problematic for southern identity, there is also significant rhetorical possibility in nostalgia if called forth in the right way (McPherson 2003; Stokes and Atkins-Sayre 2016). The ritual of cooking, for example, allows a person to enact the past, recreating foods that have been a central part of the southern region for years (Stokes and Atkins-Sayre 2016). In other words, if we learn more about how southerners have used the skillet in a variety of ways throughout its history, we appreciate how the skillet represents the South in a way that is reflective of all its people—a combination of people and histories that potentially transform the whole when combined. Rather than seeing the South through nostalgic pining or as a stand-in for all that is wrong with racist, sexist, classist America, like the basic skillet, there is more to its appearance than what we find on the Lodge Factory tour or Cracker Barrel shelves.

As a result, we argue that the skillet has the capability of using nostalgia productively, providing inventional opportunities for cooks, and making it possible to reconstruct old recipes or create new dishes. Southerners may use a skillet to embrace regional traditions, but they have found ways to reform them to develop new recipes as the South changes. They are also sharing more stories of how the tool has been used by various groups in ways that are not always celebratory. Like the production of a skillet, southerners must embrace any salvageable parts of the past and realign them to reflect a more promising future. Consequently, the southern food tradition and the ways that it has responded to changing tastes, immigration, and healthier lifestyles, shows the ways that southerners may be changing. It is possible to change, while also staying true to traditions that reflect the region's more positive elements. As Lee (2018) argues, some traditions are not problematic in and of themselves: indeed, they craft our identities. While one person might use their skillet to make the family's cornbread and another to cook while camping, both experiences shape their users. It is when particular traditions become linked rhetorically to authority, however, that they become dangerous, with words like "true," "genuine," and "real," becoming sanctimonious (Lee 2018, 6). If one group of southerners claims the "genuine" way to use the skillet, they police the borders of the southern food story and obscure the South's history. As we seek to enrich the story of the South and its foodways, then, so too should we account for its multifunctional/multivocal rhetorical symbols. The skillet both reflects where it has been and where it is now simultaneously—a rhetorically helpful way of thinking about the South. Acknowledging food's role—through taste, touch, smell, sight, sounds, and stories—in the creation and reification of southern identity is an important addition to the story.

SOUTHERN FOOD FOR THOUGHT AND RACIAL DIALOGUE

The South is often portrayed as being stuck in the past, and this image of a change-resistant region emphasizes the oppressive and violent race-based practices that are a significant part of the region's history. Ferris describes the region as torn between two time periods, "a place continually pulled back by the past and at the same time wrenched forward into a changing present" (2013, 301). In fact, much of what factors into discussions about the South being "stuck in the past" is its continued racial strife that began with the institution of slavery, but continued with the practice of sharecropping, abuse of migrant workers, use of Jim Crow laws, a rejection of "foreign" citizens, and more.

Drawing on southern foodways to talk about the region, however, can be both inclusive and restorative when recognizing that much of its food history comes from a very diverse population. Influence from enslaved cooks who came from the African tradition brought many foods (okra, legumes, rice, gumbo) to the South, where eventually free Black cooks continued the cooking traditions in obscurity. For years, those foodways were labeled as "southern" but with no acknowledgment of their longer history, in terms of labor, ingredients, or practices. There are many examples of this monomyth, with both author–chef Edward Lee (2018) and historian Rebecca Sharpless (2013) pointing out that early southern cookbooks were often published by white women appropriating the recipes of their Black female cooks without acknowledgment. As Lee asks, "What if she had been allowed to tell her story through the recipes that were likely her inventions? I see her imagined life, both tragic and uplifting, told through nuggets of the corn pone as they fry in the skillet" (2018, 2). In recent years, scholars from a variety of disciplines have made a concerted effort to write that history back into the story of the South (Stokes and Atkins-Sayre 2016; Tipton-Martin 2015; Twitty 2017). Southern cuisine grew from a system of oppression that should be acknowledged, but those traditions have also changed over time in response to political, sociological, and cultural shifts. Thus, the food is tied to the past, but responds to change, functioning to allow different types of southerners to identify with the region rather than privileging only one story or southerner.

For example, one popular skillet dish—cornbread—shows this interplay between common (mis)perceptions about the South and the rhetorical possibilities that are afforded when taking a closer look at the dish's more nuanced histories. Initially found chiefly in the mid-South, cornbread is now widespread and its versions legion: from sweet to unsweet, "there's a cornbread for everyone" (Keller 2017), with Burkette likening the difficulty in understanding the many ways of making cornbread to "the proverbial paper bag full of snakes" (2011, 312). Cornbread is often viewed simultaneously as the "simplest thing in the world" and "the most complicated," because although the dish's typical ingredients (cornmeal, leaveners, salt, and buttermilk) suggest a lack of complexity, the quality of the product depends on both using the best ingredients possible and the skill of the cook (Yonan 2015). There are heated debates in the South over whether cornbread should contain sugar, arguments about which version is superior, and omissions of the dish's Native American origins (who had been growing and using corn for up to seven thousand years). Indeed, some southerners themselves may be unfamiliar with the dish's relationship to enslaved persons and the ongoing evolution of the dish within the African American community. In fact, unfamiliarity with the dish's historical role within some Black communities is representative of the tendency to overlook cornbread's multiple stories and histories. The historically based southern restaurant, JuneBaby (n.d.), points out, for example, that cornbread was frequently consumed by enslaved persons because they did not have time to cook for themselves while forced to work in plantation fields, and that the dish was also preferred because it did not require utensils.

African American culinary historians Michael Twitty (2017) and Adrian Miller (2013) add complexity to cornbread's story by pointing out that preferences for sweet or savory cornbread in the African American community depend on history, geography, and access to particular types of cornmeal. Cornbread was not sweet initially, as sugar was expensive in pre-Emancipation times, but as Twitty explained in an interview, he uncovered enslaved cooks' recipes for cornbread containing molasses for energy (qtd. in Severson 2016). Once industrial rollers milled yellow corn instead of the traditional white, some Black cooks may have added sugar to enhance the flavor of the cheaper yellow meal (Purvis 2016). African American author Toni Tipton-Martin (2015) shows this pattern at work in the Black community in her analysis of African American cookbooks, in which nineteenth-century recipes do not contain sugar, but those written in the 1920s and 1930s include it. Miller told Kathleen Purvis (2016) in an interview that sweet cornbread became more entrenched in African American communities during the Great Migration, when cheaper industrial cornmeal available in the North called for sweetening, which then was brought back to the South through the rise of soul food restaurants. Indeed, as Purvis (2016) explains, sugar in cornbread is one of today's demarcation points between the broader southern food tradition and soul food cuisine, but, of course, "there are sweet cornbread fans in the white camp, and non-sweet cornbread fans among African-Americans."

When some, especially white, southerners decry sweet cornbread simply as a matter of "taste," they overlook how their own preferences may be shaped by the intersection of forces of history, race, class, and regionalism. Particularly for white southerners who argue that cornbread must not be sweet, they may be unwittingly hegemonic about what constitutes southern food. As Twitty explained to Kathleen Purvis in an interview, the "fight" over the correct version of cornbread is really about something much deeper than taste preferences: "It's actually a gauge of who gets to call what's Southern 'Southern,'" where the debate "is part of the larger discussion of whether or not you see Southern culture from the perspective of the big house or the slave quarters. We're still having this argument 100 years later, but we're using different vehicles to have it. Including cornbread" (2016, para. 38). That is, the rhetorical circulation of the superiority of unsweet cornbread signals a common problem with discussions of southern food in general: the omission of histories and voices of those most responsible for creating the cuisine—African Americans. What thus seems simple at first glance is a dish that carries substantial weight in representing the complexity of the South's paradoxes. That is, in the hands of a skilled cook, good skillet cornbread combines traditional ingredients with complex practices, and many southerners are only now learning about these histories.

Similarly, consider narratives about macaroni and cheese, a traditional southern, and now broadly American, dish. Some might think of it as a quick side dish that comes from a blue box, but in some southern African American families, it is a dish of honor, baked in a skillet and served for family gatherings (Okona 2018). Purvis (2017) agrees that the dish leads a secret double life, frequently serving as a cheap, filling, everyday dish in white culture and a special occasion, celebratory dish in Black culture. Miller (2013) explains that "mac and cheese" originated in Europe and was brought back to the United States in the 1800s, where enslaved people became expert in creating a special occasion dish, a history that may have influenced differing perceptions of the dish today. As Purvis (2017) writes of how the dish continues to be enjoyed in Black communities, "Who makes it, how it's made and who's allowed to bring it to a gathering involves negotiation, tradition, and tacit understanding. It's baked, and it's a side dish, but it's the side dish of honor, present at every important occasion." Talking about these differences perhaps leads to deeper, more meaningful considerations of race, identity, and possibilities for connection in the South.

Throughout both of these examples of traditional skillet-crafted southern foods, we continue to find evidence of tired assumptions in the southern food story that equates southern food with whiteness. In fact, food stories are part of a general tendency to equate southernness and whiteness in both academic and lay discourses, despite studies showing that Black southerners are more likely than whites to claim southern identity (Sloan and Thompson 2012). Whether heard in debates about cornbread or mac and cheese, or moving beyond food to think about Confederate memorials, issues of economic mobility in the South, or lingering patterns of segregation, the meaning of southern identity is in conflict between Black southerners whose "labor, and often their blood, played an important and essential role in the development of the region," and certain white southerners, who "feel that their heritage is 'under siege'" as they "still long for and wish to hold onto their southern identity" (Sloan and Thompson 2012, 73–74). Delving into southern foodways rhetoric helps scholars explore how the history of racial conflict created different Souths and southerners, where some white southerners may emphasize positive associations with the region, including its land, culture, and people, ignoring or downplaying issues of race, while for some Black southerners, "region is seen through the prism of race—region as race" (Sloan and Thompson 2012, 92). Similarly, some southerners might share a nostalgic tale of using a loved one's cast iron pan to make their own dishes, whereas that same pan might represent personal pain, hard labor, loss, or struggle for others. Sharing stories of traditional foodways provides an entry point into discussions about identity, where despite differences in how southerners may view race, our varied experiences in creating a dish sparks discussion about similarities and differences that help cross racial lines (Sloan and Thompson 2012; Stokes and Atkins-Sayre 2016).

Although the previous examples of southern food provide glimpses into the rhetorical construction of more traditional southern dishes and their relationship to identity realignment, the cuisine has changed to show foodways of the past adapting to the shifting racial and ethnic demographics of the region. The increase in crawfish consumption in the South, for example, speaks to the adaptation of southern foodways to population trends as well as its changing demographics and identities. Sharp (2017) points out that Houston became a natural fit for Vietnamese immigrants after the fall of Saigon in 1975, with the city's proximity to water, subtropical climate, and ability to work in familiar industries, such as the seafood trade. Over time, Vietnamese immigrants blended traditional flavors with Gulf South ones to create "the most delicious expression of Houston's culinary identity": Vietnamese–Cajun crawfish. Though some from states like Louisiana have been known to at first resist the culinary fusion, the blending of Cajun and Vietnamese flavors has become very popular. When discussing these cultural fusions, contemporary scholars are more likely to prefer the "salad bowl" metaphor than the "melting pot," with its reduction of individual qualities (e.g., Hanchett 2013), but the influence of other cultures on the South and resulting changes are undeniable. Houstonites, for example, now enjoy dishes like crawfish pho, crawfish fried rice, and crawfish empanadas. This type of culinary mash-up style of eating is now available throughout the country and world; tellingly, southern Viet–Cajun style preparations are also now popular back in Vietnam (Dao 2018).

Such stories of how southern foods morph and change as they encounter different populations support the "South as skillet" metonym. One might start with a traditional southern ingredient (here, a crawfish), but end up somewhere quite different from where one started. These developments not only breathe new life into the South's food story; they more accurately represent the many variations of southern identity beyond the dominant narratives of the binary Black and white South. That is, the foodways of the changing South reflect what is happening in the region. Controversial histories and difference are sometimes "spoken" through the food of the region, when these changes are not explicitly acknowledged in traditional modes of rhetoric like political discourse.

CLASS IN THE REGION

Apart from problems associated with race, the South has also long been plagued by issues of poverty (Moore 2018). Although in today's South there are pockets of prosperity, the region continues to battle all of the issues associated with poverty, including food insecurity, health crises, housing issues, struggling institutions of education, and so forth. The foodways of the region have often reflected that reality, although not always in a negative way. For example, historically southern food was influenced by the ingredients that were readily available; the crops that were more bountiful, the animals that were easiest to raise, and the ingredients that were available to purchase often drove what appeared on the table (Stokes and Atkins-Sayre 2016). Historically, the food of the region was fairly healthy because it was fresh and natural (Miller 2013).

As industrialization spread throughout the region, reformers attempted to protect traditional foodways while campaigning against external forces' bringing unwholesome and undesirable ingredients to the region (Ferris 2014). This ongoing struggle between romanticizing traditional foods while worrying about outside influences on the health and well-being of southerners continues today, especially inside Appalachia, where the issue of class and food still creates what Ferris calls a "power struggle between natives and outsiders to control regional culture" (137). For example, Ferris writes of a history of using food to divide Appalachians into classes, with "educated and moral" residents eating from "gardens of joy," with the "worst off" using handle-less skillets to cook "perhaps a few Kentucky Wonder beans among the corn and a straggling patch of onions and turnips" (170). While today's impoverished residents might be more likely to live in food deserts or be dependent on grocery outlets that provide primarily unhealthy options or offer healthier versions of foods at a much higher cost, these issues of class continue to paint southerners, especially, as in need of particular reform in order to correct their unhealthy lifestyles.

The skillet metonym helps refute claims that the South, in particular, is unhealthy, obese, and in need of intervention. Although poverty rates still drive many food practices, the tradition of choosing to use simple and fresh ingredients even when others are accessible remains strong in the region, with nonprofits such as Grow Appalachia helping families grow as much of their own food as possible. Further, it has become newsworthy to combine "poor" ingredients in a "humble" skillet to create something new and fancy. Two examples show how the skillet metaphor rehabilitates poverty-driven cooking techniques while also helping to create new understandings of the poorer, rural pockets of the South.

For instance, the image of eating cornbread and beans is frequently used as a stereotype to denigrate poor, particularly white, mountain southerners that has recently undergone a type of revisioning. Of course, cornbread does have a humble history, associated with being a white "poor people's food" (Engelhardt 2011). Today, however, cornbread has lost some of its poverty connotations and, combined with beans, is considered a beloved staple of the table. Once associated with being cheap, bland, and filling, "the foods of the hillbilly, the hick, and the redneck," the dish is now considered to be part of a "scrappy, intelligent way of cooking" (Black 2016). The classic combination is now used to rhetorically signal authenticity, skill, and resourcefulness; as Jones (2017) puts it, "The lazy-hillbilly stereotype doesn't survive scrutiny of the foods that hillbillies invented." Further, a closer look at the skillet cornbread reclaims the Mountain South for nonwhite southerners who also live there and challenges the stereotypes that associate whiteness with particular foods dominant in the southern food story. As Carey (2018) points out, cornbread is "a food symbolic of the region . . . and a staple found in the diets of Native Americans, white Appalachians, people of color, and migrant workers, all exploited in the farm-to-food-economy, all contributors to life in the region past and present." In fact, regional activists published the twenty-four-page Cornbread Communist Manifesto to advocate for the needs of the area's most vulnerable populations. Described as "decidedly intersectional" because people must move from different identities to navigate the region's conservative and radical spaces, cornbread activism displays a "particular grace at knowing how to talk about complicated political issues with someone that you don't agree with" (Carey 2018).

Thus, for mountain southerners of different identities, although it is trendy to eat "authentic" and "nostalgic comfort food" like cornbread and beans, their approachable familiarity as part of the southern culinary canon allows eaters to openly discuss issues in a more approachable and accessible way. As Appalachian writer Courtney Balestier writes regarding talking about cornbread and the "appropriate" color of soup beans with emigrated Kentucky Appalachians in Detroit, "there is a sense in which this distinction does not matter and a sense in which it says everything about the migration North: The color of my soup beans versus the color of your soup beans only mattered when we were both in a third place, talking about our soup beans" (2019, 123). What Balestier and others are doing when they write about cornbread and beans is not simply talking about the dish itself. Instead, like the skillet, the discussion of their creation and variations becomes fodder for connection and conversation, where similarly disparaged places like Appalachia and Detroit, both associated with poverty, find value and meaning from intertwined food traditions. What the skillet metonym adds to the discussion about food and class in the South is that it allows us to see how certain dishes help theorize the relationship between food and labor. Cornbread and beans served as portable meals for miners; they allowed women to do any number of other tasks as they simmered away on the stove (Morris 2007). Rather than defaulting to discussions of how "poor people" buy or cook "bad foods," these dishes and others help us understand how food does more than nourish.

Similarly, a closer look at skillet-made southern gravies and sauces shows how cooks rely on skill, ingenuity, and resourcefulness to enhance meals, revealing how southerners express adaptive and creative characteristics, rather than the backward, ignorant, and regressive qualities that are sometimes still ascribed to the region's rural poor, in particular. Taken together, for example, popular southern gravies illustrate economy and sustainable cooking techniques that enhance meals. As Sohn describes, "like a coat of fresh paint, gravy brings out the best of what it covers" (2005, 31). Just by using the drippings of chicken, sausage, or other meats, cooks create a variety of gravies that flavor dishes and leave nothing to waste. Redeye gravy is a particularly interesting example of this practice. Found frequently in the Mountain South, redeye gravy is made simply with country ham drippings, water, and a splash of coffee for color. Its unique name derives from the "appearance of a 'red eye' in the middle of the reduced gravy" (Evans 2011), though lore also tells of General Andrew Jackson demanding "country ham with gravy as red as his eyes" following a night of drinking (Lovelace 2012). Popular in the 1930s and 1940s, redeye gravy now shows up on food trucks, at Cracker Barrel, and in Hawaii, where it is made from the state's famous Kona coffee. Although class snobbery would likely prevent the moniker, the gravy can also be considered as one of the classic "pan sauces" created by cooking meat. Fine cooks created sauces from oils and labor-intensive whisking in copper saucepans, while southerners were denigrated for combining grease and water in their skillets. The inputs and outputs were never all that different—what mattered was the relative savoir faire and economic standing of the cook. As some small degree of economic mobility and attempts at diversity in fine dining kitchens change who cooks elite food and who rates and writes those recipes, such hierarchy begins to shift.

Southern food has often struggled with its image as being unhealthy, and at first glance, these dishes play into the stereotype. There is no doubt that an overuse of lard, butter, and carbohydrate-based ingredients represented by the gravy traditions may be unhealthy. It is also the case that the region does have high rates of obesity and obesity-related diseases. But, similar to the "there's more to the white southern food story," there's rhetorical meaning in the ongoing popularity of cornbread and beans and gravy. For middle-class, lower middle-class, and poor southerners, the calories offered by these dishes could once be expended through agricultural or other forms of labor, but as jobs shifted from the fields to the factory or office, the dishes still symbolized family and community for those used to eating them. As Tomlinson puts it, "Food was our one source of wealth. . . . Those great meals carried with them tons of fat and calories, salt, and all the things that are bad for you. But it was the one sort of tangible expression of what mattered to them, and what they considered to be the riches they could share with me" (qtd. in Keane 2019).

Indeed, the continued use of such ingredients and practices can also be read not of the South's caloric excess or reliance on unhealthy ingredients, but instead as a way to offer special treats, honor special occasions, and provide enjoyment. The South may be known for its fried chicken, heavy desserts, or unfortunately, Paula Deen's over-the-top donut burger, but these dishes continue to be the outlier, not the norm, for many southerners. There is a reason that fried chicken was called the "gospel bird." It was meant traditionally to be enjoyed on Sundays (Miller 2013). The continuing use of these traditional recipes means that southern food can both reflect its agricultural past but also be used to make caloric changes in its white-collar present. Today's cast iron cook might make gravy in her skillet on the weekend but roast okra in it (with Indian spices) on a weekday to maintain a healthier lifestyle.

In addition, continuing consumption of some of the South's more "notorious" dishes serves an identity-supporting function, used to deflect criticism and stereotypes and create regional (and microregional) associations that help connect eaters, as in this humorous example from Glen Simpson's "Tomato

Gravy" lyrics: "You can have your bagels and croissants / Pour the gravy over bacon Sausage or ham / Give me eggs full of cholesterol / I don't give a spam" (qtd. in Sohn 2005, 33). What is intriguing in such (frequently humorous) defenses of traditional southern food is how they respond to arguments that pleasure is only "allowed" for certain cultures and classes. In the way that a gravy biscuit might contain a similar nutritional profile as a croissant or bagel sandwich, one is much more likely, due to class assumptions about the South, to be vilified. This is not to say that some southern food traditions do not deserve health-conscious scrutiny or should serve as edible defenses of white victimage. Trying to get beyond stereotypes of the Mountain Dew-drinking, cornbread-eating poor white southerner is not the same as arguing that all southern food traditions are equally healthy or meaningful. Rather, in addition to the examples shared here that focus on mountain southerners, significant stories about the intersection of southern food and class remain to be shared.

WOMEN AND GENDER IN THE REGION

Along with a tendency to tell the South's food story in largely white, male terms, thinking about the South through the skillet also helps emphasize how women have used the tool to create much of what constitutes southern identity, even if the women's individual histories and stories are not yet well known. There are many more women cooks and chefs beyond Paula Deen who highlight their southern roots; like the larger "great man" rhetorical canon, we do not know about them (yet).

Toni Tipton-Martin's (2015) *Jemima Code* attempts to remedy that problem. Her project, aimed at recovering African American women's stories and cultural contributions through a study of their recipes, provides another example of how telling food stories can emphasize the true multiplicity of influences on southern food (although her study extends beyond just the South). Tipton-Martin seeks to dispel the myth that "black chefs, cooks, and cookbook authors—by virtue of their race and gender—are simply born with good kitchen instincts" (2). Not only does this flawed reasoning hide much of the work of those women; it also "diminishes knowledge, skills and abilities involved in their work, and portrays them as passive and ignorant laborers incapable of creative culinary artistry" (2). Instead, a study of those food traditions, many of them influential in southern cuisine, shows these women speaking their traditions, their talents, their artistry through their food creations. Although Tipton-Martin's research focuses primarily on post-nineteenth-century creations (because of a limited amount of printed material available before those dates), her work emphasizes the fact that African American women were present in creating both the Old South foodways and those of a more contemporary South. This history, the stories of the South through food, also speaks to the gender diversity of southern culture.

Food stories themselves often point to the influence of women on the region. For example, think about how easy it is to order cornbread now at more upscale restaurants, throughout the South and elsewhere. As Lee (2018) puts it, "nowadays you couldn't throw a stone without hitting a cornbread skillet" (303). What he observes, though, is that in the crush of the cornbread's popularity, hipster credibility, and news articles featuring elaborate recipes, we lose the individual stories of the women who cooked the bread for years in cafeterias, small restaurants, diners, or churches. The cornbread Lee most frequently eats, for instance, is tied to two women who cook the dish quite differently and who have different southern African American backgrounds: one grew up on a farm in rural Tennessee, the other in downtown Louisville during the civil rights movement. To think that their cornbread would be similar assumes their stories would be too, when in fact, as Lee says, "their choices in their cornbread recipes tell an intimate story of their past" (305). The ingredients (and therefore their stories) often speak to differences in regions, race, class, upbringing, traditions, and so forth. Shirley Mae, for example, resists the term "soul food," identifying more with her rural southern upbringing, while Janice reflects about how the neighborhood in which her restaurant sits used to be more integrated. In this way, their food's individuality speaks beyond the lives of women whose foodways create the South as region; in fact, sampling their dishes combats the notion, described by Rice (2012), that regions in a capitalist system create a monotonous menu of sameness. Cracker Barrel always serves the same cornbread, but if you eat in different kitchens throughout the South, you might find hot water cornbread in one and a corn pancake in another. Southern women's dishes are not the same, and only in recent years have publishing venues been receptive to their stories (or social media and blogging have made the barrier to entry sufficiently low). The need to better understand southern women as rhetorically influenced by their various identities and histories is seen in other stories. For example, southern chef and TV personality Carla Hall describes her soul food cookbook as being on a mission to "reclaim black American cuisine from the stereotype of delicious but rich and caloric (verging on deadly) celebration food," while also seeking to create an environment that is more welcoming to female professional chefs (qtd. in Howard 2018). Her work also speaks to the history of praising Black women's home cooking but not recognizing them as chefs.

Similarly, the Soul Food Sessions movement, a pop-up dinner series seeking to highlight the culinary talents of people of color by applying "fine-dining techniques to traditionally African-American ingredients," is an example of the need to circulate more, and different, stories about gender and southern food (Purvis 2018). At a recent "Soul Sisters" dinner, eight up-and-coming Black female chefs chose to pay homage to the "Black Granny," considered in the Black community to be the originator of soul food (Louis 2018). Designed to "dispel the myth that Black women's soul food is synonymous with only collard greens and chitterlings," according to Louis, the women each chose a famous muse to inspire their six-course, upscale menu. Here, traditional notions of "Granny's cooking" are used productively, with one attendee enthusing, "These women have a skill set that's on a level of all chefs, not just Black chefs. That's what we're celebrating" (qtd. in Louis 2018). Significantly, the positive image of the Black matriarch, seeing her as a "Strong Black Woman" or a "black superwoman," helps establish the centrality of African American women to southern regionalism (Reid 2011, 52). The Soul Sisters dinner is another example of how rhetor-chefs pull from the past traditions of the South to productively challenge the southern food narrative, and thus the region's story as a whole, to reflect a more intricate, interesting, and promising present and future. It is rhetorical invention through food.

CONCLUSIONS

The main conclusion that we draw from an examination of the South through the image of the cast iron skillet is that it motivates critical conversations about race, class, gender, and more because it is able to reflect the region's past and present. The Old and New South are forged together in cast iron, disrupting and restarting conversations. As this volume puts forth, there are parts of the Old South that are worth salvaging as rhetorical resources for a reconstruction, providing a firm narrative footing for understanding the region today. At the same time, moving beyond the past to consider a changed and continually changing region is vital. Southern food provides us with an outlet to do this work. The food found on southern tables reflects our diverse history. Although many of the dishes are tied to histories of oppression and exploitation, they also reflect the culture and invention of the cooks and the people who eat the food. The story of southern food can speak the truth about the Old South history even when some individuals are not comfortable broaching the subject. Similarly, the foodways of the South also reflect the changes that the region has undergone over the years, including changes in race relations, an influx of immigrants, changing industries, altered gender roles, and so forth. Again, the food on our tables, in the stores, and in local restaurants may speak a clearer truth of the region than traditional forms of rhetoric have done. Disingenuous politicians may pull on white-dominated southern in-group identity to say that contemporary immigrants are not welcome, but that is certainly not true when it comes to food history or variety in the region. Consequently, southern food stays consistent to tradition while changing in response to immigration, the movement toward healthier lifestyles, and the need to account for the diversity of people who have always lived here or who continue to move here.

In examining southern rhetoric through the skillet image, we shared examples that add complexity to claims about race, class, and gender in the Old South regional monomyth. This view combines the region's past and present, and the tensions present in our food stories intersect to encapsulate a fuller picture of the South. After all, the weight of the South's past cannot be attributed to each of these problems alone. Still, it is important to consider how they collectively define southern food as regional topoi that, as Rice (2012) argues, are strategic. That is, we pointed out that one value of southern foodways rhetoric is its ability to allow the region's controversial histories and differences to "speak" through the food of the region, even when these changes are not (or are not yet) explicitly acknowledged in traditional rhetoric such as "polite" campaign speaking or contentious political discourse (Rice 2012). What foodways rhetorics provide is an emphasis on process, as food is a "living thing, not only historical" where oftentimes "the best cooking is not about perfection, but rather the flawed process of how we aim for a desired flavor" (Lee 2018, 306). The skillet metonym grants that the region is not solely driven by its problematic past, but is attempting to come to terms with where it has been and where it is headed; food reflects that transformation and, in turn, changes the relational identities that are created.

We also must be careful in thinking about regions without falling prey to nostalgia. Although we have discussed how the skillet metonym is able to resist what Rice (2012) calls "bleeding into kitschy or nostalgic regionalism" (203), it is worth underscoring here how we see the skillet as a disruptor, not an object that symbolizes and valorizes a white, religious, gun-loving, and isolated South. Rather, nostalgia may be productive as well as problematic (Stokes and Atkins-Sayre 2016). When we think about nostalgia in southern food, it is often from the vantage point of the old (white) South, in which white southerners pine for a white southern history that did not exist, or at least, did not exist for them. If we enrich these narratives with stories of how southerners of all races and backgrounds used their skillets to construct meals that shaped different identities, these untraditional texts illustrate how their stories were here all along; we just were not interested in recognizing and archiving their work. At a minimum, by moving foodways into a conversation on rhetoric traditionally indexed by political oratory, we create a space for disruption. Attempts at whitewashing its history, in Lodge or Cracker Barrel, are conspicuous. Whereas the rostrum can be *de facto* white and male as a space of southern identity, the skillet durably unsettles it.

Ultimately, the skillet has a place in the effort to re-establish the southern region as a way to resist rhetorical metanarratives. As famed African American culinary historian Michael Twitty (2017) has explained in his reenactment of slave cooking traditions, "Southern food is my vehicle because it is **not** apolitical. It is also drenched in all the dreadful funkiness of the history it was created in." Thus, when chefs such as Twitty present southern food dishes in a new light, they take nostalgic ingredients into new realms, helping to circulate familial and cultural intergenerational stories. Those chefs also help to change the conversation; in 2017, only 16 percent of head chefs and cooks were Black (United States Bureau of Labor Statistics 2017). Twitty's observation underscores our view as the skillet for a metonym that allows for consideration of the past while offering a measure of possibility. The object remains the same: handed down from family to family or purchased anew, ingredients and traditions remain. As one writer argues, "This pan, this mute dense tool, roots us to our parents and grandparents and the hundreds of generations that came before them. Every one that was ever made . . . is basically the same: a heavy, unbending piece of metal that picks up a patina with long use and grows to fit the hands that hold it" (Ozersky 2012). Those hands might place traditional and new ingredients together to make something completely different, and maybe their work creates a conversation with another southerner about why their story, too, helps define the southern region. In the end, there's enough room in the skillet for all of those ingredients.

REFERENCES

Balestier, Courtney. 2019. "Eating to Go." In *The Food We Eat, the Stories We Tell: Contemporary Appalachian Tables*, edited by Elizabeth Engelhardt and Lora Smith, 116–31. Athens: Ohio University Press.

Black, Jane. 2016. "The Next Big Thing in American Regional Cooking: Humble Appalachia." *Washington Post*, March 29, 2016. https://www.washingtonpost.com/lifestyle/food /the-next-big-thing-in-american-regional-cooking-humble-appalachia/2016/03/28 /77da176a-f06d-11e5-89c3-a647fcce95e0_story.html.

Black, Jason Edward, and Vernon Ray Harrison. 2015. "Southern Paternal Generationalism and the Rhetoric of the Drive-By Truckers." *Western Journal of Communication* 79 (May): 283–306. https://doi.org/10.1080/10570314.2015.1035398.

Burkette, Allison. 2011. "Stamped Indian: Finding History and Culture in Terms for American 'Cornbread.'" *American Speech* 86, no. 3 (December): 312–39. https://doi.org/10.1215 /00031283-1503919.

Carey, Leigh Ann. 2018. "Raise Hell and Eat Cornbread, Comrades! Looking for Radical Politics in the Hollers and Backroads of the South." *Slate*, November 5, 2018. https://slate .com/human-interest/2018/11/queer-appalachia-radical-politics-south.html.

Cooper, Christopher A., and H. Gibbs Knotts. 2013. "Overlapping Identities in the American South." *The Social Science Journal* 50, no. 1 (March): 6–12. https://doi.org/10.1016 /j.soscij.2012.04.001.

Cooper, Christopher A., and H. Gibbs Knotts. 2017. *The Resilience of Southern Identity: Why the South Still Matters in the Minds of Its People*. Chapel Hill: University of North Carolina Press.

Dao, Dan Q. 2018. "Vietnamese-Cajun Crawfish Is the American Food of the Future." *Munchies/Vice Magazine*, February 27, 2018. https://munchies.vice.com/en_us/article /vbpqnm/vietnamese-cajun-crawfish-houston.

de Velasco, Antonio. 2019. "'I'm a Southerner, Too': Confederate Monuments and Black Southern Counterpublics in Memphis, Tennessee." *Southern Communication Journal* 84 no. 4 (July): 233–45. https://doi.org/10.1080/1041794X.2019.1636129.

Editors of *Garden and Gun*. 2013. *The Southerner's Handbook: A Guide to Living the Good Life*. New York: HarperCollins.

Elie, Lolis Eric. n.d. "Affirmation After Katrina." Southern Foodways Alliance. Accessed July 25, 2019. https://www.southernfoodways.org/film/lolis-eric-elie-affirmation -after-katrina/.

Engelhardt, Elizabeth D. 2011. *A Mess of Greens: Southern Gender & Southern Food*. Athens: University of Georgia Press.

Evans, Judith. 2011. "Redeye Gravy Often Made from Just Two Ingredients." *St. Louis Post-Dispatch*, May 4, 2011. https://www.stltoday.com/lifestyles/food-and-cooking/red-eye -gravy-often-made-from-just-two-ingredients/article_6840f9c3-6142-5477-90a1 -6c9f58e1fddf.html.

Ferris, Marcie Cohen. 2013. "The 'Stuff' of Southern Food: Food and Material Culture in the American South." In *The Larder: Food Studies Methods from the American South*, edited by John T. Edge, Elizabeth Engelhardt, and Ted Ownby, 276–311. Athens: University of Georgia Press.

Ferris, Marcie Cohen. 2014. *The Edible South: The Power of Food and the Making of an American Region*. Chapel Hill: University of North Carolina Press.

Hanchett, Tom. 2013. "Salad Bowl Suburbs: Global Food Geography in Charlotte, N.C.... and Beyond." In *The Larder: Food Studies Methods from the American South*, edited by John T. Edge, Elizabeth Engelhardt, and Ted Ownby, 165–83. Athens: University of Georgia Press.

Harrison, Alferdteen. 1991. "Preface." In *Black Exodus: The Great Migration from the American South*, edited by Alferdteen Harris, vii–x. Jackson: University Press of Mississippi.

Hood, M. V. Trey. 2018. "Review: The Resilience of Southern Identity—Why the South Still Matters in the Minds of Its People." *Journal of Southern History* 84, no. 1 (February): 233–34. https://doi.org/10.1353/soh.2018.0072.

Howard, Manny. 2018. "Carla Hall Corrects the Record with 'Soul Food.'" *Slate*, November 3, 2018. https://www.salon.com/2018/11/03/carla-hall-corrects-the-record-with-soul-food/.

Inabinet, Brandon, and Christina Moss. 2019. "Complicit in Victimage: Imagined Marginality in Southern Communication Criticism." *Rhetoric Review* 38, no. 2 (April): 160–72. https:// doi.org/10.1080/07350198.2019.1582228.

Jackson, Blyden. 1991. "Introduction: A Street of Dreams." In *Black Exodus: The Great Migration from the American South,* edited by Alferdteen Harris, xi–xx. Jackson: University Press of Mississippi.

Jones, Sarah. 2017. "Can Local Food Help Appalachia Build a Post-Coal Future?" *The Nation,* October 11, 2017. https://www.thenation.com/article/can-local-food-help-appalachia-build-a-post-coal-future/.

JuneBaby. n.d. "Encyclopedia." *JuneBaby.* Accessed August 12, 2019. https://www.junebaby seattle.com/encyclopedia.

Keane, Erin. 2019. "Tommy Tomlinson's Book about Losing Weight Is Really about 'The Things That Haunted Me.'" *Salon,* January 15, 2019. https://www.salon.com/2019/01/15/tommy-tomlinsons-book-about-losing-weight-is-really-about-the-things-that-haunted-me/.

Keller, Annaliese. 2017. "Cornbread—Made in the USA." *Edible Paradise,* October 15, 2017. https://edibleparadise.com/home-page-stories/cornbreadnnmade-in-the-usa/.

Lee, Edward. 2018. *Buttermilk Graffiti: A Chef's Journey to Discover America's New Melting-Pot Cuisine.* New York: Artisan.

Leopold, Todd. 2012. "The South: Not All Bubbas and Banjos." *CNN,* April 14, 2012. https://www.cnn.com/2012/04/14/us/bubba-southern-stereotypes/index.html.

Lodge. n.d. "About." Accessed August 12, 2019. http://www.lodgemfg.com/about.

Louis, Katrina. 2018. "Female Chefs Shine at Soul Food Session Year-End Dinner." *Q City Metro,* December 14, 2018. https://qcitymetro.com/2018/12/14/female-chefs-shine-at-soul-food-sessions-year-end-dinner/.

Lovelace, Melba. 2012. "Dear Melba; Keep an Eye on the Gravy." *Daily Oklahoman,* April 18, 2012. https://newsok.com/article/3667166/keep-an-eye-on-the-gravy.

McFee, Michael. 2016. "Skillet Laureate." *Southern Cultures* 22, no. 2 (Summer): 88–104. http://www.southerncultures.org/article/skillet-laureate/.

McPherson, Tara. 2003. *Reconstructing Dixie: Race, Gender, and Nostalgia in the Imagined South.* Durham, NC: Duke University Press.

Miller, Adrian. 2013. *Soul Food: The Surprising Story of an American Cuisine.* Chapel Hill: University of North Carolina Press.

Moore, Roger. 2018. "Poverty Statistics for Southern States." Southern Legislative Conference, September 2018. https://www.slcatlanta.org/research/index.php?pub=580.

Morris, Kendra Bailey. 2007. "Beans and Cornbread: Feeding Souls a Mile Deep." *NPR's Kitchen Window,* March 7, 2007. https://www.npr.org/templates/story/story.php?storyId=7743821.

National Museum of African American History & Culture. n.d. "Popular and Pervasive Stereotypes of African Americans." Accessed July 25, 2019. https://nmaahc.si.edu/blog-post/popular-and-pervasive-stereotypes-african-americans.

Okona, Nneka. 2018. "Rooted in Tradition, Baked Mac and Cheese Is a Fixture in Life's Big Events." *Chicago Tribune,* December 26, 2018. https://www.chicagotribune.com/dining/ct-food-southern-mac-and-cheese-20181221-story.html.

Ozersky, Josh. 2012. "A Pan for All Seasons." *Time,* March 26, 2012. http://content.time.com/time/magazine/article/0,9171,2109125,00.html.

Paasi, Anssi. 2003. "Region and Place: Regional Identity in Question." *Human Geography* 27, no. 4 (August): 475–85. https://doi.org/10.1191/0309132503ph439pr.

Powell, Douglas R. 2007. *Critical Regionalism.* Chapel Hill: University of North Carolina Press.

Purvis, Kathleen. 2016. "Why Does Sugar in Cornbread Divide Races in the South?" *Charlotte Observer*, March 29, 2016. https://www.charlotteobserver.com/living/food-drink /article68763427.html.

Purvis, Kathleen. 2017. "This American Comfort Food Leads a Double Life—But Only Some of Us Know the Secret. Do You?" *Charlotte Observer*, November 15, 2017. https://www .charlotteobserver.com/living/food-drink/article184866748.html.

Purvis, Kathleen. 2018. "We Just Won the Superbowl: A Charlotte Chef Is Going National." *Charlotte Five*, June 7, 2018. https://www.charlottefive.com/soul-food-sessions-national/.

Reid-Brinkley, Shanara Rose. 2011. "Mammies and Matriarchs: Feminine Style and Signifyin(g) in Carol Moseley Braun's 2003–2004 Campaign for the Presidency." In *Standing in the Intersection: Feminist Voices, Feminist Practices in Communication Studies*, edited by Karma R. Chávez and Cindy L. Griffin, 35–58. Albany: SUNY Press.

Rice, Jenny. 2012. "From Architectonic to Tectonics: Introducing Regional Rhetorics." *Rhetoric Society Quarterly* 42, no. 3 (June): 201–213. https://doi.org/10.1080/02773945 .2012.682831.

Severson, Kim. 2016. "How I Mastered the Art (and Politics) of Cornbread Dressing." *New York Times*, November 8, 2016. https://www.nytimes.com/2016/11/09/dining/cornbread -dressing-thanksgiving.html.

Sharp, Ellie. 2017. "Viet-Cajun Crawfish is the Most Delicious Expression of Houston's Diverse Culinary Identity." *Eater*, February 27, 2017. https://houston.eater.com/2017/2/27 /14707856/houston-vietnamese-cajun-crawfish.

Sharpless, Rebecca. 2013. *Cooking in Other Women's Kitchens: Domestic Workers in the South, 1865–1960*. Chapel Hill: University of Chapel Hill Press.

Sloan, Melissa M., and Ashley B. Thompson. 2012. "Race as Region, Region as Race: How Black and White Southerners Understand Their Regional Identities." *Southern Cultures* 18, no. 4 (Winter): 72–95. http://www.southerncultures.org/article/race-as-region-region -as-race-how-black-and-white-southerners-understand-their-regional-identities/.

Sohn, Mark. 2005. *Appalachian Home Cooking*. Lexington: University Press of Kentucky.

St. George, Zach. 2014. "America's Last King of Cast Iron Finds His Time Has Come Again." *Bloomberg*, May 19, 2014. https://www.bloomberg.com/news/articles/2014-05-19 /lodge-skillets-endure-americas-last-king-of-cast-iron-finds-his-time-has-come-again.

Stokes, Ashli Q., and Wendy Atkins-Sayre. 2016. *Consuming Identity: The Role of Food in Redefining the South*. Jackson: University Press of Mississippi.

Tell, Dave. 2012. "The Meanings of Kansas: Rhetoric, Regions, and Counter Regions." *Rhetoric Society Quarterly* 42, no. 3 (June): 214–32. https://doi.org/10.1080/02773945.2012.682843.

Tipton-Martin, Toni. 2015. *The Jemima Code: Two Centuries of African American Cookbooks*. Austin: University of Texas Press.

Twitty, Michael W. 2017. *The Cooking Gene: A Journey through African American Culinary History in the Old South*. New York: Amistad.

United States Bureau of Labor Statistics. 2017. Labor force characteristics by race and ethnicity, 2017. https://www.bls.gov/opub/reports/race-and-ethnicity/2017/home.htm.

Watts, Rebecca. 2008. *Contemporary Southern Identity: Community through Controversy*. Jackson: University Press of Mississippi.

Wood, Andrew. 2012. "Regionalization and the Construction of the Ephemeral Co-Location." *Rhetoric Society Quarterly* 42, no. 3 (June): 290–96. https://doi.org/10.1080/02773945 .2012.682847.

Yonan, Joe. 2015. "Sean Brock on His Cracklin' Cornbread, Where the South Comes Together in a Skillet." *Washington Post*, January 22, 2015. https://www.washingtonpost.com/lifestyle /food/sean-brock-on-his-cracklin-cornbread-where-the-south-comes-together-in-a -skillet/2015/01/22/03a81af8-9dc7-11e4-bcfb-059ec7a93ddc_story.html?utm_term =.039067a6727a.

York, Paul S. n.d. "Cooking in Your Cast Iron Skillet." *Southern Living*. Accessed July 1, 2019. https://www.southernliving.com/food/how-to/cast-iron-skillet-recipes-cooking.

Chapter 12

CONVERGENCES OF SOUTHERN IDENTITY AND THE GLOBAL SOUTH IN THE NATIONAL CENTER FOR CIVIL AND HUMAN RIGHTS

CAROLYN WALCOTT

As a Black, Caribbean-born, female scholar situated in the South, I often consider myself an "insider" among the growing migrant community, but yet grapple with the "outsider" syndrome based on the evocative anti-Blackness that has characterized the rise of the white Right in the state of Georgia. The "othering" of Black communities has also been a source of personal unease as Black Caribbean migrants are sometimes perceived to be less susceptible to and lacking the history of racism in the US South.

The American South has a tricky relationship with the Global South. Framed within the understanding that a substantial part of the population has roots in Africa, who experienced conquest and trauma, we at least have to note the parallel.[1] And yet, some white southerners would certainly look to other parts of the world (Africa, Asia, Latin America, and the Caribbean) as developing, not developed. Shome (2019) traces the origin of the term "Global South" to the postcolonial era of the early 1980s. The Global South is constituted, according to Shome, by "economically impoverished nations, most of which were hemispherically in the South and were emerging from the darkness of colonialism" (198). Given this nationalist interpretation of the postcolonial 1980s, then, it makes no sense to cleanly include the African American experience as part of the Global South.

However, as a Guyanese scholar, I read the diaspora experience as vividly linked through economic hardship, traumatic history, and identity. A recent visit to the National Center for Civil and Human Rights in Atlanta, Georgia, makes this connection clear. The center was established in 2007 and officially opened to the public in 2014 (Chapman 2014), in the unveiling of a major rhetorical representation of the civil rights era in the United States while connecting those events to global human rights issues. Atlanta is home to a growing population of African migrants from the Global South, including the Caribbean, and African Americans who continue to migrate inwardly from other states.

Thus, the center is an important place for connecting Caribbean and African American memory of slavery, as civil rights struggles in the United States coincided with anticolonial resistance in the Global South. While African Americans marched down the streets of Atlanta for change, Afro-Caribbean citizens joined the wave of Pan-African anticolonial activism during the 1950s. These events signified the collective anticolonial struggle among members of the African diaspora (Dunn and Lewis 2011). Migrants from the Global South have the possibility to unite in a common relational identity connected to collective memory of slavery and oppressed civil rights (Rice 2010). In this chapter, I would like to help extend the analyses about US Black southern identity, pushing us to read it as globally regional. I will conclude with some areas of the center that could better support such a diaspora reading of regions.

Scholarship on colonization grounds this analysis. In colonized territories, stories of revolt and rebellion against colonizers are a key feature of historical narrative. Southerners are beginning to narrate their history via the Stono Rebellion (1739), Prosser's Rebellion (1800), German Coast Uprising (1811), Denmark Vesey conspiracy (1822), Nat Turner's revolt (1831), the *Amistad* mutiny (1839), Creole Revolt (1841), and John Brown's raid on Harper's Ferry (1859)—rather than the "gallant" heroes between 1861 and 1865. Moreover, the facilitation of the slave trade's "lower third" (the production of sugar, cocoa, and cotton, among other commodities) means that it was not exactly congruent with the European financial, insurance, and shipping businesses that constituted its northern leg (Morgan 2007). While an estimated ten million enslaved Africans were transported to the Caribbean under the transatlantic slave trade, the United States imported a significantly smaller labor force of enslaved Africans before and after its independence (Trouillot 1995). However, slavery in southern states persisted years after it was abolished in the British West Indies. Plantation settlements were spread across states including Georgia, Mississippi, Alabama, Virginia, and the Carolinas to support the production of such commodities as sugar, cotton, and coffee.

Similarly, in my Caribbean home, the eighteenth and nineteenth centuries are primarily read through a lens of rebellion (Craton 1979). Revolts in Jamaica (Burnard 2011) and British Guiana (Matthews 2006), especially the two-day Demerara Uprising of 1823, are understood as unsettling white planters enough that their relative power eventually vanished, paving the way for abolition

(Howard 2015). It would be useful to view American history before the twentieth century similarly, focusing on the increased paranoia and moral wrestling caused by African Americans in the South. Even if such revolts did not bring down the empire of slavery all at once, they created the powder keg that led to emancipation. As enslaved Africans in the British West Indies continued to fuel the Industrial Revolution (Williams, Tomich, and Darity 2014), so too did cotton production in the US South (Jung 2020). Fear of British expansion to the US South, for the exploitation of its raw goods economy, emerged as a significant source of concern for white planters who continued to profit from enslaved labor in that region of the United States (Narayan 2018). The southern states were, to an extent, foreign countries when it came to their relational identity to the world.

Bringing this argument up to the twentieth and twenty-first centuries as the South industrialized is, of course, a bit complicated, given ways that American discourses functioned to prioritize white southerners. And yet, the economic disparities make it clear that global racism and regionalism intersect. In *Six Ways America Is like a Third World Country,* McElwee (2014) cites inequality, gun violence, and problems in criminal justice, healthcare, education, and infrastructure as characteristics of underdevelopment in regions of the United States. Specifically, he singles out healthcare as comparably poor in the "Deep South" as in Algeria, Nicaragua, and Bangladesh, countries classified by the United Nations as developing countries. Similarly, Tomasky (2010) compared the social well-being of citizens in the US South to those in developing countries by citing the high incidence of low births, particularly in the states where the enslavement of African Americans persisted for decades. These states include Mississippi, Louisiana, Alabama, South Carolina, Tennessee, and North Carolina. Regional narratives of social inequity, layered with the unique experiences of enslaved African Americans in the southern region of the US, tell of a situation that is comparable to that exhibiting the legacies of colonialism in the Global South.

Beyond scientific indicators, in the world of cultural and literary artifacts, relational identity is strongly similar. As an essay in *Africology* puts it, members of "the modern African Diaspora share an emotional bond with one another and with their ancestral continent, and . . . broadly similar problems in constructing and realizing themselves" (Palmer 2000, 32). Paul Theroux, in *Deep South* (2015), compares his journeys in South Carolina to his journalistic work in parts of Africa and Afghanistan. Stories from Theroux's journeys include Gullah Geechee culture that is still substantially African on the Sea Islands; parts of Allendale County, South Carolina, that resemble Africa; and foreign aid and missionary zeal that flows from the Global North to African relief, bypassing the US South through a web of bureaucracy (40). The memories of

External view of the National Center for Civil and Human Rights in Atlanta. Photo by Carolyn Walcott.

Black communities, including African Americans and Africans in the diaspora, intersect in profound ways, an important direction for public memory studies (Gallager and LaWare 2010).

The National Center for Civil and Human Rights functions as a regional space for capturing such memory that evades national parameters, even as it works hard to create civil rights as a uniquely *American* experience. Located in the heart of downtown Atlanta, adjacent to the World of Coca-Cola and the Georgia Aquarium, the center has been described as a museum of many colors (Kopanek 2014)—one that embodies white economic interests while facilitating historical and cultural narratives of the African American struggle (Pelak 2015).

But it can do more. Woods, Ewalt, and Baker (2013) posit that critical regionalism is necessary for "disrupting the narratives of a place through the production of alternative relational cartographies" (345). Staton (2015) has suggested that the rhetorical appeal of its photographic texts should be critically analyzed to counteract subjective representation of historical events. Critical analysis of the center therefore offers an alternative lens to explore connections as a way out of a uniquely nationalistic reading that defies the global logics of colonialism that operated in the American South.

This focus joins a trend in southern studies. Public memorials and oral histories on the experiences of enslaved African Americans in southern states are part of a growing body of knowledge on memory, trauma, and narrative that has global scope (see Mattern 2017; Savage 2009; and Conner and Wheeler 2018). Scholars have also conducted case studies that demonstrate global connections, including the rhetoric of civil disputes between former slave owners and newly freed individuals in the South (Milewski 2018; Milewski

2019), contestation surrounding monuments (Denson 2017), and the absence of marginalized voices in the constructions of southern identity (Davis 2016). The center gives scholars an opportunity to push this work further and see how memory space opens up possibilities for a global diaspora (Gilberti 2013; Arbona 2015). My chapter does so with the additional argument that such space also cultivates regionalism that defies the nation-state's borders.

While this chapter acknowledges both historical and contemporary accounts of southern slavery, including the prevailing trauma still experienced by African Americans, it also considers the collective experiences of Black migrants whose histories are not far removed from the African American narrative. Although Hummel (2013) argues that the Black experience in the United States has been protracted, I contend that Blacks in the diaspora are excluded from the conversation around race and place in the creation of Black identity. Black Americans have largely influenced the shaping of the African diaspora and differences in the perspectives that have informed scholarship on African history and identity, both in scholarship and in expensive internationally curated museum spaces. Thus, in this chapter, I rely on critical regionalism to demonstrate convergence between the two.

To understand how others in the African diaspora could draw inspiration from the National Center for Civil and Human Rights, I begin with the way memory is structured in four parts (collective, public, cultural, and social memory) for southern identity with African Americans. Then I proceed to a critique of exhibits at the center to discuss how it bears witness to this memory. I conclude with the global turn toward human rights in the center's exhibits, especially attending to the issue of human trafficking. Convergence of the experiences of southern African Americans with a broader African diaspora may begin to help cities like Atlanta uncover its potential to deliver regionalism as a trauma healing point between the Global North and Global South.

AFRICAN AMERICAN IDENTITY, MEMORY, AND MEMORIALS

Collective memory, first studied by Maurice Halbwachs (1992), is associated with the broad psyche of others across place and time. Bodnar (1992) gives examples in his work of "flashbulb moments," in which we recall where we were and what we were doing at the time of the event in history. According to Halbwachs (1992), there is really no such thing as "individual memory." The only real memory is collective and cocreated through narration with someone else. Collective memory is built around storytelling, which, in effect, collides with excluded stories.

Bodnar (1992) defines public memory, the second category, as "a body of beliefs and ideas about the past that help a society to understand its past, present, and by implication, its future" (15). Bodnar posits that commemorative events are predicated upon language centered on "social unity and civic loyalty," aimed at influencing public memory and ultimately gaining patriotic support. Bodnar's nationalist frame fits well with the current framing of the National Center for Civil and Human Rights, with its attention to militant manhood (and, by association, later womanhood) in demanding rights previously denied. This collectivist approach is reflected in memorializing Vietnam War heroes as a means of drawing public attention to the valor necessary to maintain nationhood. As Bodnar explains, public memory is thus directed to a past built on resistance that built the foundation for the current liberties now enjoyed, as the nation responds to contestation undergirded by loyalty.

And yet for many reasons, the South's diaspora narrative clearly does not fit with this theory. Patricia Davis's (2016) critiques call out the exclusion in the South and southern identity when we forget the African American story as fundamentally centered in the region. She notes that the absence of African American narratives obscures critical appraisal of the events and people that shaped southern history. Going one step further, then, we see how Bodnar's mode of "public memory" does not engage identity and trauma. Rather than appealing through patriotic displays that carve small spaces for subgroup and ethnic stories to be included in a dominant national identity, African Americans were often appealing through their pain.

Trauma is reconstructed in memorial spaces regarding slavery and war, for example (Edkins 2003). These displays are not just attempts at expanding civil rights, but an attempt for a deeper rupture with the past, even if the media often subjugate such memories to a nationalist frame when they attempt to make sense of such spaces (Zelizer 2014). Visual artifacts ignite such cultural memory, the third category, among spectators.

For Sturken (1997), cultural memory represents "a field of cultural negotiation through which different stories vie for a place in history" (1). Cultural memory, Sturken explains, is "a field of contested meanings in which Americans interact with cultural elements to produce concepts of the nation, particularly in events of trauma, where both the structures and fractures of a culture are exposed" (2–3). This broader theory than public memory shows how shared ideology is coconstructed—the nation can be produced in the National Center for Civil and Human Rights itself, rather than as something against which individual enactments appeal (for rights and inclusion). Trauma, in such a space, can define the region or nation—not merely serve as a support for an appeal. Often, we understand this best through photos, cinema, and television that shock us with scenes of the brutality of slavery and its legacies. We still see that scholars frame all memory at the level of the nation, although Sturken too is interested in how the *nation* is constructed—not the regions or diasporas.

The fourth category of memory, social (or popular) memory, refers to memory constructed in spheres among people who converge to discuss social issues. Here, I argue that the center provides that space for memorializing and discussing social issues, even in the way its name operates as an issue. Visitors to the center get to consider future implications for race and identity with liberal democracies, beyond any necessary building of a particular narrative, civic strategy of rights creation, or nation-building—even as all three are also there in the space. But the surplus of trauma and global understanding in the museum calls our attention to something about relations, dialogue, and identity that are regionally organized, not just civic in the traditional sense of rights-giving and duty-requiring. African Americans and others, including other marginalized groups and whites who witnessed the era directly or vicariously, recall and claim those experiences as part of their regionality as Global South or southern, in a social way that defies the nation.

A close reading of the center's exhibits can thus help show how the past impacts the current and future discourse around Blackness and identity. The center's articulated purpose is "to create a space for visitors to explore the fundamental rights of all human beings so that they leave inspired and empowered to join the ongoing dialogue about human rights in their communities" ("About Us" n.d.). With its universal mission captured in three words—Reflect, Inspire, Transform—the center aims to maintain the city's civil rights legacy inspired by significant activists including Martin Luther King Jr., while providing a place for visitors to "reflect on the past, transform the present and inspire the future" ("About Us" n.d.).

Arguably, the Black Lives Matter movement draws inspiration from the historical nonviolent resistance of the civil rights era. It is clearly a national rights-focused project, too. The movement reignites public memory of civil injustices, while advocating for legislative transformation to secure the future of Black lives in America. Nevertheless, social memory for all of us who see ourselves as outside the national civic body in some way can enter a discussion of civil and human rights.

The selection of historical accounts for the displays magnifies what Sturken (1997) describes as negotiated spaces for sustaining cultural memory. Social memory of civil and human rights at the center is therefore negotiated, and it positions the viewer to look deeper for resonance of memory between African Americans and Africans in the diaspora. In so doing, the outsider cocreates popular or social memory, even while drawing on the particular public and cultural experiences of nation-bound, public communities.

BRIDGING CIVIL AND HUMAN RIGHTS
IN THE US SOUTH

Within the walls of the picturesque forty-three-thousand-square-foot structure are narratives of trauma that memorialize and honor key actors of the civil rights era who challenged white supremacy as part of the struggle for equal rights and justice for Black Americans, such as the right to live, work, and become citizens (Staton 2015). The passage of laws that privileged white people was among the actions and situations that triggered civil rights activism across the southern states from the 1950s to the 1970s, known as the civil rights era. Among the key events were acts of civil disobedience, nonviolent protests, and marches across southern states. Sights, sounds, and recollections are all captured in exhibits titled "Rolls Down like Water: The American Civil Rights Movement."

Among the major rhetorical features on the main level of the three-story center are a lunch counter sit-in simulation inspired by the sit-in by students in Greensboro, North Carolina, in 1960; news of the assassination of Martin Luther King Jr. in 1968; and audio and visual representations of antisegregationists. Global human rights and human rights contraventions are also central features of the center's major exhibits on its upper level. By connecting the past with the present, narratives cast victims of human trafficking as slaves of the syndicates that operate globally, including in Atlanta.

Visitors are also introduced to global leaders who have committed crimes against humanity in various parts of the world. As this chapter argues, slavery's dark history lurks behind the present and continues to impact migrant populations mainly from the Global South in their pursuit of a better life. While images of slavery and civil rights activism inspire nostalgia for the African diaspora, they also evoke memory of a past built on human rights abuse. Such imagery is strongly rhetorical (Dickinson, Blair, and Ott 2010), in which "events, objects, and practices carry evocative, affective weight [as] they create and/or sustain emotional affiliation" (Palmer 2000, 3). Profoundly emotive images under one roof reflect a bridging of the Global South with the local South where human trafficking, like slavery, is recognized as both a global and local problem at the level of ongoing trauma. Regardless of economic or political oversight by a US government that has seen "progress," slavery is not extinct from the South, including Atlanta, where a growing number of Black people have migrated and continue to evolve.

As I walked through the center, I felt echoes of Guyana's oral histories of resistance against colonialism, including the vilification and ultimate fate of those who openly rebelled against civil injustice. Cuffy, whose real name was Koffie, an enslaved African, met his demise as the result of leading other enslaved Africans in a revolt against white planters in 1763. The 1763 memorial in the city of Georgetown is a testimony of that struggle. Although Cuffy lived in an era before King, both fought for human rights and dignity for Black people irrespective of geographies. Ultimately, both Cuffy and King suffered a similar fate for giving voice to the oppressed. I also at this moment remembered how modest Guyana's collection of African artifacts is to tell such a story. The African Museum in the capital of Georgetown can only tell of oppression based on fragments, while African Americans tell their story at the center as it has been carefully curated from primary documents.

That difference made me want to attend to the vacuum in scholarship on intersections between the historical experiences of Black migrant populations from the Global South and their counterparts in the North. Very few scholars have acknowledged the burgeoning population of Black migrants to the Global North, including the United States, and their exclusion from ideations of Black history, identity, and memory. Despite dialectical differences among the Black communities across the United States based on nationality and regional locale, African Americans and Africans in the diaspora share a common history of slavery and civil rights contraventions. Boxer (2011) captured this argument when he stated that "the link between decolonisation and the civil rights movement in the USA was also well understood by African Americans, and there is no doubt that they drew inspiration from, and also helped to influence, developments in other parts of the world" (1).

The link is tangible. The Caribbean diaspora in the United States is comprised of almost eight million individuals, and the number has been increasing by 50 percent every ten years (Zong and Batalova 2019).[2] Despite the growing population of Black migrants in the United States, the concept of a Black identity and the cultural memory associated with slavery differ among diasporas. For instance, Black Americans often call themselves African Americans, but that term excludes a significant portion of the Black population who migrated here from Africa, South America, and the Caribbean. Questions pertaining to African identity are largely unanswered (Okpalaoka 2014), causing scholars of history to confront challenges and clarify misperceptions in academic spaces regarding who holds the right to narrate the history of slavery.

As a native of Haiti who completed his doctoral studies in the United States, Trouillot (1997) recalls his own reflexivity in response to African American students who questioned historical accounts of slavery and western narratives. Trouillot was not merely a scholar with theoretical knowledge, but one who had conducted extensive field work in Haiti. His scholarship was informed by interviews and observation of the remnants of Haiti's battlefield following the Haitian revolution. Trouillot therefore understood and developed an insider's perspective on the historical experiences of revolt against slavery and its effects years later, as reported in his *Silencing the Past: Power and the Production of History*. This was not a past with which African Americans were familiar. So, for Trouillot, the classroom became a space for discourse and clarification. In his response to one student who questioned Western narratives of African American slavery and its effects on the Black community, Trouillot stated, "I wanted them to learn that the African connection was more complex and tortuous than they had ever imagined, [and] that the US monopoly on both Blackness and racism was itself a racist plot" (71).

Knowledge of slavery's impact in other parts of the world, like the Caribbean experience, seemed limited among African Americans based on Trouillot's encounter. Museums in the United States, including the center in Atlanta, tend to do a good job with the African American story substantiated through reference to high numbers of Africans stolen, dehumanized, and terrorized. But when it comes to telling the stories of individuals, revolts, and independence movements throughout the Global South and the African diaspora, they tend to have a very limited presentation. The center provides a space where Africans in the diaspora could draw inspiration, especially since what it means in the American South is quite different from what it means in other areas of the nation. The museum could actively assert that the dominant narrative identity in the South is Black. Instead of simply making reference to contemporary global issues as "parallels" to a specifically American civil rights history, the museum could reflect on how the narrative of trauma and experiences of overcoming bear similar features across the world.

A WALK-THROUGH: GATEKEEPING VISUALITY
OF CIVIL AND HUMAN RIGHTS

As an Afro-Caribbean immigrant from the Global South, my knowledge of slavery was based on a small mix of oral history, formal education, and social memory within the local public sphere in Guyana. I was therefore curious about the National Center for Civil and Human Rights as a space for critical gaze on Black identity. On one summer afternoon in July 2019, I encountered the sweltering heat of downtown Atlanta for the fifteen-minute walk from Georgia State University to the center. The journey took me past downtown sites such as Centennial Park, the epicenter for the 1996 Olympic Games hosted by the city of Atlanta, situated less than five minutes from the center. After paying for my tour, I followed the multitude of visitors who gravitated toward the middle level of the obviously well-funded, three-story edifice. I first encountered historical images of southern segregation and Jim Crow laws that prohibited

Black people from enjoying basic civil liberties such as using public facilities including restrooms and restaurants. The images evoked a deep sense of anxiety and sadness that I once felt as I watched *Best of Enemies*, a film set in the civil rights era based on the racial tensions associated with desegregation of the school system in the South. Artifacts labelled "Colored," "White," and "White Men's Rest Room" that demarcated public spaces during the Jim Crow era and images of segregationists in southern states also appear in this area. Apart from restricting spaces and places for occupation by whites only, Jim Crow laws also prohibited interracial unions as seen in a sign in uppercase letters: "PERSONAL RELATIONSHIPS—THE LEGISLATURE SHALL NEVER PASS ANY LAW TO LEGALISE ANY MARRIAGE BETWEEN ANY WHITE PERSON AND A NEGRO, OR DESCENDANT OF A NEGRO."

In addition to laws that restricted unions, Black and white people were also denied other forms of social interaction. From an outsider perspective, the rhetorical significance of the Jim Crow laws featured at the center gave me a personal sense of indignity and empathy for African Americans. The cultural memory of enslaved Africans in the Global South appeared to diverge from the experiences of Black Americans, although both groups experienced forced migration from the continent of Africa to expand white economic interests. While an elitist culture pervaded spaces in the Caribbean, where the planter class once settled, the eventual occupation of those spaces by Caribbean-born leaders facilitated political and socioeconomic mobility once reserved for colonists. Despite social and political leadership in the Caribbean, the economic stagnation of the Black South was held in common with white dominance of international trade and relations.

As shown in other displays at the center, narratives cloaked in resentment for the Black populace were also reflected in the language deployed by southern segregationists to mobilize support for their cause. For instance, Alabama Senator Sam Engelhardt, who was openly segregationist, voiced anti-Black sentiments during a social gathering. He assured his supporters that they should "have no fear, the white and the right will win." Whether winning was confined to the county or state level, over the years political leaders utilized racial rhetoric to secure and maintain power, as described by Mendelberg (2001). Racial utterances by state officials during the civil rights era created a strong rhetorical force against social change and cemented the idea that the South was solidly white and resentful of outside influence. Such foregrounding of course ignores research by Crenshaw (1988) that found that regionalized populism for centuries before and decades after have targeted American Indians, individuals of mixed race, and Blacks, and cultivated the idea that federal control created "divisive" societies. In other words, the museum does not help visitors understand the ways that Black southerners were also audiences of such discourse or could even buy into ideas of their own inferiority and, minimally, for a need for calm patience and civil obedience in the face of white political terrorism.

An exhibit labelled "White Men Only" caused me to consider the once-restricted spaces of power and leadership that some Black people have come to occupy in the United States. The euphoria felt by many African Americans when the nation's first Black president, Barack Obama, was sworn into office in 2008 reached beyond the United States. Many who were familiar with the civil rights struggles felt that President Obama represented the realization of the dream espoused by Martin Luther King Jr. At the same time, when I visited the museum in 2019, it appeared very little had changed over the post-civil rights decades in the United States. The birther arguments surrounding President Obama's "outside" origins were especially keenly felt and mirrored closely the psyche of racial prejudice reflected in this area of the museum.

The oral history that visitors can experience via recordings in the center's exhibits also shows how many political and judicial leaders publicly and repeatedly advocated white supremacy. Judge Tom P. Brady illustrated the use of hate language when he told a gathering, "I don't want the Negro as I've known him and contacted him in my lifetime, as a class, to control the making of law that controls me, to control the government under which I live." In the audio recording, Brady responds to a question posed by an audience member, perhaps a reporter, by saying, "I'd feel better off and I think this country would be better off if all Negroes were removed from it because I think it's a potential source of racial strife." Framed as the "Negro problem," one can imagine from these voices a very small minority group in the United States causing significant trouble, as if a deportation convoy was feasible. This section of the museum pushes the fact of white male leadership so strongly, especially in its strong archive of historical video footage, that it is easy to see the American project as a purely white project.

More famous than Brady's statements were those of Governor Ernest Vandiver of Georgia. Vandiver's statement that "We can and we must protect the children of Georgia" emphasized that he felt an obligation to protecting only the state's white children and implied that white children were under threat from Black people. In another recording, William S. Pritchard, an Alabama attorney and colonel in the military, described Black people as African savages sold into slavery because of a permanent state of delinquency and lack of work ethic. As I played the videos, I could hear deep sighs emerging from African American visitors who walked by. As I processed the sights and sounds of the center, I was reminded of Toni Morrison's statement that "Oppressive language does more than represent violence; it is violence" (1993, para. 13). Among the visitors who strolled in and out of the main hallway were an interracial couple and their two biracial daughters. I allowed my mind a moment to contemplate their family's relationship to the enduring wounds of the civil rights era as a time in which sometimes unspoken white supremacy became voiced as dominant sentiment, especially in the South.

In Guyana, I had observed that interracial tensions among Guyanese of African and Indian descent created similar social restrictions for conjugal relations between Afro-Guyanese and Indo-Guyanese couples. Interracial couples were disparaged and, in some instances, disavowed by family members. The "whites only" signifier also rekindled my memory of Guyana's political history and the pursuit of independence from Britain. In the process, Guyanese leaders of African and Indian descent presided over ethnic conflict to secure votes and ultimately the nation's resources. Voting for your own "race" became synonymous with racial superiority although, as in the American civil rights struggle, interracial unity was evident among Guyanese.

With respect to land ownership, I also considered the laws that disenfranchised African Americans from obtaining land alongside the privileges of formerly enslaved persons in Guyana who purchased the first few villages, including Victoria, thus reclaiming the land they once tilled for their owners. I also juxtaposed the African American exclusion from businesses owned by white people with the privileging of Portuguese entrepreneurs who immigrated to Guyana after enslaved Africans. Like African Americans, Afro-Guyanese pursued equality and human dignity in a post-slavery setting.

Guyanese historian and scholar Kean Gibson (2003) describes a cycle of racial oppression as a result of primordial instinct for preservation. Gibson argues that Afro-Guyanese are economically marginalized by Indo-Guyanese based on the Indian caste system maintained and perpetuated by these new elites, after the fall of European colonialism. Indo-Guyanese continue to hinder development by oppressing Afro-Guyanese. Members of the Indo-Guyanese political and academic communities have attempted to refute such claims, and yet in the space of this museum, they clearly reflect Martin Luther King Jr.'s idea of a transcendent evil of racism, not to be merely eliminated by Black power against white supremacy alone. The linguistic and cultural oppression in the South has all sorts of effects, including those on white residents as well as Black. Revolution, redistribution, and Black political leadership only become effective under the broader shared goal of mutual uplift in such racially heterogeneous environments.

After being transfixed for two hours on the pictorial history of the civil rights era in the museum, I next moved to the lunch counter simulation showing how passive nonviolent resistance among southern Black people took the civil rights movement to another level. On February 1, 1960, four African American students from Greensboro, North Carolina's Agricultural and

Technical College staged a sit-in at the Woolworth's lunch counter to protest the segregated accommodations for whites and people of color established under the 1890 Louisiana law (Wynn 1991). The students' demand for service was met with resistance from the white community, but inspired wide support for their nonviolent defiance of the Jim Crow laws that designated separate public eating places for Black and white customers.

Sturken (1997) notes, "Reenactment is a form of re-experiencing; within the codes of realism, viewers are allowed to feel that they, too, have undergone the trauma" (96). The lunch counter simulation at the National Center for Civil and Human Rights fed that truly global feeling of trauma. There were noticeable departures from the space designed to evoke a sense of presence as the narrator asked, "How long can you last?" I sat down, carefully placed the headset over my ears, put my palms on the counter, and closed my eyes as directed. What came next were the sounds of torment. As the audio grew louder, my anxiety intensified over the loud and aggressive yells of antisegregationists. Every fiber in my being froze as the beating increased upon the Black protestors who dared to defy the sign "whites only."

Although the entire simulation lasted for only forty-three seconds, it seemed like hours. Afterwards, I took a few minutes to regain my composure as my heart continued to race over thoughts of "what if I'd actually been at the sit-in; what would have been my end?" I returned to the reenactment a second time, closed my eyes, and waited once more to be led down the dark history of rejection. This time, each forceful sound took me back to Guyanese and Caribbean history and the oral histories of descendants of African runaways from slavery who received merciless whippings when they were recaptured.

I left the lunch counter disturbed by the racial exclusion experienced by Black Americans during slavery and the post-slavery era, as well as the current resurgence of racism. Following Black Lives Matter protests and the increased ease of digital exposure, many African Americans have experienced resurgent anxieties in public spaces including restaurants and parks. President Donald Trump's political rhetoric has aggravated a resurgence of white nationalism that punctuated the civil rights era (Abramsky 2016). And yet, despite a similar persecution for just being born Black, one visitor said to me after the lunch counter reenactment, "I don't know that I would have the same amount of resolve to do it. How could someone remain nonviolent through all of that?" Perhaps under the lens of a historically unique event in national history, such a reaction especially makes sense. Activists were trained to react using methods of nonviolence and civil disobedience, resulting in their arrest in a specific set of historical circumstances. The museum visitor, though, did see the connection and was angry that "people still feel this way today about Black people," as being undesirable in certain spaces.

The author at the lunch counter sit-in exhibit, where visitors can hear the sounds of the protests. Courtesy of Carolyn Walcott.

The nonviolent resistance of African Americans in spaces where they were unwelcome connects them to Caribbean history and collective memory of Africans through similar resistance movements led by notable scholars like Walter Rodney. In 1968, Jamaica's prime minister, Hugh Shirer, expelled Rodney from the Caribbean due to his political activism that inspired civil disturbances in Jamaica. As a Caribbean historian, Rodney led the Black power movement in the Caribbean and anticolonial discourses in Jamaica. Rodney would later emerge as a professor of history and Guyanese exemplar who openly challenged European imperialism. His seminal work, *How Europe Underdeveloped Africa*, emerged from his activism and his doctoral degree on African history, earned in London at the age of twenty-four. Although I was an outsider to the events of the US civil rights era, my memories of Rodney's resistance gave me an insider perspective on the lunch counter events.

As I viewed the center's pictorial collection of national support for the slain Martin Luther King Jr., I vividly recalled the similarly mournful atmosphere that permeated the Caribbean region as news of Rodney's assassination spread. The Guyanese historian and Pan African scholar had not only gained notoriety but met a fate similar to that of King. In 1980, Rodney was assassinated for his strong anti-imperialist posture that drew a growing national and international following. This collective memory, experienced as my own flashbulb, saw me in the back seat of my mom's car, as the horse-drawn funeral procession for the Rodney left a legacy of rhetorical canons still echoed by many today. Throngs of supporters attended and rallied around the clarion call "enough is enough" aimed at the ruling political administration. Like King's assassination, Rodney's assassination attracted public debate, social, collective, and cultural memory among the African diaspora. Although Rodney was assassinated twelve years after King, the vitriol experienced by both activists establishes the shared experience of African Americans and Africans in the diaspora. Guyana's Rodney is America's King. The museum, however, made no reference to a shared sense of loss for leadership across the diaspora; it instead worked to portray the King assassination as a unique event in American history.

Following the representations of King's death, the museum took its global turn. I spent the final hour of my tour on the upper level, which features the International Gallery. Human rights is a prominent theme among the various depictions, with visual narratives complementing the rights-based appeal to various communities including women, LGBTQ persons, persons with disabilities, and immigrants. Global human rights, including contemporary issues around LGBTQ and women's rights, were striking features of the human rights exhibits. Exhibits were themed around emancipation, justice, and equality, but very little on human dignity. Visitors have a choice of three screens to view powerfully narrated accounts of human rights abuses, including global human trafficking, which piqued my interest most.

As a global phenomenon, human trafficking permeates countries across the Global South including Latin America and the Caribbean, but is also felt in the Global North. My awareness of human trafficking is informed by my memory of stories of victims in Guyana who reported being captive to both male and female perpetrators disguised as employment recruiters. Victims were

A section of the human rights exhibit, where visual narratives are presented of documented human trafficking cases. Photo by Carolyn Walcott.

transported to rural locations and forced to work under inhumane conditions without remuneration as part of forced labor and sex trafficking, the two major activities of the human trafficking syndicate globally.

According to the center's human trafficking narrative, eleven million un-documented immigrants are among the forty million victims held hostage by perpetrators of human trafficking globally. Due to their illegal status, many of these victims suffer in silence within the syndicate. As an illicit transnational industry, human trafficking accrues $43.3 billion through forced labor and $99 billion from sexual exploitation. Women and girls constitute 98 percent of sex trafficking victims globally. The hallowed grounds of the center suddenly felt unstable as I considered the numerous reported incidents of human trafficking and sex trafficking in the state of Georgia. As one of the fastest growing cities in the United States, Atlanta is a major hub. The Hartsfield–Jackson International Airport, named after the city's first Black mayor (Maynard Jackson) as well as a former white mayor, is considered the world's busiest airport and a conduit for human and sex trafficking (Yamanouchi 2017).

The FBI named Atlanta one of fourteen US cities with the highest rate of child sex trafficking (Covenant House Georgia 2020). In addition, according to that report, 12,400 men purchase sex with young women monthly, while one hundred adolescent women are sexually exploited forcibly every night in the state of Georgia. It is therefore a firmly articulated paradox that the city that houses the National Center for Civil and Human Rights also harbors such profound human rights abuses. Johnson (2019) posits that art representing Black agency has created a Black public sphere that has played a major role in educating, exploring, and (re)defining what it means to be Black locally, nationally, and globally. In the area of global sex trafficking, at least, the museum is doing a good job in actually articulating a global linkage that is firmly rooted in local trauma. It can be hoped that these efforts might allow the museum to see itself as, through its name and mission, articulating a dialogue for the Global South and thus urgently in need of a reframing of its history as a transnational (or at least trans-Atlantic) story, even after the American ban of the African slave trade. This story, too, might help express a regional frame as well—that the movement of ideas, duties, and rights is not just a sign of a "charitable" America. Rather, the trauma of racism and the life-generating experience of Black people in the diaspora form an unending chain stronger than the chains of oppression.

CONCLUSION

African Americans and Africans in the diaspora share a similar history of colonization dispersed across geographies in the Global South and the Global North. Differences among the African American and foreign-born African communities are socially constructed via assimilation and interaction. The National Center for Civil and Human Rights, viewed from the perspective of outsider, brought me inside by presenting exhibits that stimulated my recollection of Guyanese civil rights. At the same time, the center highlights the convergence of memory among African Americans and Africans in the diaspora through experiences and aspirations for civil and human rights.

The center's exhibits on civil rights illustrate the Black struggle in America and the resilience of that community to contest public memory—that is, to transgress the idea of a "Black problem" and show its members as a dominant constituent in the American South. Concomitantly, Africans in the diaspora draw inspiration from nonviolent resistance through their assimilation in spaces such as Atlanta and disrupt the fear of the Black outsider. In other words, in our experience of the museum itself, we push from the American safe zone of public memory work into the more radical space of social memory. Our very presence in such a museum space articulates a Black diaspora reading and dialogue that can reframe the South as an intersection.

The center's focus on global human trafficking in a city where victims are often trafficked represents, in a rather indirect way, an initial attempt at addressing such an audience for dialogue. However, with a focus on a distinctly American civil rights memory and I-85 sex trafficking, it likely leaves most visitors more focused on the need for individual charity than any such dialogue. Europe and North America's leadership in a global economy that promotes human trafficking industry, plucking my friends from developing areas and the Global South, is unattached to a continuous history of trauma based on forced exploitation.

Such a focus also discredits the problematizing of the Black community as the source of global conflict. In global sex trafficking, traffickers often use the allure of freedom as an initial deception: they present young women with the "escape" of visiting the Global North, getting a job there, and attaining its level of consumption (based on historical and ongoing exploitation of the Global South). The curation lacks a focus on social memory that would overcome such mistakes. For example, international stories of Black activism and Black success would remove the sense that Americans have a sort of special or unique place in fighting issues like global sex trafficking. Stories about migrants and the fluidity across borders historically would refute the idea that a uniquely American history is the answer for a uniquely non-American problem that has crept onshore. In this way, the center can keep from playing into the hands of a new human rights problem, in the form of immigrants, LGBTQ minorities, or traffic victims. Ethnocentric biases are evident in the legal justification of past acts of human rights contraventions, but a deeper conversation is necessary to counteract normalizing of human rights violations against African Americans and Africans in the diaspora.

NOTES

1. Hopefully, I do not overstate the case, as the demographics of the US South jumped dramatically depending on immigration and economic trends, and antebellum urban centers typically go the other way, with substantial white majorities. From 1850 to 1860, for example, the US white urban population was double and in some cases triple the Black urban enslaved population (US Census Bureau 1850). In Richmond, Virginia, where the total population stood at 38,000, 62 percent were whites, 7 percent were free Blacks, and 31 percent were enslaved persons (US Census Bureau 1850; US Census Bureau 1860). Similarly, in Charleston, South Carolina, 58 percent of the population of 41,000 were whites, 8 percent were free Blacks, and 34 percent were enslaved persons, while in Mobile, Alabama, 71 percent were whites, 3 percent were free Blacks, and 26 percent were enslaved persons in a total population of 30,000 (Berlin and Gutman 2001). In Baton Rouge, Louisiana, according to Berlin and Gutman, the white population was almost triple that of the enslaved population: in a population of only 5,000 people, 68 percent were whites, 23 percent were enslaved persons, and 9 percent were free Blacks.

2. Individuals who were either born in a Caribbean island nation or reported ancestry of a given country in the Caribbean, according to the the American Community Survey (n.d.). According to the same survey, between 1980 and 2000, the Caribbean immigrant population reached 2.9 million and increased by more than 50 percent every ten years; in 2000, the population reached 3.7 million and had increased by 18 percent in 2010. Whereas in 2014, approximately four million immigrants from the Caribbean resided in the United States, accounting for 9 percent of the nation's 42.4 million immigrants, by 2017 the steady inflow of migrants accounted for 4.4 million in 2017 (Anderson 2015). In terms of Black migrants from the Global South, the Pew Research Center analysis of the US Census conducted in 2010 revealed that 3.8 million Black immigrants resided in the United States, quadrupling the number in 1980 (Zong and Batalova 2019). In addition, Black immigrants accounted for 8.7 percent of the US Black population tripling the share in 1980, with the immigrant Black population projected to reflect 16.5 percent of US Blacks by 2060, according to Zong and Batalova. In certain metropolitan areas, foreign-born Black people make up a significant share of the overall Black population.

REFERENCES

Abramsky, S. 2016. "Make America Hate Again." *New Statesman* 145, no. 5338: 24–29.
"About Us." n.d. *The National Center for Civil and Human Rights.* Accessed January 20, 2020. https://www.civilandhumanrights.org/about-us/.
American Community Survey. n.d. Data Profiles. US Census Bureau. Accessed January 20, 2020. https://www.census.gov/acs/www/data/data-tables-and-tools/data-profiles/2017/.
Anderson, M. 2015. "A Rising Share of the U.S. Black Population Is Foreign Born, 9 Percent Are Immigrants; and While Most Are from the Caribbean, Africans Drive Recent Growth." Pew Research, April 4, 2015. https://www.pewresearch.org/social-trends/2015/04/09/a-rising-share-of-the-u-s-black-population-is-foreign-born/.
Arbona, Javier. 2015. "Anti-Memorials and World War II Heritage in the San Francisco Bay Area: Spaces of the 1942 Black Sailors' Uprising." *Landscape Journal* 34, no. 2: 177–92.
Berlin, Ira, and Herbert G. Gutman. 2001. "Natives and Immigrants, Free Men and Slaves: Urban Workingmen in the Antebellum American South." *American Historical Review* 88 (December): 1175–201.
Bodnar, John. 1992. *Remaking America: Public Memory, Commemoration, and Patriotism in the Twentieth Century.* Princeton, NJ: Princeton University Press.
Boxer, Andrew. 2011. "Civil Rights—The International Dimension." *History Review* 70 (September): 21–26.
Burnard, Trevor. 2011. "Powerless Masters: The Curious Decline of Jamaican Sugar Planters in the Foundational Period of British Abolitionism." *Slavery & Abolition* 32, no. 2: 185–98. https://doi.org/10.1080/0144039X.2011.568231.
Chapman, Gray. 2014. "Center for Civil and Human Rights Opens Its Door to Atlanta." *Architectural Record* 202, no. 8 (July 28). https://www.architecturalrecord.com/articles/3202-the-freelon-group-and-hoks-center-for-civil-and-human-rights-opens-its-doors-to-atlanta.
Conner, Thomas H., and James Scott Wheeler. 2018. *War and Remembrance: The Story of the American Battle Monuments Commission.* Lexington: University Press of Kentucky.

Covenant House Georgia. 2020. Human Trafficking and Child Slavery. https://covenant housega.org/Human-Trafficking.

Craton, Michael. 1979. "Proto-Peasant Revolts? The Late Slave Rebellions in the British West Indies 1816–1832." *Past & Present* 85, no. 99 (November): 99–125.

Crenshaw, Kimberlé Williams. 1988. "Race, Reform, and Retrenchment: Transformation and Legitimation in Antidiscrimination Law." *Harvard Law Review* 101, no. 7 (May): 1331–87.

Davis, Patricia G. 2016. *Laying Claim: African American Cultural Memory and Southern Identity.* Tuscaloosa: University of Alabama Press.

Denson, Andrew. 2017. *Monuments to Absence: Cherokee Removal and the Contest over Southern Memory.* Chapel Hill: University of North Carolina Press.

Dickinson, Greg, Carole Blair, and Brian L. Ott, eds. *Places of Public Memory: The Rhetoric of Museums and Memorials.* Tuscaloosa: University of Alabama Press.

Dunn, Hopeton S., and Rupert Lewis. 2011. "Communicating Pan-Africanism: Caribbean Leadership and Global Impact." *Critical Arts: A South-North Journal of Cultural & Media Studies* 25, no. 4: 467–72.

Edkins, Jenny. 2003. *Trauma and the Memory of Politics.* Cambridge, UK: Cambridge University Press.

Gallager, Victoria G., and Margaret R. LaWare. 2010. "Sparring with Public Memory: The Rhetorical Embodiment of Race, Power, and Conflict in the Monument to Joe Louis." In *Places of Public Memory: The Rhetoric of Museums and Memorials*, edited by Greg Dickinson, Carole Blair, and Brian L. Ott, 87–112. Tuscaloosa: University of Alabama Press.

Gibson, K. 2003. *The Cycle of Racial Oppression in Guyana.* Lanham, MD: University Press of America.

Gilberti, Marco. 2013. "Rethinking the Memorial in a Black Belt Landscape: Planning, Memory, and Identity of African-Americans in Alabama." *Urbani Izziv* 24, no. 1: 144–59.

Halbwachs, Maurice. 1992. *On Collective Memory.* Edited and translated by Lewis A. Coser. Chicago: University of Chicago Press. Originally published in 1925.

Howard, Martin R. 2015. *Death Before Glory: The British Soldier in the West Indies in the French Revolutionary and Napoleonic Wars, 1793–1815.* Barnsley, South Yorkshire, UK: Pen and Sword Military.

Hummel, Jeffrey Rogers. 2013. *Emancipating Slaves, Enslaving Free Men: A History of the American Civil War.* New York: Open Court.

Johnson, Stephanie Anne. 2019. "Education, Art, and the Black Public Sphere." *Journal of Pan African Studies* 12, no. 10 (March): 41–58.

Jung, Yeonha. 2020. "The Long Reach of Cotton in the US South: Tenant Farming, Mechanization, and Low-Skill Manufacturing." *Journal of Development Economics* 143 (March). https://doi.org/10.1016/j.jdeveco.2019.102432.

Kopanek, Christopher. 2014. "George C. Wolfe Brings the Civil Rights Museum to Vivid Life in Atlanta." *American Theatre*, November 2014, 50–53.

Mattern, Joanne. 2017. *Martin Luther King, Jr. National Memorial: A Stone of Hope.* South Egremont, MA: Red Chair Press.

Matthews, Gelien. 2006. *Caribbean Slave Revolts and the British Abolitionist Movement.* Baton Rouge: Louisiana State University Press.

McElwee, Sean. 2014. "Six Ways America Is like a Third-World Country." *Rolling Stone Magazine*, March 5, 2014. https://www.rollingstone.com/politics/politics-news/six -ways-america-is-like-a-third-world-country-100466/.

Mendelberg, Tali. 2001. *The Race Card: Campaign Strategy, Implicit Messages, and the Norm of Equality*. Princeton, NJ: Princeton University Press.

Milewski, Melissa. 2018. "Justice in an Unjust World: The Untold Story of African-Americans' Civil Cases in the Segregated South." *History Today* 68, no. 6: 65–77.

Milewski, Melissa. 2019. "Taking Former Masters to Court: Civil Cases between Former Masters and Slaves in the US South, 1865–1899." *Slavery & Abolition* 40, no. 2 (May): 240–55.

Morgan, Kenneth. 2007. *Slavery and the British Empire: From Africa to America*. Oxford, UK: Oxford University Press.

Morrison, Toni. 1993. The Nobel Prize Lecture. https://www.nobelprize.org/prizes/literature /1993/morrison/lecture/.

Narayan, Rosalyn. 2018. "'Creating Insurrections in the Heart of Our Country': Fear of the British West India Regiments in the Southern US Press, 1839–1860." *Slavery & Abolition* 39, no. 3 (August): 497–517. https://doi.org/10.1080/0144039X.2018.1489796.

Okpalaoka, Chinwe L. Ezueh. 2014. *(Im)migrations, Relations, and Identities: Negotiating Cultural Memory, Diaspora, and African (American) Identities*. New York: Peter Lang.

Palmer, Colin A. 2000. "Defining and Studying the Modern African Diaspora." *Africology: The Journal of Pan African Studies* 11, no. 2 (Winter-Spring): 214–20.

Pelak, Cynthia Fabrizio. 2015. "Institutionalizing Counter-Memories of the U.S. Civil Rights Movement: The National Civil Rights Museum and an Application of the Interest-Convergence Principle." *Sociological Forum* 30, no. 2: 305–327.

Rice, Alan J. 2010. *Creating Memorials, Building Identities: The Politics of Memory in the Black Atlantic.* Liverpool, UK: Liverpool University Press.

Savage, Kirk. 2009. *Monument Wars: Washington, D.C., the National Mall, and the Transformation of the Memorial Landscape*. Berkeley: University of California Press.

Shome, Raka. 2019. "Thinking Culture and Cultural Studies—from/of the Global South." *Communication and Critical/Cultural Studies* 16, no. 3: 196–218.

Staton, Hilarie. 2015. *Civil Rights: Uncovering the Past—Analyzing Primary Sources.* St. Catharine's, Ontario, Canada: Crabtree Publishing Company.

Sturken, Marita. 1997. *Tangled Memories: The Vietnam War, the AIDS Epidemic, and the Politics of Remembering*. Berkeley: University of California Press.

Theroux, Paul. 2015. *Deep South: Four Seasons on Back Roads*. Boston: Houghton Mifflin Harcourt.

Tomasky, Michael. 2010. "South and the Third World." *The Guardian*, August 10, 2010. https:// www.theguardian.com/commentisfree/michaeltomasky/2010/aug/10/usa-infant -mortality-south-v-world.

Trouillot, Michel-Rolph. 1997. *Silencing the Past: Power and the Production of History*. Boston: Beacon Press.

US Census Bureau. 1850. The Seventh Census of the United States. https://www.census.gov /library/publications/1853/dec/1850a.html.

US Census Bureau. 1860. Population of the United States. https://www.census.gov/library /publications/1864/dec/1860a.html.

Wallace, Elizabeth Kowaleski. 2006. *The British Slave Trade and Public Memory*. New York: Columbia University Press.

Williams, Eric, Dale W. Tomich, and William Darity Jr., eds. 2014. *The Economic Aspect of the Abolition of the West Indian Slave Trade and Slavery*. Lanham, MD: Rowman & Littlefield Publishers.

Woods, Carly, Joshua P. Ewalt, and Sara J. Baker. 2013. "A Matter of Regionalism: Remembering Brandon Teena and Willa Cather at the Nebraska History Museum." *Quarterly Journal of Speech* 99, no. 3 (August): 341–63.

Wynn, Linda T. 1991. "The Dawning of a New Day. The Nashville Sit-Ins, February 13–May 10, 1960." *Tennessee Historical Quarterly* 50, no. 1 (Spring): 42–54.

Yamanouchi, Kelly. 2017. "Airport Training Targets Human Trafficking." *Atlanta Journal-Constitution*, May 3, 2017. https://www.ajc.com/travel/airport-training-targets-human-trafficking/BSRnXUPAt1wT29yUq2C8sN/.

Zelizer, Barbie. 2014. "Memory as Foreground, Journalism as Background." In *Journalism and Memory*, edited by Barbie Zelizer et al. London, UK: Palgrave Macmillan.

Zong, Jie, and Jeanne Batalova. 2019. *Caribbean Immigrants in the United States*. Washington, DC: Migration Policy Institute.

Chapter 13

WHAT LIES BENEATH

Recovering an African Burial Ground and Black Nationalism's
Cultural Influence in the Capital of the Confederacy

MEGAN FITZMAURICE

*I moved to Athens, Georgia, for graduate school. As a young, white Californian,
I was surprised to see a Confederate memorial and a proslavery legislator memorialized at the campus entrance. Though not a southerner by birth, I've now
lived in three southern states for over a decade, making me feel more invested in
the South's complex commemorative culture. I find myself alternately protesting
and celebrating various changes in the memorial landscape. Most recently, I have
been celebrating the city of Richmond's decision to provide $25–$50 million for
a new memorial at the African Burial Ground to honor the city's earliest Black
residents.[1]*

Throughout the United States, many historic Black cemeteries are subject to
chronic neglect, vandalism, or even repavement (Rothstein 2010). Such was
the case in Richmond, Virginia, where one of the nation's oldest cemeteries
had been turned into a parking lot for Virginia Commonwealth University
(VCU). The burial ground was likely the interment site for many free and
enslaved Black Richmonders between 1750 and the early 1800s (V. Davis 2003,
11; Stevenson 2008, 7–8). This chapter follows the efforts of Black activists to
recover the cemetery known as the African Burial Ground (ABG) in the former
capital of the Confederacy.

The ABG's chief advocates were known as the "Defenders for Freedom,
Justice & Equality" (DFJE), a group formed in 2002 committed to "working for
the survival of our communities through education and social justice projects"
("Defenders for Freedom, Justice & Equality" 2013). In 2004, member Ana
Edwards established a new initiative for the DFJE known as the Sacred Ground
Historical Reclamation Project (SGHRP). This initiative aimed "to apply

historical insight to contemporary dynamics to help oppressed peoples exercise their right to self-determination" ("About the Sacred Ground Project" n.d.). The SGHRP's first campaign centered on recovering the ABG and preserving "Shockoe Bottom" as a historic site—the neighborhood where both the ABG and the city's slave-trading enterprise were located. Free Egunfemi (2015), the self-proclaimed "Guardian of Ancestral Remembrance," worked to ensure that there was a spiritual element to the SGHRP's commemoration of these spaces. The campaign expanded and encompassed a diverse coalition of activists who attended city council meetings, held memorial services, and led protests to memorialize the city's Black history.

In this chapter, I argue that as these activists campaigned to recover the ABG and Shockoe Bottom, they invoked a rhetoric of Black Nationalism that also recovered regional narratives of Black resistance and African influence. In other words, the SGHRP challenged racially and ideologically homogeneous narratives of southern history and redefined the region as one that is, and always has been, shaped by Black voices and bodies. I make the case that invoking these themes created a sense of continuity between the Black ancestors they sought to commemorate and the current Black residents they sought to empower. This rhetorical continuity demonstrates that while Black Nationalism as a *movement* may have climaxed in the North, its ideological foundation as a *rhetorical strategy* of racial solidarity and resistance has long flourished in the South. Thus, this study aims to diversify and nuance the strategies used by Black southerners as movers and shakers of regional identity.

While Black Nationalism is difficult to define because of its long history and varied usage, it has consistently referred to a range of ideological commitments that center around Black liberation,[2] self-determination,[3] and Pan-Africanism[4] (Williams 2015, xiii; Ogbar 2005, 3; Breitman 1965, 38). This last tenet calls for African descendants across the globe to stand in solidarity against anti-Black racism and to embrace a shared African heritage (Odamtten 2014, 172–78).[5] Though Black Nationalism is often remembered as an ideology of the urban North, its earliest expressions can be traced back to the slave revolts and expressions of African spirituality in southern slave communities (Moses 1988, 6–11).[6] So rather than insinuating that these contemporary activists are unprecedented in their approach to challenging white supremacy, I suggest that they echo the Black Nationalist rhetoric of their ancestors as they shape the region's political culture and commemorative landscape.

Not only are regional memories largely devoid of Black Nationalism's legacy; they are also saturated with Lost Cause nostalgia, resulting in whitewashed narratives of southern history. While scholars concur that no one really agrees on what it means "to be a southerner," the region is frequently associated with memories of enslavement and white supremacy (Watts 2007, 3–9). Such narratives however have a tendency to sideline stories of Black agency and empowerment (Ramsey 2007, 769–70).[7] This chapter challenges linear narratives of progress that frame the "Old South" as one solely shaped by white supremacy and the "New South" as the dawn of multicultural influence (Kuklinski, Cobb, and Gilens 1997; Bartley 1995).[8] Rather, the activists studied here invoke Black Nationalist precepts of African spirituality and Black liberation to frame the South as a continuously contested space of voices and values.

Moreover, the SGHRP's desire to secure physical and symbolic space expresses a key tenet of Black Nationalism—the desire of Black Americans for a self-determined space of their own. As Robin D. G. Kelley notes, these territorial desires are about "looking for a new beginning, a place where they can be free and develop their own culture without interference" (2003, 126). Burial grounds function as particularly important spaces for Black southerners because they allow for both the celebration of their heritage and the remembrance of their ancestors' suffering (Clark 2005; Hong 2017). Indeed, this case study demonstrates that ancestor reverence, symbolic spaces, and racial distinctiveness are commitments reflective of both southern and Black Nationalist rhetorical traditions. Thus, this analysis enters into conversation with this volume's other chapters by troubling myopic constructions of regional memory, echoing Douglas Reichert Powell's call to view regions as "vital spaces of cultural strife" where ideas about race, class, and gender are (re)shaped (2012, 28). In this chapter, I chronicle several key phases in the SGHRP's campaign to save the ABG and commemorate Shockoe Bottom: the protests to remove the parking lot, the spiritual ceremonies at the ABG, and the plans for a museum on the site. For each phase, I analyze their performances and public discourse by unpacking the central themes of their rhetoric and comparing them to the historical themes of Black Nationalism.

REMEMBERING SLAVERY IN THE CAPITAL
OF THE CONFEDERACY

Between the 1840s and 1850s, Richmond was the second-largest hub of the US slave trade, surpassed only by New Orleans. Although the United States outlawed involvement with the transatlantic slave trade in 1808, the internal slave trade continued until the Civil War's end. Richmond served as one of the busiest destinations for this domestic trafficking. The city witnessed the sale of some two million Africans—*four times* as many as were stolen from Africa and brought to the United States (McInnis 2014, 102). Because most of these individuals were sold from the Upper South (Delaware, Maryland, Virginia) to the plantations of the Deep South (Alabama, Louisiana, Mississippi), Richmond's location on the James River made it an epicenter for the regional sale and transportation of enslaved Africans. Traffickers sold, some estimates suggest, between 300,000 and 350,000 enslaved persons out of Virginia between 1830 and 1865. Most of these transactions took place in Richmond's holding jails and auction houses, located in the dockside neighborhood known as Shockoe Bottom (Edwards and Wilayto 2015, 5–6).

Shockoe Bottom was named as such because of the area's low-lying location along Shockoe Creek. The area flooded frequently, but its riverside location made it a prime hosting ground for the region's slave-trading activities. Prior to 1808, slave traders brought many of the Africans who endured the Middle Passage to Richmond's docks, where they were marched off the slave ships in coffles to the holding pens in Shockoe Bottom (Edwards and Wilayto 2015, 5–6). The buying and selling of humanity were so rampant along Shockoe Creek that this area became known as the "Wall Street of the Confederacy" (Jefferson 2012, 4).

One of the most notorious of these holding pens was "Lumpkin's Jail," named after Robert Lumpkin, its owner and manager from 1800 to 1832. However, most of the city's Black residents knew this establishment as "Devil's Half Acre" (Campbell 2012, 111–12). The history of this site exemplifies the need for a more complex approach to how we remember former sites of enslavement as well as those who were enslaved. Robert eventually married a woman named Mary, whom he had formerly enslaved and the mother of his seven children (Crowell 2012, 43). Once Robert passed away in 1866, Mary Lumpkin took over as sole proprietor and turned the former slave pen into a theological school for individuals who were formerly enslaved. Eventually, this seminary was incorporated into what is now Virginia Union University (Hylton 2014, 9–10). Mary Lumpkin's efforts to repurpose this space highlight ways that Black southerners were not just victims of white oppression, but active agents in their own empowerment and the reshaping of the postwar regional landscape.

Richmond's history as the second-largest hub of the US slave trade and the capital of the Confederacy has resulted in a contested commemorative culture for this majority-Black city (Ogline Titus 2014, 338–47). Though at one point over 30 percent of the city's residents were enslaved, the first and only formal memorial recognizing this history was erected in 2007 (Smith and Miller 1997, 647). The Slavery Reconciliation Statue is one of three identical memorials symbolizing the triangular slave trade. The other two statues are located in Liverpool, England, and the republic of Benin, West Africa ("Our History" n.d.). Thanks to the city's Slave Trail Commission established in 1998, there are also seventeen placards located throughout Richmond that commemorate historical sites of slavery ("Richmond City Council Slave Trail Commission" n.d.).

In 2004, the SGHRP successfully lobbied the city for an additional placard at a significant site of Black resistance: Gabriel's execution. Gabriel was an enslaved blacksmith who planned an uprising in which he recruited hundreds of slaves to kill every white person in Richmond (excluding Methodists, Quakers, and Frenchmen). However, two of his enslaved accomplices alerted authorities of Gabriel's plan before it was implemented. He was captured and executed on October 7, 1800, at the ABG (Aptheker 1969, 219–26). The stones used for the city's gallows remain at the ABG, where Egunfemi (2015) pours libations and leads an annual processional to honor Gabriel's memory, as well as others who suffered his fate.

In contrast, Richmond boasts eight Confederate monuments in addition to numerous schools, highways, and holidays named for Lost Cause leaders ("A List of Virginia's 200-Plus Confederate Monuments and Public Symbols" 2017). Many notable Confederate political and military leaders are given elaborate memorials in Hollywood Cemetery, a designated landmark on the National Register of Historic Places ("Hollywood Cemetery" 2021). The city's most prominent landmark though is "Monument Avenue," a street strewn with five memorials to Confederate leaders erected between 1890 and 1929.[9] When the city unveiled a statue featuring the renowned Black tennis player and humanitarian Arthur Ashe in 1996, it brought a visible and ideological shift to Monument Avenue's makeup (Driggs, Wilson, and Winthrop 2001). Ashe's monument was highly contested among both Black and white residents, which, according to Watts (2007), reflected a regional conflict over commitments to change and tradition. Some Black residents, noted Watts, resented integrating Ashe into a space that venerated the South's racist past and advocated for a commemorative place of their own (47). This commitment to self-determination and spatial representation—southern displays of Black Nationalism—would surface again in the campaign to recover the ABG.

PROTESTING A PARKING LOT

Chidester and Linenthal assert that "a sacred space is not merely discovered, or founded, or constructed; it is claimed, owned, and operated by people advancing specific interests" (1995, 15). Thus, the SGHRP not only had to prove the ABG's existence; its members also had to assert their rightful ownership of this space. This section explains ways their campaign worked to both liberate their ancestors' memory from desecration and affirm the self-determination of Black southerners to reshape Richmond's commemorative landscape.

In response to mounting protests regarding VCU's parking lot, Virginia's Department of Historic Resources (DHR) published a report on the ABG's location in 2008 (Hong 2017, 12–15). Yet, Dr. Michael Blakey, anthropologist and advisor for SGHRP, found the report gravely inaccurate: the DHR had merely drawn a box around the label "Burial Ground for Negroes" on a historical city map to determine the site's boundary. Blakey's anthropological team at the College of William & Mary published their own study later that year to expose the DHR's flawed findings and prove the expansive boundaries of the burial ground (Blakey and Turner 2008). Despite this evidence, VCU continued to use the site as a parking lot, repaving it the following year and fencing off only a fifty by 110-foot portion to use as a memorial.

Not only was the state incapable of accurately assessing the burial ground's existence, but Blakey argued that it was also unqualified to recognize its cultural and spiritual significance. His study noted that the DHR could not release definitive findings while "Richmond community groups representing African American concerns" were working "to restore [the ABG] as sacred or cultural space" (Blakey and Turner 2008, 1–2). The DHR's findings represented yet another hindrance to the long-standing efforts of Black southerners to protect their ancestors' gravesites as culturally distinct commemorative spaces.[10] Subjugated peoples are not just interested in correcting the state's history, as Ronald W. Walters explains, but in acquiring "a share in the resources involved in creating it" (2003, 1–2). For this reason, Blakey asserted that individuals with "expertise in African-Diasporic mortuary traditions" and members of "the descendant community" should be consulted throughout the investigation (Blakey and Turner 2008, 6). Blakey's research invalidated the DHR's assumed expertise on the site and showcased ways Africans and their descendants have shaped the southern landscape culturally and topographically through their burial practices. These arguments justified the burial ground's return to its original stewards: the city's Black residents.

The SGHRP organized several demonstrations at the ABG to reclaim it as a sacred site of Black memory. In 2009, King Salim Khalfani, executive director of Virginia's NAACP chapter, spoke at a vigil held the day before VCU would repave over the ABG. He told the press: "Now, without regard to the sacredness of the Africans buried there, VCU will pave the site and utilize it for parking. No sane or rational people would allow this without a fight. If VCU moves forward with this plan and we cannot stop them, we will seek restitution, reparations, and possibly begin a direct-action campaign to express our outrage" (qtd. in Slayton 2009). By suggesting that the ABG's repavement served as grounds for reparations, Khalfani framed VCU's actions as a manifestation of the systemic racism that those buried below the parking lot endured. Indeed, this was not merely a local struggle, but a reflection of regional and national power dynamics that have long been executed at the nexus of race and space (P. Davis 2013, 108–111). While Black Nationalists have frequently been criticized for their reparation demands, Kelley explains that reparations have never been "entirely, or even primarily, about money"; rather, this discussion is concerned with issues of "social justice, reconciliation, reconstructing the internal life of Black America, and eliminating institutional racism" (2003, 114). And for Black southerners, spatial and racial reparations remain deeply intertwined given the region's history of commemorative intimidation: the systemic erection of Confederate statues as a means of maintaining white control over public space even after slavery's demise (Cox 2003, 150). So as the SGHRP fought to reclaim the ABG, it also sought restitution for slavery's material, symbolic, and spatial legacies.

Activists convened yet again on April 12, 2011—the 150th anniversary of the start of the Civil War—to occupy the site of the burial ground. By planning the protest on this anniversary, the activists worked to capitalize on the public's fixation with this battle to highlight the battle for liberation that continues to be fought on southern soil (or in this case—asphalt). The time and space of this protest upended Lost Cause memories of the war in exchange for what Patricia Davis describes as memories of "the war that ended slavery," where "Southern Blackness, rather than whiteness" is at the narrative's center (2016, 13).

The protestors blocked the parking lot for over an hour until the police arrived. While many protestors dispersed at that time, police officers arrested four participants who refused to move on trespassing charges. These activists were protesting the state's new signage that commended the asphalt's removal while the parking lot was still actively in use (Pourzal 2011). The protest occurred just hours before Virginia's governor formally agreed to purchase the lot from VCU for the asphalt's removal. The VCU spokesperson, Anne Buckley, stated that the lot would be closed as soon as the university found an alternative parking site (Kapsidelis 2011).

Although the administration may have acknowledged the need to memorialize this site in word, they had yet to follow through in deed. Such dissonance only contributed to the group's skepticism about white institutional change, aligning these southern activists with a long history of Black Nationalists who have proclaimed that "Africans in America must take responsibility for liberating themselves" (Stuckey 1972, 6). In this case, reclaiming the burial ground was about recovering an ideological commitment that prized Black bodies and African spirituality above property values and transportation convenience. Such a platform resonated with past Black power activists who viewed the country's fixation on capitalism and private property as part and parcel of its racist agenda.[11] Although the activists were arrested for "trespassing" on the parking lot, they pinned the university as the site's "real" trespassers because of their disregard for its original inhabitants. As Khalfani pointed out, "no sane or rational people" would tolerate the desecration of their ancestors' resting place (qtd. in Slayton 2009). Such criticism carries heavy weight in a region that has expended millions of dollars to protect the resting places of their Confederate ancestors. By invoking the importance of Civil War history and ancestor reverence, these activists engaged in a strategic rhetoric at the nexus of both traditionally southern and Black Nationalist values.

LIBERATING THE BURIAL GROUND THROUGH ANCESTRAL SOLIDARITY

While SGHRP supporters were a racially diverse group, the activists who claimed an ancestral connection to those buried in the cemetery saw the parking lot as a threat to their heritage. For these descendants, recovering the burial ground was also a means of recovering genealogies and reclaiming ancestors. This rhetoric of kinship reflected the ideals of Pan-Africanism among Black southerners. As Sterling Stuckey explains, Pan-Africanism holds that many cultural and geographical differences among African descendants "were virtually destroyed on the anvil of American slavery," allowing Black Americans to maintain a sense of solidarity despite their ancestral diversity (1972, 1). In the American South, this critical framework functions to resist those traditional narratives that erase the lives of enslaved Africans before their transatlantic kidnapping, as well as those political structures that deny Black southerners' legal right to their ancestral land. As the activists called for the ABG's restoration as a means of respecting "*their* ancestors," they framed their demands as no different from the privileges already enjoyed by many of the region's white residents.

Shawn Utsey, a professor of African American studies at VCU, created a documentary about the controversy surrounding the burial ground called *Meet Me at the Bottom* (2010). In one of Utsey's interviews, a Black VCU student who was watching the lot's repavement exclaimed, "the burial ground means a lot because this could be a gateway to someone else's ancestry or someone else's heritage and they might never have a chance to know about it because we're building over it." Ja'nel Edens, another VCU student, questioned what the parking lot meant for her own ancestral research: "There's no way we can fully know what was here. What if I want to go back and trace my history? And what if that remain is right here and they're building over it?" (qtd. in DePompa 2009). For these students, the burial ground was a potential key to unlocking their past, and ironically, their university was hindering this quest for knowledge.

Burial grounds are unique sites of southern Black memory for they are not just places of mourning; they are also places of celebration where descendants can commemorate the rich culture of their African ancestors. Janine Bell of the Elegba Folklore Society in Richmond exclaimed, "Can't we have something in our memory that makes us proud? Africans everywhere, then and now, there and here, recognize in one way or another, the significance of our ancestors" (qtd. in Utsey 2010). For Bell, reclaiming this burial ground would help expand memories of the southern Black experience beyond slavery and beyond the South. This site held the potential to celebrate her ancestors' self-determination and honor a transhistorical, transglobal African community. Indeed, this burial ground was likely one of the few spaces where free and enslaved Black people were given relative freedom to engage in their own traditions and rituals. This often involved a combination of both Christian and African spiritual elements—an act of defiance toward those slaveholders who attempted to control the enslaved persons' religious beliefs (Adkins 2008). Thus, the site symbolized memories of oppression, resistance, *and* celebration, embodying the complex ways African bodies and voices have long shaped the southern landscape.

Framing the ABG's recovery as an issue of spiritual and cultural significance to the African diaspora at large, the SGHRP invited leaders from the Nzema tribe of Princes Town, Ghana, to perform an "atonement ceremony" at the ABG. Traditionally, this ceremony represents an "official apology for the participation of African rulers in the enslavement and sell-out of African people" (Schramm 2016, 239–40). So on November 6, 2008, Chief Nana Ndama Kundumuah IV poured water from an African gourd onto the ground to atone for "the pain and agony that the fallen heroes went through" during enslavement (Utsey 2010). By hosting this ceremony, the SGHRP fostered a sense of reconciliation and racial solidarity between the descendants of the enslaved persons and the African rulers and their people. Another Ghanaian leader, Sebastian Yami Kofi Essien, instructed descendants at the ceremony: "You must uphold and hold the heritage you know you have. Step by step you know the whole place will be taken and there will be no history; there will be nothing for us. . . . As Africans, as Americans, as blacks—we do not play with our culture" (qtd. in Utsey 2010). Essien encouraged the SGHRP to preserve this burial ground as a means of joining the Pan-African fight against neocolonial legacies that continue to threaten Black spaces, histories, and cultures, as described by Fierce (1993, xx). Essien's unifying rhetoric framed the Ghanaian ceremony as a synecdochal representation of all African cultures from which those buried there descended. By drawing on histories and traditions older than the state itself, these African leaders gave the SGHRP a renewed cultural justification for the ABG's reclamation.

On November 18, 2010, the Black Student Union (BSU) at VCU sought to join the SGHRP in resisting institutional control of the ABG by organizing a silent protest on campus. Students dressed in all black and marched to the campus quad, lying down on the concrete for over two hours. They held signs that read: "Get your asphalt off my ancestors!" and "If I died would you park on me?" Student Kiara Green explained that participants were "standing for justice" and remaining silent "for our ancestors buried beneath the VCU parking lot" (qtd. in Trice 2010). Amie Tudor, one of the organizers, told news cameras, "These people are lying down silently, as a demonstration for the voices that cannot be heard" (qtd. in Bell 2010). The students' rhetoric accused the university of desecrating their ancestors and framed its indifference as racial injustice.

This demonstration reflected southern Black protest traditions that applaud students as powerful change-agents and engage silence as a form of nonviolent activism (Carson 1995). Strategic silence has often been used to seize not just equal rights, but equal access to spaces in which to exercise those rights—i.e., a lunch counter to eat at, a bus seat to sit down on, a sidewalk to tread across (Morgan and Davies 2013). As a means of space making and rights claiming, silence is a strategic rhetorical choice as it spotlights one's embodied actions in real time (Glenn 2004, 20–48). Activists are not fighting *for* the right to occupy that space—they are *already doing it.* As George Lipsitz explains, "it takes places for racism to take place," and so challenging ideological structures of racism often involves challenging its physical structures as well (2011, 5).

For VCU's Black students, the university's violation of this burial ground was a spatial expression of racism that violated both them and their ancestors. By lying on their backs throughout the quad, the BSU took on the physical form of those individuals whose memory they were looking to protect. While the deceased buried below the parking lot were unseen, these activists gathered at the university's center and were impossible to ignore. Such a performative gesture pushed the university to acknowledge that the Black bodies below the parking lot have occupied the site long before the campus's construction. The protestors crafted a rhetorical equivalence between their ancestors' bodies and their own, embodying a transhistorical Black identity that is a hallmark of Pan-Africanism. As Stuckey explains, Black communities are able to maintain Pan-African solidarity across time and space primarily because of their "shared experience of oppression at the hands of white people" (1972, 6). The thought of parking a car over these students' bodies is unfathomable, yet these protestors' signs implied that parking a car over their ancestors' bodies is an act just as heinous. This performance made visible the invisible desecration of those buried at the ABG as well as the sustained apathy of white institutions toward Black bodies.

In 2010, the city finally made arrangements to buy the lot from VCU and transfer the property to the Slave Trail Commission. On May 21, 2011, Mayor

Dwight C. Jones hosted an "Asphalt-Breaking Ceremony" at the site. Participants included city council members, Chair Edwards (SGHRP), Director Khalfani (NAACP), Janine Bell (Elegba Folklore Society), and President Rao (VCU). In the summer of 2011, three local contractors donated the labor to remove the asphalt from the burial ground and cover the site with sod ("Asphalt Being Removed from Lot over Slave Burial Ground" 2011). The Richmond Slave Trail Commission placed a small historical marker at the site, but the ABG lacked any additional commemorative or interpretive display. While the DFJE named the site's memorialization as a top priority for the organization, the burial ground faced a more urgent threat just three years after the asphalt's removal.

LIBERATING THE BURIAL GROUND THROUGH SELF-DETERMINATION

In 2014, this sacred space was again at risk of desecration due to the city's "Revitalize RVA" initiative. Mayor Dwight Clinton Jones proposed a $200 million development plan that included a minor-league baseball stadium, hotel, and retail center in Shockoe Bottom (Sheir 2014). Despite the fact that this proposal also included a promise to raise $30 million for a local slavery museum, the SGHRP expressed fear and anger that yet again, the city's Black history was at risk of being sidelined by commercial interests (King 2014). By rejecting government proposals for both the slavery museum and commercial development, the activists attempted to liberate the site from political leaders' control of the commemorative landscape and retain their self-determination of this space. This response captures the hesitations many Black activists hold toward partnerships with predominately white institutions—namely, the long history of white cooptation of Black political action (Malcolm X 1984; Dawson 2001, 21–22).

Mayor Jones's plans for the baseball stadium ultimately failed after he could not get a majority vote for the proposal from city council. The city moved forward with commemorative plans for Shockoe Bottom that were substantial in funding, but small in scope. Specifically, the city's $19 million proposal focused solely on the site of Lumpkin's Jail—an effort deemed insufficient by many community members who desired to see a larger picture of Africans' impact on Richmond. In its autumn 2014 newsletter, the DFJE reminded readers that "stopping the stadium has always been just the first part of a two-part struggle. The task now is to create a real memorial to the mass suffering and resistance that took place in Richmond." The DFJE affirmed that "the essential element will be a real community discussion in which the Black community *must* play the leading role" (qtd. in Edwards and Wilayto 2014, 6).

Thus, activists voiced their concerns at community forums organized by the city's architectural design team. Waite Rawls, president of the American Civil War Museum Foundation, observed: "I've been to dozens of these meetings, and at every one of them the broad consensus is that it should be bigger than Lumpkin's jail, yet every time we get something back from the city, it says Lumpkin's jail." Pamela Bingham affirmed that the commemoration "cannot just be about the jail. . . . I'm here to represent the descendants of Gabriel. It is very important to my family that this be right" (Culbertson 2017). As the descendant of an enslaved man executed at Shockoe Bottom, Bingham engaged her family history as evidence of the ways that the city's history of Black oppression and resistance expanded far beyond the jail.

Moreover, the DFJE argued that the city's commemoration would neglect to portray the cultural, technological, and political accomplishments of enslaved individuals. In its September 2015 newsletter, the DFJE reminded readers that "Shockoe Bottom was a place of great misery, but also of great resistance. It deserves to be properly memorialized" (qtd. in "Welcome to the UCI Road World Championships" 2015). The city's limited proposal would thus tell only half of the story, a form of selective amnesia that would obscure memories of the early Black abolitionists who laid the foundation for slavery's demise (Hoerl 2012).[12] This obfuscation reinforced the same patronizing logics of slavery and diminished the agency of these Black individuals by selectively circulating memories that testified to their victimage and not their victories.

Many citizens also voiced concern that the city's commemoration would paint a misleading picture of what actually occurred at this site. They suggested that rather than simply calling it "Lumpkin's Jail," as was the case on the city's historical map, the site should be referred to as "Devil's Half Acre"—the name that enslaved people used. By claiming an alternate name for the site, these activists enacted a powerful political exercise. Lisa Corrigan suggests the act of renaming works " to exert more control over the rhetorical landscape and redefine Black interest through new vocabulary" (2016, 10). As Corrigan further explains, Black power activists frequently renamed themselves and their environment as a means of establishing "rhetorical power" and "expressing agency." She spotlights the the Black Panthers, for example, who appropriated terms like "guerilla warfare" and "armed struggle" to align their antiracist mission with the revolutionary struggles of oppressed groups around the globe (9–11). Egunfemi also argued that using the term "jail" mirrored racist frameworks that pinned Black people as inherently criminal and might allow "young people [to] assume their enslaved ancestors did something wrong to end up there" (qtd. in Komp 2016). These community members fought for a commemoration that acknowledged the power and agency of their ancestors in both name and design.

By arguing for an expanded memorialization, these community members advocated for a more comprehensive, nuanced representation of the city's Black history. Lumpkin's Jail/Devil's Half Acre was a site of torture, and thus, limiting commemoration to this site would fail to represent ways that the city's Black population resisted these violent logics of white supremacy. The activists' assertion of their collective agency, moral sensibilities, and ancestral ties helped liberate the Black community from these historical rhetorics that have attempted to restrict Black subjectivity. As Laura Helton et al. note, the historical record "often records Blackness only as an absence of human subjecthood" (2015, 5). This absence was magnified by the city's decision to commemorate Black slavery while denying Black agency. In the same way that VCU's treatment of the burial ground as a parking lot desecrated the memory of those buried below, the city's co-option of Shockoe Bottom's commemoration stripped political agency from the city's Black community. The SGHRP's activism served to humanize both the Black bodies who passed through this epicenter of the slave trade and the Black individuals who voiced their right to define this space. Their words and their actions exemplified Stokely Carmichael's (1971) conception of Black power as "the right to create our own terms through which to define ourselves, and our relationship to society, and to have these terms recognized."

The SGHRP sought commemorations at Shockoe Bottom that would not just bear witness to the evils of slavery, but would also recognize ongoing forms of racialized oppression. On the organization's website, its members elaborated that their commemorative plans would encourage "Pride in living, in resisting enslavement and white supremacy, in surviving sharecropping, lynching, vagrancy laws, old Jim Crow, systemic racism and desegregation. . . . And more recently we have come to understand that this struggle and every one of its public victories forces the established leadership, white and Black, to acknowledge that Black Lives Do Matter" ("Richmond's African Burial Ground" 2017).

The SGHRP's commemorative vision recognized what Saidiya V. Hartman describes as "the legacy of slavery that still haunts us" (2002, 766). This group pushed for a memorial site that acknowledged that slavery was not the only "southern problem," but one of many ongoing attempts to oppress the region's Black population (Hart 1905, 644). Moreover, the activists testified that slavery was not *just* a "southern" problem, but it reflected global systems of white supremacy "with direct impact on the apartheid and eugenicist systems of South Africa and Nazi Germany" ("Richmond's African Burial Ground" 2017). Such arguments discredit erroneous beliefs that characterize the South as the sole perpetrator of anti-Black and white supremacist violence (Yuhl 2013). The SGHRP desired a museum that would reflect white supremacy's global pervasiveness, engaging the Black Nationalist belief that racism is deeply tied to systems of colonization and imperialism (Davies and M'Bow 2007, 17–18). For the SGHRP, any museum about slavery needed to recognize the ongoing, universal struggle to convince white culture that "Black lives do matter."

The activists' discourse also framed their commemorative campaign in terms of a progress narrative that celebrated the Black community's strength and survival amidst two centuries of racial violence. By praising the Black community's history of "resisting" and "surviving," these activists engaged commemoration as a means of countering slavery's haunting legacy with memories of Black agency and social change. The activists explained that reclaiming Shockoe Bottom from government control would help give Black Richmonders a sense of "pride" in both their surroundings and their history. It was important that they were the chief decision makers of the museum to ensure it would be a space of self-empowerment and protection against spatial and ideological encroachment. Because "identity *depends* on memory," securing a commemorative site was one means of materializing Black Richmond's racial solidarity, ancestral pride, and historical resilience (Davis and Starn 1989, 1–6).

Indeed, SGHRP activists declared self-determination to be their chief objective in the fight to reclaim and commemorate Shockoe Bottom. In an article for *RVA News*, Egunfemi (2015) explained that the project's goal was "to impact the historical record so that it reflects the views of those who support the Self Determined right for Black people to speak our own truth about the complex legacy of enslavement and resistance in our beloved city." Such commitments expressed the legacies of Black Nationalism, which frame "self-determination" as an integral component of "Black freedom" and "Black power" (McCartney 2010, 120). Clearly, even the city's proposed slavery museum would be an affront to the Black community's history—the very subject they sought to commemorate.

CONCLUSION

On April 3, 2015, citizens in Richmond gathered at the burial ground on the 150th anniversary of the Civil War's end. Egunfemi and other activists organized a "posthumous emancipation" of the formerly enslaved persons buried at the site. People gathered to play instruments, light candles, and leave offerings of fruit, wine, and coins on a makeshift altar. During the day's events, Egunfemi affixed paper slips to the trees bearing the names of three hundred enslaved men and women who lived in Richmond. In a libation ceremony titled "Anointing the Veil," Egunfemi led the crowd in a call-and-response chant that declared to the men and women buried below: "You are now free" (Kinte 2015; Komp 2016).

This posthumous emancipation ceremony highlighted the spiritual, cultural, and spatial significance of the burial ground. After years of struggle, activists reclaimed this site as a sacred gathering place where Richmond's Black citizens could honor their ancestors and their history of oppression and resilience. This commitment to ancestor reverence, sacred space, and racial distinctiveness reflected both Black Nationalist and southern rhetorical traditions, demonstrating that these traditions are not mutually exclusive, but mutually constitutive.

This chapter holds several historical and theoretical implications. First, this case study affirmed that Black Nationalism is exemplified in the ways that Black southerners have sought and continue to seek self-determination, liberation, and racial solidarity. While Black Nationalism is often associated with slave revolts, the "Back-to-Africa" movement of the 1910s–1920s, and the Black Power movement of the 1960s–1970s, this chapter exemplified ways the main ideological tenets of Black Nationalism have circulated prior and subsequent to these eras, as well as beyond the urban North (Turner 1969; Martin 1976; Gordon 2006). The rhetoric of Black solidarity and empowerment invoked by the SGHRP reflected these long-standing commitments and provided a strong ideological counterforce to logics of white supremacy and institutional apathy. Indeed, the posthumous emancipation ceremony clearly demonstrated ways that Black resilience and African pride continue to shape the South's cultural landscape.

Second, this chapter contributed to the growing body of scholarship working to expand narrow conceptions of southern identity. Because Richmond is still known as the "Capital of the South," this case study holds regional implications for how the South's racialized history is remembered (Lewis 2018). As Powell explains, "a critical regionalism works in solidarity with the historically disempowered populations . . . to transform their local material circumstances while linking their particular struggles to larger ones" (2012, 33). These activists' efforts to challenge myopic narratives of the city's slave history are prismatic of regional narratives that portray Black Americans only as disempowered subjects. Even in instances where citizens are challenging ideologies of white supremacy, narrative roles for Black southerners are often limited to slave and victim (Morrison 1992). The SGHRP worked to trouble this binary between white agency and Black subjugation, showcasing ways that Black communities actively created physical places and cultural spaces of resistance, spirituality, celebration, and innovation, even during eras of intense racial violence in the region. Indeed, if the South continues to be discussed only in terms of Lost

Cause mythology, there will be a continued silencing of those Black voices that crafted spaces of joy and resistance—whether such mythology is being celebrated or disparaged.

Third, this chapter demonstrated the significance of securing physical and symbolic space as a rhetorical strategy for combatting racism and strengthening solidarity. As Don Mitchell argues, "rights have to be exercised somewhere, and sometimes that 'where' has itself to be actively produced by taking, by wresting, some space and transforming both its meaning and its use—by producing a space in which rights can exist and be exercised" (2003, 81). The SGHRP "actively produced" a sacred place where Black voices and bodies were venerated, "transforming" a parking lot into an African gathering place. This spatial recovery act worked to symbolically resist centuries of Black displacement and restore the region's ties to the African continent. Pan-Africanism holds that Africa is not just a geographical place, but "a psychological space from which Blacks could trace their ancestry and reclaim a lost dignity" (Gordon 2006, 180). By recovering the ABG, the activists also helped recover a "psychological space" in which the city's Black residents could reconnect with their ancestors.

As of March 2021, the city has yet to decide exactly how it will commemorate Shockoe Bottom. Whether or not the city's plan for a museum or the SGHRP's commemorative proposal will come to fruition is hard to say. However, what Shockoe Bottom is *not*—namely, a parking lot or a baseball stadium—speaks to the power of activists to reshape a region's physical and cultural landscape.

NOTES

1. Megan Fitzmaurice would like to thank Shawn Parry-Giles and the editors for their guidance on earlier drafts of this chapter. Elizabeth Gardner, Allison Prasch, and Jedidiah Mahan also provided valuable insight on the fieldwork and analysis.

2. Efforts to resist enslavement during the eighteenth and nineteenth centuries marked the beginning of Black liberation struggles in the United States. However, the fight for freedom from economic, political, and social injustice continues to this day. Yohuru Williams explains that "Black freedom movements" work as an umbrella term for the numerous—sometimes conflicting but often overlapping—historical movements "geared toward addressing issues of Black inequality" in the United States (2015, xiii).

3. Black Americans have consistently proclaimed racial solidarity and self-determination as key components of liberation. Such principles embolden Black communities to seek political and cultural freedom from white-dominated institutions through the creation of their own establishments (Ogbar 2005, 3).

4. George Breitman describes Black Nationalism as "The tendency for Black people in the United States to unite as a group, as a people into a movement of their own to fight for freedom, justice, and equality. . . . This tendency holds that Black people must control their

own movement and the political, economic, and social institutions of the Black community" (1965, 38).

5. Africa has served as both a literal and figurative site of empowerment for Black activists throughout the long Black freedom movement (Odamtten 2014, 172–78).

6. Wilson Jeremiah Moses explains that Black Nationalism arose as a guiding philosophy not only for Africans brought to what would become the United States in the 1700s, but also for Africans enslaved across the Americas. Thus, this ideology was shaped by a geographically diverse range of Black communities who had endured enslavement (1988, 6–11).

7. William Ramsey argues that the "essentialist assumptions" of the region crafted largely by white discourses have denied "the full and central place of Black folk in the South" (2007, 769–70).

8. Scholarly and popular accounts attest to the significant decrease in antiblack prejudice and the rise of Black political representation in the region as evidence of a "New South" that emerged after the civil rights movement of the 1960s (Kuklinski, Cobb, and Gilens 1997, 323–49; Bartley 1995).

9. Those memorialized are Robert E. Lee, J. E. B. Stuart, Jefferson Davis, Thomas "Stonewall" Jackson, and Matthew Fontaine Maury.

10. African Americans have been fighting to reclaim African Burial Grounds across the South, including sites in Texas, Missouri, Tennessee, and South Carolina, among other places (Wessler 2015).

11. For example, Huey Newton explained: "The Black Panther Party is a revolutionary Nationalist group and we see a major contradiction between capitalism in this country and our interests. We realize that this country became very rich upon slavery and that slavery is capitalism in the extreme. We have two evils to fight, capitalism and racism. We must destroy both racism and capitalism" (1995, 51).

12. "Selective amnesia" refers to the routine omission of historical events from public discourse that "defy seamless narratives of national progress and unity" (Hoerl 2012, 180).

REFERENCES

"About the Sacred Ground Project." n.d. *Sacred Ground Historical Reclamation Project* (blog). Accessed November 8, 2017. http://www.sacredgroundproject.net/p/richmonds-african -burial-ground.html.

Adkins, LaTrese. 2008. "Burial, African Practices in the Americas." In *Africa and the Americas: Culture, Politics, and History*, edited by Richard M. Juang and Noelle Morrissette. Santa Barbara, CA: ABC-CLIO.

Aptheker, Herbert. 1969. *American Negro Slave Revolts*. New York: International Publishers.

"Asphalt Being Removed from Lot over Slave Burial Ground." 2011. *NBC12 News*, May 24, 2011. https://www.nbc12.com/story/14706065/asphalt-being-removed-from-parking -lot-over-burial-ground.

Bartley, N. V. 1995. *The New South, 1945–1980*. Baton Rouge: Louisiana State University Press.

Bell, Valerie. 2010. *African Burial Ground (VCU Students Protest) Uncovering the Silence (Doc Preview)*. YouTube. https://www.youtube.com/watch?v=_Y3eyAbojoU.

Blakey, Michael L., and Grace S. Turner. 2008. "Institute for Historical Biology (IHB) Review of the Virginia Department of Historic Resources (DHR) Validation and Assessment

Report on the Burial Ground for Negroes, Richmond, Virginia by C. M. Stephenson, June 25." Williamsburg, VA: Institute for Historical Biology of the College of William and Mary.

Breitman, George, ed. 1965. *Malcolm X Speaks: Selected Speeches and Statements.* Evergreen Books. New York: Grove Press.

Campbell, Benjamin. 2012. *Richmond's Unhealed History.* Richmond: Brandylane Publishers.

Carmichael, Stokely. 1971. "From Black Power to Pan-Africanism." Speech, Whittier College, CA, March 22, 1971. http://americanradioworks.publicradio.org/features/Blackspeech /scarmichael-2.html.

Carson, Clayborne. 1995. *In Struggle: SNCC and the Black Awakening of the 1960s.* Cambridge, MA: Harvard University Press.

Chidester, David, and Edward Tabor Linenthal, eds. 1995. *American Sacred Space.* Bloomington: Indiana University Press.

Clark, Mary L. 2005. "Treading on Hallowed Ground: Implications for Property Law and Critical Theory of Land Associated with Human Death and Burial." *Kentucky Law Journal* 94, no. 3: 487–534.

Corrigan, Lisa M. 2016. *Prison Power: How Prison Influenced the Movement for Black Liberation.* Jackson: University Press of Mississippi.

Cox, Karen L. 2003. "The Confederate Monument at Arlington: A Token of Reconciliation." In *Monuments to the Lost Cause: Women, Art, and the Landscapes of Southern Memory,* edited by Cynthia Mills and Pamela H. Simpson. Knoxville: University of Tennessee Press.

Crowell, Cheryl. 2012. *New Richmond.* Charleston, SC: Arcadia Publishing.

Culbertson, Todd. 2017. "Todd Culbertson Column: Reconciliation Depends on Acknowledging the Truth about Slavery." *Richmond Times-Dispatch,* March 11, 2017. http://www .richmond.com/opinion/our-opinion/todd-culbertson/todd-culbertson-column -reconciliation-depends-on-acknowledging-the-truth-about/article_896cce11-0e1c -5330-bd64-c3b6c352d6af.html.

Davies, Carole Boyce, and Babacar M'Bow. 2007. "Politicizing an Existing Global Geography." In *Black Geographies and the Politics of Place,* edited by Katherine McKittrick and Clyde Woods, 14–45. Cambridge, MA: South End Press.

Davis, Natalie Zemon, and Randolph Starn. 1989. "Introduction: Special Issue on Memory and Countermemory." *Representations,* no. 26 (April): 1–6.

Davis, Patricia. 2013. "Memoryscapes in Transition: Black History Museums, New South Narratives, and Urban Regeneration." *Southern Communication Journal* 78, no. 2: 107–127.

Davis, Patricia. 2016. *Laying Claim: African American Cultural Memory and Southern Identity.* Tuscaloosa: University of Alabama Press.

Davis, Veronica A. 2003. *Here I Lay My Burdens Down: A History of the Black Cemeteries of Richmond, Virginia.* Richmond: Dietz Press.

Dawson, Michael C. 2001. *Black Visions: The Roots of Contemporary African-American Political Ideologies.* Chicago: University of Chicago Press.

"Defenders for Freedom, Justice & Equality." 2013. *The Black Activist,* no. 1 (Summer). http:// jblun.org/issue/1/docs/black-activist-issue-1.htm#_Toc360386816.

DePompa, Rachel. 2009. "Groups Protest VCU Re-Paving of Parking Lot." *NBC 12,* August 4, 2009. http://www.nbc12.com/story/10847440/groups-protest-vcu-re-paving -of-parking-lot.

Driggs, Sarah Shields, Richard Guy Wilson, and Robert P. Winthrop. 2001. *Richmond's Monument Avenue*. Chapel Hill: University of North Carolina Press.

Edwards, Ana, and Phil Wilayto. 2014. "Major Breakthroughs on Shockoe Stadium Struggle." *The Virginia Defender*, Autumn 2014. https://drive.google.com/file/d/0BzmgRd6803ZCXzhoQ3BQcFF2c0U/view.

Edwards, Ana, and Phil Wilayto. 2015. "The Significance of Richmond's Shockoe Bottom: Why It's the Wrong Place for a Baseball Stadium." *African Diaspora Archaeology Newsletter* 15, no. 1: 5–11.

Egunfemi, Free. 2015. "KUJICHAGULIA Means Self Determination: Reclaiming the Untold Stories of the Shockoe Bottom Resistance Movement—Part I." *RVAnews* (blog). September 30, 2015. https://rvanews.com/news/kujichagulia-means-self-determination-reclaiming-the-untold-stories-of-the-shockoe-bottom-resistance-movement-part-i/129567.

Fierce, Mildred C. 1993. *The Pan-African Idea in the United States, 1900–1919: African-American Interest in Africa and Interaction with West Africa*. New York: Garland Publishing.

Glenn, Cheryl. 2004. *Unspoken: A Rhetoric of Silence*. Carbondale: Southern Illinois University Press.

Gordon, Dexter B. 2006. *Black Identity: Rhetoric, Ideology, and Nineteenth-Century Black Nationalism*. Carbondale: Southern Illinois University Press.

Hart, Albert Bushnell. 1905. "Conditions of the Southern Problem." *The Independent* 58: 644–50.

Hartman, Saidiya V. 2002. "The Time of Slavery." *The South Atlantic Quarterly* 101, no. 4: 757–77.

Helton, Laura, Justin Leroy, Max A. Mishler, Samantha Seeley, and Shauna Sweeney. 2015. "The Question of Recovery: An Introduction." *Social Text* 33, no. 4: 1–18.

Hoerl, Kristen. 2012. "Selective Amnesia and Racial Transcendence in News Coverage of President Obama's Inauguration." *Quarterly Journal of Speech* 98, no. 2: 178–202.

"Hollywood Cemetery." 2021. Virginia Department of Historic Resources, January 28, 2021. https://www.dhr.virginia.gov/historic-registers/127-0221/.

Hong, Mai-Linh K. 2017. "'Get Your Asphalt Off My Ancestors!': Reclaiming Richmond's African Burial Ground." *Law, Culture, and the Humanities* 13, no. 1: 81–103.

Hylton, Raymond Pierre. 2014. *Virginia Union University*. Charleston, SC: Arcadia Publishing.

Jefferson, Alphine W. 2012. "Foreword." In *The Richmond Slave Trade: The Economic Backbone of the Old Dominion*, by Jack Trammell. Charleston, SC: The History Press.

Kapsidelis, Karin. 2011. "Four Arrested for Blocking VCU Parking Lot." *Richmond Times-Dispatch*, April 13, 2011. http://www.richmond.com/news/four-arrested-for-blocking-vcu-parking-lot/article_0393cb85-022a-5af1-8fe6-7b6b41de4d63.html.

Kelley, Robin D. G. 2003. *Freedom Dreams: The Black Radical Imagination*. Boston: Beacon Press.

King, Dean. 2014. "The Battle of the Ballpark." *Virginia Living* (blog). August 28, 2014. http://www.virginialiving.com/baseball/.

Kinte, K. 2015. *Emancipation African Burial Ground Celebration (Rva 150 Years)*. YouTube. https://youtu.be/Mo7k4IOkl5E.

Komp, Catherine. 2016. "Community Work Shapes Ideas for Shockoe Bottom Memorial Park." *Virginia Currents*, June 16, 2016. VPM, National Public Radio. http://ideastations.org/radio/news/community-work-shapes-ideas-shockoe-bottom-memorial-park.

Kuklinski, James H., Michael D. Cobb, and Martin Gilens. 1997. "Racial Attitudes and the New South." *The Journal of Politics* 59, no. 2: 323–49.

Lewis, Monique Antonette. 2018. "Richmond, Capital of the South." *Huffington Post*, January 10, 2018. https://www.huffingtonpost.com/entry/richmond-the-capital-of-the -South_us_597feb83e4b07c5ef3dc17cf.

Lipsitz, George. 2011. *How Racism Takes Place*. Philadelphia: Temple University Press.

"A List of Virginia's 200-Plus Confederate Monuments and Public Symbols." 2017. *Richmond Times-Dispatch*, August 17, 2017. http://www.richmond.com/news/virginia/a-list-of -virginia-s--plus-confederate-monuments-and/article_258a50dc-5f98-5c21-b325 -54c8edfe0303.html.

Malcolm X. 1984. "Ballot or the Bullet." In *The Sixties Papers: Documents of a Rebellious Decade*, edited by Judith Clavir Albert and Stewart Edward Albert. New York: Praeger.

Martin, Tony. 1976. *Race First: The Ideological and Organizational Struggles of Marcus Garvey and the Universal Negro Improvement Association*. Westport, CT: Greenwood Press.

McCartney, John. 2010. *Black Power Ideologies: An Essay in African American Political Thought*. Philadelphia: Temple University Press.

McInnis, Maurie D. 2014. "Mapping the Slave Trade in Richmond and New Orleans." *Buildings & Landscapes: Journal of the Vernacular Architecture Forum* 20, no. 2: 102–125.

Mitchell, Don. 2003. *The Right to the City: Social Justice and the Fight for Public Space*. New York: Guilford.

Morgan, Iwan, and Philip Davies, eds. 2013. *From Sit-Ins to SNCC: The Student Civil Rights Movement in the 1960s*. Gainesville: University Press of Florida.

Morrison, Toni. 1992. *Playing in the Dark: Whiteness and the Literary Imagination*. Cambridge, MA: Harvard University Press.

Moses, Wilson Jeremiah. 1988. *The Golden Age of Black Nationalism, 1850–1925*. New York: Oxford University Press.

Newton, Huey P. 1995. "Huey Newton Talks to the Movement about the Black Panther Party, Cultural Nationalism, SNCC, Liberals, and White Revolutionaries." In *The Black Panthers Speak*, edited by Philip S. Foner. New York: Da Capo Press.

Odamtten, Harry. 2014. "Critical Departures in the Practice of Pan-Africanism in the New Millennium." In *Pan-Africanism and the Politics of African Citizenship and Identity*, edited by Toyin Falola and Kwame Essien. New York: Routledge.

Ogbar, Jeffrey O. G. 2005. *Black Power: Radical Politics and African American Identity*. Baltimore: Johns Hopkins University Press.

Ogline Titus, Jill. 2014. "An Unfinished Struggle: Sesquicentennial Interpretations of Slavery and Emancipation." *Journal of the Civil War Era* 4, no. 2: 338–47.

"Our History." n.d. Initiatives of Change. Accessed July 15, 2019. https://us.iofc.org/our -history.

Pourzal, Jonathan. 2011. "The Root: The Sad History of Cemented Cemeteries." National Public Radio, May 23, 2011. http://www.npr.org/2011/05/23/136574853/the-root-the-sad -history-of-cemented-cemeteries.

Powell, Douglas Reichert. 2012. *Critical Regionalism: Connecting Politics and Culture in the American Landscape*. Chapel Hill: University of North Carolina Press.

Ramsey, William. 2007. "An End of Southern History: The Down-Home Quests of Toni Morrison and Colson Whitehead." *African American Review* 41, no. 4: 769–85.

"Richmond City Council Slave Trail Commission." n.d. City of Richmond. Accessed July 15, 2019. http://www.richmondgov.com/CommissionSlaveTrail/HistoryOfTheSlaveTrail Commission.aspx.

"Richmond's African Burial Ground." 2017. *Sacred Ground Historical Reclamation Project* (blog). http://www.sacredgroundproject.net/p/richmonds-african-burial-ground.html.

Rothstein, Edward. 2010. "African Burial Ground, and Its Dead, Are Given Life." *New York Times*, February 25, 2010. https://www.nytimes.com/2010/02/26/arts/design/26burial.html.

Schramm, Katharina. 2016. *African Homecoming: Pan-African Ideology and Contested Heritage*. New York: Taylor & Francis.

Sheir, Rebecca. 2014. "Opponents Balk at Mayor's Stadium Proposal in Shockoe Bottom, VA." *WAMU 88.5*, September 12, 2014. https://wamu.org/story/14/09/12/opponents_balk_at _mayors_stadium_proposal_in_shockoe_bottom_va/.

Slayton, Jeremy. 2009. "VCU Parking Lot Paving Draws Protests." *Richmond Times-Dispatch*, August 4, 2009. http://www.richmond.com/news/vcu-parking-lot-paving-draws -protests/article_5500bfa7-57b9-5df2-a99c-a19ba152b6bc.html.

Smith, John David, and Randall M. Miller, eds. 1997. "Slavery in Richmond, Virginia." In *Dictionary of Afro-American Slavery*, 647. Westport, CT: Greenwood Press.

Stevenson, Christopher M. 2008. "Burial Ground for Negroes, Richmond, Virginia: Validation and Assessment." Richmond: Virginia Department of Historic Resources.

Stuckey, Sterling. 1972. *The Ideological Origins of Black Nationalism*. Boston: Beacon Press.

Trice, Jamie. 2010. "VCU Parking Lot Sparks Controversy, Student Protest." *Commonwealth Times*, December 9, 2010. http://www.commonwealthtimes.org/2010/12/09/vcu-parking -lot-sparks-controversy-student-protest/.

Turner, James. 1969. "The Sociology of Black Nationalism." *The Black Scholar* 1, no. 2: 20–30.

Utsey, Shawn O. 2010. *Meet Me in the Bottom: The Struggle to Reclaim Richmond's African Burial Ground*. Richmond: Burn Baby Burn Productions.

Walters, Ronald W. 2003. "The Politics of Black Memory." *Souls: A Critical Journal of Black Politics, Culture, and Society* 5, no. 3: 1–7.

Watts, Rebecca Bridges. 2007. *Contemporary Southern Identity: Community through Controversy*. Jackson: University Press of Mississippi.

"Welcome to the UCI Road World Championships." 2015. *Virginia Defender*, September 2015. https://drive.google.com/file/d/1husyfjkW1lvkZsFWSxIBzbi8pzqt5qhI/view.

Wessler, Seth Freed. 2015. "Black Deaths Matter." *The Nation*, October 15, 2015. https://www .thenation.com/article/black-deaths-matter/.

Williams, Yohuru. 2015. *Rethinking the Black Freedom Movement*. New York: Routledge.

Yuhl, Stephanie. 2013. "Hidden in Plain Sight: Centering the Domestic Slave Trade in American Public History." *The Journal of Southern History* 79, no. 3: 593–624.

ABOUT THE EDITORS AND CONTRIBUTORS

Whitney Jordan Adams is visiting assistant professor of English, rhetoric, and writing at Berry College. Her research interests include southern rhetoric, discord and resentment rhetoric, and ethnography. Her work has been published in the *K.B. Journal: The Journal of the Kenneth Burke Society*. She has taught English in five foreign countries and was the recipient of the Versailles Fellowship in 2012. She spent a year lecturing at the Université de Versailles Saint-Quentin-en-Yvelines (UVSQ) in Versailles, France, and researching how the American South is viewed in France. She has also helped lead a summer writing center at the Harbin Institute of Technology in Harbin, China.

Wendy Atkins-Sayre is professor and chair of the Department of Communication & Film at the University of Memphis. Her research centers on identity as constructed through discourse, with an emphasis on regional and social movement studies. Her most recent book, edited with Ashli Stokes, looks at the role that rhetoric plays in building an urban–rural divide in America: *City Places, Country Spaces: Rhetorical Explorations of the Urban–Rural Divide* (Peter Lang).

Jason Edward Black (he/his/him) is professor of communication studies at UNC Charlotte and Fulbright Research Chair in Canadian Studies at Brock University. His research involves rhetoric and social change with an emphasis on Indigenous resistance and LGBTQIA activism. Black is the coauthor of *Mascot Nation: The Controversy over Native American Representations in Sports* (University of Illinois Press, 2018) and author of *American Indians and the Rhetoric of Removal and Allotment* (University Press of Mississippi, 2015). He is also coeditor of *Returning to Rhetorical History* (University of Alabama Press, 2021), *Decolonizing Native American Rhetoric* (Peter Lang, 2018), and *An Archive of Hope: Harvey Milk's Speeches and Writings* (University of California Press, 2013). Black's work appears in the *Quarterly Journal of Speech, Rhetoric & Public Affairs, Argumentation and Advocacy, American Indian Quarterly*,

American Indian Culture and Research Journal, and in numerous journals and book chapters.

Patricia G. Davis is associate professor in the Communication Studies Department at Northeastern University. Her work foregrounds the intersection of race, memory, and representation in a variety of communicative contexts. She has had essays published in *Text and Performance Quarterly, Rhetoric Review, Feminist Media Studies,* and the *Journal of Intercultural and International Communication,* as well as a number of edited collections. Her book *Laying Claim: African American Cultural Memory and Southern Identity* (University of Alabama Press, 2016) is the winner of outstanding book awards from the American Studies and Critical/Cultural divisions of the National Communication Association.

Cassidy D. Ellis is a doctoral student at the University of New Mexico where she studies critical intercultural communication and autoethodologies. Her work is interested in discourses of race and personhood within abortion rhetoric. She is specifically interested in the ways in which race is evoked and centered by pro- and anti-abortion rhetoric, affecting the way "life" is constructed. She situates her work in the histories and cultures of the US South and Southwest.

Megan Fitzmaurice is adjunct assistant professor in the Department of Communication at the University of Texas at Arlington. Her research examines Black activism, public memory, and rhetorical theory and has been published in the *Southern Journal of Communication, Feminist Media Studies,* and *Rhetoric & Public Affairs.* She is an associate editor of Recovering Democracy Archives, a public digital humanities project housed in the Center for Political Communication and Civic Leadership at the University of Maryland.

Michael L. Forst serves as director of the Maine Youth Action Network, a youth engagement nonprofit based in Portland, Maine. He is a doctoral candidate at Southern Illinois University Carbondale, where his research is positioned at the intersection of critical intercultural communication and leadership development. He is specifically interested in the ways in which whiteness, regionality, and cultural performance inform leadership training pedagogy.

Jeremy R. Grossman is lecturer at the University of Maryland. He received his BA and MA from Colorado State University and his PhD from the University of Georgia in communication studies. His areas of scholarly focus include rhetoric and psychoanalysis, rhetorical simulation, disaster policy in an era of climate change, and public memory studies. His doctoral dissertation interrogates discourses surrounding Hurricane Katrina and its public memory, specifically the ways in which such memory is displaced by means of rhetoric. The chapter in this volume is a tangential derivation of that research. He also spent several years as the editorial assistant to Barbara A. Biesecker at the *Quarterly Journal of Speech*, including acting as coeditor of the journal's Centennial Issue in 2015. He has published on Hurricane Katrina in the *Quarterly Journal of Speech* and *Rhetoric & Public Affairs*.

Brandon Inabinet is associate professor of communication studies at Furman University. He studies rhetoric in intergenerational arguments, circulation, and regionalism. His most recently published work appears in *Rhetoric Review* and *Public Culture*.

Cynthia P. King has taught in the Department of Communication Studies at Furman University since 2006, where she is currently chair of the department. Dr. King teaches in the areas of strategic public discourse, public speaking, African American rhetoric, and media studies. In 2015, she was awarded Furman's prestigious Meritorious Teaching Award and appointed chair of the Department of Communication Studies. Beyond her work in the academy, Dr. King has led communication workshops for organizations that include the Hope Leadership Program sponsored by the United States Agency for International Development (USAID), the National Albania American Council in Pristina Kosovo, the Academy for Educational Development (AED), the McNair Scholars Programs at the University of Maryland and American University, the Women's Leadership Initiative at Furman University, and the Riley White Peterson Policy Fellowship Program in the Riley Institute at Furman University.

Julia M. Medhurst is a writing center administrator and a doctoral student in the Department of Communication at Texas A&M University. She is interested in how whiteness works rhetorically, as well as how communicative acts build collective identity. Currently, she is investigating ways to put this knowledge to work in building and sustaining equitable writing and oral communication centers.

Christina L. Moss is assistant professor of rhetoric at the University of Memphis. She studies southern regional rhetoric and the intersections of regional identity with race and gender as related to visual and commemorative rhetoric. She has most recently published work in *Rhetoric Review* and *The Howard Journal of Communications*.

Ryan Neville-Shepard is assistant professor of communication at the University of Arkansas, where he teaches classes in rhetorical criticism, argumentation, and political communication. His work in the area of modern American political rhetoric has been published in journals such as *Communication Studies, Western Journal of Communication, Argumentation & Advocacy, Southern Communication Journal, Communication Quarterly,* and *American Behavioral Scientist.*

Jonathan M. Smith is a doctoral candidate in rhetoric and media studies at the University of Memphis. His current research examines public address, presidential campaigns, and news media from both rhetorical and critical cultural perspectives. Employing theories related to ideology, identity, and affect, his dissertation examines the ways presidential candidates construct identities during the campaign surfacing stages and navigate the ever-changing and evolving contexts of American culture. Smith is specifically concerned with how racism, sexism, LGBTQ+ prejudice, nativism, and religious intolerance affect identity construction and public reception. His work has appeared in *The Journal of Contemporary Rhetoric* (2017), *Citizen Critics* (2017), *Southwestern Journal of Mass Communication* (2018), and the edited collection *Gender, Race, and Social Identity in American Politics: The Past and Future of Political Access* (2019).

Ashli Quesinberry Stokes is professor of communication studies and director of the Center for the Study of the New South at the University of North Carolina at Charlotte. She recently edited *City Places, Country Spaces: Rhetorical Explorations of the Urban–Rural Divide* (Peter Lang) and coauthored *Consuming Identity: The Role of Food in Redefining the South* with Wendy Atkins-Sayre. Her research exploring intersections between identity, activism, and regions has also been published in *Global Public Relations: Spanning Borders, Spanning Cultures, Why Does No One in My Books Look Like Me?,* and in journals including the *Southern Communication Journal, Public Relations Inquiry, Journal of Public Interest Communications,* and *Journal of Public Relations Research,* among others.

Dave Tell is professor of communication studies at the University of Kansas. He is the author of *Confessional Crises and Cultural Politics in Twentieth Century America* (Penn State University Press, 2012) and *Remembering Emmett Till* (University of Chicago Press, 2019). He is a former fellow of the National Endowment for the Humanities and a codirector of the Emmett Till Memory Project. His writing on the Till murder has been published in the *Chicago Tribune, Atlantic Monthly, LitHub, The Conversation,* and a wide range of academic journals. He is a past president of the American Society for the History of Rhetoric and the inaugural Public Humanities Officer for the Rhetoric Society of America.

Carolyn Walcott is a former graduate student at Georgia State University where she obtained her PhD in communication in 2020. Her doctoral dissertation explored Guyana's newspaper framing of Exxon Mobil's oil discoveries and the challenges journalists confront in covering the oil and gas sector. Her research interests include political communication, international communication, and media pedagogy. She is the author of "Guyana: The Rebirth of University Journalism Studies" in *Global Journalism Practice & New Media Performance* (2014) and "Cross-Cultural Issues in Administrative Leadership in the Academy: Personal Experiences of Diaspora Administrators and Experts" in *Multidisciplinary Issues Surrounding African Diasporas* (2019). She is also the former director of the University of Guyana Center for Communication Studies.

INDEX

References to illustrations appear in **bold**.

9 781496 836151